RED HOT!

RED HOT!

A Cook's Encyclopedia of Fire and Spice

Consultant Editor: Jenni Fleetwood

HERMES
HOUSE

This edition is published by Hermes House, an imprint of Anness Publishing Ltd,
Hermes House, 88–89 Blackfriars Road, London SE1 8HA; tel. 020 7401 2077; fax 020 7633 9499

www.hermeshouse.com; www.annesspublishing.com

If you like the images in this book and would like to investigate using them for publishing, promotions or advertising,
please visit our website www.practicalpictures.com for more information.

Publisher: Joanna Lorenz
Editorial Director: Helen Sudell
Editor: Joy Wotton
Consultant Editor: Jenni Fleetwood
Designer: Nigel Partridge
Production Controller: Ben Worley

ETHICAL TRADING POLICY
Because of our ongoing ecological investment programme,
you, as our customer, can have the pleasure and reassurance of knowing
that a tree is being cultivated on your behalf to naturally replace the
materials used to make the book you are holding. For further
information about this scheme, go to www.annesspublishing.com/trees

A CIP catalogue record for this book is available from the British Library.

Previously published in two volumes as *Red Hot Chili Pepper* and *The Ultimate Hot and Spicy Cookbook*

Recipes contributed by: Pepita Aris, Catherine Atkinson, Alex Barker, Judy Bastyra, Angela Boggiano,
Carla Capalbo, Kit Chan, Maxine Clark, Jacqueline Clarke, Trish Davies, Roz Denny, Patrizia Diemling,
Matthew Drennan, Tessa Evelegh, Joanna Farrow, Rafi Fernandez, Christine France, Silvano Franco,
Sarah Gates, Shirley Gill, Brian Glover, Rosamund Grant, Nicola Graimes, Deh-Ta Hsuing, Shehzad Husain,
Christine Ingram, Becky Johnson, Manisha Kanani, Lucy Knox, Lesley Mackley, Sally Mansfield, Norma Miller,
Jane Milton, Sallie Morris, Annie Nichols, Elisabeth Lambert Ortiz, Jennie Shapter, Marlena Spieler, Liz Trigg,
Hilarie Walden, Laura Washburn, Pamela Westland, Steven Wheeler, Judy Williams, Jeni Wright

The consultant editor would like to thank chilli grower Michael Michaud and Christine McFadden,
fellow members of the Guild of Food Writers, for sharing their knowledge of and enthusiasm for chillies.
Michael and Joy Michaud are market gardeners, and from July to December each year they can supply
fresh chillies by mail order. Contact them at Peppers by Post, Sea Spring Farm, West Bexington,
Dorchester, Dorset DT2 9DD, UK, tel: 01308 897892; http://www.peppersbypost.biz/

PUBLISHER'S NOTE
Although the advice and information in this book are believed to be accurate and true at the time of
going to press, neither the authors nor the publisher can accept any legal responsibility or liability for
any errors or omissions that may be made nor for any inaccuracies nor for any harm or injury that
comes about from following instructions or advice in this book.

NOTES

Bracketed terms are intended for American readers.
For all recipes, quantities are given in both metric and imperial measures and, where
appropriate, in standard cups and spoons. Follow one set of measures, but not a mixture,
because they are not interchangeable.
Standard spoon and cup measures are level. 1 tsp = 5ml, 1 tbsp = 15ml, 1 cup = 250ml/8fl oz.
Australian standard tablespoons are 20ml. Australian readers should use 3 tsp in place of 1 tbsp
for measuring small quantities.
American pints are 16fl oz/2 cups. American readers should use 20fl oz/2.5 cups
in place of 1 pint when measuring liquids.
Electric oven temperatures in this book are for conventional ovens. When using a fan oven, the
temperature will probably need to be reduced by about 10–20°C/20–40°F. Since ovens vary,
you should check with your manufacturer's instruction book for guidance.
Medium (US large) eggs are used unless otherwise stated.

CONTENTS

INTRODUCTION 6

THE CHILLI FAMILY 8

CHILLI PRODUCTS 13

CHOOSING, STORING
  AND EQUIPMENT 15

PREPARATION AND
  COOKING TECHNIQUES 16

SPICE POWDERS 18

SPICE PASTES 22

SAMBALS 24

AFRICAN SPICE MIXTURES 26

BARBECUE SPICE MIXTURES 28

CAJUN SPICE MIXTURES
  AND BASTES 30

CHILLI PASTA 31

CHILLI GIFTS 32

SCORCHING SALSAS, SAUCES, DIPS,
  RELISHES AND NIBBLES 34

SPICY SOUPS 84

RED HOT APPETIZERS AND SNACKS 122

FIERY FISH AND SEAFOOD 178

SIZZLING POULTRY
  AND MEAT DISHES 236

FLAME-FILLED PASTA, NOODLE
  AND RICE MAIN DISHES 306

VIBRANT VEGETARIAN
  AND SIDE DISHES 370

PIQUANT SALADS 422

SWEET AND SPICY DISHES 462

SPICED DRINKS 486

NUTRITIONAL INFORMATION 496
INDEX 504

INTRODUCTION

There's a ring of fire encircling the globe, and it has nothing to do with volcanic activity. This is fire we're very much in favour of: the warmth that comes from red hot chilli peppers. These powerful little pods originated in South America, but now form a very important part of many of the world's major cuisines.

India is the largest producer and exporter of chillies, with much of the crop used for local consumption. Thailand, Mexico, Japan, Turkey, Nigeria, Ethiopia, Uganda, Kenya and Tanzania are also prime producers, exporting chillies to other countries around the globe.

The word chilli is spelt in different ways. Sometimes it is chile, sometimes chili, sometimes chilli pepper. This last description is accurate insofar as it recognizes that chillies are members of the *Capsicum* family, like the sweet peppers. It also forms a link with all those spicy powders – chilli, cayenne and paprika – which are an essential part of many national dishes.

WHAT'S IN A NAME?

The great explorer Columbus was responsible for confusing chillies with peppers. When he set sail in 1492, hoping to find a sea route to the spice islands, it was a source of black pepper (*Piper nigrum*) he was seeking.

Not only did he fail to find his intended destination, discovering instead the Caribbean island of San Salvador (now Watling Island), but he also made the incorrect assumption that the hot spice flavouring the local food was black pepper. By the time it was realized that the fleshy pods of a fruit were responsible, rather than tiny black peppercorns, it was too late.

Below: Mexican chillies, clockwise from top left: small green chillies, chipotle chillies, mulato chillies, dried habanero chillies, pasilla chillies, green (bell) peppers, green jalapeño chillies, Anaheim chillies, and (centre left) Scotch bonnets, (centre right) red chillies.

Above: Chillies form an important part of many of the world's major cuisines.

The Spanish called the flavouring pimiento (pepper) and the name stuck, and it has led to confusion ever since.

It was the Aztecs who coined the name chilli. Like the Mayas and Incas, they were greatly enamoured of the brightly coloured fruit that had originated in the rainforests of South America, and used chillies both as food and for medicinal purposes. When the Spanish invaded Mexico in 1509, they found many different varieties of both fresh and dried chilli on sale at the market at Tenochtitlan and still more being cultivated in Montezuma's botanical gardens at Huaxtepec.

Mexico remains a mecca for chilli-lovers, with every region having its own special varieties. Chillies are valued for their heat and for their flavour, and accomplished Mexican cooks will often use several different types – fresh and dried – in a single dish.

A CHAIN OF CHILLIES

Columbus is credited with introducing chillies to Europe, bringing back "peppers of many kinds and colours" when he returned to Europe in 1493. Soon after this, Vasco da Gama succeeded in finding the sea route to the spice islands. By the middle of the 16th century, a two-way trade had been established. Spices such as nutmeg, cinnamon and black pepper were brought to Europe from the East, and chillies and other plants from the New World went to Asia.

The spice trade created a culinary explosion, and the chilli rapidly became an important ingredient in the food of

Above: Chillies in all their different guises add both flavour and heat to many kinds of dishes. Here, they are shown fresh and dried, preserved in oil and ground into rich and fragrant powders.

Below: Asian chillies

South-east Asia, India and China. Portuguese and Arab traders introduced it to Africa. It was enthusiastically adopted, and when West African slaves were taken to the Southern States of America to work the cotton plantations, the chillies that were part of their diet went with them.

THE CHILLI IN EUROPE

Although parts of Europe adopted the chilli with great enthusiasm, universal acceptance has been relatively slow. Spain and Portugal use chillies quite extensively, which is not surprising, given the influence of those early explorers, but in France their use is limited to a few signature dishes, like the fiery rouille traditionally served with bouillabaisse.

It used to be the case that the further north you went, the less likely you would be to encounter chilli dishes. All this is changing, however, as Asian food becomes increasingly popular. Don't be

surprised if you encounter chilli lollipops (popsicles) or chilli ice cream. The flavour of chillies can be subtle as well as strident, and their affinity for fruit means that, used judiciously, they can make as valuable a contribution to fruit salads as they do to salsas and spicy Mexican dishes.

In response to public demand, most supermarkets stock chillies. Chillies are easy to grow, and many gardeners enjoy cultivating and then cooking them.

Chillies are Good for You

An excellent source of vitamin C, chillies also yield beta carotene, folate, potassium and vitamin E. They stimulate the appetite and improve circulation, but can irritate the stomach if eaten to excess. Chillies are also a powerful decongestant, and can help to clear blocked sinuses.

THE CHILLI FAMILY

There are more than two hundred different types of chilli, all members of the nightshade *(solanaceae)* family, like tomatoes and potatoes. Most of those used for culinary purposes belong to the genus *Capsicum annuum*. These were originally thought to be annuals, which explains the name, but can be perennial when cultivated in the tropics. The plants grow to a height of 1m/1yd, and chillies of this type include jalapeños, cayennes, Anaheim chillies and poblanos, as well as the common sweet (bell) peppers.

Tabasco chillies and the very hot Punjab chillies belong to a group called *Capsicum frutescens*, while Scotch bonnets and habaneros – the fragrant hot chillies that look like tam-o'-shanters – are *Capsicum chinense*. Some of the largest chilli plants are *Capsicum baccatum*. Ajis fall into this category, as do peri-peri chillies. Finally, there is a small group called *Capsicum pubescens*. The most notable chilli in this group is the manzano. The name means "apple", and these chillies resemble crab apples in size and shape.

Unless you grow chillies or are lucky enough to live near a farmer's market that features these flavoursome ingredients, you are unlikely to encounter more than a few of the more common varieties, such as serranos, jalapeños

Below: Chillies are members of the nightshade (solanaceae) *family, like tomatoes and potatoes.*

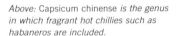

Above: Capsicum chinense *is the genus in which fragrant hot chillies such as habaneros are included.*

and cayennes, and even these may not be identified as such. Supermarkets have a habit of limiting their labelling to the obvious, like "red chillies" or – one step better – "hot red chillies".

This raises another issue. How do you know whether a chilli is hot or not? Are small chillies hotter than big ones? Or red chillies hotter than green? The answer to the last two questions is no. Although some of the world's hottest chillies are tiny, there are some large varieties that are real scorchers. Colour isn't an infallible indicator either. Most chillies start out green and ripen to red, but some start yellow and become red, and yet others start yellow and stay yellow, and across the spectrum you'll find hot varieties. To confuse the issue still further, chillies on the same plant can have different degrees of heat, and in at least one type of chilli, the top of the fruit is hotter than the bottom. Fortunately for those of us who like to have some warning as to whether the contents of our shopping basket will be fragrant or fiery, there are rating systems for the heat in chillies. The best known of these grades chillies in Scoville units. Until relatively recently, the world's hottest chilli was reckoned to be the Mexican red savina habanero, which scores 557,000 on the Scoville

scale, but a new contender, the tezpur chilli, has been discovered in India. The tezpur registers a blistering 855,000 Scoville units, and is so hot that it is said to have triggered heart attacks in the unwary or novice taster. Scoville units are useful when it comes to fine comparisons such as these, but working with units measured in this way can be unwieldy. For general classification, a simpler system, which rates chillies out of ten, is more often used.

What makes one chilli hotter than another is the amount of the chemical capsaicin contained in the seeds and fibrous white lining. Apart from producing anything from a tingle to a tidal wave of heat, capsaicin also contributes to the feel-good factor by stimulating the brain to produce hormones called endorphins.

A less appealing aspect to capsaicin is that it is an irritant, and can cause severe burning to delicate parts of the face (and other parts of the anatomy) with which it comes into contact. It is therefore vital to handle chillies with care. Wear gloves while preparing them, or cut them up using a knife and fork. If you do handle chillies directly, wash your hands thoroughly in soapy water immediately afterwards (capsaicin does not dissolve in water alone) or use vegetable oil to remove any residue.

THE BURNING QUESTION

If you bite into a chilli that is unpleasantly hot, don't drink a glass of water. That will only spread the discomfort around your mouth making the burning sensation much worse. Instead, try one of these simple solutions:
• Take a large drink of creamy milk, hold it in your mouth for a minute or so, then spit it out discreetly. Repeat as necessary.
• A similar effect can be achieved with water or ice cream, as long as you do not swallow it.
• Eat a piece of fresh bread, a cooked potato or some rice. These will absorb the offending capsaicin oil.

NAMING THE CHILLI

You will find both fresh and dried chillies on sale. Dried chillies can be stored like other spices, and can be rehydrated with excellent results. Some chillies actually taste better when they have been dried. It is well worth getting to know as many different varieties as possible. Then, like a true aficionado, you can start blending several types for the ultimate in chilli pleasure.

The following descriptions of chillies are listed by their heat scale, with 10 being the hottest.

Anaheim

Heat scale 2–3: Their alternative name of "California long green" gives some idea of what these large chillies look like (they are also known as New Mexico). The pods are about 15cm/6in long and about 5cm/2in wide, making them good candidates for stuffing. The flavour is fresh and fruity, like a cross between tart apples and green (bell) peppers. Anaheim skins can be a bit tough, so these chillies are best roasted and peeled. The dried chillies are used to make a mild chilli powder.

Below: Ancho chillies

Ancho

Heat scale 3: Dried poblanos, these are larger than most other dried chillies. Open the packet and savour the wonderful fruity aroma – like dates or dried figs. After rehydration, anchos can be stuffed, and they also taste great sliced or chopped in stir-fries and similar dishes.

Guajillo

Heat scale 3: These dried chillies are about 15cm/6in long, with rough skin. The mature fresh pods are a deep reddish brown and have a smooth texture. It is thought they might be related to Anaheim chillies, as they have a similar look. They have a mild, slightly bitter flavour, suggestive of green tea. Guajillos are used in many classic salsas.

Italia

Heat scale 3: Juicy and refreshing, these dark green chillies ripen to a rich, dark red. They taste great in salads and have an affinity for tropical fruit, especially mangoes.

Below: Mulato chillies

Mulato

Heat scale 3: A dried chilli with a thin, wrinkled, dark brown skin, this is related to the ancho. The flavour is smoky and herby.

Poblano

Heat scale 3: Big and beautiful, poblanos look like sweet (bell) peppers, and are perfect for stuffing. They start off a deep green and ripen to a bright, clear red or rich, dark brown. The flavour is spicier than that of a sweet pepper, with peachy overtones. Poblanos taste wonderful with other chillies, whose flavour they appear to boost.

Below: Poblano chillies

Above: Anaheim chilli

Above: Guajillo chillies

Below: Pasado chillies

Cherry Hot

Heat scale 4: Pungent, with thick walls, these chillies look like large versions of the fruit for which they are named. The skins can be tough, so they are best peeled. Cherry hot chillies have a sweetish flavour and make good pickles.

Below: Cherry hot chillies

Above: Fresno chillies

Fresno

Heat scale 5: Plump and cylindrical, with tapered ends, these fresh chillies are most often sold red, although you will sometimes find green or yellow ones in the shops. They look rather similar to jalapeños, and can be substituted for them if necessary.

Pasado

Heat scale 3–4: Very dark brown, skinny, dried chillies, these are generally about 10cm/4in long. When rehydrated, they taste lemony, with a hint of cucumber and apple. Pasados have an affinity for black beans, and make a fine salsa. Strips taste good on pizzas.

Below: Cascabel chillies

Costeno Amarillo

Heat scale 4: Not to be confused with the much hotter aji amarillo, this is a pale orange dried chilli, which is ideal for use in yellow salsas and Mexican *mole* sauce. It has a citrus flavour and is often used to give depth to the flavour of soups and stews.

Pasilla

Heat scale 4: Open a packet of these deep purple dried chillies and the first thing you notice is their rich liquorice aroma. Quite large at about 15cm/6in in length, pasillas have a spicy, fruity flavour that is good with shellfish, *moles* and mushrooms. Pureés made from rehydrated pasillas do not need to be sieved, as the skin is thin.

Cascabel

Heat scale 4: The name translates as "little rattle", and refers to the sound the seeds make inside this round dried chilli. The woody, nutty flavour is best appreciated when the skin is removed. Soak them, then either scrape the flesh off the skin or sieve it. Cascabels are great in stews, soups and salsas.

Chilli Boost

For an instant lift, sprinkle some dried crushed chilli on your food.

Above: Pasilla chillies

Cultivating Chillies

If you can grow tomatoes, then you'll be able to try your luck with chillies. They enjoy similar conditions, prefer higher temperatures, need watering more often and like slightly acid soils. You can grow them in tubs, hanging baskets or pots on the windowsill. Raise the plants under glass in spring, or buy them from a good plantsman. Plant out when frost is no longer a problem and the first flowers are visible. Water well in dry weather, mulch thickly and feed fortnightly with a high-potash fertilizer. Stake taller varieties. Pinch out growing tips if sideshoots are not being made and stop these once they have set fruit. During the growing season, watch for aphids, cutworms or slugs, and treat. Harvest about 12–16 weeks after planting out. Pull up plants and hang under glass in a sunny place when frost threatens to encourage the fruit to continue ripening.

Above: Jalapeño chillies

Jalapeño

Heat scale 4–7: These are frequently seen in supermarkets. Plump and stubby, like fat fingers, they have shiny skins. They are sold at both the green and the red stage, although the former seem to be marginally more popular. Jalapeños have a piquant, grassy flavour, and are widely used in salsas, salads, dips and stews; they are also canned and bottled. Their fame is due to the fact that they are the best known and most commonly used chilli in Mexican food. A heat-free jalapeño has been developed in the US. Too thick-skinned to be sun-dried, jalapeños are generally smoke-dried and acquire a name change. In this form they are known as chipotle chillies.

Below: Pickled jalapeño chillies

Hungarian Wax Chillies

Heat scale 5: These really do look waxy, like novelty candles. Unlike many chillies, they start off yellow, not green. It is not necessary to peel them, and they are often used in salads and salsas.

Aji Amarillo

Heat scale 6–7: There are several different varieties of this chilli, including one that is yellow when fully ripe, and a large brown aji that is frequently dried. The chillies average about 10cm/4in in length and look rather like miniature windsocks. Red ajis originated in Peru, and were popular among the Incas.

Below: Cayenne chillies

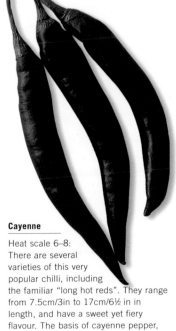

Cayenne

Heat scale 6–8: There are several varieties of this very popular chilli, including the familiar "long hot reds". They range from 7.5cm/3in to 17cm/6½ in in length, and have a sweet yet fiery flavour. The basis of cayenne pepper, these chillies are also used in sauces.

Above: Chipotle chillies

Chipotle

Heat scale 6–10: This smoke-dried jalapeño has wrinkled, dark red skin and thick flesh. Chipotles need long, slow cooking to soften them and bring out their full flavour, which is hot and tasty with a deep intriguing smokiness.

Serrano

Heat scale 7: Usually sold green, these are small (about 4cm/1½in long) and quite slender. Serranos are the classic Mexican green chilli (*chiles verdes*), and are an important ingredient in guacamole. The flavour is clean and crisp, with a suggestion of citrus. Serranos are thin-skinned and do not need to be peeled. They dry well, but are seldom sold that way, although you may come across them occasionally for sale in a Mexican or Spanish market.

Above: Serrano chillies

Left: Bird's
eye chillies

De Arbol

Heat scale 8: More often sold dried than fresh, these smooth cayenne-type chillies are slim and curvaceous. A warm orange-red, they are about 7.5cm/3in long. De arbols combine blistering heat with a clean, grassy flavour. Add them to soups or use to enliven vinegar or oil. Unlike most dried chillies, which must be soaked in hot water for 20–30 minutes before use, dry de arbol pods can be crumbled and added straight to stews or similar dishes. To reduce the heat, slit them and shake out the seeds first.

Above: Dried habanero chillies

Bird's Eye

Heat scale 8: Small and extremely hot, these come from a highly volatile family of chillies that are found in Africa, Asia, the United States and the Caribbean, and often labelled simply as "Thai chillies". Thin-fleshed and explosively hot, they are sold green and red, often with the stems still attached. Dried, they are widely available in jars. They are called bird's eyes because they are much liked by mynah birds.

Below: Dried bird's eye chillies

reminds them of chardonnay wine; others that it is redolent of sun-warmed apricots. Don't sniff them too enthusiastically, however, and be ultra-cautious when handling habaneros, for they are excessively hot. Always wear strong gloves when preparing them, and don't stand over a food processor or blender when using them to make a paste, or the fumes may burn your face. When cooking with habaneros, a little goes a long way. They are very good with fruit and in salsas. Dried habaneros have medium-thick flesh and wrinkled skins. When rehydrated, they have a rich tropical-fruit flavour.

Scotch Bonnets

Heat scale 10: Often confused with habaneros, which they closely resemble. Scotch bonnets are grown in Jamaican and are the principal ingredient of jerk seasoning.

Below: Scotch bonnet chillies

Above: Dried de arbol chillies

Manzano

Heat scale 9: This delicious chilli is very hot and fruity. About the size of a crab apple, it is the only chilli to have purple/black seeds.

Habanero

Heat scale 10: Don't imagine that intense heat is the only defining feature of this lantern-shaped chilli. Habaneros have a wonderful, fruity flavour, and a surprisingly delicate aroma. Some say it

Use Scotch bonnets very cautiously as they are one of the hottest chillies. It is advisable to deseed them before use unless you can tolerate their intense and lingering flavour.

Tiny Terrors

Thailand grows many different varieties of chillies. The smallest are so tiny they are popularly referred to as *prik kee noo* (mouse droppings). Use cautiously as they are fiery hot.

CHILLI PRODUCTS

Specialist shops, devoted to chillies and chilli products, are springing up all over the world. Alongside mugs, plates, bowls and aprons rioting with chilli motifs, you'll find an astonishing array of powders, pastes, sauces and oils.

POWDERS

Anything connected with chillies tends to be confusing, and chilli powder is no exception. The name suggests that this product is simply powdered chilli, but it is in fact a blend of several ingredients, designed specifically for making chilli con carne. In addition to ground hot chillies, it typically contains cumin, oregano, salt and garlic powder.

Pure powders – the whole chilli and nothing but the chilli – are less easy to come by, but are available from specialist shops and by mail order. Ancho, caribe and Anaheim (New Mexico) red powders are mild (heat scale 3). Pasilla, a rich, dark powder, registers 4 on the heat scale, while chipotle is a little hotter still.

Right: Chilli powder

Left: Ancho powder

Right: Pasilla powder

Left: Paprika

Right: Cayenne pepper

Convenient Chillies

Jars of whole chillies in white wine vinegar are handy for the home cook. Also look out for minced (ground) chillies. After opening, jars must be tightly closed, kept in the refrigerator and the contents consumed by the use-by date.

Cayenne pepper is a very fine ground powder from the *Capsicum frutescens* variety of chilli. The placenta (the fibrous white inner lining) and seeds are included, so it is very hot. Tiny amounts of cayenne are often added to cheese and egg dishes, and it is sprinkled over smoked fish and prawns (shrimp). It is also added to some curries.

Paprika is a fine, rich red powder made from mild chillies. The core and seeds are removed, but the flavour can still be quite pungent. Hungarians have adopted this as their national spice, but it is also widely used in Spanish and Portuguese cooking. Look out for *pimentón dulce*, a delicious smoked paprika from Estramadura in Spain.

Right: Crushed chilli flakes

CRUSHED CHILLIES

Dried chilli flakes are widely available. Italians call them *peperoncini* and add them to their famous arrabbiata sauce. Sprinkle them on pizzas or add to cooked dishes for a last-minute lift. Crushed dried green jalapeños are a useful pantry item, combining considerable heat with a delicious, melting sweetness.

CHILLI PASTE

It is worth keeping a few jars of ready-made chilli paste, such as harissa or *ras-el-hanout*, on your shelves. A hot chilli paste is quite easy to make at home. Simply seed fresh chillies, then purée them in a blender or food processor until smooth. Store small amounts in the refrigerator for up to 1 week, or freeze for up to 6 months. Chilli paste can also be made from dried chillies. Having rehydrated them, purée as for fresh chillies. You may have to sieve tough-skinned varieties.

Below: Hot chilli paste

Left: Red Tabasco sauce

Left: Green Tabasco sauce

CHILLI SAUCES

There are many varieties of these and the names appear to prove that chillies stimulate the imagination as well as the appetite. Some of the printable ones include Endorphin Rush, Lethal Weapon and Global Warming, along with the unforgettable Scorned Woman Hot Sauce.

The most famous chilli sauce, however, is Tabasco, developed in Louisiana by E. McIlhenny in the latter half of the 19th century. Chillies are matured in oak barrels to develop the sauce's unique flavour. Try mixing a few drops with fresh lime juice as a baste next time you grill salmon steaks, or add to sauces, soups or casseroles. Also available is Tabasco Jalapeño Sauce – often referred to as green Tabasco sauce. Milder in flavour than the red version, it is good with nachos, hamburgers or on pizza.

Chilli sauces are also widely used in Asia. Chinese chilli sauce is quite hot and spicy, with a hint of fruitiness thanks to the inclusion of apples or plums. For an even milder flavour, look out for sweet chilli sauce, which is a blend of red chillies, sugar and tamarind juice from Sichuan. There is also a thick Chinese sauce made solely from chillies and salt. This is usually sold in jars, and is much hotter than the bottled version. Vietnamese chilli sauce is very hot, while the Thai sauce tends to be thicker and more spicy. Bottled chilli sauces are used both for cooking and as a dip.

CHILLI OILS

Various types of chilli oil are on sale. Toss them with pasta, add a dash to a stir-fry, or drizzle them over pizzas.

Chilli oils also make a good basis for salad dressings. You can make your own chilli oil by heating chillies in oil, or use a ready-made mixture. Olive oil, flavoured with chipotle and de arbol chillies, with a hint of rosemary, is a particularly good blend. It can also be used for light cooking.

Chilli oil is seldom used for cooking in China and South-east Asia, but is a popular dipping sauce. Two types are widely sold. The first is a simple infusion of dried chillies, onions, garlic and salt in vegetable oil. The second, XO chilli oil, is flavoured with dried scallops and costs considerably more. Chilli oil has a pleasant smell, and a concentrated flavour, much stronger than chilli sauce. It is often drizzled over fish and shellfish just before serving. It should be used sparingly.

Below: Chilli oil

Chilli and Tomato Oil
Heating oil with chillies intensifies the rich flavour. This tastes great sprinkled over pasta.

1 Heat 150ml/¼ pint/⅔ cup olive oil in a pan. When it is very hot, but not smoking, stir in 10ml/2 tsp tomato purée (paste) and 15ml/1 tbsp dried red chilli flakes.

2 Leave to cool, then pour into an airtight jar and store in the refrigerator for up to 2 months.

Above: Sweet chilli sauce (top) and chilli sauce

CHOOSING, STORING AND EQUIPMENT

Below is some helpful advice on selecting and storing chillies and tips on equipment that will make their preparation simpler.

CHOOSING AND STORING CHILLIES

• When buying fresh chillies, apply the same criteria as when buying sweet (bell) peppers. The fruit should look bright and unblemished.
• Some chillies are naturally wrinkled when ripe, however, so a smooth skin is not essential.

Above: Chillies dried on string or canes will keep well for many months.

• Avoid any chillies that seem limp or dry, or that have bruising on the skin.
• In the supermarket, wrap your hand in a plastic bag when picking out chillies, or you may have an unpleasant surprise if you later touch your face.
• To store chillies, wrap them in kitchen paper, place in a plastic bag and keep in the salad compartment of the refrigerator for a week or more.
• Chillies can also be frozen. There is no need to blanch them if you plan to use them fairly soon.
• Frozen chillies are a huge boon to the busy cook, as they can be sliced when only partially thawed, and crushed with garlic and ginger to make a fragrant spice paste.
• To dry chillies, thread them on a string, hang them in a warm place until dry, then crush them and store in a sealed jar.

EQUIPMENT

Gloves may not seem obvious pieces of equipment, but they are invaluable for the dedicated chilli cook. The fine disposable gloves used in hospitals can be used for most chillies, but you need the heavy-duty type for really hot varieties such as habaneros. Of course, you can prepare chillies without wearing gloves, either by using a knife and fork for cutting, or by taking a chance and washing your hands in soapy water afterwards, but burns from capsaicin, the chemical found in the seeds and fibrous white lining, can be very unpleasant.

A mortar and pestle is ideal for grinding chillies and making chilli pastes, but it does involve a fair amount of hard work. Traditional Indian or Asian granite or stone sets are generally fairly large, with deep, pitted or ridged bowls. The rough surface acts like pumice, increasing the grinding effect. Porous volcanic rock is also used for the Mexican mortar – the *molcajete* – which traditionally stands on wide legs, and is very sturdy. The Mexican *tejolote* tends to be shorter

Left: A smooth mortar and pestle for crushing dry ingredients.

Above: A rough mortar and pestle for making wet pastes.

Left: If you like to make your own spice mixtures, then a spice or coffee grinder kept solely for this purpose is very useful.

than the traditional pestle, and fits neatly into the hand. *Molcajetes* must be tempered before being used. To do this, a mixture of dry rice and salt is spooned into the bowl, then ground into the surface to remove any loose sand or grit before being discarded.

A food processor is faster and easier, if less satisfying, than a mortar and pestle, especially for pastes, but must be very carefully cleaned after use. If you intend preparing chillies and spice pastes frequently, it may be worth investing in a mini food processor, and reserving it for spices.

A spice grinder, or coffee grinder kept specifically for spices, is handy when making dry spice mixtures.

Left: A food processor or a blender will process chillies very efficiently, and is especially useful for large quantities.

PREPARATION AND COOKING TECHNIQUES

Every cook handling chillies has had the same experience, that unthinking moment when the hand goes to the face and the burning, tingling sensation of chilli oil is experienced, especially around the sensitive areas of the eyes, nose and mouth. It's not worth it! So be warned, be careful. Wear rubber gloves or wash your hands thoroughly in plenty of hot soapy water when handling chillies. Water alone will not remove the chemical capsaicin, and even after using soap, traces may remain. Baby oil or olive oil can be used to remove it from sensitive areas. This advice applies to dried and fresh chillies as the burning properties are equally strong for both.

Preparing Fresh Chillies

1 If the chilli is to be stuffed, and kept whole, merely slit it without separating the 2 halves. For all other purposes, hold the chilli firmly at the stalk end, and cut it neatly in half lengthwise with a sharp knife.

2 Cut off the stalk from both halves of the chilli, removing a thin slice containing the stalk from the top of the chilli at the same time. This will help to free the white membrane (placenta) and make it easier to scrape out the seeds to be discarded.

3 Carefully scrape out all the seeds and discard them. Remove the core with a small sharp knife.

4 Cut out any white membrane from the centre of each chilli half. Keep the knife blade close to the flesh so that all the membrane is removed. This is usually easy to do. Discard the membrane.

5 Slice each piece of chilli into thin strips. If diced chilli is needed, bunch the strips together and cut across them to produce tiny pieces.

COOK'S TIP
Much of the capsaicin, the fiery oil in chillies, is concentrated in the fibrous white section that contains the seeds. Many recipes suggest removing and discarding this, but true chilli lovers usually leave it in.

Soaking Dried Chillies

Most dried chillies must be rehydrated before being used. In some instances, a recipe will recommend toasting as a first step, to intensify the flavour. This can be done by putting the seeded chillies in a roasting pan in the oven for a few minutes, or by pressing them on to the surface of a hot, dry, heavy frying pan. Do not let them burn, or they could become bitter. Once this is done, continue as below.

1 Wipe the chillies to remove any surface dirt. If you like, you can slit them and shake out the seeds before soaking. Alternatively, just brush away any seeds you can see.

2 Put the chillies in a bowl and pour over hot water to cover. If necessary, fit a saucer in the bowl to keep the chillies submerged. Soak for 20–30 minutes (up to 1 hour if possible), until the colour is restored and the chillies have softened and swelled.

3 Drain the chillies, cut off the stalks if necessary, then slit them and scrape out the seeds. Slice or chop the flesh. If the chillies are to be puréed, process them with a little of the soaking water. Sieve the purée if necessary.

Roasting Fresh Chillies

There are several ways of roasting fresh chillies. You use the grill, roast in the oven, dry-fry as explained below, or hold them over a gas flame.

1 Put the chillies in a dry frying pan and place over the heat until the skins are charred and blistered. Alternatively, roast the chillies in a griddle pan.

2 For larger chillies that are to be stuffed, make a neat slit down the side of each one. Place in a dry frying pan over a moderate heat, turning frequently until the skins blister.

3 To roast chillies on a skewer over a flame, spear them on a long-handled metal skewer and roast them over the flame of a gas burner until the skins blister and darken.

4 Slip the roasted chillies into a strong plastic bag and tie the top to keep the steam in.

5 Set aside for 20 minutes. Take the chillies out of the bag and remove the skins, either by peeling them off, or by rubbing the chillies with a clean dishtowel. Cut off the stalks, then slit the chillies and, using a sharp knife, scrape out and discard the seeds.

Grinding Chillies

When making chilli powder, this method gives a distinctive and smoky taste.

1 Soak the chillies, if dried, pat dry and then dry fry in a heavy pan until crisp. You can also do this on a griddle. In either case, watch the chillies carefully because they can suddenly burn, and then you have to start all over again!

2 Transfer to a mortar and grind to a fine powder with a pestle. Store in an airtight container.

Making a Chilli Flower

This makes a very attractive garnish for a special dish.

1 Wearing rubber gloves and using a small pair of scissors or a slim-bladed knife, cut a chilli carefully lengthwise from the tip to within 1cm/½in of the stem end. Repeat this at regular intervals around the chilli – more cuts will produce more petals.

2 Rinse the chilli in cold water and remove all the seeds. Place in a bowl of iced water and chill for at least 4 hours. For very curly flowers, leave the chilli overnight. When ready to use, lift the chilli out and drain it on kitchen paper.

SPICE POWDERS

The name "curry powder" used to be attached to any ground spice mixture used for making hot or highly flavoured foods. It isn't an authentic term, but is a corruption of the Tamil word "karhi", which simply means a food cooked in a sauce. During the days of the Raj, British merchants and soldiers returning home were eager to continue enjoying the flavours they had encountered in India, and demand for a commercial curry powder was the result. The first of these were crude mixtures, bearing little resemblance to the sophisticated and often subtle blends that Indian cooks produced every day. These differed according to whether they were to be used for meat, poultry, fish or vegetables, and reflected the personal tastes of the maker.

Above: Ancho powder

Today, although bought curry powders have improved greatly, many individuals prefer to make their own spice mixtures in the traditional fashion, roasting and grinding whole spices and savouring the wonderful aroma that is part and parcel of the procedure.

Chillies do not feature in all spice blends, but are typical of those that originated in hot spots such as Madras, Mysore or Goa (the home of vindaloo).

Dry spice mixes – or curry powders – are popular in India, Pakistan and Sri Lanka. Each region has its own favourite blend of spices. When making your own spice powders and pastes, feel free to experiment with different types of dried or fresh chillies. Where chilli powder is listed in recipes, you can opt for the blended spice or a pure powder from a specific type of chilli.

Classic Curry Powder

This mixture can be modified to suit your own personal taste. Try not to keep it too long, or it will lose its aroma.

MAKES ABOUT 115G/4OZ/1 CUP

INGREDIENTS
    6–8 dried red chillies
    105ml/7 tbsp coriander seeds
    60ml/4 tbsp cumin seeds
    10ml/2 tsp fenugreek seeds
    10ml/2 tsp black mustard seeds
    10ml/2 tsp black peppercorns
    15ml/1 tbsp ground turmeric
    5ml/1 tsp ground ginger

1 Unless you like a fiery mixture, snap off the stalks from the dried chillies and shake out and discard most of the seeds and all the stalks.

2 Heat a heavy pan and dry-fry the chillies with the seeds and black peppercorns over a medium heat until they give off a rich aroma. Shake the pan constantly so that the spices are evenly roasted.

3 Tip the roasted spices into a mortar and grind them to a smooth powder. Alternatively, use a spice grinder or a coffee grinder reserved for spices.

4 Stir in the ground turmeric and the ginger. Use immediately or store in an airtight jar protected from strong light.

Below: Classic curry powder

Mild Curry Powder

This is a basic recipe for a mild Indian curry powder, but you can adjust the quantities to suit your taste.

MAKES ABOUT 115G/4OZ/1 CUP

INGREDIENTS
Whole spices
    50g/2oz/½ cup coriander seeds
    60ml/4 tbsp cumin seeds
    30ml/2 tbsp fennel seeds
    30ml/2 tbsp fenugreek seeds
    4 dried red chillies
    5 curry leaves
Ground spices
    15ml/1 tbsp chilli powder
    15ml/1 tbsp ground turmeric
    2.5ml/½ tsp salt

1 Dry-roast the whole spices in a large heavy-based frying pan for 8–10 minutes, shaking the pan from side to side until the spices begin to darken and release a rich aroma. Allow them to cool slightly.

2 Put the spices in a spice grinder or mini food processor and process gently to achieve a fine powder.

3 Add the remaining ground spices and store in an airtight jar.

Garam Masala

Garam means "hot" and masala means "spices" so the spices used are those that "heat" the body, such as chillies, black peppercorns, cinnamon and cloves. Garam masala is added at the end of cooking and sprinkled over dishes as a garnish.

Below: Garam masala

MAKES ABOUT 50G/2OZ/½ CUP

INGREDIENTS
    10 dried red chillies
    2 × 2.5cm/1in cinnamon sticks
    2 curry leaves
    30ml/2 tbsp coriander seeds
    30ml/2 tbsp cumin seeds
    5ml/1 tsp black peppercorns
    5ml/1 tsp cloves
    5ml/1 tsp fenugreek seeds
    5ml/1 tsp black mustard seeds
    1.5ml/¼ tsp chilli powder

1 Dry-fry the chillies, cinnamon sticks and curry leaves in a large heavy frying pan for 2 minutes until you smell the spices as they roast.

2 Add the coriander and cumin seeds, peppercorns, cloves, fenugreek and mustard seeds, and dry-fry for a further 8–10 minutes, shaking the pan from side to side until the spices begin to darken and release a rich aroma.

3 Allow the mixture to cool slightly before grinding. Put the mixture into a spice grinder or electric coffee grinder, kept for spice grinding, or use a pestle and mortar. Grind to a fine powder. Add the chilli powder, mix together and store the powder in an airtight jar.

COOK'S TIP
Garam masala will keep for 2–4 months in an airtight container and the flavours will mature during storage.

Keep a lid on it
If your pan is a fairly shallow one, put a lid over it when frying the mustard seeds. When they pop, they can travel a surprising distance. Shiver the pan from side to side while the seeds are frying, so that they do not stick to the base. Fry over a gentle heat. You can use this technique for other small seeds, such as cumin.

Sambaar Powder

This blend of spices and dhal is used in South Indian cooking to flavour vegetable and lentil combinations, braised dishes and spicy broths. The powder also acts as a thickening agent.

MAKES ABOUT 105ML/7 TBSP

INGREDIENTS
    8–10 dried red chillies
    90ml/6 tbsp coriander seeds
    30ml/2 tbsp cumin seeds
    10ml/2 tsp black peppercorns
    10ml/2 tsp fenugreek seeds
    10ml/2 tsp urad dhal (white split
        gram beans)
    10ml/2 tsp channa dhal (yellow
        split peas)
    10ml/2 tsp mung dhal (yellow
        mung beans)
    25ml/1½ tbsp ground turmeric

1 Snap off the stalks from the dried chillies and shake out most of the seeds. Heat a heavy frying pan and add the first 5 ingredients.

2 Toss all the spices together over a medium heat until they give off a rich aroma, then turn into a bowl.

3 Repeat the process with the pulses, to toast them without letting them burn.

4 Mix the spices and pulses together, then grind them to a fine powder. Stir in the turmeric. Use immediately or store in an airtight jar away from strong light.

Below: Sambaar powder

Sri Lankan Curry Powder

This has totally different characteristics from Indian curry powders. The spices are roasted separately, and chilli powder is used instead of whole dried chillies. The result is a rich, dark curry powder that is ideal for fish, poultry, meat and vegetable curries.

In Sri Lanka, coriander, cumin, fennel and fenugreek seeds are roasted separately before being combined with roasted cinnamon, cloves and cardamom seeds. After grinding, chilli powder is stirred into the mixture, which is aromatic, rather than fiery. Colour and presentation are key features of Sri Lankan cuisine, and you will often find red, yellow and even black curries artistically arranged around a central bowl of rice.

MAKES ABOUT 75G/3OZ/¾ CUP

INGREDIENTS
   90ml/6 tbsp coriander seeds
   45ml/3 tbsp cumin seeds
   15ml/1 tbsp fennel seeds
   5ml/1 tsp fenugreek seeds
   5cm/2in piece cinnamon stick
   5ml/1 tsp cloves
   8 green cardamom pods
   6 dried curry leaves
   5–10ml/1–2 tsp chilli powder

1 Dry-fry or roast the coriander seeds, cumin seeds, fennel seeds and fenugreek seeds separately, because they all turn dark at different stages. Do not let the spices burn; remove them as soon as they give off a rich aroma.

2 Dry-fry the cinnamon stick, cloves and cardamom pods together for a few minutes until they give off a pungent aroma.

Above: Sri Lankan Curry powder

3 As soon as they are cool enough to handle, remove the seeds from the cardamom pods and place them in a mortar. Add the remaining dry-fried ingredients, then the curry leaves. Grind to a smooth powder. Alternatively, use a spice grinder.

4 Stir in the chilli powder. Use immediately or store in an airtight jar away from strong light.

Singapore-style Curry Powder

Chillies are a key ingredient in this curry powder for poultry and meat dishes.

MAKES ABOUT 75G/3OZ/¾ CUP

INGREDIENTS
   3–4 dried red chillies
   90ml/6 tbsp coriander seeds
   15ml/1 tbsp cumin seeds
   15ml/1 tbsp fennel seeds
   10ml/2 tsp black peppercorns
   2.5cm/1in piece cinnamon stick
   4 green cardamom pods
   6 cloves
   10ml/2 tsp ground turmeric

1 Unless you like a fiery mixture, snap off the stalks from the dried chillies and shake out most of the seeds.

2 Heat a heavy pan and add all the seeds, with the chillies, peppercorns, cinnamon stick, cardamoms and cloves. Dry-fry over a medium heat, stirring, until the spices give off a rich aroma.

Above: Singapore-style curry powder

3 When cool enough to handle, break the cinnamon stick into small pieces and remove the seeds from the cardamom pods.

4 Grind all the roasted spices to a fine powder in a mortar. Alternatively, use a spice grinder or an electric coffee grinder reserved for spices.

5 Stir in the ground turmeric. Use immediately or store in an airtight jar away from strong light.

> **VARIATION**
> To adapt Singapore-style curry powder for using with fish and shellfish, use only 2–3 chillies and 5ml/1 tsp black peppercorns, but increase the fennel seeds to 30ml/ 2 tbsp. Add 5ml/1 tsp fenugreek seeds. Leave out the cinnamon stick, cardamom pods and cloves.

Seven-seas Curry Powder

Like Sri Lankan Curry Powder, this uses chilli powder rather than whole dried chillies. Milder than some of the other mixtures, it combines the fiery taste of chilli with the warm flavours of cumin, cinnamon and cloves. It is widely used in Indonesian and Malaysian cooking.

MAKES ABOUT 90G/3½OZ/SCANT 1 CUP

INGREDIENTS
  6–8 white cardamom
    pods, bruised
  90ml/6 tbsp coriander seeds
  45ml/3 tbsp cumin seeds
  25ml/1½ tbsp celery seeds
  5cm/2in piece cinnamon stick
    or cassia
  6–8 cloves
  15ml/1 tbsp chilli powder

1 Put the cardamom pods in a heavy frying pan with all the other whole spices. Dry-fry the mixture, stirring it and shaking the pan constantly, until the spices give off a rich, heavy aroma.

2 When they are cool enough to handle, remove the cardamom seeds from the pods, then grind them finely with all the other roasted ingredients.

3 Add the chilli powder and mix. Use immediately or store in an airtight jar.

Below: Seven-seas curry powder

Malayan-Chinese Curry Powder

This is good for poultry, especially chicken, and robust fish curries. You can double or even treble the quantities, but it is better to make a smaller amount and use it fairly quickly, as curry powder will stale if stored for too long.

MAKES ABOUT 60ML/4 TBSP

INGREDIENTS
  2 dried red chillies
  6 whole cloves
  1 small cinnamon stick
  5ml/1 tsp coriander seeds
  5ml/1 tsp fennel seeds
  10ml/2 tsp Sichuan peppercorns
  2.5ml/½ tsp grated nutmeg
  2.5ml/½ tsp ground star anise
  5ml/1 tsp ground turmeric

1 Snap or cut the tops off the dried chillies and shake out most of the seeds. Use a small, sharp knife to remove any remaining seeds.

2 Put the chillies, cloves, cinnamon stick, coriander seeds and fennel seeds in a wok or heavy frying pan. Add the Sichuan peppercorns. Dry-fry over a medium heat, tossing the spices frequently, until they give off a rich, spicy aroma.

3 Tip the spices into a mortar and grind them to a smooth powder. Alternatively, use a spice grinder or an electric coffee grinder reserved for spices.

4 Stir in the grated nutmeg, star anise and turmeric. Use immediately or store in an airtight jar away from strong light to keep its flavour.

COOK'S TIPS
• When you are buying spices, always go to stores where there will be a good turnover. Indian or Asian speciality stores would be ideal. Whole spices do not have an indefinite shelf life, and you want to get the best flavour from your spice mix. Buy individual spices in small quantities and write the date of purchase on the packet if you are buying them loose and they do not have a "best before" date stamped on them. Then you can check them regularly and throw out any that have been stored for more than a couple of months.
• Although it is best to make curry powder and similar spice mixes in small quantities, a trip to a market with a fine selection of fresh spices might tempt you to make a large amount. Put some of the surplus in small jars as gifts for friends who like to cook, and store the rest in airtight tubs in the freezer.

SPICE PASTES

Unlike powdered blends, pastes are made from what are called "wet spices": lemon grass, fresh ginger, garlic, galangal, shallots, tamarind and chillies. These are traditionally ground using a mortar and pestle, but today a food processor is often used for convenience and speed. Supermarkets stock some excellent ready-made spice pastes, but making your own is simple and highly satisfying. Any surplus paste can be stored in a tub in the freezer.

Thai cooking is based on curry pastes. Thai cooks strive to create a balance between spicy hot, sweet, sour and salty tastes, and their curries reflect this. There are three principal types of curry paste – red, green and sour. Fresh ingredients such as chillies, lemon grass and shallots are given a salty tang with shrimp paste, while citrus juice and rind adds a touch of sourness. Fresh pastes can be bought from any Thai market, but most cooks prefer to make their own as needed. You will find commercial curry powder in Thailand – used in dishes such as stir-fried crab in curry sauce – but pastes are preferred.

Madrasi Masala

Masalas can be dry mixes or pastes. This one belongs to the latter category, and is a blend of dry and wet spices. The paste is cooked in oil to develop the flavours.

MAKES ABOUT 450G/1LB/2½ CUPS

INGREDIENTS
  120ml/8 tbsp coriander seeds
  60ml/4 tbsp cumin seeds
  15ml/1 tbsp black peppercorns
  15ml/1 tbsp black mustard seeds
  165ml/11 tbsp ground turmeric
  45–60ml/3–4 tbsp chilli powder
  15ml/1 tbsp salt
  8 garlic cloves, crushed
  7.5cm/3in piece fresh root ginger,
    peeled and finely grated (shredded)
  about 60ml/4 tbsp cider vinegar
  175ml/6fl oz/¾ cup sunflower oil

1 Heat a heavy frying pan and dry-fry the coriander seeds, cumin seeds and peppercorns for 1–2 minutes, stirring.

Above: Madrasi masala

2 Add the mustard seeds and toss constantly over the heat until they start to pop and the mixture gives off a rich aroma. Do not let the spices become too dark.

3 Grind the mixture to a fine powder, then add the turmeric, chilli and salt. Stir in the garlic, ginger and enough of the vinegar to make a paste.

4 Heat the oil in a large frying pan and fry the paste, stirring and turning it constantly, until the oil begins to separate from the spicy mixture.

5 Spoon the masala into a clean jar. Make sure that there is a film of oil floating on top. This will form an airtight seal and act as a preservative, ensuring that the paste keeps its colour. Store in the refrigerator for 2–3 weeks.

Thai Red Curry Paste

Some excellent versions of this classic paste are now produced commercially, but if you prefer to make your own, here's how.

MAKES ABOUT 175G/6OZ/1 CUP

INGREDIENTS
  3 lemon grass stalks
  10 fresh red chillies, seeded
    and sliced
  115g/4oz dark red onions or
    shallots, chopped
  4 garlic cloves
  1cm/½in piece fresh galangal,
    peeled, sliced and bruised
  stems from 4 fresh coriander
    (cilantro) sprigs
  15–30ml/1–2 tbsp groundnut
    (peanut) oil
  5ml/1 tsp grated (shredded) dried
    citrus rind
  1cm/½in cube of shrimp paste,
    wrapped in foil and warmed in a
    frying pan
  15ml/1 tbsp coriander seeds
  10ml/2 tsp cumin seeds
  5ml/1 tsp salt

1 Slice the tender lower portion of the lemon grass stalks and bruise them with a cleaver. Put them in a large mortar and add the chillies, onions or shallots, garlic, galangal and coriander stems.

2 Grind with a pestle, gradually adding the oil until the mixture forms a paste. Alternatively, purée the ingredients in a food processor or blender. Add the citrus rind and the shrimp paste. Mix well.

3 Dry-fry the coriander seeds and cumin seeds in a frying pan, then tip them into a large mortar and grind to a powder. Stir into the spice paste, with the salt.

4 Use the paste immediately, or scrape it into a glass jar. Cover with clear film (plastic wrap) and an airtight lid, then store in the refrigerator for 3–4 weeks.

Left: Thai red curry paste

Green Curry Paste

This medium-hot curry paste with its vivid green colour is based on chillies. It is good used with lamb, beef or chicken.

MAKES ABOUT 75G/3OZ/½ CUP

INGREDIENTS
2 lemon grass stalks
15 fresh hot green chillies
3 shallots, sliced
2 garlic cloves
15ml/1 tbsp chopped fresh galangal
4 kaffir lime leaves, chopped
2.5ml/½ tsp grated (shredded) kaffir lime rind
5ml/1 tsp chopped coriander (cilantro) root
6 black peppercorns
5ml/1 tsp coriander seeds, roasted
5ml/1 tsp cumin seeds, roasted
15ml/1 tbsp granulated sugar
5ml/1 tsp salt
15–30ml/1–2 tbsp groundnut (peanut) oil

1 Slice the tender lower portion of the lemon grass and bruise with a cleaver. Put them in a large mortar and add all the remaining ingredients except the oil. Grind to a paste. Add the oil, a little at a time, blending between each addition.

2 Use the paste immediately, or scrape it into a glass jar. Cover with clear film (plastic wrap) and an airtight lid. Store in the refrigerator for 3–4 weeks.

Below: Green curry paste

Thai Mussaman Curry Paste

Originating from the Malaysian border area, this paste can be used with beef, chicken or duck.

MAKES ABOUT 175G/6OZ/1 CUP

INGREDIENTS
12 large dried red chillies
1 lemon grass stalk
60ml/4 tbsp chopped shallots
5 garlic cloves, roughly chopped
10ml/2 tsp chopped fresh galangal or fresh root ginger
5ml/1 tsp cumin seeds
15ml/1 tbsp coriander seeds
2 cloves
6 black peppercorns
1cm/½ in cube of shrimp paste, wrapped in foil and warmed in a frying pan
5ml/1 tsp salt
5ml/1 tsp granulated sugar
30ml/2 tbsp oil

1 Snap the dried chillies and shake out most of the seeds. Discard the stems. Soak the chillies in a bowl of hot water for 20–30 minutes.

2 Cut the tender lower portion of the lemon grass stalk into small pieces, using a small sharp knife. Place in a dry wok. Add the chopped shallots, roughly chopped garlic and galangal or ginger and dry-fry for a moment or two until the mixture gives off an aroma.

3 Stir in the whole cumin seeds, coriander seeds, cloves and peppercorns, and continue to dry-fry over a low heat for 5–6 minutes, stirring constantly. Spoon the mixture into a large mortar.

Above: Thai Mussaman curry paste

4 Drain the chillies and add them to the mortar. Use a pestle to grind the mixture finely, then add the prepared shrimp paste with the salt, granulated sugar and oil. Pound to form a rough paste. Use as required, then spoon any leftover paste into a jar, seal tightly and store in the refrigerator for up to 4 months.

COOK'S TIP
Shrimp paste is made from fermented shrimps. Also known as blachan, terasi, kapi or ngapi, it is widely used in the cooking of South-east Asia. It is available from Asian food stores and comes in block form, or packed in tiny tubs or jars. It smells rather vile because it is fermented, but the odour vanishes as soon as the paste is cooked. Warming it tempers the raw taste; the easiest way to do this is to wrap a small cube in foil and dry-fry it in a frying pan for about 5 minutes, turning it occasionally to heat evenly.

SAMBALS

When Westerners speak of sambals, they are usually referring to the side dishes served with curry – diced cucumber, sliced bananas and yogurt. These dishes are designed to cool the palate, but true sambals are something else entirely. They are extremely hot sauces or relishes based on chillies. Traditionally, they are served in small bowls, and used like mustard, to pep up other dishes. A sambal can also be a dish cooked with a hot chilli paste.

Chilli Sambal

This Indonesian speciality – *sambal oelek* – is a very simple mixture, made by pounding hot chillies with salt. Tamarind water is sometimes added, and Asian cooks will occasionally temper its heat by stirring ground roasted peanuts into the mixture.

MAKES 450G/1LB/2½ CUPS

INGREDIENTS
    450g/1lb fresh red chillies, seeded
    10ml/2 tsp salt

1 Cut the chillies in half and remove the stems. Using a sharp knife, scrape out and discard the seeds. Bring a pan of water to the boil, add the chillies and cook for 5–8 minutes.

2 Drain the chillies and tip them into a food processor or blender. Process to a rough paste.

3 Add the salt, process briefly to mix, then scrape the paste into a glass jar. Cover with clear film (plastic wrap) and a lid and store in the refrigerator. To serve, spoon into small dishes and offer the sambal as an accompaniment, or use it as suggested in recipes.

Sambal Blachan

Hot chillies can hold their own against strong flavours, as this sambal proves. The shrimp paste gives it a pungent quality, while the lemon or lime juice adds a welcome sharpness. Sambal blachan is frequently served with rice dishes. The rice tempers the heat.

MAKES ABOUT 30ML/2 TBSP

INGREDIENTS
    2–4 fresh red chillies, seeded
    salt
    1cm/½in cube of shrimp paste
    juice of ½ lemon or lime

1 Chop the chillies roughly and place them in a mortar. Add a little salt, then use a pestle to pound them to a paste.

2 Warm the shrimp paste, either by moulding it on to the end of a metal skewer and heating it in a gas flame until the outside begins to look dry, or by wrapping the paste in foil and heating it in a dry frying pan for about 5 minutes.

3 Add the shrimp paste to the chillies and pound to mix well. Stir in lemon or lime juice to taste.

Above: Sambal kecap

Sambal Kecap

Frequently served as a dip with chicken or beef satays, instead of the more usual peanut sauce, this is also delicious with deep-fried chicken.

MAKES ABOUT 150ML/¼ PINT/⅔ CUP

INGREDIENTS
    1 fresh red chilli, seeded and
        finely chopped
    2 garlic cloves, crushed
    60ml/4 tbsp dark soy sauce
    20ml/4 tsp lemon juice or 15ml/
        1 tbsp tamarind juice
    30ml/2 tbsp hot water
    30ml/2 tbsp deep-fried onion
        slices (optional)

1 Place the chopped chilli, crushed garlic and soy sauce in a small bowl. Stir in the lemon or tamarind juice, mix well, then thin with the hot water.

2 Stir in the deep-fried onion slices, if using. Cover and leave the sambal to stand for about 30 minutes before using.

COOK'S TIP
Deep-fried onion slices are very easy to make. Cut 2–3 onions in half, then into very thin slices. Blot these dry on kitchen paper, then add them to hot oil. Lower the heat slightly and cook until the onions have firmed up and browned. Lift out with a slotted spoon, drain on kitchen paper and leave until cold.

Above: Chilli sambal and sambal blachan (right)

Nam Prik Sauce

This is the universal Thai sauce, served solo, with rice or as a dip for fresh vegetables. The quantities can be varied.

MAKES ABOUT 275G/10OZ/1½–2 CUPS

INGREDIENTS
    50g/2oz dried prawns (shrimp)
    1cm/½in cube of shrimp paste, wrapped in foil and warmed in a frying pan
    3–4 garlic cloves, crushed
    3–4 fresh red chillies, seeded and sliced
    50g/2oz peeled cooked prawns (shrimp)
    a few coriander (cilantro) sprigs
    8–10 tiny baby aubergines (eggplant)
    45–60ml/3–4 tbsp lemon or lime juice
    30ml/2 tbsp Thai fish sauce (*nam pla*) or to taste
    10–15ml/2–3 tsp soft light brown sugar

1 Soak the dried prawns in water for 15 minutes. Drain and put in a mortar with the shrimp paste, garlic and chillies. Pound to a paste with a pestle, or process in a food processor. Add the cooked prawns and coriander. Pound or process again until combined.

2 Chop the aubergines roughly and gradually pound them into the sauce. Add the lemon or lime juice, fish sauce and sugar to taste.

Below: Nam prik sauce

Above: Sambal Salamat

Sambal Salamat

This hot tomato sambal is very popular in Indonesia. It has a very strong flavour and should be used sparingly.

MAKES ABOUT 120ML/4FL OZ/½ CUP

INGREDIENTS
    3 ripe tomatoes
    2.5ml/½ tsp salt
    5ml/1 tsp chilli sauce
    60ml/4 tbsp Thai fish sauce (*nam pla*)
    15ml/1 tbsp chopped fresh coriander (cilantro) leaves

1 Cut a small cross in the base of each tomato. Place them in a heatproof bowl and pour over boiling water to cover. Leave the tomatoes in the water for 30 seconds.

2 Lift out the tomatoes with a slotted spoon and plunge them into a bowl of cold water. The skins will have begun to peel back from the crosses. Remove the skins completely, cut the tomatoes in half and squeeze out the seeds. Chop the flesh finely and put it in a bowl.

3 Add the salt, chilli sauce, fish sauce and coriander. Mix well. Set aside for at least 2 hours before serving, so that the flavours can blend.

VARIATION
Use a fresh red chilli instead of chilli sauce, if you prefer. Slit it, remove the seeds and then chop the flesh finely. To give the sambal a slightly smoky flavour, roast the chilli under the grill (broiler) until the skin blisters and begins to blacken, then remove the skin and seeds before chopping the flesh.

Above: Nuoc Cham

Nuoc Cham

In Vietnam, this fiery sauce is used as a condiment, and serves much the same purpose as salt and pepper does in the West. It tastes good with fried spring rolls. Chillies are widely used in Vietnamese cooking, especially in the centre of the country, where it is believed that eating them frequently keeps mosquitoes away and malaria at bay.

MAKES ABOUT 105ML/7 TBSP

INGREDIENTS
    2 fresh red chillies, seeded
    2 garlic cloves, crushed
    15ml/1 tbsp granulated sugar
    45ml/3 tbsp Thai fish sauce. (*nam pla*)
    juice of 1 lime or ½ lemon

1 Chop the chillies roughly, place them in a large mortar and use a pestle to pound them to a paste.

2 Scrape the paste into a bowl and add the garlic, sugar and fish sauce. Stir in lime or lemon juice to taste.

AFRICAN SPICE MIXTURES

Chillies are not native to Africa. They were introduced by Portuguese and Arab traders, but Africans really warmed to them, partly for the flavour they brought to a diet that was sometimes rather bland, and partly for the cooling effect they had on the skin by promoting perspiration. Today, Africa is an important chilli producer, with Nigeria, Ethiopia, Uganda, Kenya and Tanzania leading the field.

One of the world's most famous chilli pastes – harissa – comes from North Africa. A spicy blend of red chillies, coriander and cumin, it has a host of uses. Moroccan and Tunisian cooks serve it solo or with puréed tomatoes as a side dish for dipping pieces of barbecue-cooked meat. It is wonderful for adding to soups and stews and also serves as the basis of a sauce for serving over couscous.

Right: Large dried red chillies are used in harissa.

Dried chilli spice mixes are also popular in Africa. They invariably include warm spices such as cardamom, cumin, coriander and ginger, and are used with fish, meat and vegetables. The best-known spice mixes are Berbere, which comes from Ethiopia, and *Ras-el-hanout*, a Moroccan chilli powder that can include upwards of 20 different spices. This also comes as a paste. Tsire powder is a simple peanut and spice mixture used in West Africa for coating kebabs.

Harissa

Serve this hot, spicy condiment as a dipping sauce, or stir it into soups or stews. When added to natural (plain) yogurt, it makes a very good marinade for pork or chicken.

MAKES ABOUT 120ML/4FL OZ/½ CUP

INGREDIENTS
    12 dried red chillies
    15ml/1 tbsp coriander seeds
    10ml/2 tsp cumin seeds
    2 garlic cloves
    2.5ml/½ tsp salt
    60–90ml/4–6 tbsp olive oil

1 Snap the chillies and shake out some, but not all, of the seeds. Discard the stems, then put the chillies in a bowl and pour over warm water to cover. Soak for 20–30 minutes, until softened.

2 Meanwhile, dry-fry the coriander seeds and cumin seeds in a frying pan until they give off a rich aroma. Tip them into a mortar and grind them to a powder with a pestle. Tip them into a bowl and set them aside.

3 Put the garlic in the mortar, sprinkle it with the salt, and pound to a paste. Drain the chillies, add them to the paste and pound until it is smooth.

4 Add the spices, then gradually work in the oil, trickling it in and mixing until the sauce is well blended and has a consistency like that of mayonnaise.

Below: Harissa

Above: Tsire powder

Tsire Powder

This simple spice mixture is used as a coating for kebabs throughout West Africa. Cubes of raw meat are first dipped in oil or beaten egg and then coated in the powder. The cooked kebabs are dusted with a little more tsire powder before being served.

MAKES ABOUT 60ML/4 TBSP

INGREDIENTS
    50g/2oz/½ cup salted peanuts
    5ml/1 tsp mixed spice or apple
        pie spice
    2.5–5ml/½–1 tsp chilli powder
    salt

1 Grind the peanuts to a coarse powder in a mortar, blender or food processor.

2 Add the mixed spice or apple pie spice, chilli powder and a little salt. Mix or process until well blended.

3 Use immediately or transfer to an airtight container, close tightly and store in a cool place for up to 6 weeks.

COOK'S TIP
Mixed spice is a commercial mixture of ready ground spices. It typically contains allspice, cinnamon, cloves, ginger and nutmeg. Similar blends are marketed as apple pie spice or pumpkin pie spice. It is best used within 6 months of purchase to enjoy the best flavour.

Above: Berbere

Berbere

Ethiopia produces some of Africa's most delicious food. Dishes, such as the spicy stews, fuelled by the fire of this hot spice mixture, are served on large discs of bread, called *injera*.

MAKES ABOUT 50G/2OZ/SCANT ½ CUP

INGREDIENTS
  10 dried red chillies
  8 white cardamom pods
  5ml/1 tsp cumin seeds
  5ml/1 tsp coriander seeds
  5ml/1 tsp fenugreek seeds
  8 cloves
  5ml/1 tsp allspice berries
  10ml/2 tsp black peppercorns
  5ml/1 tsp ajowan seeds
  5ml/1 tsp ground ginger
  2.5ml/½ tsp grated nutmeg
  30ml/2 tbsp salt

1 Snap the chillies and shake out some of the seeds. Remove the stalks. Heat a heavy frying pan. Bruise the cardamom pods and add them to the pan with the chilli, cumin, coriander, fenugreek, cloves, allspice berries, peppercorns and ajowan seeds. Roast the spices, shaking the pan over a medium heat, until they give off a rich aroma.

2 Seed the cardamoms, then tip all the roasted spices into a large mortar, spice mill or coffee grinder kept specifically for spices. Grind to a fine powder. Stir in the ginger, nutmeg and salt. Use immediately or transfer to an airtight jar.

Baharat

Variations on this spice are to be found in all the countries that border the eastern Mediterranean, from Egypt and Jordan to the Lebanon and Syria. Its use has also spread south, to the Sudan and Ethiopia. An indication of just how fundamental it is to the cooking of these areas is to be found in its Arabic name, which simply translates as "spice". The recipe here is a basic one, but there are umpteen variations, some including cassia bark.

MAKES ABOUT 115G/4OZ/1 CUP

INGREDIENTS
  1 cinnamon stick
  30ml/2 tbsp coriander seeds
  30ml/2 tbsp cumin seeds
  90ml/6 tbsp cardamom seeds
  30ml/2 tbsp cloves
  30ml/2 tbsp black peppercorns
  60ml/4 tbsp paprika
  5ml/1 tsp ground allspice
  10ml/2 tsp grated nutmeg
  10ml/2 tsp chilli powder

1 Grind the cinnamon stick in a spice mill or a coffee grinder kept especially for spices. Tip the ground cinnamon into a bowl.

2 Heat a frying pan. Add the coriander seeds, cumin seeds, cardamom seeds, cloves and peppercorns. Roast the spices, shaking the pan over a medium heat, until they give off a rich aroma and just begin to change colour.

3 Grind the whole roasted spices, in batches if necessary, until they form a fine powder. This can be done using a mortar and pestle. Alternatively use an electric spice mill or coffee grinder.

4 Add the ground spice mixture to the cinnamon and mix well to blend the flavours.

5 Stir in the paprika, ground allspice, grated nutmeg and chilli powder. Use immediately, or transfer to an airtight jar and store out of the light to retain its colour and strength.

COOK'S TIPS
• Ajowan seeds resemble cumin seeds in appearance. When crushed, they release a powerful aroma reminiscent of thyme. If you can't locate these seeds, use extra cumin instead, or stir in a little dried thyme just before using the spice.
• If you are unlikely to use the Berbere spice mix quickly, store it in an airtight plastic container in the freezer where it will keep for several months.

Ras-el-hanout
What distinguishes this traditional Moroccan spice mixture is its complexity. It can contain more than 20 different ingredients, including dried rose petals. Every spice merchant seems to have a different blend, and recipes are jealously guarded. Chillies are usually in there somewhere, along with cinnamon, cardamom, coriander seeds, cloves, salt, peppercorns, ginger, nutmeg, turmeric, but it is the secret extras – some of which are rumoured to have aphrodisiac qualities – that really set it apart.

BARBECUE SPICE MIXTURES

Spice rubs and marinades are a boon to the barbecue cook, improving the appearance and flavour of cooked meats, poultry and fish while filling the air with a tantalizing aroma. Many of the mixtures are also delicious on roast chicken; just brush the bird lightly with olive oil before cooking, sprinkle the barbecue spice over it and rub in.

Basic Barbecue Spice Mix

Rub this on chops, steaks or portions of chicken. To make a marinade, add the mixture to a glass of red or white wine. Add a few slices of onion and stir in 60ml/4 tbsp of garlic-flavoured oil (or chilli oil if you are feeling adventurous).

MAKES ABOUT 60ML/4 TBSP

INGREDIENTS
    10ml/2 tsp celery seeds
    5ml/1 tsp paprika
    5ml/1 tsp grated nutmeg
    5ml/1 tsp chilli powder
    5ml/1 tsp garlic powder
    5ml/1 tsp onion salt
    10ml/2 tsp dried marjoram
    5ml/1 tsp salt
    5–10ml/1–2 tsp soft light brown sugar
    5ml/1 tsp lightly ground black pepper

1 Put the celery seeds in a mortar and grind to a powder with a pestle, or use a spice mill. Tip the powder into a bowl and stir in the remaining ingredients. Use the spice mixture immediately or store in an airtight jar.

Below: Basic barbecue spice mix

Above: Old-fashioned Philadelphia spice powder

Old-fashioned Philadelphia Spice Powder

This only has a trace of chilli, but the taste combines well with the warm, rounded flavours of the nutmeg and mace. The mixture makes a truly great seasoning for a pork joint, or can be rubbed both on steaks and chops. Do this in plenty of time before you plan to roast or cook on the barbecue, to allow the flavours to develop.

MAKES ABOUT 30–45ML/2–3 TBSP

INGREDIENTS
    8 cloves
    5ml/1 tsp chilli powder
    2.5ml/½ tsp grated nutmeg
    1.5ml/¼ tsp ground mace
    5ml/1 tsp dried basil
    5ml/1 tsp dried thyme
    2 dried bay leaves
    salt

1 Grind the cloves to a coarse powder, then add the other ingredients and continue grinding until fine.

2 Use immediately or store in an airtight container, away from strong light.

COOK'S TIP
All spices and spice mixtures start to deteriorate soon after being ground, so try to use them as soon as possible. Store in airtight and preferably tinted glass jars in a cool place, away from direct light, or keep them in the freezer.

Jamaican Jerk Paste

Give pork chops or chicken pieces a taste-lift with this delectable paste. Scotch bonnet chillies would be used in Jamaica, but they are extremely hot, so unless you are a devout chilli-head, you might prefer to substitute a milder variety, or reduce the quantity.

SUFFICIENT FOR FOUR MEAT PIECES

INGREDIENTS
    15ml/1 tbsp oil
    2 onions, finely chopped
    2 fresh red chillies, seeded and
        finely chopped
    1 garlic clove, crushed
    2.5cm/1in piece of fresh root
        ginger, grated (shredded)
    5ml/1 tsp dried thyme
    5ml/1 tsp ground allspice
    5ml/1 tsp Tabasco sauce or other
        hot pepper sauce
    30ml/2 tbsp rum
    grated (shredded) rind and juice
        of 1 lime
    salt and ground black pepper

1 Heat the oil in a frying pan. Add the onions and cook for 10 minutes until soft. Stir in the chillies, garlic, ginger, thyme and allspice, and fry for 2 minutes more. Stir in the Tabasco sauce or hot pepper sauce, rum, lime rind and juice.

2 Simmer until the mixture forms a dark paste with a rich aroma. Season with salt and pepper, and leave to cool.

3 To use, rub over chops or chicken pieces, place in a shallow dish, cover and chill for 8 hours or overnight before barbecuing (grilling) or roasting.

Chermoula

This Moroccan mixture makes a very good marinade for meaty fish, but you can also use it as a cold sauce for fried fish. It is important to not use too much onion.

SUFFICIENT FOR 675G/1½LB FISH FILLETS

INGREDIENTS
    1 small red onion, finely chopped
    2 garlic cloves, crushed
    1 fresh red chilli, seeded and
      finely chopped
    30ml/2 tbsp chopped fresh
      coriander (cilantro)
    15ml/1 tbsp chopped fresh mint
    5ml/1 tsp ground cumin
    5ml/1 tsp paprika
    generous pinch of saffron threads
    60ml/4 tbsp olive oil
    juice of 1 lemon
    generous pinch of salt

1 Mix the onion, garlic, chilli, coriander, mint, cumin, paprika and saffron threads in a bowl. Add the olive oil, lemon juice and the salt. Mix well.

2 To use, add cubed fish to the bowl and toss until coated. Cover and leave in a cool place to marinate for 1 hour. Thread onto skewers and barbecue or grill (broil).

Thai Chilli and Citrus Marinade

This delectable combination of hot and sour flavours is perfect for chicken and seafood. Marinate fish or shellfish for about 1 hour; chicken for 3–4 hours.

MAKES ABOUT 175ML/6FL OZ/¾ CUP

INGREDIENTS
    2 small fresh red chillies
    15ml/1 tbsp granulated sugar
    2 garlic cloves, crushed
    white parts of 3 spring onions
      (scallions), chopped
    2.5cm/1in piece of fresh galangal or
      ginger, peeled and finely chopped
    grated (shredded) rind and juice of
      1 mandarin
    15ml/1 tbsp tamarind juice
    15ml/1 tbsp Thai fish sauce
      (*nam pla*)
    30ml/2 tbsp light soy sauce
    juice of 1 lime
    15ml/1 tbsp vegetable oil

1 Slit the chillies and scrape out the seeds. Chop the flesh roughly and put it in a mortar. Add the sugar and grind to a paste with a pestle.

2 Add the crushed garlic, chopped spring onions and chopped fresh galangal or ginger. Add the grated rind of the mandarin to the mortar. Grind to a paste.

3 Scrape the paste into a bowl. Squeeze the juice from the mandarin and add it to the paste, with the tamarind juice, fish sauce and soy sauce. Stir in the lime juice and oil, mixing well. Set the marinade aside for 30 minutes, to allow the flavours to blend before using as a marinade.

Peri-peri Barbecue Marinade

Peri-peri is a hot chilli sauce that originated in Portugal, but which is now popular wherever there are large Portuguese communities. It is widely used in South Africa and Mozambique, and makes a marvellous marinade that is particularly good with shellfish.

MAKES ABOUT 75ML/5 TBSP

INGREDIENTS
    1 fresh red chilli
    2.5ml/½ tsp paprika
    2.5ml/½ tsp ground coriander
    1 garlic clove, crushed
    juice of 1 lime
    30ml/2 tbsp olive oil
    salt and ground black pepper

1 Slit the chilli using a small sharp knife and scrape out and discard the seeds. Chop the flesh finely and put it in a small bowl.

2 Stir in the paprika, ground coriander, crushed garlic and lime juice, then whisk in the olive oil, using a fork or salad dressing whisk. Season to taste with salt and pepper. This makes an excellent marinade for prawns (shrimp) and can also be used with chicken. Marinate prawns for about 30 minutes; chicken for several hours. When cooking the shellfish or chicken on the barbecue, baste it with any of the remaining marinade.

COOK'S TIP
Tamarind pods yield a sour, fruity pulp that is as widely used in South-east Asia as lemon is in the West. Buy tamarind as a compressed block, in slices or as a concentrate. To use block tamarind, pinch off the equivalent of 15ml/1 tbsp and soak this in 150ml/¼ pint/⅔ cup warm water for 10 minutes. Swirl the tamarind with your fingers to release the pulp from the seeds, then strain the liquid through a nylon sieve into a bowl. Tamarind slices must also be soaked in warm water, while the concentrate is mixed with warm water in the ratio of 15ml/1 tbsp concentrate to 75ml/ 5 tbsp water.

CAJUN SPICE MIXTURES AND BASTES

Louisiana is home to some of the world's most exciting food, the marriage of French and Creole cooking with Spanish and African influences. The more sophisticated, cosmopolitan style is called Creole, while Cajun cooking is the food of rustic, country people; the trappers and fishers descended from the French who were exiled from Nova Scotia by the British in 1765. They like their food hot and spicy.

Cajun Spice Mix

This can be used as a seasoning for fish steaks, chicken or meat. It can also be used for gumbo, a thick soup or stew that generally contains okra, and for jambalaya.

MAKES ABOUT 150ML/¼ PINT/⅔ CUP

INGREDIENTS
1 onion
2 garlic cloves
5ml/1 tsp black peppercorns
5ml/1 tsp cumin seeds
5ml/1 tsp white mustard seeds
10ml/2 tsp paprika
5ml/1 tsp chilli powder or
  cayenne pepper
5ml/1 tsp dried oregano
10ml/2 tsp dried thyme
5ml/1 tsp salt

1 Finely chop the onion. Press the garlic firmly with the flat side of a wide-bladed knife to release the skin, then peel and chop it very finely. Set aside until ready to use.

2 Dry-fry the peppercorns, cumin and mustard seeds over a medium heat, to release their flavours, but do not allow them to burn.

3 Grind the dry-fried spices to a fine powder, then add the paprika, chilli powder or cayenne, oregano, thyme and salt. Grind again to achieve a uniformly fine mixture.

4 If the mix is to be used immediately, add the spices to the finely chopped garlic and onion in a blender or food processor and process until well combined. Alternatively, store the dry mixture in an airtight container, and add the garlic and onion only when ready to use the spice mix.

Below: Cajun spice mix

COOK'S TIP
A simple way to use this spice mix is as a coating for fish steaks, chicken pieces, pork chops or beef steaks that have been dipped in melted butter to help the spices adhere to the flesh. Fry the coated fish or meat in a large frying pan in hot oil or butter in a kitchen that has a good extractor fan, because the cooking process will produce a lot of smoke that can sting the eyes and produce unpleasant smells.

Chilli Pepper Baste

This sauce was developed by the McIlhenny family, producers of Tabasco sauce, and is quite fiery. Cautious cooks should start off by using less Tabasco in the mixture, adding an extra dash or two at the end if necessary rather than making the sauce too hot initially. It is sufficient to baste four pork chops, duck breast portions or lamb steaks.

MAKES ABOUT 115G/4OZ/½ CUP

INGREDIENTS
115g/4oz/½ cup butter
juice of 1 lemon
15ml/1 tbsp Worcestershire sauce
7.5ml/1½ tsp Tabasco sauce
1 garlic clove, finely chopped
salt and ground black pepper

1 Melt the butter in a small non-aluminium pan. Add the lemon juice and bring the mixture to simmering point over a low heat. Do not let the butter burn or it will taste bitter.

2 Add the Worcestershire and Tabasco sauces and the chopped garlic. Continue cooking over a low heat, without letting the garlic brown, for another 5 minutes. Season with salt and pepper. Meanwhile, preheat the grill (broiler) until hot.

3 Use the baste immediately it is ready, otherwise the butter will solidify, preventing application. Using a large pastry brush, spread the baste over the top of the chosen meat or poultry, grill (broil) for about 5 minutes, then turn over and brush the other side with more baste. Grill until the meat or poultry is cooked to your liking.

CHILLI PASTA

Making your own pasta is great fun, and when you add chillies to the dough, it not only looks good, but it tastes excitingly different, too. A flavoured pasta such as this needs to be served with a simple sauce, or stuffed with crab meat for a special treat.

SERVES FOUR TO SIX

INGREDIENTS
    300g/11oz/2¾ cups flour
        (see Cook's Tip)
    3 eggs
    5–10ml/1–2 tsp dried red
        chilli flakes
    5ml/1 tsp salt

1 Mound the flour on a clean work surface and make a large, deep well in the centre with your hands. Keep the sides of the well quite high, so that when the eggs are added they will not run out. Crack the eggs into the well, then add the chilli flakes and salt.

2 With a table knife or fork, mix the eggs, chilli and salt together, then gradually start incorporating the flour from the sides of the well. Try not to break the sides of the well or the runny mixture will escape and quickly spread over the work surface.

3 As soon as the egg mixture is no longer liquid, dip your fingers in the flour and use them to work the ingredients together until they form a rough and sticky dough. Scrape up any dough that sticks to the work surface with a knife, then scrape this off the knife with your fingers. If the dough is too dry, add a few drops of cold water; if it is too moist, sprinkle a little flour over it.

4 Press the dough into a rough ball and knead it as you would bread. Push it away from you with the heel of your hand, then fold the end of the dough back on itself so that it faces towards you and push it out again. Continue folding the dough back a little further each time and pushing it out until you have folded it back all the way towards you.

5 Give the dough a quarter turn anti-clockwise, then continue kneading, folding and turning for 5 minutes if you intend shaping the dough in a pasta machine, or for 10 minutes if you will be rolling it out by hand. Wrap the kneaded dough in clear film (plastic wrap) and leave to rest for about 15–20 minutes at room temperature before rolling and shaping for cooking.

Making Pasta in a Food Processor

This is a quick and simple way of making pasta.

1 Sift the flour into the bowl of the food processor and add the salt and chilli flakes.

2 Crack the eggs into the flour and process the mixture until the dough begins to come together. Tip it out and knead until smooth. Wrap in clear film (plastic wrap) and leave for 30 minutes.

Rolling and Shaping Pasta

For rounded spaghetti shapes, you need a machine, but you can easily make flat shapes or filled pasta by hand.

After the dough has rested, sprinkle plenty of flour over your work surface and begin rolling the dough, rotating it in quarter turns. Roll out until you have a sheet 3mm/⅛in thick. Fold into a wide, flat sausage.

For tagliatelle, cut the rolled pasta into 5mm/¼in strips. For ravioli, cut out two equally sized pieces 35 x 23cm/ 14 x 9in. Space the filling evenly across the pasta and moisten with egg to make the seal. Place the second piece on top, pressing down around the filling to push out the air. Divide using a serrated pastry wheel.

COOK'S TIP
The best flour to use is Farina Bianca 00 or Tipo 00, which is available from some larger supermarkets and good Italian delicatessens. Imported from Italy, this is a fine, soft white wheat flour. If you use ordinary plain (all-purpose) flour, you will find the dough quite difficult to knead and roll, especially by hand. If you can't get 00 flour, use a strong white (bread) flour.

CHILLI GIFTS

Bright and colourful, chillies make beautiful gifts. For a simple "thank you" to a friend who loves cooking spicy foods, simply tie a bunch of chillies together with a raffia bow. When the occasion calls for a more elaborate present, fill a basket with spices, including bunches of small red and green chillies. Chilli oils and vinegars are always welcome, and you can include a pot of chilli mustard as a special treat.

Above: A decorative chilli and cinnamon rope

Chilli Rope

To make a dried chilli rope, thread red chillies on a long piece of fine string and hang in a cool, airy place. They should retain their rich colour and can be used when quite dry. If you are making the rope as a gift, add a little label with the above instructions.

Chilli Spice Basket

The perfect gift for a house-warming! Choose a pretty basket, preferably a coloured one that will set off the contents. Fill with any or all of the following, or make up your own selection of spices.

6–7 fresh red chillies, tied
  with ribbon
6–7 fresh green chillies, tied
  with ribbon
cinnamon sticks, tied with ribbon
whole nutmegs
cardamom pods packed in a muslin
  or cheesecloth bag
lemon grass sticks wrapped in kaffir
  lime leaves and tied with raffia
dried pomegranates
vanilla pods (beans) tied with raffia
dried orange peel
coriander seeds and cumin seeds
          packed in muslin or
          cheesecloth "purses"

Right: Chilli spice oil

Chilli Spice Oil

This looks very pretty on the kitchen shelf and makes a thoughtful gift. The quantities given are just a guide – use your own artistic flair!

MAKES ABOUT 600ML/1 PINT/2½ CUPS

600ml/1 pint/2½ cups extra virgin
  olive oil
1 garlic clove, peeled and halved
3 dried red chillies
5ml/1 tsp coriander seeds
3 allspice berries
6 black peppercorns
4 juniper berries
2 bay leaves

1 Pour oil into a sterilized bottle, filling it three-quarters full. Add the garlic, chillies, coriander, allspice, peppercorns, juniper and bay, then top up with more oil to fill the bottle. Seal tightly and label clearly. Leave in a cool, dark place for 2 weeks. If the flavour is not sufficiently pronounced, leave for another week.

COOK'S TIP
Moulds can grow in oil, so long-term storage is not recommended.

Right: Chilli spice basket

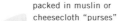

Chilli Spirit

For a drink with a real kick, steep chillies in sherry or vodka. Choose a pale spirit to show off the chillies.

MAKES 1 LITRE/1¾ PINTS/4 CUPS

INGREDIENTS
  25–50g/1–2oz small fresh
  red chillies
  1 litre/1¾ pints/4 cups pale dry
  sherry or vodka

1 Wash and dry the chillies thoroughly with kitchen paper, discarding any that are less than perfect, as these will look unsightly in the bottle. Using a fine cocktail stick or toothpick, prick the chillies all over to release their flavours into the alcohol.

2 Sterilize an attractive glass bottle with a wide enough neck to allow the chillies to pass easily. Pack the chillies tightly in the bottle, pushing them down with a metal or wooden skewer.

3 Top up with sherry or vodka to reach almost to the top of the bottle. Cork tightly and leave in a dark, cool place for at least 10 days, or up to 2 months, shaking the bottle occasionally for the chilli flavour to mingle evenly.

Right: Chilli vinegar

Chilli Vinegar

Pep up soups and sauces with this spicy vinegar, or use to deglaze a pan after cooking beef steaks.

MAKES ABOUT 600ML/1 PINT/2½ CUPS

  8 dried red chillies
  600ml/1 pint/2½ cups red wine
  vinegar or sherry vinegar

1 Place the chillies in a sterilized preserving jar or heatproof bottle. Pour the vinegar into a pan and bring to the boil. Carefully pour the vinegar into the jar or bottle. Cool, cover tightly, and leave to steep for 2 weeks, shaking the jar occasionally.

2 Taste for flavour and strain when sufficiently strong, pouring the vinegar into a clean, sterilized bottle, filled right to the top. Cover tightly, label and store.

VARIATION
Chilli Ho Ho Fill a sterilized bottle with small whole chillies. Top up with sherry vinegar, or spirits such as gin or vodka. Cover tightly or seal with a cork, label clearly and leave for 2 weeks, shaking occasionally.

Chilli and Garlic Mustard

A jar of this makes a great gift to add to a basket of mixed chilli goodies.

MAKES ABOUT 300ML/½ PINT/1¼ CUPS

INGREDIENTS
  1 dried red chilli
  40g/1½oz/¼ cup white mustard seeds
  40g/1½oz/¼ cup black mustard seeds
  50g/2oz/¼ cup soft light brown sugar
  5ml/1 tsp salt
  5ml/1 tsp whole peppercorns
  10ml/2 tsp tomato purée (paste)
  1 large garlic clove
  200ml/7fl oz/scant 1 cup distilled
    malt vinegar

1 Snap the top off the chilli and shake out the seeds. Discard the stem. Put the chilli in a food processor or blender with the mustard seeds, sugar, salt, peppercorns, tomato purée and garlic.

2 Whizz until mixed. Add 15ml/1 tbsp vinegar at a time, processing the mixture until it forms a coarse paste.

3 Leave to stand for 10–15 minutes, to thicken slightly. Spoon into a 300ml/½ pint/1¼ cup jar or several smaller jars. Cover the surface of the mustard with clear film (plastic wrap) or a waxed paper disc, seal tightly and label.

Below: Chilli and garlic mustard

Turn up the heat with these sizzling sauces, selected to show just how versatile chillies can be in a supporting role. A spoonful of Mango and Chilli Salsa adds sweetness and spice to all sorts of dishes, from baked ham to crackers and cheese. Hot Hot Habanero Salsa stokes the fire, while Guacamole cools and comforts. Some sauces and dips are based on specific chillies, like chipotle and guajillo, while others leave the choice to you. Add chutneys, relishes, breads and nibbles, and it's easy to see why this is your passport to chilli heaven.

Scorching Salsas, Sauces, Dips, Relishes and Nibbles

SALSA VERDE

*ALSO KNOWN AS GREEN FIRE, THIS IS A CLASSIC GREEN SALSA IN WHICH CAPERS PLAY AN
IMPORTANT PART. MAKE IT WITH GREEN CAYENNE CHILLIES OR THE MILDER JALAPEÑOS.*

SERVES FOUR

INGREDIENTS
  2–4 fresh green chillies
  8 spring onions (scallions)
  2 garlic cloves
  50g/2oz/½ cup salted capers
  1 fresh tarragon sprig
  bunch of fresh parsley
  grated (shredded) rind and juice
    of 1 lime
  juice of 1 lemon
  90ml/6 tbsp olive oil
  15ml/1 tbsp green Tabasco sauce
  ground black pepper

1 Cut the chillies in half and scrape out
and discard the seeds. Trim the spring
onions and cut them into short lengths.
Cut the garlic in half. Mix in a food
processor and pulse until chopped.

2 Use your fingertips to rub the excess
salt off the capers but do not rinse them
(see Cook's Tip). Add the capers,
tarragon and parsley to the food
processor and pulse again until they are
quite finely chopped.

3 Transfer the mixture to a small bowl.
Stir in the lime rind and juice, lemon
juice and olive oil. Stir lightly so the
citrus juice and oil do not emulsify.

4 Add green Tabasco and black pepper
to taste. Chill until ready to serve but
do not prepare more than 8 hours
in advance.

COOK'S TIP
If you can only find capers pickled in
vinegar, they must be rinsed well in cold
water before using.

AVOCADO <u>AND</u> SWEET RED PEPPER SALSA

*THIS SIMPLE SALSA IS A FIRE-AND-ICE MIXTURE THAT COMBINES HOT CHILLI WITH COOLING
AVOCADO. SERVE IT WITH CORN CHIPS FOR DIPPING.*

SERVES FOUR

INGREDIENTS
  2 ripe avocados
  1 red onion
  1 sweet red (bell) pepper
  4 fresh green chillies
  30ml/2 tbsp chopped fresh
    coriander (cilantro)
  30ml/2 tbsp sunflower oil
  juice of 1 lemon
  salt and ground black pepper

1 Cut the avocados in half and remove
the stone (pit) from each. Scoop out
the flesh and dice it. Finely chop the
red onion.

2 Slice the top off the sweet red pepper
and pull out the central core. Shake out
any remaining seeds. Cut the pepper
into thin strips, then into dice.

3 Cut the chillies in half lengthways,
scrape out and discard the seeds and
finely chop the flesh. Put it in a jug
(pitcher) and mix in the coriander,
oil, lemon juice and season with salt
and pepper to taste.

4 Place the avocado, red onion
and pepper in a bowl. Pour in
the chilli dressing and toss well.
Serve immediately.

COOK'S TIP
Serrano chillies would be a good choice,
or moderate them with the milder
Anaheim if you like.

CHILLI AND PESTO SALSA

USE LONG SLIM RED CHILLIES TO MAKE THIS AROMATIC SALSA, WHICH IS DELICIOUS
OVER CHICKEN AND FISH OR USED TO DRESS A FRESH AVOCADO AND TOMATO SALAD.
MAKE IT INTO A DIP BY MIXING IT WITH A LITTLE MAYONNAISE OR SOUR CREAM.

SERVES FOUR

INGREDIENTS
50g/2oz/1⅓ cups fresh coriander
   (cilantro) leaves
15g/½oz/¼ cup fresh parsley
2 fresh red chillies
1 garlic clove, halved
50g/2oz/½ cup shelled pistachio nuts
25g/1oz/⅓ cup freshly grated
   (shredded) Parmesan cheese
90ml/6 tbsp olive oil
juice of 2 limes
salt and ground black pepper

1 Process the coriander and parsley in a food processor until finely chopped. Cut the chillies in half, scrape out and discard seeds. Add to the herbs, with the garlic and process until finely chopped.

2 Add the pistachio nuts to the herb mixture and pulse until they are roughly chopped. Scrape the mixture into a bowl and stir in the Parmesan cheese, olive oil and lime juice.

3 Add salt and pepper to taste. Spoon the mixture into a serving bowl, cover and chill until ready to serve.

FIERY CITRUS SALSA

THIS UNUSUAL SALSA, WHICH COMBINES FRUIT WITH CHILLIES, MAKES A FANTASTIC
MARINADE FOR SHELLFISH AND IS DELICIOUS DRIZZLED OVER BARBECUE-COOKED MEAT.

SERVES FOUR

INGREDIENTS
1 orange
1 green apple
2 fresh red chillies
1 garlic clove
8 fresh mint leaves
juice of 1 lemon
salt and ground black pepper

1 Slice the base off the orange so that it will stand firmly on a chopping board. Using a sharp knife, remove the peel and pith in sections.

2 Holding the orange over a bowl to catch the juices, cut away the segments from the membrane, letting them fall into the bowl. Squeeze any juice from the remaining membrane into the bowl.

3 Peel, quarter and core the apple. Put it in a food processor. Cut the chillies in half and scrape out and discard the seeds. Add them to the food processor with the orange segments and juice, garlic and fresh mint.

4 Process until smooth. Then, with the motor running, pour in the lemon juice through the feeder tube. Season to taste. Pour into a bowl and serve immediately.

VARIATION
If you're feeling really daring, don't seed the chillies! They will make the salsa particularly hot and fierce.

CLASSIC MEXICAN TOMATO SALSA

THIS IS THE TRADITIONAL TOMATO-BASED SALSA THAT MOST PEOPLE ASSOCIATE WITH MEXICAN FOOD. THERE ARE INNUMERABLE RECIPES FOR IT, BUT THE BASICS OF ONION, TOMATO, CHILLI AND CORIANDER ARE COMMON TO EVERY ONE OF THEM. SERVE THIS SALSA AS A CONDIMENT WITH A WIDE VARIETY OF DISHES.

SERVES SIX AS AN ACCOMPANIMENT

INGREDIENTS

  3–6 fresh serrano chillies
  1 large white onion
  grated rind and juice of 2 limes, plus
    strips of lime rind, to garnish
  8 ripe, firm tomatoes
  large bunch of fresh coriander
  1.5ml/¼ tsp caster sugar
  salt

1 Use three chillies for a salsa of medium heat; up to six if you like it hot. To peel the chillies spear them on a long-handled metal skewer and roast them over the flame of a gas burner until the skins blister and darken. Do not let the flesh burn. Alternatively, dry fry them in a griddle pan until the skins are scorched.

2 Place the roasted chillies in a strong plastic bag and tie the top of the bag to keep the steam in. Set aside for about 20 minutes.

3 Meanwhile, chop the onion finely and put it in a bowl with the lime rind and juice. The lime juice will soften the onion.

VARIATIONS
Use spring onions or mild red onions instead of white onion. For a smoky flavour, use chipotle chillies instead of fresh serrano chillies.

4 Remove the chillies from the bag and peel off the skins. Cut off the stalks, then slit the chillies and scrape out the seeds with a sharp knife. Chop the flesh roughly and set aside.

5 Cut a small cross in the base of each tomato. Place the tomatoes in a heatproof bowl and pour over boiling water to cover.

6 Leave the tomatoes in the water for 3 minutes, then lift them out using a slotted spoon and plunge them into a bowl of cold water. Drain. The skins will have begun to peel back from the crosses. Remove the skins completely.

7 Dice the peeled tomatoes and put them in a bowl. Add the chopped onion which should have softened, together with the lime mixture. Chop the fresh coriander finely.

8 Add the coriander to the salsa, with the chillies and the sugar. Mix gently until the sugar has dissolved and all the ingredients are coated in lime juice. Cover and chill for 2–3 hours to allow the flavours to blend. The salsa will keep for 3–4 days in the fridge. Garnish with the strips of lime rind just before serving.

CHUNKY CHERRY CHILLI AND TOMATO SALSA

PUNGENT CHERRY CHILLIES AND SWEET CHERRY TOMATOES ARE MIXED WITH COOLING CUCUMBER IN THIS DELICIOUS DILL-SEASONED SALSA.

SERVES FOUR

INGREDIENTS
    1 ridge cucumber
    5ml/1 tsp sea salt
    500g/1¼lb cherry tomatoes
    1–2 fresh hot cherry chillies
    1 lemon
    1 garlic clove, crushed
    45ml/3 tbsp chilli oil
    30ml/2 tbsp chopped fresh dill
    salt and ground black pepper

1 Trim the ends off the cucumber and cut it into 2.5cm/1in lengths, then cut each piece lengthways into thin slices.

2 Spread out the cucumber slices in a colander and sprinkle them with the sea salt. Leave for 5 minutes until the cucumber has wilted.

COOK'S TIPS
• Cherry chillies are usually only moderately hot, but have quite a pungent, biting flavour. One could easily be sufficient to flavour the salsa.
• If you do not have gas roast the chillies under a hot grill (broiler) until blistered and blackened.

3 Wash the cucumber slices well under cold water and pat them dry with kitchen paper.

4 Quarter the cherry tomatoes and place in a bowl with the wilted cucumber. Skewer the chilli (or chillies) on a metal fork and hold in a gas flame for 2–3 minutes, turning often, until blistered and blackened. Slit, scrape out the seeds, then finely chop the flesh. Add it to the bowl.

5 Grate the lemon rind finely and place in a small bowl. Squeeze the lemon and add the juice to the bowl, with the garlic, chilli oil and dill. Add salt and pepper to taste, and whisk the ingredients together with a fork.

6 Pour the chilli oil dressing over the tomato and cucumber and toss well. Leave the salsa to marinate at room temperature for at least 2–3 hours before serving.

DOUBLE CHILLI SALSA

THIS IS A SCORCHINGLY HOT SALSA MADE WITH TWO TYPES OF CHILLIES, AND SHOULD BE SPREAD SPARINGLY ON COOKED MEATS AND BURGERS.

3 Use a clean dishtowel to rub the skins off the blistered chillies.

4 Try not to touch the chillies with your bare hands: use a fork to hold them and slice them open with a sharp knife. Scrape out and discard the seeds, then finely chop the flesh.

SERVES FOUR TO SIX

INGREDIENTS
    6 fresh habanero chillies or
     Scotch bonnets
    2 ripe tomatoes
    4 fresh green jalapeño chillies
    30ml/2 tbsp chopped fresh parsley
    30ml/2 tbsp olive oil
    15ml/1 tbsp balsamic or
     sherry vinegar
    salt

1 Skewer a habanero or Scotch bonnet chilli on a metal fork and hold it in a gas flame for 2–3 minutes, turning until the skin darkens and blisters. Repeat with the remaining chillies. Set aside.

2 Skewer the tomatoes one at a time and hold in a gas flame for 1–2 minutes, until the skin splits and wrinkles. Slip off the skins, halve the tomatoes, then use a teaspoon to scoop out and discard the seeds. Chop the flesh very finely.

5 Cut the jalapeño chillies in half lengthways, remove the seeds, then finely slice them into tiny strips. Mix both types of chilli, the tomatoes and the chopped parsley in a bowl.

6 Make a dressing by mixing the olive oil and vinegar with a little salt, pour this over the salsa and toss to mix. Cover the bowl. Chill for up to 3 days.

ROASTED TOMATO SALSA

SLOW ROASTING THESE TOMATOES TO A SEMI-DRIED STATE RESULTS IN A VERY RICH, FULL-FLAVOURED SWEET SAUCE. THE COSTENO AMARILLO CHILLI IS MILD AND HAS A FRESH LIGHT FLAVOUR, MAKING IT THE PERFECT PARTNER FOR THE RICH TOMATO TASTE. THIS SALSA IS GREAT WITH TUNA OR SEA BASS.

SERVES SIX AS AN ACCOMPANIMENT

INGREDIENTS
500g/1¼lb tomatoes
8 small shallots
5 garlic cloves
sea salt
1 fresh rosemary sprig
2 costeno amarillo chillies
grated rind and juice of ½
   small lemon
30ml/2 tbsp extra virgin olive oil
1.5ml/¼ tsp soft dark brown sugar

1 Preheat the oven to 160°C/325°F/ Gas 3. Cut the tomatoes into quarters and place them on a baking tray.

2 Peel the shallots and garlic and add them to the roasting tin. Sprinkle with sea salt. Roast in the oven for 1¼ hours or until the tomatoes are beginning to dry. Do not let them burn or blacken or they will have a bitter taste.

3 Leave the tomatoes to cool, then peel off the skins and chop the flesh finely. Place in a bowl. Remove the outer layer of skin from any shallots that have toughened.

4 Using a large, sharp knife, chop the shallots and garlic roughly, place them with the tomatoes in a bowl and mix.

5 Strip the rosemary leaves from the woody stem and chop them finely. Add half to the tomato and shallot mixture and mix lightly.

6 Soak the chillies in hot water for about 10 minutes until soft. Drain, remove the stalks, slit them and scrape out the seeds with a sharp knife. Chop the flesh finely and add it to the tomato mixture.

7 Stir in the lemon rind and juice, the olive oil and the sugar. Mix well, taste and add more salt if needed. Cover and chill for at least an hour before serving, sprinkled with the remaining rosemary. It will keep for up to a week in the fridge.

COOK'S TIP
Use plum tomatoes or vine tomatoes, which have more flavour than tomatoes that have been grown for their keeping properties rather than their flavour.

MANGO AND CHILLI SALSA

THIS HAS A FRESH, FRUITY TASTE AND IS PERFECT WITH FISH OR AS A CONTRAST TO RICH,
CREAMY DISHES. THE BRIGHT COLOURS MAKE IT AN ATTRACTIVE ADDITION TO ANY TABLE.

SERVES FOUR

INGREDIENTS
    2 fresh red fresno chillies
    2 ripe mangoes
    ½ white onion
    small bunch of fresh
        coriander (cilantro)
    grated (shredded) rind and
        juice of 1 lime

1 To peel the chillies, spear them on a long-handled metal skewer and roast them over the flame of a gas burner, turning the chillies continually, until the skins blister and darken. Do not let the flesh burn. Alternatively, dry-fry them in a frying pan until the skins are scorched.

2 Place the roasted chillies in a strong plastic bag and tie the top. Set aside.

VARIATION
For a refreshing change, look out for juicy Italia chillies, which have a wonderful affinity for mangoes.

3 Meanwhile, put one of the mangoes on a board and cut off a thick slice close to the flat side of the stone (pit). Turn the mango round and repeat on the other side. Score the flesh on each thick slice with criss-cross lines at 1cm/½in intervals, taking care not to cut through the skin. Repeat with the second mango.

4 Fold the mango halves inside out so that the mango flesh stands proud of the skin, in neat dice. Carefully slice these off the skin and into a bowl. Cut off the flesh adhering to each stone, dice it and add it to the bowl.

5 Remove the roasted chillies from the bag and carefully peel off the skins. Cut off the stalks, then slit the chillies and scrape out the seeds with a sharp knife. Discard the seeds.

6 Chop the white onion and the coriander finely and add them to the diced mango. Chop the chilli flesh finely and add it to the mixture in the bowl, together with the lime rind and juice. Toss the ingredients in the bowl thoroughly, then cover and chill for at least 1 hour before serving. The salsa will keep for 2–3 days in the refrigerator.

ROASTED SERRANO AND TOMATO SALSA

ROASTING THE CHILLIES GIVES A GREATER DEPTH TO THE TASTE OF THIS SALSA, WHICH
ALSO BENEFITS FROM THE ROUNDED FLAVOUR OF ROASTED TOMATOES.

SERVES SIX

INGREDIENTS
    500g/1¼lb tomatoes
    2 fresh serrano chillies
    1 onion
    juice of 1 lime
    large bunch of fresh
        coriander (cilantro)
    salt

1 Preheat the oven to 200ºC/400ºF/ Gas 6. Cut the tomatoes into quarters and place them in a roasting pan. Add the chillies. Roast for 45–60 minutes, until charred and softened.

2 Place the roasted chillies in a strong plastic bag. Tie the top to keep the steam in and set aside for 20 minutes. Leave the tomatoes to cool slightly, then remove the skins and dice the flesh.

3 Chop the onion finely, then place in a bowl and add the lime juice and the diced tomatoes.

4 Remove the chillies from the bag and peel off the skins. Cut off the stalks, then slit the chillies and scrape out the seeds with a sharp knife. Chop the chillies roughly and add them to the onion mixture. Mix well.

5 Chop the coriander and add most to the salsa. Add salt, cover and chill for at least 1 hour before serving, sprinkled with the remaining coriander. This salsa will keep in the refrigerator for 1 week.

SWEET POTATO AND JALAPEÑO SALSA

COLOURFUL AND SWEET, WITH JUST A HINT OF HEAT, THIS SALSA MAKES THE PERFECT ACCOMPANIMENT TO HOT, SPICY MEXICAN DISHES.

SERVES FOUR

INGREDIENTS

675g/1½lb sweet potatoes
juice of 1 small orange
5ml/1 tsp crushed dried
  jalapeño chillies
4 small spring onions (scallions)
juice of 1 small lime (optional)
salt

COOK'S TIP

This fresh and tasty salsa is also very good served with a simple grilled (broiled) salmon fillet or other fish dishes, and makes a delicious accompaniment to veal escalopes (scallops) or chicken breast portions.

1 Peel the sweet potatoes and dice the flesh finely. Bring a pan of water to the boil. Add the sweet potato and cook for 8–10 minutes, until just soft. Drain off the water, cover the pan and put it back on the stove top, having turned off the heat.

2 Leave for 5 minutes to dry out, tip it into a bowl and set aside.

3 Mix the orange juice and crushed dried chillies in a bowl. Chop the spring onions finely and add them to the juice and chillies.

4 When the sweet potatoes are cool, add the orange juice mixture and toss carefully until all the pieces are coated. Cover the bowl and chill for 2 hours.

5 Taste the salsa and season with salt. Stir in the lime juice if you think the mixture needs to be sharpened slightly. The salsa will keep for 2–3 days in a covered bowl in the refrigerator.

HOT HOT HABANERO SALSA

THIS IS A VERY FIERY SALSA WITH AN INTENSE HEAT LEVEL. A DAB ON THE PLATE ALONGSIDE A MEAT OR FISH DISH ADDS A FRESH, CLEAN TASTE.

SERVES FOUR

INGREDIENTS
5 dried roasted habanero chillies
4 dried costeno amarillo chillies
3 spring onions (scallions), chopped
juice of ½ large grapefruit or
  1 Seville (Temple) orange
grated (shredded) rind and juice
  of 1 lime
small bunch of fresh
  coriander (cilantro)
salt

COOK'S TIP
Dried habanero chillies are just as hot as when fresh. Lantern shaped and deep orange in colour, they release a lovely fruity aroma when reconstituted, and go very well with the milder, citrus-flavoured costeno amarillo chillies.

1 Soak the habanero and costeno amarillo chillies in hot water for about 20 minutes until softened. Drain, reserving the soaking water.

2 Wear rubber gloves to handle the habaneros. Remove the stalks from all the chillies, then slit them and scrape out the seeds with a small sharp knife and discard. Chop the flesh roughly.

3 Put the chillies in a food processor and add a little of the soaking liquid. Purée to a fine paste. Do not lean over the processor – the fumes may burn your face. Remove the lid and scrape the mixture into a bowl.

4 Put the chopped spring onions in another bowl and add the grapefruit or orange juice, with the lime rind and juice. Roughly chop the coriander.

5 Carefully add the chopped coriander to the chilli mixture and then combine the ingredients very thoroughly. Add salt to taste. Cover the bowl and chill for at least 1 day before use. Serve this salsa very sparingly and warn your guests that it is hot.

CACTUS PEAR SALSA

NOPALES ARE THE TENDER, FLESHY LEAVES OR "PADDLES" OF AN EDIBLE CACTUS KNOWN VARIOUSLY AS THE CACTUS PEAR AND THE PRICKLY PEAR CACTUS. THIS PLANT GROWS WILD IN MEXICO, BUT IS ALSO CULTIVATED. ALTHOUGH FRESH NOPALES ARE DIFFICULT TO TRACK DOWN OUTSIDE MEXICO, IF YOU DO LOCATE A SUPPLY, THEN LOOK FOR PADDLES THAT ARE FIRM AND SMOOTH SKINNED.

SERVES FOUR AS AN ACCOMPANIMENT

INGREDIENTS
  2 fresh red fresno chillies
  250g/9oz *nopales* (cactus paddles)
  3 spring onions
  3 garlic cloves, peeled
  ½ red onion
  100g/3½oz fresh tomatillos
  2.5ml/½ tsp salt
  150ml/¼ pint/⅔ cup cider vinegar

1 Spear the chillies on a long-handled metal skewer and roast them over the flame of a gas burner until the skins blister and darken. Do not let the flesh burn. Alternatively, dry fry them in a griddle pan until the skins are scorched. Place the roasted chillies in a strong plastic bag and tie the top to keep the steam in. Set aside for 20 minutes.

2 Remove the chillies from the bag and peel off the skins. Cut off the stalks, then slit the chillies and scrape out the seeds. Chop the chillies roughly and set them aside.

COOK'S TIP
Fresh *nopales* are sometimes available from specialist fruit and vegetable stores. Like okra, they yield a sticky gum, and are best boiled before being used. Fresh cactus will lose about half its weight during cooking. Look out for canned *nopales* (sometimes sold as *nopalitos*) packed in water or vinegar.

3 Carefully remove the thorns from the nopales. Wearing gloves or holding each cactus paddle in turn with kitchen tongs, cut off the bumps that contain the thorns with a sharp knife.

4 Cut off and discard the thick base from each cactus paddle. Rinse the paddles well and cut them into strips then cut the strips into small pieces.

5 Bring a large saucepan of lightly salted water to the boil. Add the cactus paddle strips, spring onions and garlic. Boil for 10–15 minutes, until the paddle strips are just tender.

6 Drain the mixture in a colander, rinse under cold running water to remove any remaining stickiness, then drain again. Discard the spring onions and garlic.

7 Chop the red onion and the tomatillos finely. Place in a bowl and add the cactus and chillies.

8 Spoon the mixture into a large preserving jar, add the salt, pour in the vinegar and seal. Put the jar in the fridge for at least 1 day, turning the jar occasionally to ensure that the *nopales* are marinated. The salsa will keep in the fridge for up to 10 days.

PINTO BEAN SALSA

THESE BEANS HAVE A PRETTY, SPECKLED APPEARANCE. THE SMOKY FLAVOUR OF THE CHIPOTLE CHILLIES AND THE HERBY TASTE OF THE PASILLA CHILLI CONTRAST WELL WITH THE TART TOMATILLOS. UNUSUALLY, THESE ARE NOT COOKED.

2 Soak the chipotle and pasilla chillies in hot water for about 10 minutes until softened. Drain, reserving the soaking water. Remove the stalks, then slit each chilli and scrape out the seeds with a small sharp knife. Chop the flesh finely and mix it to a smooth paste with a little of the soaking water.

3 Roast the garlic in a dry frying pan over a moderate heat for a few minutes until the cloves start to turn golden. Crush them and add them to the beans.

SERVES FOUR AS AN ACCOMPANIMENT

INGREDIENTS
130g/4½oz/generous ½ cup pinto beans, soaked overnight in water to cover
2 chipotle chillies
1 pasilla chilli
2 garlic cloves, peeled
½ onion
200g/7oz fresh tomatillos
salt

1 Drain the beans and put them in a large saucepan. Pour in water to cover and place the lid on the pan. Bring to the boil, lower the heat slightly and simmer the beans for 45–50 minutes or until tender. They should still have a little bite and should not have begun to disintegrate. Drain, rinse under cold water, then drain again and tip into a bowl. Leave the beans until cold.

COOK'S TIP
Canned tomatillos can be substituted, but to keep a clean, fresh flavour add a little lime juice.

4 Chop the onion and tomatillos and stir them into the beans. Add the chilli paste and mix well. Add salt to taste, cover and chill before serving.

BLACK BEAN SALSA

THIS SALSA HAS A STRIKING APPEARANCE. IT IS RARE TO FIND A BLACK SPICE AND IT PROVIDES A GOOD CONTRAST TO THE MORE COMMON REDS AND GREENS ON THE PLATE.

SERVES FOUR

INGREDIENTS
   130g/4½oz/generous ½ cup black
     beans, soaked overnight in water
   1 pasado chilli
   2 fresh red fresno chillies
   1 red onion
   grated (shredded) rind and juice
     of 1 lime
   30ml/2 tbsp Mexican beer (optional)
   15ml/1 tbsp olive oil
   small bunch of fresh coriander
     (cilantro), chopped
   salt

1 Drain the beans, rinse them thoroughly and put them in a large pan. Pour in water to cover. Do not add salt as this toughens the outside skin and stops the bean cooking properly. Place the lid on the pan and bring to the boil. Lower the heat slightly and simmer the beans for about 40 minutes or until tender. They should still have a little bite and should not have begun to disintegrate. Drain, rinse under cold water, then drain again and leave the beans until cold.

2 Soak the pasado chilli in hot water for about 20 minutes until softened. Drain, remove the stalk, then slit the chilli and, using a small sharp knife, scrape out the seeds and discard them. Chop the flesh finely.

COOK'S TIP
Pasado chillies are always sold in their dried, roasted form. Dark, almost black, in colour, they have a subtle citrus flavour and are only mildly hot.

3 Spear the fresno chillies on a long-handled metal skewer and roast them over the flame of a gas burner, turning the chillies all the time, until the skins blister and darken. Do not let the flesh burn. Alternatively, dry-fry them in a griddle pan until the skins are scorched.

4 Place the roasted chillies in a strong plastic bag and tie the top to keep the steam in. Set aside for 20 minutes.

5 Meanwhile, chop the red onion finely. Remove the chillies from the bag and peel off the skins. Slit them, remove and discard the seeds, and chop them finely.

6 Tip the beans into a bowl and add the onion and both types of chilli. Stir in the lime rind and juice, and beer, if using, then add the oil and coriander. Season with salt and mix well. Leave the salsa for a day or two to allow the flavours to develop fully. Serve chilled.

GUACAMOLE

THIS POPULAR MEXICAN DIP CAN BE SERVED WITH TORTILLA CHIPS, OR USED AS A DIP WITH SUCH FRESH VEGETABLES AS CRISP CARROT BATONS AND CELERY STICKS.

MAKES 475ML/16FL OZ/2 CUPS

INGREDIENTS
    3 large ripe avocados
    3 spring onions (scallions),
        finely chopped
    1 garlic clove, crushed
    15ml/1 tbsp olive oil
    15ml/1 tbsp sour cream
    2.5ml/½ tsp salt
    30ml/2 tbsp fresh lemon or
        lime juice
    2.5ml/½ tsp cayenne pepper

COOK'S TIP
Guacamole does not keep well, but, if necessary, it can be stored in the refrigerator for a few hours. Cover the surface with clear film (plastic wrap) to prevent discolouring.

1 Halve the avocados and remove the stones (pits). Peel the halves. Put the flesh in a large bowl.

2 With a fork, mash the avocado flesh coarsely, taking care not to break up the flesh too much.

3 Add the spring onions, garlic, olive oil, cream, salt and lemon or lime juice. Mash until well blended, but do not overwork the mixture. Small chunks of avocado should still remain. Adjust the seasoning, if necessary, with salt or lemon or lime juice. Transfer the avocado mixture to a serving bowl. Serve the guacamole dip immediately, sprinkled with the cayenne pepper.

TOMATO SALSA

MAKES 900ML/1½ PINTS/3¾ CUPS

INGREDIENTS
    1 fresh hot green chilli, seeded
        and chopped
    1 garlic clove
    ½ red onion, coarsely chopped
    3 spring onions (scallions), chopped
    15g/½ oz/½ cup fresh coriander
        (cilantro) leaves
    675g/1½lb ripe tomatoes, seeded
        and coarsely chopped
    1–3 canned green chillies
    15ml/1 tbsp olive oil
    30ml/2 tbsp fresh lime or lemon juice
    2.5ml/½ tsp salt, to taste
    45ml/3 tbsp tomato juice or
        cold water

1 In a food processor or blender, combine the fresh chilli, garlic, chopped red onion, spring onions and coriander leaves. Process until everything is finely chopped.

2 Add the remaining ingredients. Pulse on and off until chopped; the tomato salsa should be chunky in texture.

3 Transfer to a bowl and taste for seasoning. Leave to stand for at least 30 minutes before serving. This salsa is best served the day it is made.

COOK'S TIP
For less heat, remove the seeds from both fresh and canned chillies.

AVOCADO AND TOMATO DIP

ONE OF THE BEST-LOVED MEXICAN SALSAS, THIS BLEND OF CREAMY AVOCADO, TOMATOES, CHILLIES, CORIANDER AND LIME NOW APPEARS ON TABLES THE WORLD OVER.

SERVES SIX TO EIGHT

INGREDIENTS
  4 medium tomatoes
  4 ripe avocados, preferably fuerte
  juice of 1 lime
  ½ small onion
  2 garlic cloves
  small bunch of fresh coriander
    (cilantro), chopped
  3 fresh red fresno chillies
  salt
  tortilla chips, to serve

1 Cut a cross in the base of each tomato. Place the tomatoes in a heatproof bowl and pour over boiling water to cover.

2 Leave the tomatoes in the water for 30 seconds, then lift them out using a slotted spoon and plunge them into a bowl of cold water. Drain. The skins will have begun to peel back from the crosses. Remove the skins completely. Cut the tomatoes in half, remove the seeds with a teaspoon, then chop the flesh roughly and set it aside.

3 Cut the avocados in half and remove the stones (pits). Scoop the flesh into a food processor or blender. Process until almost smooth, then scrape into a bowl and stir in the lime juice.

4 Chop the onion finely, then crush the garlic. Add both to the avocado and mix well. Stir in the coriander.

5 Remove the stalks from the chillies, slit them and scrape out and discard the seeds. Chop the chillies finely and add them to the avocado mixture, with the chopped tomatoes. Mix well.

6 Check the seasoning and add salt to taste. Cover closely with clear film (plastic wrap) or a tight-fitting lid and chill for 1 hour before serving as a dip with tortilla chips. If it is well covered, guacamole will keep in the refrigerator for 2–3 days.

COOK'S TIP
Smooth-skinned fuerte avocados are native to Mexico, so would be ideal for this dip. If they are not available, use any avocados, but make sure they are ripe. To test, gently press the top of the avocado; it should give a little.

SPICY TOMATO AND CHILLI DIP

GET YOUR TASTE BUDS TINGLING WITH THIS TANGY DIP, SPIKED WITH FRESH GREEN CHILLIES.
IT IS DELICIOUS SERVED WITH DEEP-FRIED POTATO SKINS OR HASH BROWNS.

SERVES FOUR

INGREDIENTS
1 shallot, halved
2 garlic cloves, halved
handful of fresh basil leaves, plus
  extra, to garnish
500g/1¼lb ripe tomatoes
30ml/2 tbsp olive oil
2 fresh green chillies
salt and ground black pepper

COOK'S TIP
Use green serrano or jalapeño chillies.
Anaheims are also suitable, and will
give a milder result.

1 Place the shallot and garlic in a
blender or food processor. Add the basil
leaves and process until very finely
chopped. You may need to scrape down
the sides of the bowl with a spatula.

2 Cut the tomatoes in half and add
them to the shallot mixture. Pulse until
the mixture is well blended and the
tomatoes are finely chopped.

3 With the motor still running, slowly
pour in the olive oil through the feeder
tube. Add salt and pepper to taste and
pulse briefly to mix. Spoon the mixture
into a bowl.

4 Cut the chillies lengthways and scrape
out the seeds with a sharp knife and
discard. Finely slice across the chillies,
cutting them into tiny strips and stir
them into the tomato mixture. Garnish
with a few torn basil leaves. Serve the
dip at room temperature. Refrigerated,
this will keep for 3–4 days.

SPICED CARROT DIP

THIS IS A DELICIOUS LOW-FAT DIP WITH A SWEET AND SPICY FLAVOUR. SERVE WHEAT CRACKERS OR FIERY TORTILLA CHIPS AS ACCOMPANIMENTS FOR DIPPING.

SERVES 4

INGREDIENTS

1 onion
3 carrots
grated rind and juice of
  2 oranges
15ml/1 tbsp hot curry paste
150ml/¼ pint/¾ cup low-fat
  natural (plain) yogurt
1 handful of fresh basil leaves
15–30ml/1–2 tbsp fresh lemon
  juice, to taste
red Tabasco sauce, to taste
salt and ground black pepper

1 Using a sharp vegetable knife, finely chop the onion. Peel and grate the carrots. Place the onion, carrots, orange rind and juice and hot curry paste in a small pan. Bring the mixture to the boil, cover with a lid and simmer for about 10 minutes, or until tender.

2 Process in a blender or food processor until smooth and leave to cool.

3 Stir in the yogurt, then tear the basil leaves into small pieces and stir them into the carrot mixture.

4 Add lemon juice, Tabasco, salt and pepper to taste and serve.

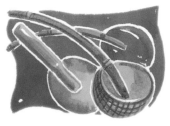

CHILLI BEAN DIP

SUBSTANTIAL ENOUGH TO SERVE FOR SUPPER ON A BAKED POTATO, THIS CREAMY BEAN DIP ALSO TASTES GREAT WITH TRIANGLES OF LIGHTLY TOASTED PITTA BREAD OR A BOWL OF CRUNCHY TORTILLA CHIPS. SERVE IT WARM TO ENJOY IT AT ITS BEST.

SERVES FOUR

INGREDIENTS

2 fresh green chillies
2 garlic cloves
1 onion
30ml/2 tbsp vegetable oil
5–10ml/1–2 tsp hot chilli powder
400g/14oz can kidney beans
75g/3oz/¾ cup grated (shredded)
  mature (sharp) Cheddar cheese
1 fresh red chilli, seeded
salt and ground black pepper

1 Slit the green chillies and use a sharp knife to scrape out the seeds. Chop the flesh finely, then crush the garlic and finely chop the onion.

2 Heat the oil in a large pan and add the garlic, onion, green chillies and chilli powder. Cook gently for 5 minutes, stirring, until the onions have softened and are transparent, but not browned.

COOK'S TIP
Fresh green chillies provide the heat in this dip. You can substitute sweet red (bell) pepper for the garnish.

3 Drain the kidney beans, reserving the liquid in which they were canned. Set aside 30ml/2 tbsp of the beans and purée the remainder in a food processor or blender.

4 Spoon the puréed beans into the pan and stir in 30–45ml/2–3 tbsp of the reserved can liquid. Heat gently, stirring to mix well.

5 Stir in the reserved whole kidney beans and the Cheddar cheese. Cook gently for 2–3 minutes, stirring regularly until the cheese melts. Add salt and pepper to taste.

6 Cut the red chilli into tiny strips. Spoon the dip into 4 individual serving bowls and sprinkle the chilli strips over the top. Serve warm.

CHILLI AND RED ONION RAITA

RAITA IS A TRADITIONAL INDIAN ACCOMPANIMENT, A COOLING AGENT TO SERVE WITH HOT CURRIES. IT IS ALSO DELICIOUS SERVED WITH POPPADUMS AS A DIP.

SERVES FOUR

INGREDIENTS
5ml/1 tsp cumin seeds
1 large red onion
1 small garlic clove
1 small fresh green chilli, seeded
150ml/¼ pint/⅔ cup natural
  (plain) yogurt
30ml/2 tbsp chopped fresh coriander
  (cilantro), plus extra, to garnish
about 2.5ml/½ tsp granulated sugar
salt

1 Heat a small pan and dry-fry the cumin seeds for 1–2 minutes, until they release their aroma and begin to pop.

2 Let the seeds cool for a few minutes, then tip them into a mortar. Crush them with a pestle or flatten them with the heel of a heavy-bladed knife.

COOK'S TIPS
• For an extra tangy raita, stir in 15ml/ 1 tbsp lemon juice.
• For a thicker consistency, drain off any liquid from the yogurt before adding the ingredients.

3 Cut the red onion in half. Cut a few thin slices for the garnish and chop the rest finely. Crush the garlic, then finely chop the chilli. Stir the onion, garlic and chilli into the yogurt with the crushed cumin seeds and coriander.

4 Add sugar and salt to taste. Spoon the raita into a small bowl, cover and chill until ready to serve. Garnish with the reserved onion slices and extra coriander before serving. The dip will keep for 2 days in the refrigerator.

PUMPKIN SEED SAUCE

THE ANCESTORS OF MODERN-DAY MEXICANS DIDN'T BELIEVE IN WASTING FOOD, AS THIS TRADITIONAL RECIPE PROVES. IT IS BASED UPON PUMPKIN SEEDS AND HAS A DELICIOUS NUTTY FLAVOUR. IT IS GREAT SERVED OVER STEAMED OR BOILED NOPALES (CACTUS PADDLES) *AND IS ALSO DELICIOUS WITH COOKED CHICKEN OR RACK OF LAMB.*

SERVES FOUR AS AN ACCOMPANIMENT

INGREDIENTS
130g/4½oz raw pumpkin seeds
500g/1¼lb tomatoes
2 garlic cloves, crushed
300ml/½ pint/1¼ cups chicken
  stock, preferably freshly made
15ml/1 tbsp vegetable oil
45ml/3 tbsp red chilli sauce
salt (optional)

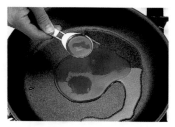

1 Preheat the oven to 200°C/400°F/ Gas 6. Heat a heavy-based frying pan until very hot. Add the pumpkin seeds and dry fry them, stirring constantly over the heat. The seeds will start to swell and pop, but they must not be allowed to scorch (see Cook's Tip). When all the seeds have popped remove the pan from the heat.

2 Cut the tomatoes into quarters and place them on a baking tray. Roast in the hot oven for 45 minutes–1 hour, until charred and softened. Allow to cool slightly, then remove the skins using a small sharp knife.

3 Put the pumpkin seeds in a food processor and process until smooth. Add the tomatoes and process for a few minutes, then add the garlic and stock and process for 1 minute more.

COOK'S TIP
When dry frying the pumpkin seeds, don't stop stirring for a moment or they may scorch, which would make the sauce bitter. It is a good idea to stand back a little as some of the hot seeds may fly out of the pan.

4 Heat the oil in a large frying pan. Add the red chilli sauce and cook, stirring constantly, for 2–3 minutes. Add the pumpkin seed mixture and bring to the boil, stirring all the time.

5 Simmer the sauce for 20 minutes, stirring frequently until the sauce has thickened and reduced by about half. Taste and add salt, if needed. Serve over meat or vegetables or cool and chill. The salsa will keep for up to a week in a covered bowl in the fridge.

SMOKY CHIPOTLE SAUCE

THE SMOKY FLAVOUR OF THIS RICH SAUCE MAKES IT IDEAL FOR BARBECUE-COOKED FOOD, AS A MARINADE OR ACCOMPANIMENT. IT IS WONDERFUL STIRRED INTO CREAM CHEESE AS A SANDWICH FILLING WITH CHICKEN. CHIPOTLE CHILLIES ARE SMOKE-DRIED JALAPEÑOS.

SERVES SIX

INGREDIENTS
500g/1¼lb tomatoes
5 chipotle chillies
3 garlic cloves, roughly chopped
150ml/¼ pint/⅔ cup red wine
5ml/1 tsp dried oregano
60ml/4 tbsp clear honey
5ml/1 tsp American mustard
2.5ml/½ tsp ground black pepper
salt

1 Preheat the oven to 200°C/400°F/ Gas 6. Cut the tomatoes into quarters and place them in a roasting pan. Roast for 45–60 minutes, until they are charred.

2 Meanwhile, soak the chillies in a bowl of cold water to cover for about 20 minutes or until soft. Remove the stalks, slit the chillies and scrape out the seeds with a small sharp knife. Discard the seeds. Chop the flesh roughly.

3 Remove the tomatoes from the oven, let them cool slightly, then remove the skins. If you prefer a smooth sauce, remove the seeds. Chop the tomatoes in a blender or food processor. Add the chillies, garlic and red wine. Process until smooth, then add the oregano, honey, mustard and black pepper. Process briefly to mix, then taste and season with salt.

4 Pour the mixture into a small pan. Bring to the boil, lower the heat and simmer the sauce for about 10 minutes, stirring occasionally, until it has reduced and thickened. Spoon into a bowl and serve hot or cold.

GUAJILLO CHILLI SAUCE

THIS SAUCE CAN BE SERVED OVER ENCHILADAS OR STEAMED VEGETABLES. IT IS ALSO GOOD EATEN HOT OR COLD WITH MEATS, AND A LITTLE MAKES A FINE SEASONING FOR SOUPS OR STEWS.

SERVES FOUR

INGREDIENTS
2 tomatoes
2 red (bell) peppers, cored, seeded and quartered
3 garlic cloves, in their skins
2 ancho chillies
2 guajillo chillies
30ml/2 tbsp tomato purée (paste)
5ml/1 tsp dried oregano
5ml/1 tsp soft dark brown sugar
300ml/½ pint/1¼ cups chicken stock

1 Preheat the oven to 200°C/400°F/ Gas 6. Cut the tomatoes into quarters and place them in a roasting pan with the peppers and whole garlic cloves. Roast for 45–60 minutes, until the tomatoes and peppers are slightly charred.

COOK'S TIP
Like chipotle chillies, guajillos are dried. They give the sauce a well-rounded, fruity flavour and do not make it too hot.

2 Put the peppers in a strong plastic bag and tie the top to keep the steam in. Set aside for 20 minutes. Remove the skin from the tomatoes. Soak the chillies in boiling water for 20 minutes.

3 Remove the peppers from the bag and rub off the skins. Cut them in half, remove the cores and seeds, then chop the flesh roughly and put it in a food processor or blender. Drain the chillies, remove the stalks, then slit them and scrape out and discard the seeds. Chop them roughly and add to the peppers.

4 Add the roasted tomatoes to the food processor. Squeeze the roasted garlic out of the skins and add to the tomato mixture, with the tomato purée, oregano, sugar and stock. Process until smooth.

5 Pour the mixture into a pan, place over a medium heat and bring to the boil. Lower the heat and simmer for 10–15 minutes until the sauce has reduced to about half. Transfer to a bowl and serve. Or leave to cool, then chill until required. The sauce will keep in the refrigerator for up to 1 week.

THAI RED CURRY SAUCE

*SERVE THIS WITH MINI SPRING ROLLS OR SPICY INDONESIAN CRACKERS, OR TOSS IT INTO
FRESHLY COOKED RICE NOODLES FOR A DELICIOUS MAIN-MEAL ACCOMPANIMENT.*

SERVES FOUR

INGREDIENTS
    200ml/7fl oz/scant 1 cup
      coconut cream
    10–15ml/2–3 tsp Thai red
      curry paste
    4 spring onions (scallions), plus
      extra, to garnish
    30ml/2 tbsp chopped fresh
      coriander (cilantro)
    1 fresh red chilli, seeded and thinly
      sliced into rings
    5ml/1 tsp soy sauce
    juice of 1 lime
    granulated sugar, to taste
    25g/1oz/¼ cup dry-roasted peanuts
    salt and ground black pepper

1 Pour the coconut cream into a small
bowl and stir in the curry paste.

COOK'S TIP
The dip may be prepared in advance up
to the end of step 3. Cover and keep in
the refrigerator for up to 4 hours.

2 Trim the spring onions and finely
slice them on the diagonal. Stir into
the coconut cream with the chopped
fresh coriander and chilli.

3 Stir in the soy sauce and fresh lime
juice, with sugar, salt and pepper to
taste. Pour the sauce into a small
serving bowl.

4 Finely chop the dry-roasted peanuts
and sprinkle them over the sauce. Garnish
with spring onions sliced lengthways
into thin curls. Serve immediately.

VARIATION
As an alternative to spring onions, try using
baby leeks. You may need only one or two
and they can be prepared in the same way.

MEXICAN VINEGAR SEASONING

ADOBO MEANS VINEGAR SAUCE, AND THIS ONE IS A PASTE MADE FROM DRIED CHILLIES, USED FOR MARINATING PORK CHOPS OR STEAKS. ADOBOS ARE USED IN MEXICAN COOKING.

MAKES ENOUGH TO MARINATE
SIX CHOPS OR STEAKS

INGREDIENTS
  1 small head of garlic
  5 ancho chillies
  2 pasilla chillies
  15ml/1 tbsp dried oregano
  5ml/1 tsp cumin seeds
  6 cloves
  5ml/1 tsp coriander seeds
  10cm/4in piece of cinnamon stick
  10ml/2 tsp salt
  120ml/4fl oz/½ cup white
    wine vinegar

1 Preheat the oven to 180°C/350°F/ Gas 4. Cut a thin slice off the top of the head of garlic, so that the inside of each clove is exposed. Wrap the head of garlic in foil. Roast for 45–60 minutes or until the garlic is soft.

2 Meanwhile, slit the chillies and shake out most of the seeds. Break up the dried chillies a little and put them in a food processor, spice mill or mortar. Add the oregano, cumin seeds, cloves, coriander seeds, cinnamon stick and salt. Process or grind to a fine powder.

3 Remove the garlic from the oven. When it is cool enough to handle, squeeze the pulp out of each clove.

4 Add the garlic and white wine vinegar to the spice mixture and process or grind to a smooth paste. Scrape into a bowl and leave to stand for 1 hour, to allow the flavours to blend. Spread over pork chops or steaks as a marinade, before cooking.

COOK'S TIP
You can buy wild Mexican oregano from Mexican food stores or by mail order.

CHILLI RELISH

FOR INSTANT HEAT, KEEP A POT OF THIS SPICY RELISH. IT TASTES GREAT WITH SAUSAGES, BURGERS AND CHEESE. IT WILL KEEP IN THE REFRIGERATOR FOR UP TO TWO WEEKS.

SERVES EIGHT

INGREDIENTS
6 tomatoes
1 onion
1 sweet red (bell) pepper, seeded
2 garlic cloves
30ml/2 tbsp olive oil
5ml/1 tsp ground cinnamon
5ml/1 tsp dried chilli flakes
5ml/1 tsp ground ginger
5ml/1 tsp salt
2.5ml/½ tsp ground black pepper
75g/3oz/scant ⅔ cup light muscovado (brown) sugar
75ml/5 tbsp cider vinegar
handful of fresh basil leaves

COOK'S TIP
This relish thickens slightly on cooling, so do not worry if the mixture seems a little sloppy when it is first made.

1 Skewer each of the tomatoes in turn on a metal fork and hold in a gas flame for 1–2 minutes, turning until the skin splits and wrinkles. Place the tomatoes on a chopping board, slip off the skins, then roughly chop.

2 Roughly chop the onion, red pepper and garlic. Gently heat the oil in a pan. Tip in the onion, red pepper and garlic, stirring lightly.

3 Cook gently for 5–8 minutes, until the pepper has softened. Add the chopped tomatoes, cover and cook for 5 minutes.

4 Stir in the cinnamon, chilli flakes, ginger, salt, pepper, sugar and vinegar. Bring gently to the boil, stirring until the sugar dissolves.

5 Simmer, uncovered, for 20 minutes, until the mixture is pulpy. Stir in the basil leaves and check the seasoning.

6 Allow to cool completely, then spoon into a glass jar or a plastic tub with a tightly fitting lid. Store, covered, in the refrigerator. This relish will keep in the refrigerator for up to a fortnight. Stir before using.

SPICY SWEETCORN RELISH

*A TOUCH OF HEAT TEMPERS THE SWEETNESS OF THIS DELICIOUS RELISH. TRY IT WITH
CRISP ONION BHAJIS OR SLICES OF HONEY-ROAST HAM FOR A SPICY SNACK.*

SERVES FOUR

INGREDIENTS

1 large onion
1 fresh red chilli, seeded
2 garlic cloves
30ml/2 tbsp vegetable oil
5ml/1 tsp black mustard seeds
10ml/2 tsp hot curry powder
320g/11¼oz can sweetcorn
grated rind and juice of 1 lime
45ml/3 tbsp chopped fresh
 coriander (cilantro)
salt and ground black pepper

1 Chop the onion, chilli and garlic. Heat
the vegetable oil in a large frying pan
and cook the onion, chilli and garlic
over a high heat for 5 minutes, until
the onions are just beginning to brown.

2 Stir in the mustard seeds and curry
powder. Cook for a further 2 minutes,
stirring, until all the seeds start to
splutter and the onions have browned.

COOK'S TIP
Opt for canned rather than frozen
sweetcorn if possible, as the kernels are
plump, moist and ready to eat.

3 Remove the fried onion mixture from
the heat and allow to cool. Place in a
glass bowl. Drain the sweetcorn and stir
it into the onion mixture.

4 Add the lime rind and juice, coriander
and salt and pepper to taste. Cover and
refrigerate until needed. The relish is
best served at room temperature.

RED ONION, GARLIC AND CHILLI RELISH

THIS POWERFUL RELISH IS FLAVOURED WITH NORTH AFRICAN SPICES AND PUNCHY PRESERVED LEMONS, AVAILABLE FROM DELICATESSENS AND LARGER SUPERMARKETS.

2 Add the garlic cloves and coriander seeds. Cover and cook gently for another 5–8 minutes, stirring occasionally to prevent the onions from browning, until the garlic is beginning to soften.

3 Add a pinch of salt, lots of pepper and the sugar, and cook, uncovered, for 5 minutes. Meanwhile, soak the saffron in the warm water for 5 minutes. Then add the saffron mixture (including the saffron threads) to the onions. Add the cinnamon, chillies and bay leaves. Stir in 30ml/2 tbsp of the sherry vinegar and the orange juice.

4 Cook gently, uncovered, until the onions are very soft and most of the liquid has evaporated. Stir in the preserved lemon and cook gently for 5 minutes. Taste and adjust the seasoning, adding sugar and/or vinegar to balance the flavours. You may not need to add more salt, since the lemons are preserved in it.

5 Serve warm or at room temperature, but not hot or chilled. The relish tastes best the day after it is made. Remove the cinnamon stick before serving.

SERVES SIX

INGREDIENTS
45ml/3 tbsp olive oil
3 large red onions, sliced
2 heads of garlic, separated into cloves and peeled
10ml/2 tsp coriander seeds, crushed but not finely ground
10ml/2 tsp light muscovado (brown) sugar, plus a little extra
pinch of saffron threads
45ml/3 tbsp warm water
10cm/2in piece of cinnamon stick
2–3 small whole dried red chillies
2 fresh bay leaves
30–45ml/2–3 tbsp sherry vinegar
juice of ½ small orange
30ml/2 tbsp chopped preserved lemon
salt and ground black pepper

1 Heat the oil in a heavy pan. Add the onions and stir, then cover and reduce the heat to the lowest setting. Cook for 10–15 minutes, stirring occasionally, until the onions are very soft but not browned.

ONION RELISH

THIS POPULAR RELISH, KNOWN AS CEBOLLAS EN ESCABECHE, IS TYPICAL OF THE YUCATAN REGION AND IS OFTEN SERVED WITH CHICKEN, FISH OR TURKEY. TRY IT WITH BISCUITS AND CHEESE — IT ADDS A SPICY, TANGY TASTE AND IS FAT AND SUGAR FREE.

MAKES ONE SMALL JAR

INGREDIENTS
   2 fresh red fresno chillies
   5ml/1 tsp allspice berries
   2.5ml/½ tsp black peppercorns
   5ml/1 tsp dried oregano
   2 white onions
   2 garlic cloves, peeled
   100ml/3½fl oz/⅓ cup white
      wine vinegar
   200ml/7fl oz/scant cup cider vinegar
   salt

1 Spear the fresno chillies on a long-handled metal skewer and roast them over the flame of a gas burner until the skins blister. Do not let the flesh burn. Alternatively, dry fry them in a griddle pan until the skins are scorched. Place the roasted chillies in a strong plastic bag and tie the top to keep the steam in. Set aside for 20 minutes.

2 Meanwhile, place the allspice, black peppercorns and oregano in a mortar or food processor. Grind slowly by hand with a pestle or process until coarsely ground.

3 Cut the onions in half and slice them thinly. Put them in a bowl. Dry roast the garlic in a heavy-based frying pan until golden, then crush and add to the onions in the bowl.

4 Remove the chillies from the bag and peel off the skins. Slit the chillies, scrape out the seeds with a small sharp knife, then chop them.

COOK'S TIP
White onions have a pungent flavour and are good in this salsa, Spanish onions can also be used. Shallots also make an exellent pickle.

5 Add the ground spices to the onion mixture, followed by the chillies. Stir in both vinegars. Add salt to taste and mix thoroughly. Cover the bowl and chill for at least 1 day before use.

PICKLED CUCUMBERS

OFTEN SERVED WITH SALT BEEF, THESE GHERKINS OR CUCUMBERS ARE SIMPLE TO PREPARE BUT IT WILL TAKE A COUPLE OF DAYS FOR THE FLAVOUR TO DEVELOP.

SERVES 6–8

INGREDIENTS
    6 small pickling cucumbers
    75ml/5 tbsp white wine vinegar
    475ml/16fl oz/2 cups
      cold water
    15ml/1 tbsp salt
    10ml/2 tsp sugar
    10 black peppercorns
    1 garlic clove
    1 bunch fresh dill (optional)

1 You will need a large lidded jar or an oblong non-metallic container with a tightly fitting lid. Cut each cucumber lengthways into six spears.

2 Mix together the wine vinegar, water, salt and sugar. Crush a few of the peppercorns and leave the rest whole. Add them to the liquid. Peel the garlic clove and cut it in half.

3 Arrange the cucumber spears in the jar or container, pour over the pickling liquid and add the garlic. Put in a few sprigs of dill if using. Make sure they are completely submerged.

4 Leave the cucumbers, covered, in the refrigerator for at least two days. To serve, lift them out and discard the garlic, dill and peppercorns. Store any uneaten cucumbers in their pickling liquid in the refrigerator.

PIQUANT PINEAPPLE RELISH

*THIS FRUITY SWEET AND SOUR RELISH IS REALLY EXCELLENT WHEN IT IS SERVED WITH
GRILLED CHICKEN OR BACON SLICES.*

SERVES 4

INGREDIENTS

   400g/14oz can crushed pineapple
     in natural juice
   30ml/2 tbsp light muscovado
     (brown) sugar
   30ml/2 tbsp wine vinegar
   1 garlic clove
   4 spring onions (scallions)
   2 red chillies
   10 fresh basil leaves
   salt and ground black pepper

1 Drain the crushed pineapple pieces
thoroughly and reserve about 60ml/
4 tbsp of the juice.

2 Place the pineapple juice in a small
pan with the muscovado sugar and
wine vinegar, then heat gently, stirring,
until the sugar dissolves. Remove the
pan from the heat and add salt and
pepper to taste.

3 Finely chop the garlic and spring
onions. Halve the chillies, remove
the seeds and finely chop the flesh.
Finely shred the basil.

4 Place the pineapple, garlic, spring
onions and chillies in a bowl. Mix well
and pour in the sauce. Leave to cool for
5 minutes, then stir in the basil.

COOK'S TIP
This relish tastes extra special when made
with fresh pineapple – substitute the juice
of a freshly squeezed orange for the
canned juice.

CHILLI STRIPS <u>WITH</u> LIME

THIS FRESH RELISH IS IDEAL FOR SERVING WITH STEWS, RICE DISHES OR BEAN DISHES. THE OREGANO ADDS A SWEET NOTE WHILE THE ABSENCE OF SUGAR OR OIL MAKES THIS A VERY HEALTHY CHOICE.

MAKES ABOUT 60ML/4 TBSP

INGREDIENTS
  10 fresh green chillies
  ½ white onion
  4 limes
  2.5ml/½ tsp dried oregano
  salt

COOK'S TIP
This method of roasting chillies is ideal if you need more than one or two, or if you do not have a gas burner. To roast over a burner, spear the chillies, four or five at a time, on a long-handled metal skewer and hold them over the flame, turning them round frequently, until the skins blister.

1 Roast the chillies in a griddle pan over a medium heat until the skins are charred and blistered but not blackened, as this might make the salsa bitter. Place the roasted chillies in a strong plastic bag and tie the top to keep the steam in. Set aside for 20 minutes.

2 Meanwhile, slice the onion very thinly and put it in a large bowl. Squeeze the limes and add the juice to the bowl, with any pulp that gathers in the strainer. The lime juice will have the effect of softening the onion. Stir in the oregano.

3 Remove the chillies from the bag and peel off the skins. Slit them, then scrape out and discard all the seeds. Cut the chillies into long strips using a sharp knife. These are called "rajas".

4 Add the chilli strips to the onion mixture and season lightly with salt. Cover the bowl and chill for at least 1 day before serving, to allow the flavours to blend. Taste the salsa and add more salt at this stage if necessary. The salsa will keep for up to 2 weeks in a covered bowl in the refrigerator.

VARIATION
White onions have a mild sweet flavour, as do red onions, which could equally well be used in their place. The colour combination of red and green would look particularly good with rice dishes.

HOT THAI PICKLED SHALLOTS <u>WITH</u> CHILLIES

THAI PINK SHALLOTS REQUIRE LENGTHY PREPARATION, BUT THEY LOOK EXQUISITE WITH
WHOLE CHILLIES IN THIS SPICED PICKLE. SERVE THEM FINELY SLICED.

MAKES TWO TO THREE JARS

INGREDIENTS
5–6 small red or green bird's
    eye chillies
500g/1¼lb Thai pink shallots, peeled
2 large garlic cloves, halved

For the vinegar
600ml/1 pint/2½ cups cider vinegar
45ml/3 tbsp granulated sugar
10ml/2 tsp salt
5cm/2in piece fresh root
    ginger, sliced
15ml/1 tbsp coriander seeds
2 lemon grass stalks, trimmed and
    cut in half lengthways
4 kaffir lime leaves or strips of lime rind
15ml/1 tbsp chopped fresh
    coriander (cilantro)

4 Pack the shallots into sterilized jars,
distributing the lemon grass, lime
leaves, chillies and garlic between
them. Pour over the hot vinegar. Cool,
then seal and leave in a dark place for
2 months before eating.

COOK'S TIPS
• When making pickles, see that bowls
and pans used for the vinegar are not
chemically affected by the acid of the
vinegar. China and glass bowls and
stainless steel pans are suitable.
• Ensure that metal lids do not come in
contact with the pickle. The acid in the
vinegar would corrode the metal. Use
plastic-coated lids or glass lids with
rubber rings. Or, when using metal lids,
cover the top of each jar with a circle of
waxed paper to prevent direct contact.
• Let hot jars cool slightly after
sterilizing. But do not let them cool
completely, or they might crack when
the hot vinegar is poured in.

1 Prick the chillies several times with
a cocktail stick or toothpick. Bring a
large pan of water to the boil. Blanch
the chillies, shallots and garlic for
1–2 minutes, then drain. Rinse all the
vegetables under cold water, then drain
again thoroughly in a colander.

2 To prepare the vinegar, put the cider
vinegar, sugar, salt, ginger, coriander
seeds, lemon grass and lime leaves or
lime rind in a pan and bring to the
boil. Reduce the heat and simmer for
3–4 minutes, then leave to cool.

3 Scoop out the ginger, then bring the
vinegar back to the boil. Add the fresh
coriander, garlic and chillies (leave the
shallots in the colander) and cook for
1 minute.

COCONUT CHUTNEY WITH ONION AND CHILLI

SERVE THIS REFRESHING COCONUT CHUTNEY AS AN ACCOMPANIMENT TO INDIAN-STYLE DISHES OR AT THE START OF A MEAL, WITH POPPADUMS, A RAITA AND OTHER CHUTNEYS.

SERVES FOUR TO SIX

INGREDIENTS
200g/7oz fresh coconut, grated
3–4 fresh green chillies, seeded
  and chopped
60ml/4 tbsp chopped fresh
  coriander (cilantro)
30ml/2 tbsp chopped fresh mint
30–45ml/2–3 tbsp lime juice
about 2.5ml/½ tsp salt
about 2.5ml/½ tsp granulated sugar
15–30ml/1–2 tbsp coconut milk
30ml/2 tbsp groundnut
  (peanut) oil
5ml/1 tsp kalonji (nigella seeds)
1 small onion, very finely chopped
fresh coriander (cilantro) sprigs,
  to garnish

1 Place the coconut, chillies, coriander and mint in a food processor. Add 30ml/2 tbsp of the lime juice, then process until thoroughly chopped.

2 Scrape the mixture into a bowl. Stir in more lime juice to taste, with the salt, sugar and coconut milk.

3 Heat the oil in a small pan and fry the kalonji until they begin to pop. Reduce the heat and add the onion. Fry, stirring frequently, until the onion is soft.

4 Stir the spiced onions into the coconut mixture and cool. Garnish with coriander sprigs before serving.

ONION, MANGO AND CHILLI RELISH

CHAATS ARE SPICED RELISHES OF VEGETABLES AND NUTS SERVED WITH INDIAN MEALS. USE GREEN JALAPEÑOS OR SERRANOS FOR MEDIUM HEAT, OR GREEN CAYENNE CHILLIES IF YOU WANT IT HOT.

SERVES FOUR

INGREDIENTS
15ml/1 tbsp groundnut (peanut) oil
90g/3½oz/1 cup unsalted peanuts
1 onion, chopped
10cm/4in piece cucumber, seeded
  and cut into 5mm/¼in dice
1 mango, peeled, stoned (pitted)
  and diced
1–2 fresh green chillies, seeded and
  finely chopped
30ml/2 tbsp chopped fresh
  coriander (cilantro)
15ml/1 tbsp chopped fresh mint
15ml/1 tbsp lime juice
pinch of granulated sugar

For the chaat masala
10ml/2 tsp ground toasted cumin seeds
2.5ml/½ tsp cayenne pepper
5ml/1 tsp mango powder (amchoor)
2.5ml/½ tsp garam masala
salt and ground black pepper

1 To make the chaat masala, grind all the spices together, then season with 2.5ml/½ tsp each of salt and pepper.

2 Heat the oil in a small pan and fry the peanuts until lightly browned, then drain on kitchen paper and set aside until cool.

COOK'S TIP
Mango powder (amchoor) is made by grinding sun-dried mango slices and mixing the powder with a little turmeric.

3 Mix the onion, cucumber, mango, chilli, fresh coriander and mint. Sprinkle in 5ml/1 tsp of the chaat masala. Stir in the peanuts and then add the lime juice and sugar to taste. Set the mixture aside for 20–30 minutes for the flavours to mature.

4 Spoon the mixture into a serving bowl, sprinkle another 5ml/1 tsp of the chaat masala over and serve. Any remaining chaat masala will keep in a sealed jar for 4–6 weeks.

APRICOT CHUTNEY

CHUTNEYS CAN ADD ZEST TO MOST MEALS, AND IN PAKISTAN YOU WILL USUALLY FIND A SELECTION OF DIFFERENT KINDS SERVED IN TINY BOWLS FOR PEOPLE TO CHOOSE FROM. DRIED APRICOTS ARE READILY AVAILABLE FROM SUPERMARKETS OR HEALTH FOOD STORES.

MAKES ABOUT 450G/1LB

INGREDIENTS
   450g/1lb/3 cups dried apricots,
      finely chopped
   5ml/1 tsp garam masala
   275g/10oz/1¼ cups soft light
      brown sugar
   450ml/16fl oz/2 cups malt vinegar
   5ml/1 tsp ginger pulp
   5ml/1 tsp salt
   75g/3oz/½ cup sultanas
      (golden raisins)
   450ml/16fl oz/2 cups water

VARIATION
For a change, you could try dried
peaches instead of the apricots. If you
like, you can add heat with green chillies.

1 Put all of the ingredients into a
medium size pan and mix them
together thoroughly.

2 Bring the mixture to the boil, then
turn down the heat and simmer for
about 30–35 minutes, stirring
occasionally as it cooks.

3 When the chutney has thickened to
a fairly stiff consistency, transfer it to
two or three clean jam jars and leave
to cool thoroughly. This chutney should
be covered tightly with a lid and stored
in the refrigerator.

TASTY TOASTS

THESE CRUNCHY TOASTS HAVE A WONDERFUL SPICY FLAVOUR. THEY MAKE AN IDEAL SNACK OR PART OF A WEEKEND BRUNCH. THEY ARE ESPECIALLY DELICIOUS WHEN SERVED WITH FRESHLY GRILLED TOMATOES AND BAKED BEANS.

SERVES 4

INGREDIENTS
   4 eggs
   300ml/½ pint/1½ cups milk
   2 fresh green chillies,
      finely chopped
   30ml/2 tbsp chopped fresh
      coriander (cilantro)
   75g/3oz/½ cup grated Cheddar
      or mozzarella cheese
   2.5ml/½ tsp salt
   1.5ml/¼ tsp ground black pepper
   4 slices bread
   corn oil, for frying

1 Break the eggs into a medium bowl
and whisk together. Slowly add the
milk and whisk again. Add the green
chillies, fresh coriander, grated cheese
and salt and pepper to taste.

2 Cut the bread slices in half diagonally,
and soak them, one at a time, in the
egg mixture.

COOK'S TIP
In place of coriander (cilantro) substitute
torn fresh basil leaves for a truly
aromatic brunch served with grilled
(broiled) tomatoes.

3 Heat the corn oil in a medium frying
pan and fry the soaked bread slices
over a medium heat, turning them once
or twice, until they are golden brown.

4 Drain off any excess oil as you
remove the toasts from the pan and
serve them immediately.

MIXED VEGETABLE PICKLE

IF YOU CAN OBTAIN FRESH TURMERIC, THEN YOU WILL FIND IT MAKES A GREAT DIFFERENCE TO THE COLOUR AND APPEARANCE OF ACAR CAMPUR. YOU CAN USE ALMOST ANY VEGETABLE, BEARING IN MIND THAT YOU NEED A BALANCE OF TEXTURES, FLAVOURS AND COLOURS.

MAKES 2–3 X 300G/11OZ JARS

INGREDIENTS
1 fresh red chilli, seeded and sliced
1 onion, quartered
2 garlic cloves, crushed
1cm/½ in cube shrimp paste
4 macadamia nuts or 8 almonds
2.5cm/1in fresh turmeric, peeled and
  sliced, or 5ml/1 tsp ground turmeric
50ml/2fl oz/¼ cup sunflower oil
475ml/16fl oz/2 cups white vinegar
250ml/8fl oz/1 cup water
25–50g/1–2oz sugar
3 carrots
225g/8oz/1½ cups green beans
1 small cauliflower
1 cucumber
225g/8oz white cabbage
115g/4oz/1 cup dry-roasted peanuts,
  coarsely crushed
salt

1 Place the chilli, onion, garlic, shrimp paste, nuts and turmeric in a food processor and blend to a paste, or pound in a mortar with a pestle.

2 Heat the oil and stir-fry the paste to release the aroma. Add the vinegar, water, sugar and salt. Bring to the boil. Simmer for 10 minutes.

3 Cut the carrots into flower shapes. Cut the green beans into short, neat lengths. Separate the cauliflower into neat, bitesize florets. Peel and seed the cucumber and cut the flesh in neat, bitesize pieces. Cut the cabbage in neat, bitesize pieces.

4 Blanch each vegetable separately, in a large pan of boiling water, for 1 minute. Transfer to a colander and rinse with cold water, to halt the cooking. Drain well.

5 Add the vegetables to the sauce. Gradually bring to the boil and cook for 5–10 minutes. Do not overcook – the vegetables should still be quite crunchy.

6 Add the peanuts and cool. Spoon into clean jars with lids.

COOK'S TIP
This pickle is even better if you make it a few days ahead.

SPICY FRIED DUMPLINGS

*THESE LITTLE DUMPLINGS ARE EASY TO MAKE. IN THE CARIBBEAN, THEY ARE OFTEN SERVED WITH
SALTFISH OR FRIED FISH, BUT THEY CAN BE EATEN SIMPLY WITH BUTTER AND JAM OR CHEESE.*

MAKES ABOUT 10

INGREDIENTS
 450g/1lb/4 cups self-raising
  (self-rising) flour
 10ml/2 tsp sugar
 2.5ml/½ tsp ground cinnamon
 pinch of ground nutmeg
 2.5ml/½ tsp salt
 300ml/½ pint/1¼ cups milk
 oil, for frying

1 Sift the dry ingredients together into
a large bowl, add the milk and mix and
knead until smooth.

2 Divide the dough into ten balls,
kneading each ball with floured hands.
Press the balls gently to flatten into
7.5cm/3in rounds.

3 Heat a little oil in a non-stick frying
pan until moderately hot. Place half the
dumplings in the pan, reduce the heat
to low and cook for about 15 minutes
until they are golden brown, turning once.

4 Stand the dumplings on their sides
for a few minutes to brown the edges,
before removing them and draining
on kitchen paper. Serve warm.

CHICKPEA BREADS

THESE FLAVOUR-PACKED UNLEAVENED BREADS ARE POPULAR IN NORTHERN INDIA. THEY ARE MADE WITH GRAM FLOUR, WHICH IS MILLED FROM CHANA DHAL, A TYPE OF CHICKPEA.

2 Mix in enough water to make a pliable, soft dough. Place the dough on a lightly floured surface and knead it until smooth, then place it in a lightly oiled bowl, cover with lightly oiled clear film (plastic wrap) and rest for 1 hour.

3 Transfer the dough to a lightly floured surface. Divide into 4 equal pieces and shape into balls. Roll out each ball of dough into a thick round, about 15–18cm/6–7in in diameter. Heat a griddle or heavy frying pan over a medium heat for a few minutes until it is hot.

4 Brush both sides of one roti with a little of the remaining oil or melted butter. Add it to the griddle or frying pan and cook for about 2 minutes, turning after 1 minute. Brush the cooked roti lightly with oil or melted butter again, slide it on to a plate and keep warm in a preheated low oven while cooking the remaining rotis in the same way. Serve warm.

VARIATION
Use 1.5–2.5ml/¼–½ tsp chilli powder instead of the fresh chilli.

MAKES FOUR

INGREDIENTS
115g/4oz/1 cup gram flour
115g/4oz/1 cup wholemeal (whole-wheat) flour
1 fresh green chilli, seeded and chopped
½ onion, finely chopped
15ml/1 tbsp chopped fresh coriander (cilantro)
2.5ml/½ tsp ground turmeric
2.5ml/½ tsp salt
45ml/3 tbsp oil or melted butter
120–150ml/4–5fl oz/½–⅔ cup lukewarm water

1 Mix the gram and wholemeal flours, chopped chilli, onion and coriander, ground turmeric and salt well together in a large bowl. Stir in 15ml/1 tbsp of the oil or melted butter.

CHILLI POORI PUFFS

THESE SMALL DISCS OF DOUGH PUFF UP INTO LIGHT AIRY BREADS WHEN FRIED. LIGHTLY STUDDED WITH PIECES OF CHILLI, THEY MELT IN YOUR MOUTH AND LEAVE YOU WITH A WARM GLOW.

MAKES TWELVE

INGREDIENTS
    115g/4oz/1 cup unbleached plain
      (all-purpose) flour
    115g/4oz/1 cup wholemeal
      (whole-wheat) flour
    2.5ml/½ tsp salt
    2.5ml/½ tsp mild chilli powder
    30ml/2 tbsp vegetable oil
    1 fresh red chilli, seeded and finely
      chopped (optional)
    100–120ml/3½–4fl oz/
      scant ½ cup–½ cup water
    oil, for frying

VARIATION
To make spinach-flavoured pooris, omit
the fresh chilli. Thaw 50g/2oz/⅓ cup
frozen chopped spinach, drain and add
to the dough with 5ml/1 tsp grated fresh
ginger and 2.5ml/½ tsp ground cumin.

1 Sift the flours, salt and chilli powder
into a large bowl. Add the vegetable
oil then mix in enough water to make
a dough. Turn the dough out on a
lightly floured surface and knead for
8–10 minutes until it is smooth, elastic
and springy.

2 Place in a lightly oiled bowl and cover
with lightly oiled clear film (plastic
wrap). Leave to rest for 30 minutes.

3 Turn out on to a lightly floured
surface. Knead in the chopped fresh
chilli, if using, then divide the dough
into 12 equal pieces. Keeping the rest
of the dough covered, roll one piece
into a 13cm/5in round. Repeat with the
remaining dough. Stack the pooris,
layered between clear film.

4 Pour oil into a deep pan to a depth of
2.5cm/1in. Heat it to 180°C/350°F or
until a cube of day-old bread, added to
the oil, browns in about 45 seconds.
Using a spatula, lift one poori and slide
it into the oil; it will sink but will rise
and begin to sizzle. Press the poori
into the oil. It will puff up. Turn it over
after a few seconds and cook for
20–30 seconds. Remove the poori from
the pan and drain on kitchen paper. Keep
warm in a preheated low oven while
cooking the remaining pooris. Serve warm.

MIXED SPICED NUTS

SPICE UP YOUR VERY OWN HAPPY HOUR WITH THESE SUPERB NUTTY SNACKS.

SERVES FOUR TO SIX

INGREDIENTS
    75g/3oz/1 cup dried unsweetened
        coconut flakes
    75ml/5 tbsp groundnut (peanut) oil
    2.5ml/½ tsp hot chilli powder
    5ml/1 tsp paprika
    5ml/1 tsp tomato purée (paste)
    225g/8oz/2 cups unsalted
        cashew nuts
    225g/8oz/2 cups whole
        blanched almonds
    60ml/4 tbsp granulated sugar
    5ml/1 tsp ground cumin
    2.5ml/½ tsp salt
    ground black pepper
    fresh herbs, to garnish

1 Heat a wok, add the coconut flakes and dry-fry until golden. Tip out on to a plate and leave to cool.

COOK'S TIP
The nuts can be stored separately for up to 1 month in an airtight tub.

2 Heat the wok again and add 45ml/3 tbsp of the oil. When it is hot, add the chilli powder, paprika and tomato purée. Stir well, add the cashew nuts and gently stir-fry until well coated. Drain, season with pepper and leave to cool.

3 Wipe out the wok with kitchen paper, heat it, then add the remaining oil. When the oil is hot, add the almonds and sprinkle in the sugar. Stir-fry gently until the almonds are golden brown and the sugar has caramelized. Place the cumin and salt in a bowl. Add the hot almonds, toss well, then leave to cool.

4 Either mix the cashew nuts, almonds and coconut flakes together or serve them in separate bowls. Garnish with sprigs of fresh herbs such as parsley and coriander.

RED-HOT ROOTS

COLOURFUL AND CRISP CHIPS, MADE FROM A SELECTION OF ROOT VEGETABLES,
TASTE DELICIOUS WITH A LIGHT DUSTING OF CHILLI SEASONING.

SERVES FOUR TO SIX

INGREDIENTS
    1 carrot
    2 parsnips
    2 raw beetroot (beets)
    1 sweet potato
    groundnut (peanut) oil, for
        deep-frying
    1.5ml/¼ tsp hot chilli powder
    5ml/1 tsp sea salt flakes

1 Peel all the vegetables, then slice the carrot and parsnips into long, thin ribbons and the beetroot and sweet potato into thin rounds. Pat dry all the vegetable ribbons and rounds on kitchen paper.

2 Half-fill a wok with oil. Heat it to 180ºC/350ºF or until a cube of day-old bread, added to the oil, browns in about 45 seconds. Add the vegetable slices in batches and deep-fry for 2–3 minutes until golden and crisp. Remove and drain on kitchen paper.

3 Place the chilli powder and sea salt in a mortar and grind with a pestle to a coarse powder. Pile up the vegetable chips on a serving plate, sprinkle over the spiced salt and serve immediately.

COOK'S TIP
To save time, you can slice the vegetables using a mandoline or a food processor fitted with a thin slicing disc.

CHILLI-SPICED PLANTAIN CHIPS

*THIS SNACK HAS A LOVELY SWEET TASTE, WHICH IS BALANCED BY THE HEAT FROM THE
CHILLI POWDER AND SAUCE. COOK THE CHIPS JUST BEFORE YOU INTEND TO SERVE THEM.*

SERVES FOUR

INGREDIENTS
  2 large plantains with very
    dark skins
  groundnut (peanut) oil, for
    shallow-frying
  2.5ml/½ tsp hot chilli powder
  5ml/1 tsp ground cinnamon
  hot chilli sauce, to serve

1 Peel the plantains. Cut off and throw
away the ends, then slice the fruit
diagonally into rounds; do not make
them too thin.

2 Pour the oil for frying into a small
frying pan, to a depth of about
1cm/½in. Heat the oil until it is very
hot, watching it closely all the time. Test
by carefully adding a slice of plantain;
it should float and the oil should
immediately bubble up around it.

3 Fry the plantain slices in small
batches or the temperature of the oil
will drop. When they are golden brown,
remove from the oil with a slotted spoon
and drain on kitchen paper.

4 Mix the chilli powder with the
cinnamon. Put the plantain chips on a
serving plate, sprinkle them with the
chilli and cinnamon mixture and serve
immediately, with a small bowl of hot
chilli sauce for dipping.

COOK'S TIP
Plantains are more starchy than the
bananas to which they are related, and
must be cooked before being eaten. When
ready to eat, the skin is almost black.

POPCORN WITH LIME AND CHILLI

*IF THE ONLY POPCORN YOU'VE HAD CAME OUT OF A CARTON AT THE CINEMA, TRY THIS
MEXICAN SPECIALITY. THE LIME JUICE AND CHILLI POWDER ARE INSPIRED ADDITIONS,
AND THE SNACK IS QUITE A HEALTHY CHOICE TO SERVE WITH DRINKS.*

MAKES ONE LARGE BOWL

INGREDIENTS
  30ml/2 tbsp vegetable oil
  225g/8oz/1¼ cups corn kernels
    for popcorn
  10ml/2 tsp mild or hot chilli powder
  juice of 2 limes

1 Heat the oil in a large, heavy frying
pan until it is very hot. Add the popcorn
and immediately cover the pan with a
lid and reduce the heat.

2 After a few minutes, the corn should
start to pop. Resist the temptation to
lift the lid to check. Shake the pan
occasionally so that all the corn will be
cooked and lightly browned.

3 When the sound of popping corn has
stopped, quickly remove the pan from
the heat and allow to cool slightly. Take
off the lid and use a spoon to lift out
and discard any corn kernels that have
not popped. Any uncooked corn will
have fallen to the base of the pan and
will be inedible.

4 Add the chilli powder to the pan.
Replace the lid firmly and shake the
pan repeatedly to make sure that all of
the corn is covered with a colourful
dusting of chilli powder.

5 Tip the popcorn into a large bowl
and keep warm. Sprinkle over the juice
of the limes immediately prior to serving
the popcorn.

TORTILLA CHIPS

THESE ARE KNOWN AS TOTOPOS *IN* MEXICO*, AND THE TERM REFERS TO BOTH THE FRIED TORTILLA STRIPS USED TO GARNISH SOUPS AND THE TRIANGLES USED FOR SCOOPING DIPS. USE TORTILLAS THAT ARE A FEW DAYS OLD; FRESH ONES WILL NOT CRISP UP SO WELL.*

SERVES FOUR

INGREDIENTS
    4–8 corn tortillas
    oil, for frying
    salt

VARIATION
When fried, wheat flour tortillas do not crisp up as well as corn tortillas, but they make a delicious sweet treat when sprinkled with ground cinnamon and caster sugar. Serve them hot with cream.

1 Cut each tortilla into six triangular wedges. Pour oil into a large frying pan to a depth of 1cm/½in, place the pan over a moderate heat and heat until very hot (see Cook's Tip).

COOK'S TIP
The oil needs to be very hot for cooking the tortillas – test it by carefully adding one of the wedges. It should float and begin to bubble in the oil immediately.

2 Fry the tortilla wedges in the hot oil in small batches until they turn golden and are crisp. This will only take a few moments. Remove with a slotted spoon and drain on kitchen paper. Sprinkle with salt.

3 *Totopos* should be served warm. They can be cooled completely and stored in an airtight container for a few days, but will need to be reheated in a microwave or a warm oven before being served.

HOT PUMPKIN SEEDS

THESE LITTLE SNACKS ARE IRRESISTIBLE, ESPECIALLY IF YOU INCLUDE CHIPOTLE CHILLIES. THEIR SMOKY FLAVOUR IS THE PERFECT FOIL FOR THE NUTTY TASTE OF THE PUMPKIN SEEDS AND THE SWEETNESS CONTRIBUTED BY THE SUGAR. SERVE THEM WITH PRE-DINNER DRINKS.

SERVES FOUR

INGREDIENTS
    130g/4½oz/1 cup pumpkin seeds
    4 garlic cloves, crushed
    1.5ml/¼ tsp salt
    10ml/2 tsp crushed dried chillies
    5ml/1 tsp caster sugar
    a wedge of lime

COOK'S TIP
It is important to keep the pumpkin seeds moving as they cook. Watch them carefully and do not let them burn, or they will taste bitter.

1 Heat a small heavy-based frying pan, add the pumpkin seeds and dry fry for a few minutes, stirring constantly as they swell.

2 When all the seeds have swollen, add the garlic and cook for a few minutes more, stirring all the time. Add the salt and the crushed chillies and stir to mix. Turn off the heat, but keep the pan on the stove. Sprinkle sugar over the seeds and shake the pan to ensure that they are all coated.

3 Tip the *pepitas* into a bowl and serve with the wedge of lime for squeezing over the seeds. If the lime is omitted, the seeds can be cooled and stored in an airtight container for reheating later, but they are best served fresh.

Dips and snacks may whet the appetite, but it's the

first course that really determines whether a meal will

go with a swing. Play safe with a humdrum soup,

and you set the scene for a staid and sensible evening;

introduce chillies and there's no telling what could

happen! Whether you select a Warming Spinach and

Rice Soup with a teasing warmth that will keep everyone

guessing as to its source, or make a more blatant

statement with classic Chicken Pepper Soup, the

conversation - and compliments - will flow like wine.

Spicy Soups

HOT AND SOUR SOUP

ONE OF CHINA'S MOST POPULAR SOUPS, THIS IS FAMED FOR ITS CLEVER BALANCE OF FLAVOURS. THE "HOT" COMES FROM PEPPER; THE "SOUR" FROM VINEGAR. SIMILAR SOUPS RELYING ON CHILLIES AND LIME JUICE ARE FOUND THROUGHOUT ASIA.

SERVES 6

INGREDIENTS
4–6 Chinese dried mushrooms
2–3 small pieces of wood ear
    and a few golden needles (lily
    buds) (optional)
115g/4oz pork fillet, cut into
    fine strips
45ml/3 tbsp cornflour
150ml/¼ pint/⅔ cup water
15–30ml/1–2 tbsp sunflower oil
1 small onion, finely chopped
1.5 litres/2½ pints/6¼ cups good
    quality beef or chicken stock, or
    2 × 300g/11oz cans consommé made
    up to the full quantity with water
150g/5oz drained fresh firm
    beancurd (tofu), diced
60ml/4 tbsp rice vinegar
15ml/1 tbsp light soy sauce
1 egg, beaten
5 ml/1 tsp sesame oil
salt and ground white or black pepper
2–3 spring onions, shredded,
    to garnish

1 Place the dried mushrooms in a bowl, with the pieces of wood ear and the golden needles (lily buds), if using. Add sufficient warm water to cover and leave to soak for about 30 minutes. Drain the mushrooms, reserving the soaking water. Cut off and discard the mushroom stems and slice the caps finely. Trim away any tough stem from the wood ears, then chop them finely. Using kitchen string, tie the golden needles into a bundle.

2 Lightly dust the strips of pork fillet with some of the cornflour; mix the remaining cornflour to a smooth paste with the measured water.

3 Heat the oil in a wok or saucepan and fry the onion until soft. Increase the heat and fry the pork until it changes colour. Add the stock or consommé, mushrooms, soaking water, and wood ears and golden needles, if using. Bring to the boil, then simmer for 15 minutes.

4 Discard the golden needles, lower the heat and stir in the cornflour paste to thicken. Add the beancurd, vinegar, soy sauce, and salt and pepper.

5 Bring the soup to just below boiling point, then drizzle in the beaten egg by letting it drop from a whisk (or to be authentic, the fingertips) so that it forms threads in the soup. Stir in the sesame oil and serve at once, garnished with spring onion shreds.

WARMING SPINACH AND RICE SOUP

*THE CHILLI ADDS JUST A FLICKER OF FIRE TO THIS LIGHT AND FRESH-TASTING SOUP,
MADE USING VERY YOUNG SPINACH LEAVES AND RISOTTO RICE.*

SERVES FOUR

INGREDIENTS
   675g/1½lb fresh spinach, washed
   45ml/3 tbsp extra virgin olive oil
   1 small onion, finely chopped
   2 garlic cloves, finely chopped
   1 small fresh red chilli, seeded and
      finely chopped
   115g/4oz/generous ½ cup risotto rice
   1.2 litres/2 pints/5 cups
      vegetable stock
   60ml/4 tbsp grated (shredded)
      Pecorino cheese
   salt and ground black pepper

1 Place the spinach in a large pan with just the water that clings to its leaves. Add a pinch of salt. Heat until the spinach has wilted, then remove from the heat and drain, reserving any liquid.

2 Either chop the spinach finely using a large knife or place in a food processor and process briefly to achieve a fairly coarse purée.

3 Heat the oil in a large pan and gently cook the onion, garlic and chilli for 4–5 minutes until softened but not browned. Stir in the risotto rice until well coated with the mixture.

4 Pour in the stock and reserved spinach liquid. Bring to the boil, reduce the heat and simmer for 10 minutes.

5 Add the spinach, with salt and pepper to taste. Cook for 5–7 minutes more, until the rice is tender. Check the seasoning and serve in heated soup plates or bowls, with the Pecorino cheese sprinkled over.

PIQUANT PUMPKIN AND COCONUT SOUP

WHEN THERE ARE PLENTY OF PUMPKINS ABOUT, SOUP SEEMS THE OBVIOUS ANSWER. THIS
THAI VERSION IS A LITTLE OUT-OF-THE-ORDINARY AND TASTES SUPERB.

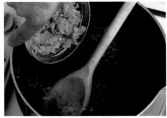

2 Pour the chicken stock into a large pan. Bring it to the boil, add the ground paste and stir gently to blend it into the stock.

3 Add the pumpkin and simmer for about 10–15 minutes or until the pumpkin is tender.

4 Stir in the creamed coconut, then bring back to a simmer. Add the Thai fish sauce, sugar and ground black pepper to taste.

SERVES FOUR TO SIX

INGREDIENTS
  1 lemon grass stalk
  2 garlic cloves, crushed
  4 shallots, finely chopped
  2.5ml/½ tsp shrimp paste
  15ml/1 tbsp dried shrimps, soaked in
    water for 10 minutes and drained
  2 fresh green chillies, seeded
  salt, to taste
  600ml/1 pint/2½ cups chicken stock
  450g/1lb pumpkin, cut into
    2cm/¾ in chunks
  600ml/1 pint/2½ cups creamed
    coconut (coconut cream)
  30ml/2 tbsp Thai fish sauce
    (*nam pla*)
  5ml/1 tsp granulated sugar
  8–12 small cooked peeled
    prawns (shrimp)
  ground black pepper
  2 fresh red chillies, seeded and
    finely sliced, to garnish
  10–12 fresh basil leaves, to garnish

1 Cut off the lower 5cm/2in of the lemon grass stalk and chop it roughly. Put it in a mortar and add the garlic, shallots, shrimp paste, dried shrimps, green chillies and salt. Grind to a paste.

COOK'S TIPS
• Chillies freeze very well and break down much more easily than fresh ones, so are perfect for pastes.
• Add salt to this soup with care. The shrimps will have been lightly salted before drying, and the shrimp paste and fish sauce may also be salty.

5 Add the prawns and cook until they are heated through. Serve in heated soup bowls, each one garnished with the finely sliced red chillies and whole basil leaves.

PUMPKIN SOUP <u>WITH</u> ANIS

*USE MILD CHILLIES FOR THIS TASTY SOUP, SO THAT THEY ACCENTUATE THE PUMPKIN FLAVOUR
AND DO NOT MASK THE LIQUORICE TASTE OF THE ANISEED-FLAVOURED APERITIF.*

SERVES FOUR

INGREDIENTS

- 1 pumpkin, about 675g/1½lb
- 30ml/2 tbsp olive oil
- 2 large onions, sliced
- 1 garlic clove, crushed
- 2 fresh red chillies, seeded
  and chopped
- 5ml/1 tsp curry paste
- 1 litre/1¾ pints/4 cups vegetable or
  chicken stock
- 15ml/1 tbsp Anis, Pernod, or aniseed
  (anise seed)-flavoured aperitif
- 150ml/¼ pint/⅔ cup single
  (light) cream
- salt and ground black pepper

1 Peel the pumpkin with a sturdy knife, cutting the skin away from the flesh, remove the seeds and then chop the flesh roughly.

2 Heat the oil in a pan and fry the onions until golden. Stir in the garlic, chillies and curry paste. Cook for 1 minute, then add the chopped pumpkin and cook for 5 minutes more, stirring frequently to prevent browning.

3 Pour over the stock and season with salt and pepper. Bring to the boil, reduce the heat, cover and simmer for about 25 minutes.

4 Spoon about one-third of the soup into a blender or food processor, process until smooth, then scrape into a clean pan. Repeat with the remaining soup, processing it in 2 batches.

5 Add the anis and reheat. Taste and season if necessary with salt and pepper. Serve the soup in individual heated bowls, adding a spoonful of cream to each portion.

HOT AND SWEET VEGETABLE AND TOFU SOUP

AN INTERESTING COMBINATION OF HOT, SWEET AND SOUR FLAVOURS THAT MAKES FOR A SOOTHING, NUTRITIOUS SOUP. IT TAKES ONLY MINUTES TO MAKE AS THE SPINACH AND SILKEN TOFU ARE SIMPLY PLACED IN BOWLS AND COVERED WITH THE FLAVOURED HOT STOCK.

SERVES FOUR

INGREDIENTS

1.2 litres/2 pints/5 cups
  vegetable stock
5–10ml/1–2 tsp Thai red
  curry paste
2 kaffir lime leaves, torn
40g/1½oz/3 tbsp palm sugar or light
  muscovado (brown) sugar
30ml/2 tbsp soy sauce
juice of 1 lime
1 carrot, cut into thin batons
50g/2oz baby spinach leaves, any
  coarse stalks removed
225g/8oz block silken tofu, diced

1 Heat the stock in a large pan, then add the red curry paste. Stir constantly over a medium heat until the paste has dissolved. Add the lime leaves, sugar and soy sauce and bring to the boil.

2 Add the lime juice and carrot to the pan. Reduce the heat and simmer for 5–10 minutes. Place the spinach and tofu in four individual serving bowls and pour the hot stock on top to serve.

HOT AND SPICY MISO BROTH WITH TOFU

THE JAPANESE EAT MISO BROTH, A SIMPLE BUT HIGHLY NUTRITIOUS SOUP, ALMOST EVERY
DAY — IT IS STANDARD BREAKFAST FARE AND IS EATEN WITH RICE OR NOODLES LATER ON.

SERVES FOUR

INGREDIENTS
1 bunch of spring onions (scallions)
  or 5 baby leeks
15g/½oz/⅓ cup fresh
  coriander (cilantro)
3 thin slices fresh root ginger
2 star anise
1 small dried red chilli
1.2 litres/2 pints/5 cups dashi stock
  or vegetable stock
225g/8oz pak choi (bok choy) or
  other Asian greens, thickly sliced
200g/7oz firm tofu, cut into
  2.5cm/1in squares
45–60ml/3–4 tbsp red miso
30–45ml/2–3 tbsp Japanese soy
  sauce (shoyu)
1 fresh red chilli, seeded
  and shredded

1 Cut the coarse green tops off half of
the spring onions or leeks and place in
a pan with the coriander stalks, ginger,
star anise and dried chilli. Pour in the
dashi or vegetable stock. Heat gently
until boiling, then simmer for
10 minutes. Strain, return to the pan
and reheat until simmering.

2 Slice the remaining spring onions or
leeks finely on the diagonal and add the
green portion to the soup with the pak
choi or greens and squares of tofu.
Cook for 2 minutes.

3 Mix 45ml/3 tbsp of the miso with a
little of the hot soup in a bowl, then stir
it into the soup. Taste the soup and add
more miso with soy sauce to taste.

4 Coarsely chop the coriander leaves
and stir most of them into the soup with
the white part of the spring onions or
leeks. Cook for 1 minute, then ladle the
soup into heated serving bowls. Sprinkle
with the remaining chopped coriander
and the shredded fresh red chilli and
serve immediately.

COOK'S TIPS
• Dashi powder is available in most Asian
and Chinese stores. Alternatively, make
your own by gently simmering 10–15cm/
4–6in kombu seaweed in 1.2 litres/
2 pints/5 cups water for 10 minutes.
Do not boil the stock vigorously as this
would make the dashi bitter. Remove the
kombu, then add 15g/½oz dried bonito
flakes and bring to the boil. Strain
immediately through a fine sieve.
• Kombu seaweed is usually dried,
pickled or shaved thinly in dry sheets.
Wash dried Kombu before using.
• Red miso is a paste made from
fermented beans and grains. Buy it from
Asian food stores. It will keep almost
indefinitely in an airtight container in
the refrigerator.

COCONUT AND PUMPKIN SOUP

THE NATURAL SWEETNESS OF THE PUMPKIN IS HEIGHTENED BY THE ADDITION OF A LITTLE SUGAR IN THIS LOVELY LOOKING SOUP, BUT THIS IS BALANCED BY THE CHILLIES, SHRIMP PASTE AND DRIED SHRIMP. COCONUT CREAM BLURS THE BOUNDARIES BEAUTIFULLY.

SERVES FOUR TO SIX

INGREDIENTS
    450g/1lb pumpkin
    2 garlic cloves, crushed
    4 shallots, finely chopped
    2.5ml/½ tsp shrimp paste
    1 lemon grass stalk, chopped
    2 fresh green chillies, seeded
    15ml/1 tbsp dried shrimp soaked
        for 10 minutes in warm water
        to cover
    600ml/1 pint/2½ cups chicken stock
    600ml/1 pint/2½ cups
        coconut cream
    30ml/2 tbsp Thai fish sauce
    5ml/1 tsp granulated sugar
    115g/4oz small cooked shelled
        prawns (shrimp)
    salt and ground black pepper

To garnish
    2 fresh red chillies, seeded and
        thinly sliced
    10–12 fresh basil leaves

1 Peel the pumpkin and cut it into quarters with a sharp knife. Scoop out the seeds with a teaspoon and discard. Cut the flesh into chunks about 2cm/¾in thick and set aside.

2 Put the garlic, shallots, shrimp paste, lemon grass, green chillies and salt to taste in a mortar. Drain the dried shrimp, discarding the soaking liquid, and add them, then use a pestle to grind the mixture into a paste. Alternatively, place all the ingredients in a food processor and process to a paste.

3 Bring the chicken stock to the boil in a large pan. Add the ground paste and stir well to dissolve.

4 Add the pumpkin chunks and bring to a simmer. Simmer for 10–15 minutes, or until the pumpkin is tender.

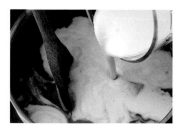

5 Stir in the coconut cream, then bring the soup back to simmering point. Do not let it boil. Add the fish sauce, sugar and ground black pepper to taste.

6 Add the prawns and cook for a further 2–3 minutes, until they are heated through. Serve in warm soup bowls, garnished with chillies and basil leaves.

COOK'S TIP
Shrimp paste is made from ground shrimp fermented in brine.

SPICED RED LENTIL AND COCONUT SOUP

HOT, SPICY AND RICHLY FLAVOURED, THIS SUBSTANTIAL SOUP IS A MEAL IN ITSELF. IF YOU ARE REALLY HUNGRY, SERVE IT WITH CHUNKS OF WARMED NAAN BREAD OR THICK SLICES OF TOAST.

SERVES FOUR

INGREDIENTS
    30ml/2 tbsp sunflower oil
    2 red onions, finely chopped
    1 bird's eye chilli, seeded and
        finely sliced
    2 garlic cloves, chopped
    1 lemon grass stalk, outer layers
        removed and inside finely sliced
    200g/7oz/scant 1 cup red lentils,
        rinsed and drained
    5ml/1 tsp ground coriander
    5ml/1 tsp paprika
    400ml/14fl oz/1⅔ cups
        coconut milk
    900ml/1½ pints/3¾ cups water
    juice of 1 lime
    3 spring onions (scallions), chopped
    20g/¾oz/½ cup fresh coriander
        (cilantro), finely chopped
    salt and ground black pepper

1 Heat the oil in a large pan and add the onions, chilli, garlic and lemon grass. Cook for 5 minutes or until the onions have softened but not browned, stirring occasionally.

COOK'S TIP
Bird's eye chillies may look insubstantial, but they pack quite a punch. Don't be tempted to add more unless you are a real chilli head!

2 Add the lentils and spices. Pour in the coconut milk and water, and stir. Bring to the boil, stir, then reduce the heat and simmer for 40–45 minutes or until the lentils are soft and mushy.

3 Stir in the lime juice and add the spring onions and fresh coriander, reserving a little of each for the garnish. Season, then ladle into heated bowls. Top with the reserved garnishes.

SPICY BEAN SOUP

THIS DELICIOUS SEPHARDI ISRAELI SOUP, OF BLACK-EYED BEANS AND TURMERIC-TINTED TOMATO BROTH, IS FLAVOURED WITH TANGY LEMON AND SPECKLED WITH CHOPPED FRESH CORIANDER. IT IS IDEAL FOR SERVING AT PARTIES — SIMPLY MULTIPLY THE QUANTITIES AS REQUIRED.

SERVES FOUR

INGREDIENTS
175g/6oz/1 cup black-eyed
  beans (peas)
15ml/1 tbsp olive oil
2 onions, chopped
4 garlic cloves, chopped
1 medium-hot or 2–3 mild fresh
  chillies, chopped
5ml/1 tsp ground cumin
5ml/1 tsp ground turmeric
250g/9oz fresh or canned
  tomatoes, diced
600ml/1 pint/2½ cups chicken,
  beef or vegetable stock
25g/1oz fresh coriander (cilantro)
  leaves, roughly chopped
juice of ½ lemon
pitta bread, to serve

1 Put the beans in a pan, cover with cold water, bring to the boil, then cook for 5 minutes. Remove from the heat, cover and leave to stand for 2 hours.

2 Heat the oil in a pan, add the onions, garlic and chilli and cook for 5 minutes, or until the onion is soft. Stir in the cumin, turmeric, tomatoes, stock, half the coriander and the beans and simmer for 20–30 minutes. Stir in the lemon juice and remaining coriander and serve at once with pitta bread.

GAZPACHO WITH AVOCADO SALSA

CHILLIES IN A CHILLED SOUP MAKE AN UNUSUAL COMBINATION. GAZPACHO TASTES DELICIOUS WITH THE ADDITION OF CHILLI AND TABASCO. THE FLAVOURS ARE ECHOED IN THE SALSA.

SERVES FOUR

INGREDIENTS
2 slices day-old bread
600ml/1 pint/2½ cups chilled water
1kg/2¼lb tomatoes
1 cucumber
1 red (bell) pepper, seeded
  and chopped
1 fresh green chilli, seeded
  and chopped
2 garlic cloves, chopped
30ml/2 tbsp extra virgin olive oil
juice of 1 lime and 1 lemon
a few drops Tabasco sauce
salt and ground black pepper
8 ice cubes, to serve
a handful of basil leaves, to garnish

For the croûtons
2 slices day-old bread, crusts removed
1 garlic clove, halved
15ml/1 tbsp olive oil

For the avocado salsa
1 ripe avocado
5ml/1 tsp lemon juice
2.5cm/1in piece cucumber, diced
½ fresh red chilli, seeded and
  finely chopped

1 Soak the bread in 150ml/¼ pint/⅔ cup of the chilled water for 5 minutes. Place the tomatoes in a bowl and cover with boiling water. Leave for 30 seconds, then peel, seed and chop the flesh.

2 Thinly peel the cucumber, then cut it in half lengthways and scoop out the seeds with a teaspoon. Discard the seeds and chop the flesh.

3 Place the bread (with any free liquid) in a food processor or blender. Add the tomatoes, cucumber, red pepper, chilli, garlic, olive oil, citrus juices and Tabasco then pour in the remaining 450ml/¾ pint/scant 2 cups chilled water. Blend until well combined but still chunky. Season to taste, pour into a bowl and chill in the refrigerator for 2–3 hours.

4 To make the croûtons, rub the slices of bread with the garlic clove. Cut the bread into cubes and place in a plastic bag with the olive oil. Seal the bag and shake until the bread cubes are evenly coated. Heat a large non-stick frying pan and fry the croûtons over a medium heat until crisp and golden.

5 Just before serving, make the salsa. Cut the avocado in half, remove the stone (pit), then peel and dice the flesh. Put it in a small bowl. Add the lemon juice, toss to prevent browning, then mix with the cucumber and chilli.

6 Ladle the soup into chilled bowls, add the ice cubes, and top each portion with a spoonful of the avocado salsa. Garnish with the basil and hand round the croûtons separately.

TORTILLA SOUP

THE SOUTH-WESTERN UNITED STATES STAKES ITS CLAIM TO THIS SIMPLE AND DELICIOUS SOUP,
BUT IT PROBABLY ORIGINATED IN MEXICO, WHERE CONSIDERABLY HOTTER VERSIONS ARE POPULAR.

SERVES FOUR TO SIX

INGREDIENTS
    15ml/1 tbsp vegetable oil
    1 onion, finely chopped
    1 large garlic clove, crushed
    2 medium tomatoes, peeled, seeded
        and chopped
    2.5ml/½ tsp salt
    2 litres/3½ pints/8 cups
        chicken stock
    1 carrot, diced
    1 courgette (zucchini), diced
    1 skinless, boneless chicken breast
        portion, cooked and shredded
    1 fresh green chilli, seeded
        and chopped

To garnish
    4 corn tortillas
    oil, for frying
    1 small ripe avocado, peeled, stoned
        (pitted) and diced
    2 spring onions (scallions), chopped
    chopped fresh coriander (cilantro)
    grated Cheddar or Monterey Jack
        cheese (optional)

1 Heat the oil in a large pan and fry the onion and garlic over a medium heat for 5–8 minutes until softened. Stir in the tomatoes and salt, and cook for 5 minutes more.

2 Stir in the stock. Bring to the boil, then cover, reduce the heat and simmer for about 15 minutes.

COOK'S TIP
To make stock, put a chicken carcass in a large pan, add water to cover, 2 chopped onions, a stick of celery and some peppercorns. Bring to the boil, cover, simmer for 40 minutes then strain.

3 Meanwhile, for the garnish, trim the tortillas into squares, then cut into strips.

4 Pour oil into a frying pan to a depth of about 1cm/½in. Heat until hot but not smoking. Add the tortilla strips, in batches, and fry until just beginning to brown. Remove with a slotted spoon and drain on kitchen paper.

5 Add the carrot to the soup. Cook, covered, for 10 minutes. Add the courgette, chicken and chilli, and continue cooking for about 5 minutes, until the vegetables are just tender.

6 Divide the tortilla strips among 4–6 heated soup bowls. Sprinkle with the avocado. Ladle in the soup, then arrange spring onions and coriander on top. Serve with grated cheese if you like.

VARIATION
Parmesan balls make a nice alternative to shredded cheese. Grate 25g/1oz Parmesan and mix well with 2 egg yolks. When the soup is ready to serve, drop half teaspoons of the mixture all over the surface. Leave for 2–3 minutes or until just firm, then serve.

VEGETABLE SOUP WITH CHILLI AND COCONUT

*ALL OVER AFRICA, CHILLIES PLAY AN IMPORTANT PART IN THE CUISINE. IN THIS HEARTY
VEGETABLE SOUP, THEY ARE PARTNERED WITH OTHER WARMING SPICES.*

SERVES FOUR

INGREDIENTS

½ red onion
175g/6oz each of turnip, sweet
    potato and pumpkin
30ml/2 tbsp butter
5ml/1 tsp dried marjoram
2.5ml/½ tsp ground ginger
1.5ml/¼ tsp ground cinnamon
15ml/1 tbsp chopped spring
    onion (scallion)
1 litre/1¾ pint/4 cups well-flavoured
    vegetable stock
30ml/2 tbsp flaked (sliced) almonds
1 fresh red chilli, seeded
    and chopped
5ml/1 tsp granulated sugar
25g/1oz creamed coconut
    (coconut cream)
salt and ground black pepper
chopped fresh coriander (cilantro),
    to garnish (optional)

1 Finely chop the onion, then peel the
turnip, sweet potato and pumpkin and
cut into 1cm/½in dice.

2 Melt the butter in a large non-stick
pan. Fry the onion for 4–5 minutes.
Add the diced vegetables and fry for
3–4 minutes.

3 Stir in the marjoram, ginger,
cinnamon and spring onion with salt
and pepper to taste. Fry over a low heat
for about 10 minutes, stirring frequently.

COOK'S TIP
Choose young small turnips. The flavour
will have a nutty sweetness.

4 Pour in the vegetable stock and add
the almonds, chopped chilli and sugar.
Stir well to mix, then cover and simmer
gently for 10–15 minutes until the
vegetables are just tender.

5 Grate the creamed coconut into the
soup and stir gently to mix. Sprinkle
with the chopped coriander, if you
like, and spoon into heated bowls
and serve.

SPICY YOGURT SOUP

SERVES 4–6

INGREDIENTS
  450ml/¾ pint/scant 2 cups natural
    (plain) yogurt, beaten
  60ml/4 tbsp gram flour
  2.5ml/½ tsp chilli powder
  2.5ml/½ tsp ground turmeric
  2–3 green chillies, finely chopped
  60ml/4 tbsp vegetable oil
  4 whole dried red chillies
  5ml/1 tsp cumin seeds
  3–4 curry leaves
  3 garlic cloves, crushed
  5cm/2in piece of fresh root
    ginger, crushed
  salt
  fresh coriander (cilantro) leaves,
    chopped, to garnish

1 Mix together the yogurt, gram flour, chilli powder, turmeric and salt and strain them into a pan. Add the green chillies and cook gently for about 10 minutes, stirring occasionally. Be careful not to let the soup boil over.

2 Heat the oil in a frying pan and fry the remaining spices, crushed garlic and fresh ginger until the dried chillies turn black.

3 Pour the oil and the spices over the yogurt soup, remove the pan from the heat, cover and leave to rest for 5 minutes. Mix well and gently reheat for a further 5 minutes. Serve hot, garnished with the coriander leaves.

VARIATION
Sugar can be added to this soup to bring out the full flavour. For an extra creamy soup, use Greek (US strained plain) yogurt instead of natural (plain) yogurt. Adjust the amount of chillies according to how hot you want the soup to be.

TAMARIND SOUP <u>WITH</u> PEANUTS <u>AND</u> VEGETABLES

*SAYUR ASAM IS A COLOURFUL AND REFRESHING SOUP FROM JAKARTA, RICH IN VEGETABLES
AND WITH MORE THAN A HINT OF SHARPNESS.*

SERVES 4 OR 8 AS PART OF A BUFFET

INGREDIENTS

For the spice paste

5 shallots or 1 medium red
   onion, sliced
3 garlic cloves, crushed
2.5cm/1in galangal, peeled
   and sliced
1–2 fresh red chillies, seeded and sliced
25g/1oz/¼ cup raw peanuts
1cm/½in cube shrimp
   paste, prepared
1.2 litres/2 pints/5 cups well-
   flavoured stock
50–75g/2–3oz/½–¾ cup salted
   peanuts, lightly crushed
15–30ml/1–2 tbsp dark brown sugar
5ml/1 tsp tamarind pulp, soaked in
   75ml/5 tbsp warm water for
   15 minutes
salt

For the vegetables

1 chayote, thinly peeled, seeds
   removed, flesh finely sliced
115g/4oz/¾ cup green beans,
   trimmed and finely sliced
50g/2oz/⅓ cup corn kernels (optional)
handful green leaves, such as
   watercress, rocket (arugula) or
   Chinese leaves (Chinese cabbage),
   finely shredded
1 fresh green chilli, sliced,
   to garnish

1 Prepare the spice paste by grinding
the shallots or onion, garlic, galangal,
chillies, raw peanuts and shrimp paste
to a paste in a food processor or with a
mortar and pestle.

2 Pour in some of the stock to moisten
and then pour this mixture into a pan or
wok, adding the rest of the stock. Cook
for 15 minutes with the lightly crushed
peanuts and sugar.

3 Strain the tamarind, discarding the
seeds, and reserve the juice.

4 About 5 minutes before serving, add
the chayote slices, beans and corn,
if using, to the soup and cook fairly
rapidly. At the last minute, add the
green leaves and salt to taste.

5 Add the tamarind juice and taste for
seasoning. Serve, garnished with slices
of green chilli.

PLANTAIN SOUP WITH CORN AND CHILLI

SERVES 4

INGREDIENTS

25g/1oz/2 tbsp butter or margarine
1 onion, finely chopped
1 garlic clove, crushed
275g/10oz yellow plantains, peeled
  and sliced
1 large tomato, peeled and chopped
175g/6oz/1 cup corn kernels
5ml/1 tsp dried tarragon, crushed
900ml/1½ pints/3¾ cups vegetable or
  chicken stock
1 green chilli, seeded and chopped
pinch of grated nutmeg
salt and ground black pepper

1 Melt the butter or margarine in a pan over a medium heat, add the onion and garlic and cook for a few minutes until the onion is soft.

2 Add the plantain, tomato and corn and cook for 5 minutes.

3 Add the tarragon, vegetable stock, chilli and salt and pepper and simmer for 10 minutes, or until the plantain is tender. Stir in the nutmeg and serve the soup immediately.

SPICY GROUNDNUT SOUP

THIS SOUP IS WIDELY EATEN IN AFRICA. GROUNDNUTS (OR PEANUTS) ARE SPICED WITH A MIXTURE OF FRESH GINGER AND CHILLI POWDER. THE AMOUNT OF CHILLI POWDER CAN BE VARIED ACCORDING TO TASTE, ADD MORE FOR A FIERY HOT SOUP.

SERVES 4

INGREDIENTS

45ml/3 tbsp pure groundnut (peanut)
  paste or peanut butter
1.5 litres/2½ pints/6¼ cups stock
  or water
30ml/2 tbsp tomato purée (paste)
1 onion, chopped
2 slices fresh root ginger
1.5ml/½ tsp dried thyme
1 bay leaf
salt and chilli powder
225g/8oz white yam, diced
10 small okra, trimmed

1 Place the groundnut paste or peanut butter in a bowl, add 300ml/½ pint/ 1¼ cups of the stock or water and the tomato purée and blend together to make a smooth paste.

2 Spoon the nut mixture into a pan and add the onion, ginger, thyme, bay leaf, salt, chilli and the remaining stock.

COOK'S TIP
Use crunchy peanut butter for an excitingly different soup, or smooth peanut butter for a combination that will combine beautifully with the sticky juice produced by the okra.

3 Heat gently until simmering, then cook for 1 hour, stirring occasionally. Add the yam and cook for 10 minutes.

4 Add the okra, and simmer until tender. Serve immediately.

SPICY PEPPER SOUP

THIS IS A HIGHLY SOOTHING BROTH FOR WINTER EVENINGS, ALSO KNOWN AS MULLA-GA-TANI.
SERVE WITH THE WHOLE SPICES, OR STRAIN AND REHEAT IF YOU LIKE. THE LEMON JUICE
MAY BE ADJUSTED TO TASTE, BUT THIS DISH SHOULD BE DISTINCTLY SOUR.

SERVES 4–6

INGREDIENTS
    30ml/2 tbsp vegetable oil
    2.5ml/½ tsp ground black pepper
    5ml/1 tsp cumin seeds
    2.5ml/½ tsp mustard seeds
    1.5ml/¼ tsp asafoetida
    2 whole dried red chillies
    4–6 curry leaves
    2.5ml/½ tsp ground turmeric
    2 garlic cloves, crushed
    300ml/½ pint/1¼ cups tomato juice
    juice of 2 lemons
    120ml/4fl oz/½ cup water
    salt, to taste
    coriander (cilantro) leaves, chopped,
      to garnish

1 In a large pan, heat the oil and fry
the pepper, cumin and mustard seeds,
asafoetida, red chillies, curry leaves,
turmeric and garlic until the chillies
are nearly black and the garlic is
golden brown.

VARIATION
If you prefer, use lime juice instead of
lemon juice. Add 5ml/1 tsp tamarind
paste for extra sourness.

COOK'S TIP
Dried red chillies may look withered
and insubstantial, but they pack quite
a punch. Don't be tempted to add
more chillies to a dish unless you are
a real chilli enthusiast.

2 Lower the heat and add the tomato
juice, lemon juice, water and salt. Bring
the soup to the boil, then simmer gently
for about 10 minutes. Pour the soup
into bowls, garnish with the chopped
coriander and serve.

PROVENÇAL FISH SOUP WITH ROUILLE

AN AUTHENTIC CHILLI-SPIKED ROUILLE LIFTS THIS EXCELLENT SOUP INTO THE REALMS OF
THE SUBLIME. A GOOD SOUP FOR A PARTY BECAUSE YOU CAN PREPARE IT ALL IN ADVANCE.

SERVES FOUR TO SIX

INGREDIENTS

30ml/2 tbsp olive oil
1 leek, sliced
2 celery sticks, chopped
1 onion, chopped
2 garlic cloves, chopped
4 ripe tomatoes, chopped
15ml/1 tbsp tomato purée (paste)
150ml/¼ pint/⅔ cup dry white wine
1 bay leaf
5ml/1 tsp saffron threads
fish trimmings, bones and heads
1kg/2¼lb mixed fish fillets and
　prepared shellfish
salt and ground black pepper
croûtons and grated (shredded)
　Gruyère cheese, to serve

For the rouille
1 slice of white bread, crusts removed
1 red (bell) pepper, cored, seeded
　and quartered
1–2 fresh red chillies, seeded
　and chopped
2 garlic cloves, roughly chopped
olive oil (optional)

1 Make the rouille. Soak the bread in 30–45ml/2–3 tbsp cold water for 10 minutes. Meanwhile, grill (broil) the red pepper, skin side up, until the skin is charred and blistered. Put into a plastic bag and tie the top to keep the steam in. Leave until cool enough to handle. Peel off the skin. Drain the bread and squeeze out excess water.

2 Roughly chop the pepper quarters and place in a blender or food processor with the bread, chillies and garlic. Process to a fairly coarse paste, adding a little olive oil, if necessary. Scrape the rouille into a small bowl and set it aside.

COOK'S TIP
If you are preparing this soup in advance, cook it for the time stated then cool and chill as rapidly as possible. A fish soup should not be left simmering on top of the stove.

3 Heat the olive oil in a large pan. Add the leek, celery, onion and garlic. Cook gently for 10 minutes until soft. Add the tomatoes, tomato purée, wine, bay leaf, saffron and the fish trimmings. Bring to the boil, reduce the heat, cover and simmer for 30 minutes.

4 Strain through a colander into a clean pan, pressing out all the liquid. Cut the fish fillets into large chunks and add to the liquid, with the shellfish. Cover and simmer for 5–10 minutes until cooked.

5 Strain through a colander into a clean pan. Put half the cooked fish into a blender or food processor with about 300ml/½ pint/1¼ cups of the soup. Process for just long enough to blend, while retaining some texture.

6 Stir the processed mixture back into the remaining soup, then add the fish and shellfish from the colander, with salt and pepper to taste. Reheat gently. Serve the soup with the rouille, croûtons and cheese.

SPICED MUSSEL SOUP

CHUNKY AND COLOURFUL, THIS FISH SOUP HAS THE CONSISTENCY OF A CHOWDER. THE CHILLI FLAVOUR COMES FROM HARISSA, A SPICY SAUCE THAT IS POPULAR IN NORTH AFRICAN COOKING.

SERVES SIX

INGREDIENTS
    1.6kg/3½lb live mussels
    150ml/¼ pint/⅔ cup white wine
    3 tomatoes
    30ml/2 tbsp olive oil
    1 onion, finely chopped
    2 garlic cloves, crushed
    2 celery sticks, thinly sliced
    bunch of spring onions (scallions),
        thinly sliced
    1 potato, diced
    7.5ml/1½ tsp harissa
    45ml/3 tbsp chopped fresh parsley
    ground black pepper
    thick yogurt, to serve (optional)

1 Scrub the mussels and remove the beards, discarding any mussels that are damaged or that fail to close when tapped with a knife.

2 Bring the wine to the boil in a large pan. Add the mussels and cover tightly with a lid. Cook for 4–5 minutes until the mussels have opened. Drain the mussels, reserving the cooking liquid. Discard any mussels that remain closed. Reserve a few mussels in their shells for the garnish. Shell the rest.

3 Cut a small cross in the base of each tomato. Put them in a heatproof bowl and pour over boiling water. Leave for 30 seconds, then lift out and plunge into cold water. Drain, peel off the skins and dice the flesh. Heat the oil in a pan and fry the onion, garlic, celery and spring onions for 5 minutes.

COOK'S TIP
Harissa can be bought in tubes or jars. Stir it into salads or cooked vegetable dishes to give them a spicy lift.

4 Add the shelled mussels, reserved liquid, potato, harissa and tomatoes. Bring just to the boil, reduce the heat and cover. Simmer gently for about 25 minutes, or until the potatoes are beginning to break up.

5 Stir in the parsley and pepper, and add the reserved mussels, in their shells. Heat through for 1 minute. Serve with a spoonful of yogurt if you like.

HOT AND SPICY SEAFOOD SOUP

FOR A SPECIAL OCCASION SERVE CREAMY RICE NOODLES IN A SPICY COCONUT-FLAVOURED SOUP, TOPPED WITH SEAFOOD. THERE IS A FAIR AMOUNT OF WORK INVOLVED IN THE PREPARATION BUT YOU CAN MAKE THE SOUP BASE AHEAD.

SERVES 4

INGREDIENTS

4 red chillies, seeded and
  roughly chopped
1 onion, coarsely chopped
1 small piece shrimp paste
1 lemon grass stalk, chopped
1 small piece fresh root ginger,
  coarsely chopped
6 macadamia nuts or almonds
60ml/4 tbsp vegetable oil
5ml/1 tsp paprika
5ml/1 tsp ground turmeric
475ml/16fl oz/2 cups stock or water
600ml/1 pint/2½ cups coconut milk
Thai fish sauce (see method)
12 king prawns (jumbo shrimp),
  peeled and deveined
8 scallops
225g/8oz prepared squid, cut
  into rings
350g/12oz rice vermicelli or rice
  noodles, soaked in warm water
  until soft
salt and ground black pepper
lime halves, to serve

For the garnish
¼ cucumber, cut into sticks
2 red chillies, seeded and
  finely sliced
30ml/2 tbsp fresh mint leaves
30ml/2 tbsp fried shallots or onions

1 In a blender or food processor, process the chillies, onion, shrimp paste, lemon grass, ginger and nuts until smooth in texture.

2 Heat 45ml/3 tbsp of the oil in a large pan. Add the chilli paste and cook for 6 minutes. Stir in the paprika and turmeric and cook for about 2 minutes more.

COOK'S TIP
Dried shrimp paste is sold in small blocks and you will find it in Asian stores and supermarkets.

3 Add the stock or water and the coconut milk to the pan. Bring to the boil, reduce the heat and simmer gently for 15–20 minutes. Season the soup to taste with Thai fish sauce.

4 Season the seafood. Heat the remaining oil in a frying pan, add the seafood and cook quickly for 2–3 minutes until tender.

5 Add the noodles to the soup and heat through. Divide among individual serving bowls. Place the seafood on top, then garnish with the cucumber, chillies, mint and fried shallots or onions. Serve with the lime halves.

COCONUT AND SEAFOOD SOUP

THE LONG LIST OF INGREDIENTS COULD MISLEAD YOU INTO THINKING THAT THIS SOUP IS COMPLICATED AND VERY TIME-CONSUMING TO PREPARE. IN FACT, IT IS EXTREMELY EASY TO PUT TOGETHER AND THE MARRIAGE OF FLAVOURS WORKS BEAUTIFULLY.

SERVES FOUR

INGREDIENTS
  600ml/1 pint/2½ cups fish stock
  5 thin slices fresh galangal or fresh
    root ginger
  2 lemon grass stalks, chopped
  3 kaffir lime leaves, shredded
  bunch garlic chives, about 25g/1oz
  small bunch fresh coriander
    (cilantro), about 15g/½oz
  15ml/1 tbsp vegetable oil
  4 shallots, chopped
  400ml/14fl oz can coconut milk
  30–45ml/2–3 tbsp Thai fish sauce
  45–60ml/3–4 tbsp Thai green
    curry paste
  450g/1lb raw large prawns (shrimp),
    peeled and deveined
  450g/1lb prepared squid
  a little fresh lime juice (optional)
  salt and ground black pepper
  60ml/4 tbsp crisp fried shallot
    slices, to serve

2 Reserve a few garlic chives for the garnish, then chop the remainder. Add half the chopped garlic chives to the pan. Strip the coriander leaves from the stalks and set the leaves aside. Add the stalks to the pan. Bring to the boil, reduce the heat to low and cover the pan, then simmer gently for 20 minutes. Strain the stock into a bowl.

3 Rinse and dry the pan. Add the oil and shallots. Cook over a medium heat for 5–10 minutes, until the shallots are just beginning to brown.

4 Stir in the strained stock, coconut milk, the remaining kaffir lime leaves and 30ml/2 tbsp of the fish sauce. Heat gently until simmering and cook over a low heat for 5–10 minutes.

5 Stir in the curry paste and prawns, then cook for 3 minutes. Add the squid and cook for a further 2 minutes. Add the lime juice, if using, and season, adding more fish sauce to taste. Stir in the remaining chives and the reserved coriander leaves. Serve in bowls and sprinkle each portion with fried shallots and whole garlic chives.

1 Pour the fish stock into a large pan and add the slices of galangal or ginger, the lemon grass and half the shredded kaffir lime leaves.

VARIATIONS
• Instead of squid, you could add 400g/14oz firm white fish, such as monkfish, cut into small pieces.
• You could also replace the squid with mussels. Steam 675g/1½lb live mussels in a tightly covered pan for 3–4 minutes, or until they have opened. Discard any that remain shut, then remove them from their shells and add to the soup.

CHILLI SQUASH SOUP

THIS HEARTY SHELLFISH, SQUASH AND GREEN BEAN SOUP COMES FROM NORTHERN THAILAND.
FULL OF CHUNKY VEGETABLES, IT IS SOMETHING OF A CROSS BETWEEN A SOUP AND A STEW.
THE BANANA FLOWER ISN'T ESSENTIAL, BUT IT DOES ADD A UNIQUE AND AUTHENTIC FLAVOUR.

SERVES FOUR

INGREDIENTS

1 butternut squash, about 300g/11oz
1 litre/1¾ pints/4 cups stock
90g/3½oz/scant 1 cup green beans,
  cut into 2.5cm/1in pieces
45g/1¾oz dried banana
  flower (optional)
15ml/1 tbsp Thai fish sauce
225g/8oz raw prawns (shrimp)
small bunch fresh basil
cooked rice, to serve

For the chilli paste
115g/4oz shallots, sliced
10 drained bottled green peppercorns
1 small fresh green chilli, seeded and
  finely chopped
2.5ml/½ tsp shrimp paste

1 Peel the butternut squash and cut it in half. Scoop out the seeds with a teaspoon and discard, then cut the flesh into neat cubes. Set aside.

2 Make the chilli paste by pounding the shallots, peppercorns, chilli and shrimp paste together using a mortar and pestle or puréeing them in a spice blender.

3 Heat the stock gently in a large pan, then stir in the chilli paste. Add the squash, beans and banana flower, if using. Bring to the boil and cook for 15 minutes.

4 Add the fish sauce, prawns and basil. Bring to simmering point, then simmer for 3 minutes. Serve in warmed bowls, accompanied by rice.

MALAYSIAN PRAWN SOUP

THIS SPICY SOUP IS NOT A DISH YOU CAN THROW TOGETHER IN 20 MINUTES, BUT IT IS GOOD PARTY FOOD. GUESTS SPOON NOODLES INTO WIDE SOUP BOWLS, ADD ACCOMPANIMENTS OF THEIR CHOICE, TOP UP WITH SOUP AND THEN TAKE A FEW PRAWN CRACKERS TO NIBBLE.

SERVES 6

INGREDIENTS

675g/1½ lb small clams
2 × 400ml/14fl oz cans coconut milk
50g/2oz ikan bilis (dried anchovies)
900ml/1½ pints/3¾ cups water
115g/4oz shallots, finely chopped
4 garlic cloves, chopped
6 macadamia nuts or blanched
  almonds, chopped
3 lemon grass stalks, root trimmed
90ml/6 tbsp sunflower oil
1cm/½in cube shrimp paste (blachan)
25g/1oz/¼ cup mild curry powder
a few curry leaves
2–3 aubergines, total weight about
  675g/1¼lb, trimmed
675g/1½lb raw peeled prawns
10ml/2 tsp sugar
1 head Chinese leaves, thinly sliced
115g/4oz/2 cups beansprouts, rinsed
2 spring onions, finely chopped
50g/2oz crispy fried onions
115g/4oz fried beancurd (tofu)
675g/1½lb mixed noodles (laksa,
  mee and behoon) or one type only
prawn crackers, to serve

2 Meanwhile, put the shallots, garlic and nuts into a mortar. Cut off the lower 5cm/2in of two of the lemon grass stalks, chop finely and add to the mortar. Pound the mixture to a paste.

3 Heat the oil in a large heavy pan, add the shallot paste and fry until the mixture gives off a rich aroma. Bruise the remaining lemon grass stalk and add to the pan. Toss over the heat to release its flavour. Mix the shrimp paste (blachan) and curry powder to a paste with a little of the coconut milk, add to the pan and toss the mixture over the heat for 1 minute, stirring all the time, and keeping the heat low. Stir in the remaining coconut milk. Add the curry leaves and leave the mixture to simmer while you prepare the accompaniments.

4 Strain the stock into a pan. Discard the ikan bilis, bring to the boil, then add the aubergines; cook for about 10 minutes or until tender and the skins can be peeled off easily. Lift out of the stock, peel and cut into thick strips.

1 Scrub the clams and then put in a large pan with 1cm/½in water. Bring to the boil, cover and steam for 3–4 minutes until all the clams have opened. Drain. Make up the coconut milk to 1.2 litres/2 pints/5 cups with water. Put the ikan bilis (dried anchovies) in a pan and add the water. Bring to the boil and simmer for 20 minutes.

5 Arrange the aubergines on a serving platter. Sprinkle the prawns with sugar, add to the stock and cook for 2–4 minutes until they turn pink. Remove and place next to the aubergines. Add the Chinese leaves, beansprouts, spring onions and crispy fried onions to the platter, along with the clams.

6 Gradually stir the remaining ikan bilis stock into the pan of soup and bring to the boil. Rinse the fried beancurd in boiling water, cool slightly and squeeze to remove excess oil. Cut each piece in half and add to the soup. Lower the heat to a very gentle simmer.

7 Cook the noodles according to the instructions, drain and pile in a dish. Remove the curry leaves and lemon grass from the soup. Place the noodles, soup and the platter of seafood and vegetables on the table, along with a bowl of prawn crackers. Guests can then help themselves.

VARIATION
You could substitute mussels for clams if preferred. Scrub them thoroughly, removing any beards, and cook them in lightly salted water until they open. Like clams, discard any that remain closed.

COOK'S TIP
Dried shrimp or prawn paste, also called blachan, is sold in small blocks and is available from Asian supermarkets.

GINGER, CHICKEN AND COCONUT SOUP

THIS AROMATIC SOUP IS RICH WITH COCONUT MILK AND INTENSELY FLAVOURED WITH GALANGAL, LEMON GRASS AND KAFFIR LIME LEAVES.

SERVES 4–6

INGREDIENTS

750ml/1¼ pints/3 cups coconut milk
475ml/16fl oz/2 cups chicken stock
4 lemon grass stalks, bruised
    and chopped
2.5cm/1in piece galangal,
    thinly sliced
10 black peppercorns, crushed
10 kaffir lime leaves, torn
300g/11oz boneless chicken, cut
    into thin strips
115g/4oz/1⅔ cups button
    (white) mushrooms
50g/2oz baby corn
60ml/4 tbsp lime juice
45ml/3 tbsp fish sauce
2 red chillies, chopped, chopped
    spring onions (scallions) and
    coriander (cilantro) leaves,
    to garnish

1 Bring the coconut milk and chicken stock to the boil. Add the lemon grass, galangal, peppercorns and half the kaffir lime leaves, reduce the heat and simmer gently for 10 minutes.

2 Strain the stock into a clean pan. Return to the heat, then add the chicken, button mushrooms and baby corn. Cook for about 5–7 minutes, or until the chicken is cooked.

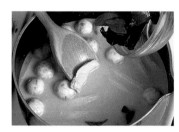

3 Stir in the lime juice, fish sauce to taste and the rest of the lime leaves.

4 Serve hot, garnished with red chillies, spring onions and coriander.

COOK'S TIP
For a milder soup omit the chillies from the garnish and reduce the number of peppercorns to five.

HOT AND SOUR PRAWN SOUP WITH LEMON GRASS

THIS IS A CLASSIC THAI SEAFOOD SOUP – TOM YAM GOONG – AND IS PROBABLY THE MOST POPULAR AND BEST KNOWN SOUP FROM THAILAND.

SERVES 4–6

INGREDIENTS

450g/1lb king prawns
    (jumbo shrimp)
1 litre/1¾ pints/4 cups chicken
    stock or water
3 lemon grass stalks
10 kaffir lime leaves, torn in half
225g/8oz can straw mushrooms,
    drained
45ml/3 tbsp fish sauce
50ml/2fl oz/¼ cup lime juice
30ml/2 tbsp chopped spring
    onion (scallion)
15ml/1 tbsp coriander
    (cilantro) leaves
4 red chillies, seeded
    and chopped
2 spring onions, finely chopped

1 Peel and devein the prawns and set aside. Rinse the prawn shells and place in a large pan with the stock or water and bring to the boil.

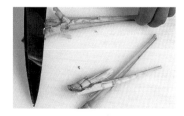

2 Bruise the lemon grass stalks with the blunt edge of a chopping knife and add them to the stock together with half of the lime leaves. Simmer gently for 5–6 minutes, until the stalks change colour and the stock is fragrant.

3 Strain the stock and return to the pan and reheat. Add the mushrooms and prawns, then cook until the prawns turn pink.

4 Stir in the fish sauce, lime juice, spring onions, coriander, red chillies and the rest of the lime leaves. Taste and adjust the seasoning. It should be sour, salty, spicy and hot.

THAI CHICKEN AND CHILLI SOUP

*THIS AROMATIC SOUP IS RICH WITH COCONUT MILK AND INTENSELY FLAVOURED WITH
GALANGAL, WHICH IS MILDLY PEPPERY AND GINGERY, LEMON GRASS AND KAFFIR LIME LEAVES.*

SERVES FOUR TO SIX

INGREDIENTS
  4 lemon grass stalks, trimmed and
    outer leaves discarded
  2 × 400ml/14fl oz/1⅔ cup cans
    coconut milk
  475ml/16fl oz/2 cups chicken stock
  2.5cm/1in piece galangal
  2 fresh red chillies
  10 black peppercorns, crushed
  10 kaffir lime leaves, torn
  300g/11oz skinless, boneless
    chicken breast portions, cut
    into thin strips
  115g/4oz/1½ cups button
    (white) mushrooms
  50g/2oz/½ cup baby corn cobs,
    quartered lengthways
  60ml/4 tbsp lime juice
  45ml/3 tbsp Thai fish sauce (*nam pla*)
  chopped spring onions (scallions)
    and fresh coriander (cilantro)
    leaves, to garnish

1 Cut off the lower 5cm/2in from each
lemon grass stalk and chop it finely.
Bruise the remaining pieces of stalk.
Bring the coconut milk and chicken
stock to the boil in a large pan. Peel
and thinly slice the galangal. Seed and
finely chop the chillies. Add all the
lemon grass, the galangal and half the
chopped chillies, then stir in the
peppercorns and half the lime leaves,
lower the heat and simmer gently for
10 minutes. Strain into a clean pan.

2 Return the soup to the heat, then
add the chicken, mushrooms and the
quartered baby corn cobs. Bring to
the boil, then lower the heat and
simmer for 5–7 minutes or until the
chicken is cooked.

3 Stir in the lime juice and fish sauce,
then add the remaining lime leaves.
Serve hot, garnished with the remaining
chopped chillies and the spring onions
and coriander.

HOT-AND-SOUR SHELLFISH SOUP

*THIS IS A CLASSIC THAI SHELLFISH SOUP – TOM YAM KUNG. THE BALANCE OF FLAVOURS IS
WHAT COUNTS, SO YOU MAY WANT TO START WITH HALF THE CHILLIES AND ADD MORE TO TASTE.*

SERVES FOUR TO SIX

INGREDIENTS
  450g/1lb raw king prawns (jumbo
    shrimp), thawed if frozen
  1 litre/1¾ pints/4 cups chicken stock
    or water
  3 lemon grass stalks, trimmed
  10 kaffir lime leaves, torn in half
  225g/8oz can straw mushrooms
  45ml/3 tbsp Thai fish sauce
    (*nam pla*)
  60ml/4 tbsp lime juice
  30ml/2 tbsp chopped spring
    onion (scallion)
  15ml/1 tbsp fresh coriander
    (cilantro) leaves
  4 fresh red chillies, seeded and
    thinly sliced
  salt and ground black pepper

1 Shell the prawns, putting the shells in
a colander. Devein the prawns and set
them aside. Rinse the shells under cold
water, drain, then put in a large pan
with the stock or water. Bring to the boil.

2 Bruise the lemon grass stalks and add
them to the stock with half the lime
leaves. Simmer gently for 5–6 minutes.

3 Strain the stock, return it to the clean
pan and reheat. Drain the straw
mushrooms and add them with the
prawns. Cook until the prawns turn
pink. Stir in the fish sauce, lime juice,
spring onion, coriander, chillies and the
remaining lime leaves. Taste and adjust
the seasoning. The soup should be
sour, salty, spicy and hot.

MULLIGATAWNY SOUP

MULLIGATAWNY (WHICH MEANS "PEPPER WATER") WAS INTRODUCED INTO ENGLAND IN THE LATE EIGHTEENTH CENTURY BY MEMBERS OF THE BRITISH ARMY AND COLONIAL SERVICE RETURNING HOME FROM INDIA.

SERVES 4

INGREDIENTS
    50g/2oz/4 tbsp butter or
      60ml/4 tbsp oil
    2 large chicken portions, about
      350g/12oz each
    1 onion, chopped
    1 carrot, chopped
    1 small turnip, chopped
    about 15ml/1 tbsp curry powder,
      to taste
    4 cloves
    6 black peppercorns, lightly crushed
    50g/2oz/¼ cup lentils
    900ml/1½ pints/3¾ cups
      chicken stock
    40g/1½ oz/¼ cup sultanas
      (golden raisins)
    salt and ground black pepper

1 Melt the butter or heat the oil in a large pan, then brown the chicken over a brisk heat. Transfer the chicken to a plate.

2 Add the chopped onion, carrot and turnip to the pan and cook, stirring occasionally, until they are lightly coloured. Stir in the curry powder, cloves and black peppercorns and cook for 1–2 minutes more before adding the lentils.

3 Pour the stock into the pan, bring to the boil, then add the sultanas and chicken and any juices from the plate. Cover and simmer gently for about 1¼ hours.

4 Remove the chicken from the pan and discard the skin and bones. Chop the flesh, return to the soup and reheat. Check the seasoning before serving the soup piping hot.

COOK'S TIP
Choose red split lentils for the best colour, although either green or brown lentils could also be used.

CHICKEN PEPPER SOUP

SERVES 4–6

INGREDIENTS
900g/2lb chicken, boned
and skinned
600ml/1 pint/2½ cups water
6 green cardamom pods
5cm/2in piece of cinnamon stick
4–6 curry leaves
15ml/1 tbsp ground coriander
5ml/1 tsp ground cumin
2.5ml/½ tsp ground turmeric
3 garlic cloves, crushed
12 whole peppercorns
4 cloves
1 onion, finely chopped
115g/4oz coconut cream
juice of 2 lemons
salt
deep-fried onions and coriander
(cilantro) leaves, chopped,
to garnish

1 Cut the chicken into pieces, then place it in a large pan with the water and cook until the chicken is tender.

2 Skim the surface, then strain, reserving the stock and keeping the chicken pieces warm.

3 Return the chicken stock to the pan and reheat.

4 Add the cardamom pods, cinnamon stick, curry leaves, ground coriander, cumin and turmeric, crushed garlic, peppercorns, cloves, finely chopped onion, coconut cream, lemon juice and salt to the pan.

5 Simmer the soup for 10–15 minutes, then strain the stock to remove the whole spices and return the chicken to the soup.

6 Reheat the soup and divide between individual bowls. Garnish each bowl with deep-fried onions and chopped coriander and serve.

COOK'S TIP
For a fast version of this soup, use ready-cooked chicken. Remove any skin and bone and chop into cubes. Add to the soup just before serving, then reheat.

THAI CHICKEN AND NOODLE SOUP

Nowadays a signature dish of the city of Chiang Mai, this delicious noodle soup originated in Burma, now called Myanmar, which lies only a little to the north. It is also the Thai equivalent of the famous Malaysian "Laksa".

SERVES FOUR TO SIX

INGREDIENTS

600ml/1 pint/2½ cups coconut milk
30ml/2 tbsp Thai red curry paste
5ml/1 tsp ground turmeric
450g/1lb chicken thighs, boned and
    cut into bitesize chunks
600ml/1 pint/2½ cups chicken stock
60ml/4 tbsp Thai fish sauce
15ml/1 tbsp dark soy sauce
juice of ½–1 lime
450g/1lb fresh egg noodles, blanched
    briefly in boiling water
salt and ground black pepper

To garnish
3 spring onions (scallions), chopped
4 fresh red chillies, chopped
4 shallots, chopped
60ml/4 tbsp sliced pickled mustard
    leaves, rinsed
30ml/2 tbsp fried sliced garlic
coriander (cilantro) leaves
4–6 fried noodle nests (optional)

1 Pour about one-third of the coconut milk into a large, heavy pan or wok. Bring to the boil over a medium heat, stirring frequently with a wooden spoon until the milk separates.

2 Add the curry paste and ground turmeric, stir to mix completely and cook until the mixture is fragrant.

3 Add the chunks of chicken and toss over the heat for about 2 minutes, making sure that all the chunks are thoroughly coated with the paste.

4 Add the remaining coconut milk, the chicken stock, fish sauce and soy sauce. Season with salt and pepper to taste. Bring to simmering point, stirring frequently, then lower the heat and cook gently for 7–10 minutes. Remove from the heat and stir in lime juice to taste.

5 Reheat the fresh egg noodles in boiling water, drain and divide among four to six warmed bowls. Divide the chunks of chicken among the bowls and ladle in the hot soup. Top each serving with spring onions, chillies, shallots, pickled mustard leaves, fried garlic, coriander leaves and a fried noodle nest, if using. Serve immediately.

RICE PORRIDGE

ORIGINATING IN CHINA, THIS DISH HAS NOW SPREAD THROUGHOUT THE WHOLE OF SOUTH-EAST ASIA AND IS LOVED FOR ITS COMFORTING BLANDNESS. IT IS INVARIABLY SERVED WITH A FEW STRONGLY FLAVOURED ACCOMPANIMENTS.

2 Pour the stock into a large pan. Bring to the boil and add the rice. Season the minced pork. Add it by taking small teaspoons and tapping the spoon on the side of the pan so that the meat falls into the soup in small lumps.

3 Stir in the fish sauce and pickled garlic and simmer for 10 minutes, until the pork is cooked. Stir in the celery.

4 Serve the rice porridge in individual warmed bowls. Sprinkle the prepared garlic and shallots on top and season with plenty of ground pepper.

COOK'S TIP
Pickled garlic has a distinctive flavour and is available from Asian food stores.

SERVES TWO

INGREDIENTS
  900ml/1½ pints/3¾ cups
    vegetable stock
  200g/7oz/1¾ cups cooked rice
  225g/8oz minced (ground) pork
  15ml/1 tbsp Thai fish sauce
  2 heads pickled garlic, finely chopped
  1 celery stick, finely diced
  salt and ground black pepper

To garnish
  30ml/2 tbsp groundnut (peanut) oil
  4 garlic cloves, thinly sliced
  4 small red shallots, finely sliced

1 Make the garnishes by heating the groundnut oil in a frying pan and cooking the garlic and shallots over a low heat until brown. Drain on kitchen paper and reserve for the soup.

NOODLE SOUP <u>WITH</u> PORK <u>AND</u> SZECHUAN PICKLE

SERVES 4

INGREDIENTS
1 litre/1¾ pints/4 cups
   chicken stock
350g/12oz egg noodles
15ml/1 tbsp dried shrimp, soaked
   in water
30ml/2 tbsp vegetable oil
225g/8oz lean pork,
   finely shredded
15ml/1 tbsp yellow bean paste
15ml/1 tbsp soy sauce
115g/4oz Sichuan hot pickle, rinsed,
   drained and shredded
pinch of sugar
salt and ground black pepper
2 spring onions (scallions), finely
   sliced, to garnish

 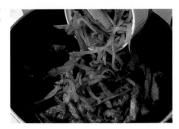

1 Bring the stock to the boil in a large pan. Add the noodles and cook until almost tender. Drain the dried shrimp, rinse them under cold water, drain again and add to the stock. Lower the heat and simmer for a further 2 minutes. Keep hot. Heat the oil in a frying pan or wok. Add the pork and stir-fry over a high heat for about 3 minutes.

2 Add the bean paste and soy sauce to the pork; stir-fry for 1 minute more. Add the hot pickle with a pinch of sugar. Stir-fry for 1 minute more.

3 Divide the noodles and soup among individual serving bowls. Spoon the pork mixture on top, then sprinkle with the spring onions and serve immediately.

SNAPPER, TOMATO <u>AND</u> TAMARIND NOODLE SOUP

TAMARIND GIVES THIS LIGHT, FRAGRANT NOODLE SOUP A SLIGHTLY SOUR TASTE.

SERVES 4

INGREDIENTS
2 litres/3½ pints/8 cups water
1kg/2¼lb red snapper (or other red
   fish such as mullet)
1 onion, sliced
50g/2oz tamarind pods
15ml/1 tbsp fish sauce
15ml/1 tbsp sugar
30ml/2 tbsp vegetable oil
2 garlic cloves, finely chopped
2 lemon grass stalks, very
   finely chopped
4 ripe tomatoes, coarsely chopped
30ml/2 tbsp yellow bean paste
225g/8oz rice vermicelli, soaked in
   warm water until soft
115g/4oz/2 cups beansprouts
8–10 fresh basil or mint sprigs
25g/1oz/¼ cup roasted peanuts,
   ground
salt and ground black pepper

1 Bring the water to the boil in a pan. Lower the heat and add the fish and onion, with 2.5ml/½ tsp salt. Simmer gently until the fish is cooked through.

2 Remove the fish from the stock; set aside. Add the tamarind, fish sauce and sugar to the stock. Cook for 5 minutes, then strain the stock into a large jug (pitcher) or bowl. Carefully remove all of the bones from the fish, keeping the flesh in big pieces.

3 Heat the oil in a large frying pan. Add the garlic and lemon grass and cook for a few seconds. Stir in the tomatoes and bean paste. Cook gently for 5–7 minutes, until the tomatoes are soft. Add the stock, bring back to a simmer and season.

4 Drain the vermicelli. Plunge it into a pan of boiling water for a few minutes, drain and divide among individual serving bowls. Add the beansprouts, fish, basil or mint, and ground peanuts. Top up each bowl with the hot soup.

SPICED LAMB SOUP

SERVES 4

INGREDIENTS

115g/4oz/⅔ cup split black-eyed
    beans (peas), soaked for 1–2 hours,
    or overnight
675g/1½lb neck (US shoulder) of
    lamb, cut into medium chunks
5ml/1 tsp chopped fresh thyme,
    or 2.5ml/½ tsp dried
2 bay leaves
1.2 litres/2 pints/5 cups stock
    or water
1 onion, sliced
225g/8oz pumpkin, diced
2 black cardamom pods
7.5ml/1½ tsp ground turmeric
15ml/1 tbsp chopped coriander
    (cilantro)
2.5ml/½ tsp caraway seeds
1 fresh green chilli, seeded and chopped
2 green bananas
1 carrot
salt and ground black pepper

1 Drain the black-eyed beans, place them in a pan and cover with fresh cold water.

2 Bring the beans to the boil, boil rapidly for 10 minutes and then reduce the heat and simmer, covered for 40–50 minutes, until tender, adding more water if necessary. Remove from the heat and set aside to cool.

3 Meanwhile, put the lamb in a large pan, add the thyme, bay leaves and stock or water and bring to the boil. Cover and simmer over a medium heat for 1 hour, until tender.

4 Add the onion, pumpkin, cardamoms, turmeric, coriander, caraway, chilli and seasoning and stir. Bring back to a simmer and then cook, uncovered, for 15 minutes, until the pumpkin is tender, stirring occasionally.

5 When the beans are cool, spoon into a blender or food processor with their liquid and blend to a smooth purée.

6 Cut the bananas into medium slices and the carrot into thin slices. Stir into the soup with the beans and cook for 10–12 minutes, until the vegetables are tender. Adjust the seasoning and serve.

BEEF AND TURMERIC SOUP

THE ADDITION OF TURMERIC AND SAFFRON COLOURS THIS SATISFYING SOUP A DEEP, VIBRANT
YELLOW. IT IS A POPULAR DISH IN IRAN.

SERVES 6

INGREDIENTS
  2 large onions
  30ml/2 tbsp oil
  15ml/1 tbsp ground turmeric
  100g/3½ oz/½ cup yellow
    split peas
  1.2 litres/2 pints/5 cups water
  225g/8oz/2 cups minced
    (ground) beef
  200g/7oz/1 cup rice
  45ml/3 tbsp each fresh chopped
    parsley, coriander (cilantro)
    and chives
  15g/½ oz/1 tbsp butter
  1 large garlic clove, finely chopped
  60ml/4 tbsp chopped fresh mint
  2–3 saffron threads dissolved
    in 15ml/1 tbsp boiling
    water (optional)
  salt and ground black pepper
  yogurt and naan bread, to serve

1 Chop one of the onions, then heat the oil in a large pan and cook the onion until golden brown. Add the turmeric, split peas and water, bring to the boil, then reduce the heat and simmer for 20 minutes.

COOK'S TIP
Fresh spinach is also delicious in this soup. Add 50g/2oz/⅔ cup finely chopped spinach leaves to the soup with the parsley, coriander (cilantro) and chives.

2 Grate the other onion into a bowl, add the minced beef and seasoning and mix well. Using your hands, form the mixture into small balls, about the size of walnuts. Carefully add to the pan and simmer for 10 minutes.

3 Add the rice, then stir in the parsley, coriander, and chives and simmer for about 30 minutes, until the rice is tender, stirring frequently.

4 Melt the butter in a small pan and gently cook the garlic for 2–3 minutes, ensuring that it does not burn. Add the mint, stir briefly and sprinkle over the soup with the saffron, if using. Spoon the soup into warmed serving dishes and serve with yogurt and naan bread.

Red hot appetizers and snacks offer lots of highly spiced,

mouth-watering morsels and searingly hot bites. Potato

Skins with Cajun Dip will set the taste buds tingling,

while Chilli Spiced Onion Koftas and Fried Dough

Balls with Fiery Salsa are perfect to hand round at a

drinks party for a quick spicy appetizer. Start off a

meal in lively style with Butterflied Prawns in Chilli

Chocolate or enjoy an easy-to-prepare supper with

Chicken Tortillas with Fresno Chilli Salsa.

Red Hot Appetizers and Snacks

SPICY PEANUT BALLS

TASTY RICE BALLS, ROLLED IN CHOPPED PEANUTS AND DEEP-FRIED, MAKE A DELICIOUS SNACK. SERVE THEM AS THEY ARE OR WITH A CHILLI SAUCE FOR DIPPING.

2 Add three-quarters of the cooked rice to the paste in the food processor, and process until smooth and sticky. Scrape into a mixing bowl and stir in the remainder of the rice. Wet your hands and shape the mixture into small balls.

3 Roll the balls, a few at a time, in the chopped peanuts, making sure they are evenly coated.

MAKES SIXTEEN

INGREDIENTS
  1 garlic clove, crushed
  1cm/½in piece of fresh root ginger, peeled and finely chopped
  1 small fresh red chilli, seeded and roughly chopped
  1.5ml/¼ tsp ground turmeric
  5ml/1 tsp granulated sugar
  2.5ml/½ tsp salt
  5ml/1 tsp chilli sauce
  10ml/2 tsp soy sauce
  30ml/2 tbsp chopped fresh coriander (cilantro)
  juice of ½ lime
  225g/8oz/2 cups cooked white long grain rice
  115g/4oz/1 cup peanuts, chopped
  vegetable oil, for deep-frying
  lime wedges and chilli dipping sauce, to serve (optional)

1 Put the crushed garlic, ginger and chilli in a food processor. Add the turmeric and process to a paste. Add the granulated sugar, salt, chilli sauce and soy sauce, with the chopped coriander and lime juice. Process briefly to mix.

COOK'S TIP
Coat the balls in the peanuts and then chill for 30 minutes before deep-frying.

4 Heat the oil for deep-frying to 180–190°C/350–375°F or until a cube of day-old bread browns in about 45 seconds. Deep-fry the peanut balls until crisp. Drain on kitchen paper, then pile on to a platter. Serve hot with lime wedges and a chilli dipping sauce, if you like.

LITTLE ONIONS COOKED WITH CHILLIES

WHOLE DRIED CHILLIES GIVE THIS SIMPLE DISH AN UNDERLYING WARMTH THAT ADDS TO ITS APPEAL. FOR A SMOKY FLAVOUR, USE CHIPOTLE CHILLIES, OR AN ANAHEIM RED CHILLI.

SERVES SIX

INGREDIENTS

105ml/7 tbsp olive oil
675g/1½lb small onions
150ml/¼ pint/⅔ cup dry white wine
2 bay leaves
2 garlic cloves, bruised
1–2 small dried red chillies
15ml/1 tbsp coriander seeds, toasted
   and lightly crushed
2.5ml/½ tsp granulated sugar
a few fresh thyme sprigs
30ml/2 tbsp currants
10ml/2 tsp chopped fresh oregano
5ml/1 tsp grated (shredded)
   lemon rind
15ml/1 tbsp chopped fresh flat
   leaf parsley
30–45ml/2–3 tbsp pine nuts, toasted
salt and ground black pepper

1 Spoon 30ml/2 tbsp of the olive oil into a wide pan. Add the onions, place the pan over a medium heat and cook gently for about 5 minutes, or until the onions begin to colour. Use a slotted spoon to remove the onions from the pan and set them aside.

2 Add the remaining oil to the pan, with the wine, bay leaves, garlic, chillies, coriander seeds, sugar and thyme. Bring to the boil and cook for 5 minutes.

3 Return the onions to the pan. Add the currants, reduce the heat and cook gently for 15–20 minutes, or until the onions are tender but not falling apart. Use a slotted spoon to transfer the onions to a serving dish.

4 Boil the liquid vigorously until it reduces considerably. Taste and adjust the seasoning, if necessary, then pour it over the onions. Sprinkle the chopped fresh oregano over the cooked onions, cool, cover and then chill them for several hours.

VARIATION
The same method can be used for courgettes (zucchini), celery, small mushrooms, fennel and baby leeks. Cut the larger vegetables in 2.5cm/1in pieces and cook as for small onions.

5 Just before serving, stir in the grated lemon rind, chopped parsley and toasted pine nuts.

CHILLI SPICED ONION KOFTAS

THESE DELICIOUS DEEP-FRIED INDIAN ONION FRITTERS ARE PEPPED UP WITH GREEN CHILLIES. SERVE THEM WITH A YOGURT DIP, TO DAMP DOWN THEIR FIRE.

SERVES FOUR TO FIVE

INGREDIENTS

675g/1½lb onions, halved and sliced
5ml/1 tsp salt
5ml/1 tsp ground coriander
5ml/1 tsp ground cumin
2.5ml/½ tsp ground turmeric
1–2 fresh green chillies, seeded and finely chopped
45ml/3 tbsp chopped fresh coriander (cilantro)
90g/3½oz/¾ cup chickpea flour
2.5ml/½ tsp baking powder
vegetable oil, for deep-frying

To serve
lemon wedges
fresh coriander (cilantro) sprigs
yogurt and herb dip (see Cook's Tips)

1 Put the onion slices in a colander, add the salt and toss well. Stand the colander on a plate or bowl and leave for 45 minutes, tossing once or twice with a fork. Rinse the onions, then squeeze out the excess moisture. Tip the onions into a bowl. Add the ground coriander, cumin, turmeric, chillies and fresh coriander. Mix well.

COOK'S TIPS
• Chickpea flour, available from supermarkets and Indian food stores, is sometimes labelled gram flour or *besan*.
• To make a yogurt and herb dip, stir 30ml/2 tbsp each of chopped fresh coriander (cilantro) and mint into 250ml/8fl oz/1 cup thick yogurt. Add salt, ground toasted cumin seeds and a pinch of sugar. Top with a chopped chilli.

2 Add the chickpea flour and baking powder, then use your hand to mix all the ingredients thoroughly.

3 Shape the mixture by hand into 12–15 koftas. They should be about the size of golf balls.

4 Heat the oil for deep-frying to 180–190°C/350–375°F or until a cube of day-old bread browns in about 45 seconds.

5 Fry the koftas, 4–5 at a time, until deep golden brown all over. Drain each batch on kitchen paper and keep warm until all the koftas are cooked. Serve with lemon wedges, coriander sprigs and a yogurt and herb dip.

CHILLI YOGURT CHEESE IN OLIVE OIL

YOGURT, HUNG IN MUSLIN TO DRAIN OFF THE WHEY, MAKES A SUPERB SOFT CHEESE. HERE IT IS BOTTLED IN OLIVE OIL WITH CHILLI AND HERBS, READY FOR SERVING ON TOAST.

FILLS TWO 450G/1LB JARS

INGREDIENTS
800g/1¾lb/about 4 cups Greek
  (US strained, plain) yogurt
2.5ml/½ tsp salt
10ml/2 tsp crushed dried chillies or
  chilli powder
15ml/1 tbsp chopped fresh rosemary
15ml/1 tbsp chopped fresh thyme
  or oregano
about 300ml/½ pint/1¼ cups olive
  oil, preferably garlic-flavoured
lightly toasted country bread, to serve

1 Sterilize a 30cm/12in square of muslin or cheesecloth by steeping it in boiling water. Drain and lay over a large plate. Mix the yogurt with the salt and tip on to the centre of the cloth. Bring up the sides of the cloth and tie firmly.

2 Hang the bag from a kitchen cabinet handle or in any convenient, cool position that allows a bowl to be placed underneath to catch the whey. Leave for 2–3 days until the yogurt stops dripping.

3 Sterilize two 450g/1lb clean glass preserving or jam jars by heating them in the oven at 150°C/300°F/Gas 2 for 15 minutes.

4 Mix the dried chillies and herbs in a bowl. Take teaspoonfuls of the cheese and roll into balls between the palms of your hands. Lower into jars, sprinkling each layer with the herb mixture.

5 Pour the oil over the cheese until the balls are completely covered. Close the jars tightly and store in the refrigerator for up to 3 weeks.

6 To serve the cheese, spoon out of the jars with a little of the flavoured olive oil and spread on to lightly toasted bread.

SPICED FETA WITH CHILLI SEEDS AND OLIVES

CHILLI SEEDS FLAVOUR MARINATED CUBES OF FETA CHEESE SPIKED WITH SPICES AND OLIVES. SPOON THE CUBES OVER GREEN LEAVES AND SERVE WITH WARM BREAD AS AN APPETIZER.

MAKES FOUR TO FIVE SMALL JARS

INGREDIENTS
500g/1¼lb feta cheese
50g/2oz/½ cup stuffed olives
10ml/2 tsp coriander seeds
10ml/2 tsp whole peppercorns
5ml/1 tsp chilli seeds
few sprigs fresh rosemary or thyme
750ml/1¼ pint/3 cups virgin olive oil

1 Drain the feta cheese, dice it and put it in a bowl. Slice the olives. Using a pestle, crush the coriander seeds and peppercorns in a mortar and add them to the cheese, with the olives, chilli seeds and rosemary or thyme leaves. Toss lightly.

2 Sterilize 4–5 small, clean, glass jars by heating them in the oven at 150°C/300°F/Gas 2 for 15 minutes.

3 Spoon the cheese into the warm, dry sterilized jars and top up with olive oil, making sure that the cheese is well covered by the oil. Close the jars tightly and store them in the refrigerator for up to 3 weeks.

COOK'S TIP
Seal the jars with screw-topped or clip-down lids. The jars need to be totally airtight to keep the cheese fresh.

FALAFEL

THESE TASTY DEEP FRIED PATTIES ARE ONE OF THE NATIONAL DISHES OF EGYPT. THEY
MAKE AN EXCELLENT APPETIZER OR ELSE CAN BE SERVED AS A BUFFET DISH.

SERVES 6

INGREDIENTS
   450g/1lb/2½ cups dried white beans
   2 red onions, chopped
   2 large garlic cloves, crushed
   45ml/3 tbsp finely chopped
     fresh parsley
   5ml/1 tsp ground coriander
   5ml/1 tsp ground cumin
   7.5ml/1½ tsp baking powder
   oil, for deep-frying
   salt and ground black pepper
   tomato salad, to serve

1 Soak the white beans overnight in water. Remove the skins and process in a blender or food processor. Add the chopped onions, garlic, parsley, coriander, cumin, baking powder and seasoning and blend again to make a very smooth paste. Leave the mixture to stand at room temperature for at least 30 minutes.

2 Take walnut-size pieces of mixture and flatten into small patties. Set aside again for about 15 minutes.

3 Heat the oil until it's very hot and then fry the patties in batches until golden brown. Drain on kitchen paper and then serve with a tomato salad.

HUMMUS

THIS POPULAR MIDDLE EASTERN DIP IS WIDELY AVAILABLE IN SUPERMARKETS, BUT NOTHING
COMPARES WITH THE DELICIOUS HOME-MADE VARIETY.

SERVES 4-6

INGREDIENTS
   175g/6oz/1 cup cooked chickpeas
   120ml/4fl oz/½ cup tahini paste
   3 garlic cloves
   juice of 2 lemons
   45–60ml/3–4 tbsp water
   salt and ground black pepper
   fresh radishes, to serve

For the garnish
   15ml/1 tbsp olive oil
   15ml/1 tbsp finely chopped
     fresh parsley
   2.5ml/½ tsp cayenne pepper
   4 black olives

COOK'S TIP
Canned chickpeas can be used for hummus. Drain and rinse under cold water before processing.

1 Place the chickpeas, tahini paste, garlic, lemon juice, seasoning and a little of the water in a blender or food processor. Process until smooth adding a little more water, if necessary.

2 Alternatively if you don't have a blender or food processor, mix the ingredients together in a small bowl until smooth in consistency.

3 Spoon the mixture into a shallow dish. Make a dent in the middle and pour the olive oil into it. Garnish with parsley, cayenne and olives and serve with the radishes.

COURGETTE FRITTERS WITH CHILLI JAM

CHILLI JAM IS HOT, SWEET AND STICKY — RATHER LIKE A THICK CHUTNEY. IT ADDS A PIQUANCY TO THESE FRITTERS BUT IS ALSO DELICIOUS WITH PIES OR CHEESE.

MAKES TWELVE

INGREDIENTS
    450g/1lb/3½ cups coarsely grated
      (shredded) courgettes (zucchini)
    50g/2oz/⅔ cup freshly grated
      Parmesan cheese
    2 eggs, beaten
    60ml/4 tbsp unbleached plain
      (all-purpose) flour
    vegetable oil, for frying
    salt and ground black pepper

For the chilli jam
    75ml/5 tbsp olive oil
    4 large onions, diced
    4 garlic cloves, chopped
    1–2 fresh Thai chillies, seeded
      and sliced
    25g/1oz/2 tbsp soft dark brown sugar

1 First make the chilli jam. Heat the oil in a frying pan until hot, then add the onions and garlic. Reduce the heat to low, then cook for 20 minutes, stirring frequently, until the onions are very soft.

VARIATION
Substitute Pecorino Romano for Parmesan cheese. It is good for grating.

2 Leave the onion mixture to cool, then scrape into a food processor or blender. Add the chillies and sugar, and blend until smooth, then return the mixture to the pan. Cook for 10 minutes, stirring frequently, until the liquid evaporates and the mixture has the consistency of jam. Cool slightly.

3 To make the fritters, squeeze the courgettes in a dishtowel to remove any excess water, then tip them into a bowl. Add the Parmesan, eggs and flour. Mix well, then season with salt and pepper.

4 Heat enough oil to cover the base of a large frying pan. Add 30ml/2 tbsp of the mixture for each fritter and cook 3 fritters at a time. Cook them for 2–3 minutes on each side until golden, then remove from the pan and keep hot while you cook the remaining fritters. Drain on kitchen paper and serve warm with a large spoonful of the chilli jam.

COOK'S TIP
Any leftover chilli jam can be kept in an airtight jar in the refrigerator for up to 1 week.

SAMOSAS

*A SELECTION OF HIGHLY SPICED VEGETABLES IN A PASTRY CASING MAKES THESE SAMOSAS
A DELICIOUS SNACK AT ANY TIME OF THE DAY.*

MAKES 30

INGREDIENTS
   1 packet spring roll pastry, thawed
      and wrapped in a damp towel
   vegetable oil, for deep-frying

For the filling
   3 large potatoes, boiled and
      coarsely mashed
   75g/3oz/¾ cup frozen peas, thawed
   50g/2oz/⅓ cup canned corn, drained
   5ml/1 tsp ground coriander
   5ml/1 tsp ground cumin
   5ml/1 tsp amchur (dry mango powder)
   1 small onion, finely chopped
   2 green chillies, finely chopped
   30ml/2 tbsp coriander (cilantro)
      leaves, chopped
   30ml/2 tbsp mint leaves, chopped
   juice of 1 lemon
   salt, to taste
   chilli sauce, to serve

1 Toss all the filling ingredients together
in a large mixing bowl until they are all
well blended. Adjust the seasoning with
salt and lemon juice, if necessary.

2 Using one strip of pastry at a time,
place 15ml/1 tbsp of the filling
mixture at one end of the strip and
diagonally fold the pastry up to form
a triangle shape.

3 Heat enough oil for deep-frying and
fry the samosas in small batches until
they are golden brown. Keep them hot
while frying the rest. Serve hot with
chilli sauce.

THAI TEMPEH CAKES WITH CHILLI SAUCE

MADE FROM SOYA BEANS, TEMPEH IS SIMILAR TO TOFU BUT HAS A NUTTIER TASTE. HERE, IT IS COMBINED WITH CHILLIES, LEMON GRASS AND GINGER AND FORMED INTO SMALL PATTIES.

MAKES EIGHT

INGREDIENTS
    2 chillies, seeded and finely chopped
    1 lemon grass stalk, trimmed
    2 garlic cloves, chopped
    2 spring onions (scallions),
        finely chopped
    2 shallots, finely chopped
    2.5cm/1in piece fresh root ginger,
        finely chopped
    60ml/4 tbsp chopped fresh coriander
        (cilantro), plus extra to garnish
    250g/9oz tempeh, thawed if
        frozen, sliced
    15ml/1 tbsp lime juice
    5ml/1 tsp granulated sugar
    45ml/3 tbsp plain (all-purpose) flour
    1 large (US extra large) egg, beaten
    vegetable oil, for frying
    salt and ground black pepper

For the dipping sauce
    45ml/3 tbsp mirin or dry sherry
    45ml/3 tbsp white wine vinegar
    2 spring onions (scallions),
        thinly sliced
    15ml/1 tbsp granulated sugar
    2 fresh red chillies, finely chopped
    30ml/2 tbsp chopped fresh
        coriander (cilantro)

1 To make the dipping sauce, mix the mirin, vinegar, spring onions, sugar, chillies, coriander and a large pinch of salt in a small bowl and set aside.

COOK'S TIP
Chill the tempeh cakes for 30 minutes in the refrigerator before frying. It will prevent them from breaking.

2 Place the chopped chillies in a food processor or blender. Cut off the lower 5cm/2in piece of the lemon grass stalk and chop it roughly. Add it to the processor or blender, with the garlic, spring onions, shallots, ginger and coriander. Process to a coarse paste; the mixture should not be too smooth at this stage.

3 Add the tempeh, lime juice and sugar, then process again until combined. Add the flour and egg, with salt and pepper to taste, and process again until the mixture forms a coarse, sticky paste.

4 Wet your hands, then take a generous spoonful of the tempeh mixture and form it into a round between your palms. Repeat with the remaining mixture, wetting your hands slightly each time.

5 Heat enough oil to cover the base of a large frying pan. Fry the tempeh cakes, in batches if necessary, for 5–6 minutes, turning once, until golden. Drain on kitchen paper. Pile on to plates and garnish with the extra coriander. Serve warm, with the dipping sauce.

POTATO SKINS WITH CAJUN DIP

DIVINELY CRISP AND NAUGHTY, THESE POTATO SKINS TASTE GREAT WITH THE PIQUANT CHILLI DIP.

SERVES TWO

INGREDIENTS
2 large baking potatoes, about
   275g/10oz each
vegetable oil, for frying

For the dip
120ml/4fl oz/½ cup natural
   (plain) yogurt
1 garlic clove, crushed
5ml/1 tsp tomato purée (paste)
2.5ml/½ tsp green chilli purée
1.5ml/¼ tsp celery salt
salt and ground black pepper

COOK'S TIP
If you prefer, you can microwave the
potatoes to save time. This will take
about 10 minutes.

1 Preheat the oven to 180°C/350°F/
Gas 4. Bake the potatoes for about 1 hour,
until tender. Cut them in half and scoop
out the flesh, leaving a thin layer on the
skins. Keep the flesh for another meal.

2 To make the piquant chilli dip, mix
all the ingredients in a bowl. Chill until
ready to serve.

3 Heat a 1cm/½in layer of oil in a large,
shallow pan. Cut each potato skin in
half again, then fry them until crisp and
golden on both sides. Drain on kitchen
paper, sprinkle with salt and black
pepper and spoon a dollop of piquant
chilli dip into each skin. Serve the
remaining dip separately so that people
can help themselves.

SPICY POTATO WEDGES WITH CHILLI DIP

THESE DRY-ROASTED POTATO WEDGES WITH CRISP SPICY CRUSTS ARE DELICIOUS WITH THE CHILLI DIP.

SERVES TWO

INGREDIENTS
 2 baking potatoes, about 225g/
  8oz each
 30ml/2 tbsp olive oil
 2 garlic cloves, crushed
 5ml/1 tsp ground allspice
 5ml/1 tsp ground coriander
 15ml/1 tbsp paprika
 salt and ground black pepper

For the dip
 15ml/1 tbsp olive oil
 1 small onion, finely chopped
 1 garlic clove, crushed
 200g/7oz can chopped tomatoes
 1 fresh red chilli, seeded and chopped
 15ml/1 tbsp balsamic vinegar
 15ml/1 tbsp chopped fresh coriander
  (cilantro), plus extra to garnish

1 Preheat the oven to 200°C/400°F/
Gas 6. Cut the potatoes in half, then
into 8 wedges.

2 Add the wedges to a pan of cold
water. Bring to the boil, then reduce the
heat and simmer gently for 10 minutes
or until the wedges have softened
slightly but the flesh has not started to
disintegrate. Drain well and pat dry on
kitchen paper.

COOK'S TIP
To save time, par-boil the potatoes and
toss them with the spices in advance,
but make sure that the potato wedges
are perfectly dry and completely covered
in the spice mixture before roasting.

3 Mix the olive oil, garlic, allspice,
coriander and paprika in a roasting pan.
Add salt and pepper to taste. Add the
potatoes to the pan and shake to coat
them thoroughly. Roast for 20 minutes,
until the wedges are browned, crisp and
fully cooked. Turn the potato wedges
occasionally during the roasting time.

4 Meanwhile, make the chilli dip. Heat
the oil in a small pan, add the onion
and garlic, and cook for 5–10 minutes
until soft.

5 Tip in the chopped tomatoes, with any
juice. Stir in the chilli and vinegar. Cook
gently for 10 minutes until the mixture
has reduced and thickened, then taste
and check the seasoning. Stir in the
chopped fresh coriander.

6 Pile the spicy potato wedges on a
plate, garnish with the extra coriander
and serve with the chilli dip.

VARIATION
Instead of balsamic vinegar, try brown
rice vinegar, which has a mellow flavour.

SPICY POTATOES

SPICY POTATOES, PATATAS PICANTES, ARE AMONG THE MOST POPULAR TAPAS DISHES IN SPAIN, WHERE THEY ARE SOMETIMES DESCRIBED AS PATATAS BRAVAS (WILD POTATOES). THERE ARE MANY VARIATIONS OF THIS CLASSIC: BOILED NEW POTATOES OR LARGE WEDGES OF FRIED POTATO MAY BE USED, BUT THEY ARE PERHAPS BEST SIMPLY ROASTED.

SERVES 2–4

INGREDIENTS
    225g/8oz small new potatoes
    15ml/1 tbsp olive oil
    5ml/1 tsp paprika
    5ml/1 tsp chilli powder
    2.5ml/½ tsp ground cumin
    2.5ml/½ tsp salt
    flat leaf parsley, to garnish

1 Preheat the oven to 200°C/400°F/ Gas 6. Prick the skin of each potato in several places with a fork, then place them in a bowl.

2 Add the olive oil, paprika, chilli, cumin and salt and toss well.

3 Transfer the potatoes to a roasting pan and bake for 40 minutes.

4 During cooking, remove the potatoes from the oven and turn occasionally, until tender. Serve hot, garnished with parsley.

FRIED DOUGH BALLS WITH FIERY SALSA

THESE CRUNCHY DOUGH BALLS ARE ACCOMPANIED BY A HOT AND SPICY TOMATO SALSA.
SERVE THEM WITH A JUICY TOMATO SALAD, IF YOU PREFER.

SERVES 10

INGREDIENTS
450g/1lb/4 cups strong white
  bread flour
5ml/1 tsp easy-blend (rapid-rise)
  dried yeast
5ml/1 tsp salt
30ml/2 tbsp chopped fresh parsley
2 garlic cloves, finely chopped
30ml/2 tbsp olive oil, plus extra
  for greasing
vegetable oil, for frying

For the salsa
6 hot red chillies, seeded and
  coarsely chopped
1 onion, coarsely chopped
2 garlic cloves, quartered
2.5cm/1in piece of root ginger,
  coarsely chopped
450g/1lb tomatoes, coarsely
  chopped
30ml/2 tbsp olive oil
pinch of sugar
salt and ground black pepper

1 Sift the flour into a large bowl. Stir in the yeast and salt and make a well in the centre. Add the parsley, garlic, olive oil and enough warm water to make a firm dough.

2 Gather the dough in the bowl together, then tip out on to a lightly floured surface or board. Knead for about 10 minutes, until the dough feels very smooth and elastic.

3 Rub a little oil into the surface of the dough. Return it to the clean bowl, cover with clear film (plastic wrap) or a clean dishtowel and leave in a warm place to rise for about 1 hour, or until doubled in bulk.

4 Meanwhile, make the salsa. Combine the chillies, onion, garlic and ginger in a food processor and process together until very finely chopped. Add the tomatoes and olive oil and process until smooth.

5 Sieve the mixture into a pan. Add sugar, salt and pepper to taste and simmer gently for 15 minutes. Do not allow the salsa to boil.

6 Roll the dough into about 40 balls. Shallow fry in batches in hot oil for 4–5 minutes, until crisp and golden. Drain on kitchen paper and serve hot, with the fiery salsa for dipping.

COOK'S TIP
These dough balls can be deep-fried for 3–4 minutes or baked at 200°C/ 400°F/Gas 6 for 15–20 minutes.

CHEESE FRITTERS

THESE CRISP FRITTERS OWE THEIR INSPIRATION TO ITALY. A NOTE OF CAUTION — DO
BE CAREFUL NOT TO BURN YOUR MOUTH WHEN YOU TAKE YOUR FIRST BITE, AS THE
SOFT, RICH CHEESE FILLING WILL BE VERY HOT.

MAKES 15–16

INGREDIENTS
 115g/4oz/½ cup ricotta cheese
 50g/2oz/⅓ cup finely grated
  fontina cheese
 25g/1oz/½ cup grated
  Parmesan cheese
 2.5ml/½ tsp cayenne pepper
 1 egg, beaten, plus a little extra to
  seal the wontons
 15–16 wonton wrappers
 oil for deep-frying

1 Line a large baking sheet with
greaseproof (waxed) paper or sprinkle it
with flour. Set aside. Combine the three
cheeses in a bowl, then add the cayenne
and beaten egg and mix well.

2 Place one wonton wrapper at a time
on a board. Brush the edges with egg.
Spoon a little filling in the centre; pull
the top corner down to the bottom
corner, to make a triangle.

3 Transfer the filled wontons to the
prepared baking sheet.

4 Heat the oil in a deep-fryer or large
pan. Slip in as many wontons at one
time as can be accommodated without
overcrowding. Fry them for 2–3 minutes
on each side, or until the fritters are
golden. Remove with a slotted spoon.
Drain on kitchen paper and serve the
fritters immediately.

CHILLED SOBA NOODLES WITH NORI

SERVES 4

INGREDIENTS
 350g/12oz dried soba noodles
 1 sheet nori seaweed

For the dipping sauce
 300ml/½ pint/1¼ cups fish stock
 120ml/4fl oz/½ cup dark soy sauce
 60ml/4 tbsp mirin
 5ml/1 tsp sugar
 15ml/1 tbsp fish sauce

Flavourings
 4 spring onions (scallions),
  finely chopped
 30ml/2 tbsp grated mooli (daikon)
 wasabi paste
 4 egg yolks (optional)

COOK'S TIP
Mooli is a slim white vegetable,
sometimes also known as daikon.

1 Make the dipping sauce. Combine the
stock, soy sauce, mirin and sugar in a
pan. Bring rapidly to the boil, add the
fish sauce, then remove from the heat.
When cool, strain the sauce into a bowl
and cover. This can be done in advance
and the dipping sauce kept chilled for
up to a week.

2 Cook the soba noodles in a pan of
lightly salted, boiling water for
6–7 minutes, or until just tender,
following the manufacturer's
instructions on the packet.

3 Drain and rinse the noodles under
cold running water, agitating them
gently to remove the excess starch.
Drain well.

4 Toast the nori over a high gas flame
or under a hot grill (broiler), then
crumble into thin strips. Divide the soba
noodles among four serving dishes and
top with the nori. Serve each portion
with an individual bowl of dipping sauce
and offer the flavourings separately.

STUFFED CHILLIES WITH CHEESE

STUFFED CHILLIES ARE POPULAR ALL OVER MEXICO. THE TYPE OF CHILLI USED DIFFERS FROM REGION TO REGION, BUT LARGER CHILLIES ARE EASIER TO STUFF THAN SMALLER ONES.

MAKES SIX

INGREDIENTS
6 fresh poblano or Anaheim chillies
2 potatoes, total weight about
   400g/14oz
200g/7oz/scant 1 cup cream cheese
200g/7oz/1¾ cups grated (shredded)
   mature (sharp) Cheddar cheese
5ml/1 tsp salt
2.5ml/½ tsp ground black pepper
2 eggs, separated
115g/4oz/1 cup plain
   (all-purpose) flour
2.5ml/½ tsp white pepper
oil, for frying
dried chilli flakes, to garnish (optional)

1 Make a neat slit down one side of each chilli. Place them in a dry frying pan over a medium heat, turning them frequently until the skins blister.

2 Place the chillies in a strong plastic bag and tie the top to keep the steam in. Set aside for 20 minutes, then carefully peel off the skins and remove the seeds through the slits, keeping the chillies whole. Dry the chillies with kitchen paper and set them aside.

COOK'S TIP
Take care when making the filling; mix gently, in order to avoid breaking up the diced potato.

VARIATION
Whole ancho (dried poblano) chillies can be used instead of fresh chillies, but will need to be reconstituted in water before they can be seeded and stuffed.

3 Scrub or peel the potatoes and cut them into 1cm/½in dice. Bring a large pan of water to the boil, add the potatoes and let the water return to boiling point. Lower the heat and simmer for 5 minutes or until the potatoes are just tender. Do not overcook. Drain them thoroughly.

4 Put the cream cheese in a bowl and stir in the grated Cheddar cheese, with 2.5ml/½ tsp of the salt and all the black pepper. Add the par-cooked potato and mix gently.

5 Spoon some of the potato filling into each chilli. Put them on a plate, cover with clear film (plastic wrap) and chill for 1 hour so the filling becomes firm.

6 Put the egg whites in a clean, grease-free bowl and whisk them to firm, dry peaks. In a separate bowl, beat the yolks until pale, then carefully fold in the whites. Scrape the mixture into a large, shallow dish. Spread out the plain flour in another large shallow dish and season it with the remaining salt and the white pepper.

7 Heat the oil for frying to 190°C/375°F. Coat a few chillies first in seasoned flour and then in egg before adding carefully to the hot oil.

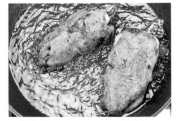

8 Fry the chillies in batches until golden and crisp. Drain on kitchen paper and serve hot, garnished with a sprinkle of chilli flakes, if you like.

PEPPERS WITH CHEESE AND CHILLI FILLING

SWEET PEPPERS AND CHILLIES ARE NATURAL COMPANIONS, SO IT ISN'T SURPRISING THAT
THEY WORK SO WELL TOGETHER IN THIS TRADITIONAL BULGARIAN APPETIZER.

3 Using a sharp knife, carefully peel away the skin from the peppers.

4 Beat together all the ingredients for the filling in a bowl. Divide evenly among the 4 peppers.

5 Reshape the peppers to look whole. Dip them into the seasoned flour, then in the egg and then the flour again.

SERVES TWO TO FOUR

INGREDIENTS
    4 red, yellow or green sweet peppers,
      either bell peppers or long peppers
    50g/2oz/½ cup plain (all-purpose)
      flour, seasoned
    1 egg, beaten
    olive oil, for shallow frying
    cucumber and tomato salad, to serve

For the filling
    1 egg
    90g/3½oz/generous ½ cup finely
      crumbled feta cheese
    30ml/2 tbsp chopped fresh parsley
    1 small fresh red or green chilli,
      seeded and finely chopped

1 Preheat the grill (broiler). Slit open the peppers lengthways on one side only, enabling you to scoop out the seeds and remove the cores, but leaving them in one piece.

2 Place the peppers in a grill (broiling) pan. Cook under medium heat until the skin is charred and blackened. Place the peppers in a plastic bag, tie the top to keep the steam in and set aside for 20 minutes.

COOK'S TIP
Feta cheese should have a bland, salt-edged taste. If kept in brine for some time it will be saltier and may need to be first soaked in water.

6 Heat the olive oil for shallow frying in a large pan and fry the peeled peppers gently for 6–8 minutes, turning once with a spatula, until they are golden brown and the filling is set. Drain the peppers thoroughly on kitchen paper before serving with a cucumber and tomato salad.

COURGETTES WITH CHEESE AND GREEN CHILLIES

THIS IS A VERY TASTY WAY TO SERVE COURGETTES, OFTEN A RATHER BLAND VEGETABLE, AND IT LOOKS GOOD TOO WITH TOMATOES AND FRESH OREGANO ADDING COLOUR.

SERVES SIX

INGREDIENTS
30ml/2 tbsp vegetable oil
½ onion, thinly sliced
2 garlic cloves, crushed
5ml/1 tsp dried oregano
2 tomatoes
50g/2oz/⅓ cup drained pickled
 jalapeño chilli slices, chopped
500g/1¼lb courgettes (zucchini)
115g/4oz/½ cup cream
 cheese, cubed
salt and ground black pepper
fresh oregano sprigs, to garnish

1 Heat the oil in a frying pan. Add the onion, garlic and dried oregano. Fry for 3–4 minutes, until the onion is soft and translucent.

2 Cut a cross in the base of each tomato. Place in a heatproof bowl and cover with boiling water. Leave in the water for 3 minutes, then lift out on a slotted spoon and plunge into a bowl of cold water. Drain. The skins will have begun to peel back from the crosses. Remove the skins and cut the tomatoes in half and squeeze out the seeds. Chop the flesh into strips.

3 Top and tail the courgettes, then cut them lengthways into 1cm/½in wide strips. Slice the strips into matchsticks.

4 Stir the courgettes into the onion mixture and fry for 10 minutes, stirring occasionally, until just tender. Add the tomatoes and chopped jalapeños and cook for 2–3 minutes more.

5 Add the cream cheese. Reduce the heat to the lowest setting. As the cheese melts, stir gently to coat the courgettes. Season with salt, pile into a heated dish and serve, garnished with fresh oregano.

TOASTED CHEESE TORTILLAS

FILLED WITH CHEESE AND CHILLIES, THESE ARE THE MEXICAN EQUIVALENT OF TOASTED SANDWICHES. SERVE THEM AS SOON AS THEY ARE COOKED, OR THEY WILL BECOME CHEWY.

2 Spear the chilli on a long-handled metal skewer and roast it over the flame of a gas burner until the skin blisters and darkens. Do not let the flesh burn. Alternatively, dry-fry it in a griddle pan until the skin is scorched. Place the roasted chilli in a strong plastic bag and tie the top to keep the steam in. Set aside for 20 minutes.

3 Remove the chilli from the bag and peel off the skin. Cut off the stalk, then slit the chilli and scrape out the seeds. Cut the flesh into 8 thin strips.

SERVES FOUR

INGREDIENTS
    200g/7oz mozzarella, Monterey Jack
        or mild Cheddar cheese
    1 fresh fresno chilli
    8 wheat flour tortillas, about
        15cm/6in across
    onion relish or classic tomato salsa,
        to serve

VARIATIONS
Try spreading a thin layer of your favourite Mexican salsa on the tortilla before adding the cheese, or adding a few pieces of cooked chicken before folding the tortilla in half.

1 If using mozzarella cheese, place it in the freezer for 30 minutes to make it easier to slice. Drain it thoroughly and pat it dry, then slice it into thin strips. Monterey Jack and Cheddar cheese should both be coarsely grated (shredded), as finely grated cheese will melt and ooze away when cooking. Set the cheese aside in a bowl.

4 Warm a large frying pan or griddle. Place 1 wheat tortilla on the pan or griddle at a time, sprinkle about one-eighth of the cheese on to 1 half and add a strip of chilli. Fold the tortilla over the cheese and press the edges gently together. Cook the tortilla for 1 minute, then turn over and cook the other side for 1 minute. You can prepare these in advance but cook only when needed.

5 Remove the filled tortilla from the pan or griddle, cut it into 3 triangles or 4 strips and serve at once, with the onion relish or tomato salsa.

PIMIENTO TARTLETS

KNOWN AS TARTALITAS DE PIMIENTO IN SPAIN, THESE PRETTY LITTLE TARTLETS ARE
FILLED WITH STRIPS OF ROASTED SWEET PEPPERS AND A DELICIOUSLY CREAMY, CHEESY
CUSTARD. THEY MAKE THE PERFECT SNACK TO SERVE WITH DRINKS.

SERVES FOUR

INGREDIENTS
  1 red (bell) pepper
  1 yellow (bell) pepper
  175g/6oz/1½ cups plain
    (all-purpose) flour
  75g/3oz/6 tbsp chilled butter, diced
  30–45ml/2–3 tbsp cold water
  60ml/4 tbsp double (heavy) cream
  1 egg
  15ml/1 tbsp grated fresh
    Parmesan cheese
  salt and ground black pepper

VARIATION
Use strips of grilled aubergine (eggplant)
mixed with sun-dried tomatoes in place
of the roasted peppers.

1 Preheat the oven to 200°C/400°F/
Gas 6, and heat the grill (broiler). Place
the peppers on a baking sheet and grill
for 10 minutes, turning occasionally,
until blackened. Cover with a dishtowel
and leave for 5 minutes. Peel away the
skin, then discard the seeds and cut
the flesh into very thin strips.

2 Sift the flour and a pinch of salt into
a bowl. Add the butter and rub it in
until the mixture resembles fine
breadcrumbs. Stir in enough of the
water to make a firm, not sticky, dough.

3 Roll the dough out thinly on a lightly
floured surface and line 12 individual
moulds or a 12-hole tartlet tin (muffin
pan). Prick the bases with a fork and
fill the pastry cases with crumpled foil.
Bake for 10 minutes.

4 Remove the foil from the pastry cases
and divide the pepper strips among the
pastry cases.

5 Whisk the cream and egg in a bowl.
Season well and pour over the peppers.
Sprinkle each tartlet with Parmesan
cheese and bake for 15–20 minutes
until firm. Cool for 2 minutes, then
remove from the moulds and transfer
to a wire rack. Serve warm or cold.

DESERT NACHOS

TORTILLA CHIPS ARE LIVENED UP WITH JALAPEÑOS IN THIS QUICK-AND-EASY SNACK. SERVED WITH A VARIETY OF SPICY MEXICAN DIPS, THIS ALWAYS PROVES TO BE A POPULAR DISH.

SERVES 2

INGREDIENTS
450g/1lb tortilla chips
45ml/3 tbsp chopped pickled jalapeño
   chillies, according to taste
12 black olives, sliced
225g/8oz/2 cups grated Cheddar cheese
Guacamole, tomato salsa and sour
   cream, to serve

1 Preheat the oven to 180°C/350°F/ Gas 4. Put the tortilla chips in a 23 × 33cm/9 × 13in ovenproof dish and spread them out evenly. Sprinkle the jalapeños, olives and cheese evenly over the tortilla chips.

2 Place the prepared tortilla chips in the top of the oven and bake for 10–15 minutes, until the cheese melts. Serve the nachos immediately, with the guacamole, tomato salsa and sour cream for dipping.

TORTILLAS WITH ENCHILADA SAUCE

SERVES 4

INGREDIENTS
450g/1lb can refried beans
300ml/½ pint/1¼ cups enchilada sauce
oil, for frying
4 corn tortillas
4 eggs
150g/5oz/1½ cups grated
   Cheddar cheese
salt and ground black pepper

1 Heat the refried beans in a pan. Cover and set aside.

2 Heat the enchilada sauce in a small pan. Cover and set aside.

COOK'S TIP
For a simple enchilada sauce, blend a can of tomatoes with 3 garlic cloves, 1 chopped onion, 45ml/3 tbsp chilli powder, 5ml/ 1 tsp each cayenne and cumin, and 2.5ml/½ tsp each dried oregano and salt.

3 Preheat the oven to 110°C/225°F/ Gas ¼. Put a 5mm/¼in layer of oil in a small non-stick frying pan and heat . When the oil is hot, add the tortillas, one at a time, and fry for about 30 seconds on each side, until just crisp. Remove and drain the tortillas on kitchen paper and keep them warm on a baking sheet in the oven. Discard the oil used for frying. Let the pan cool slightly, then wipe it with kitchen paper to remove all but a film of oil.

4 Heat the frying pan over a low heat. Break in two eggs and cook until the whites are just set. Season with salt and pepper, then transfer to the oven to keep warm. Repeat to cook the remaining eggs.

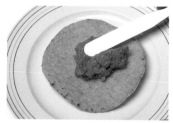

5 To serve, place a tortilla on each of four plates. Spread a layer of refried beans over each tortilla, then top each with an egg. Spoon over the warm enchilada sauce, then sprinkle with the cheese. Serve hot.

BUTTERFLIED PRAWNS IN CHILLI CHOCOLATE

THE COMBINATION OF HOT AND SWEET FLAVOURS MAY SEEM ODD, BUT THIS IS A DELICIOUS
APPETIZER. THE USE OF BITTER CHOCOLATE ADDS RICHNESS WITHOUT SWEETNESS.

SERVES 4

INGREDIENTS
  8 large raw prawns (shrimp),
    in the shell
  15ml/1 tbsp seasoned flour
  15ml/1 tbsp dry sherry
  juice of 4 clementines
    or 1 large orange
  15g/½ oz unsweetened dark
    (bittersweet) chocolate, chopped
  30ml/2 tbsp olive oil
  2 garlic cloves, finely chopped
  2.5cm/1in piece fresh root ginger,
    finely chopped
  1 small red chilli, seeded
    and chopped
  salt and ground black pepper

1 Peel the prawns, leaving just the tail
sections intact. Make a shallow cut
down the back of each prawn and
carefully pull out and discard the dark
intestinal tract. Turn over the prawns
so that the undersides are uppermost,
then carefully split them open from
tail to top, using a small sharp knife,
cutting almost, but not quite, through
to the back.

2 Press the prawns down firmly to
flatten them out. Coat the prawns with
the seasoned flour and set aside.

3 Gently heat the sherry and clementine
or orange juice in a small pan. When
warm, remove from the heat and stir in
the chopped chocolate until melted.

4 Heat the olive oil in a frying pan.
Cook the garlic, ginger and chilli over
a medium heat for 2 minutes, until
golden. Remove with a slotted spoon
and reserve. Add the prawns, cut side
down, to the pan; cook for 2–3 minutes,
until golden brown with pink edges.
Turn and cook for a further
2 minutes.

5 Return the garlic mixture to the pan
and pour over the chocolate sauce.
Cook for 1 minute, turning the prawns
to coat them in the glossy sauce.
Season to taste and serve hot.

PARTY PIZZETTES WITH A HINT OF CHILLI

*BRUSHING PIZZA DOUGH WITH CHILLI OIL BEFORE ADDING A FLAVOURSOME TOPPING GIVES
A TANTALIZING SUGGESTION OF WARMTH WHEN YOU BITE INTO THESE DELICIOUS SNACKS.*

SERVES FOUR

INGREDIENTS

150g/5oz packet pizza dough mix
5ml/1 tsp salt
120ml/4fl oz/½ cup lukewarm water
30ml/2 tbsp chilli oil
75g/3oz mozzarella cheese, grated
1 garlic clove, chopped
½ small red onion, thinly sliced
4–6 pieces sun-dried tomatoes in oil,
   drained and thinly sliced
115g/4oz cooked, peeled
   prawns (shrimp)
30ml/2 tbsp chopped fresh basil
salt and ground black pepper
shredded basil leaves, to garnish

1 Preheat the oven to 220°C/425°F/
Gas 7. Tip the pizza dough mix into a
mixing bowl and stir in the salt. Pour
in the water and mix to a soft dough.

2 Knead the dough on a lightly floured
surface for 5 minutes until smooth and
elastic. Divide it into 8 equal pieces.

3 Roll out each piece to a small oval
5mm/¼in thick. Place well apart on
2 greased baking sheets.

4 Prick each of the pizza bases all over
with a fork and brush lightly with
15ml/1 tbsp of the chilli oil. Top with
the grated mozzarella cheese, being
careful to leave a 1cm/½in border
all round.

5 Divide the garlic, onion, sun-dried
tomatoes, prawns and basil among the
pizza bases. Season and drizzle over
the remaining chilli oil. Bake for 8–10
minutes until crisp and golden. Garnish
with basil leaves and serve immediately.

PERI-PERI PRAWNS <u>WITH</u> AIOLI

THE NAME PERI-PERI REFERS TO THE SMALL, EXTREMELY HOT ANGOLAN CHILLIES FROM
WHICH THIS PORTUGUESE DISH IS TRADITIONALLY MADE.

<u>SERVES FOUR</u>

INGREDIENTS
    1 fresh red chilli, finely chopped
    2.5ml/½ tsp paprika
    2.5ml/½ tsp ground coriander
    1 garlic clove, crushed
    juice of ½ lime
    30ml/2 tbsp olive oil
    20 large raw prawns (shrimp) in shells
    salt and ground black pepper
    whole chillies, to garnish (optional)

For the aioli (quick method)
    150ml/¼ pint/⅔ cup mayonnaise
    2 garlic cloves, crushed
    5ml/1 tsp Dijon mustard

For the aioli (classic method)
    2 egg yolks
    2 crushed garlic cloves
    5ml/1 tsp granulated sugar
    5ml/1 tsp Dijon mustard
    10ml/2 tsp lemon juice
    250ml/8fl oz/1 cup mixed olive oil
      and sunflower oil

1 To make the aioli by the quick method, mix the mayonnaise, garlic and mustard in a small bowl and set aside. For the classic method, put the egg yolks in a blender or food processor and add the garlic, sugar, mustard and lemon juice. Process until mixed, then, with the motor running, add the oil through the hole in the lid or feeder tube, drip by drip at first, then in a steady stream, until all the oil has been added and the aioli is smooth.

2 Devein the prawns and remove their heads, but leave the shells on.

3 Make a peri-peri marinade by mixing the chilli, paprika, coriander, garlic, lime juice and olive oil in a non-metallic bowl. Add salt and pepper to taste. Pour over the prawns and mix well. Cover and leave in a cool place to marinate for 30 minutes, turning the prawns in the mixture from time to time.

4 Thread the prawns on to metal skewers and cook under the grill (broiler) or on the barbecue, basting and turning frequently, for 6–8 minutes until pink. Serve with the aioli, garnished with extra chillies, if you like.

FIENDISH FRITTERS

THESE DELECTABLE FRITTERS COME FROM THE PHILIPPINES. UNUSUALLY, THEY ARE FIRST SHALLOW FRIED, THEN DEEP-FRIED. EAT THEM FRESH FROM THE PAN, DIPPED IN THE PIQUANT SAUCE.

SERVES TWO TO FOUR

INGREDIENTS
16 raw prawns (shrimp),
  in the shell
225g/8oz/2 cups plain
  (all-purpose) flour
5ml/1 tsp baking powder
2.5ml/½ tsp salt
1 egg, beaten
1 small sweet potato
1 garlic clove, crushed
115g/4oz/2 cups beansprouts,
  soaked in cold water for
  10 minutes and well drained
vegetable oil, for shallow and
  deep-frying
4 spring onions
  (scallions), chopped

For the dipping sauce
1 jumbo garlic clove, sliced
45ml/3 tbsp rice or wine vinegar
15–30ml/1–2 tbsp water
salt, to taste
6–8 small fresh red chillies

1 Mix together all the 5 ingredients for the dipping sauce and divide between 2–4 small wide bowls. The garlic slices and whole chillies will float on top.

2 Put the prawns in a pan with cold water to cover. Bring to the boil,reduce the heat and then simmer for about 4–5 minutes or until the prawns are pink and tender when pierced with the tip of a sharp knife. Lift them out with a slotted spoon and drain well. Discard the heads and the body shell, but leave the tails on. Strain and reserve the cooking liquid. Set aside and leave to cool.

VARIATIONS
• Use cooked tiger prawns (jumbo shrimp) if you prefer. In this case, make the batter using ready-made fish stock or chicken stock.
• You could substitute 15ml/1 tbsp very finely sliced fresh ginger for the garlic in the dipping sauce, if you like.

3 Sift the flour, baking powder and salt into a bowl. Add the beaten egg and about 300ml/½ pint/1¼ cups of the reserved prawn stock and beat to make a batter that has the consistency of double (heavy) cream.

4 Peel the sweet potato and grate it coarsely. Add it to the batter, then stir in the crushed garlic. Pat the beansprouts dry in kitchen paper and add to the batter.

5 Pour the oil for shallow frying into a large frying pan. It should be about 5mm/¼in deep. Pour more oil into a wok for deep-frying. Heat the oil in the frying pan. Taking a generous spoonful of the batter, drop it carefully into the frying pan so that it spreads out to a fritter about 10cm/4in across.

6 Add more batter to the pan but do not let the fritters touch. As soon as the fritters have set, top each one with a single prawn and a few pieces of chopped spring onion. Continue to cook over a medium heat for 1 minute, then remove with a spatula.

7 Heat the oil in the wok to 190°C/ 375°F and deep-fry the fritters in batches until they are crisp and golden brown. Drain on kitchen paper and then arrange on a serving plate or platter. Serve with the dipping sauce.

PAN-STEAMED CHILLI MUSSELS

IF YOU CAN TAKE THE HEAT, USE BIRD'S EYE CHILLIES FOR THIS SIMPLE DISH, OR SUBSTITUTE ONE RED CAYENNE OR TWO RED FRESNO CHILLIES. LEMON GRASS ADDS A REFRESHING TANG.

2 Cut off the lower 5cm/2in of each lemon grass stalk and chop finely. Add to the pan, with the shallots, kaffir lime leaves, chillies, Thai fish sauce and lime juice.

3 Cover the pan with a lid and place it over medium-high heat. Steam for 5–7 minutes, shaking the pan occasionally, until the mussels open. Discard any of the mussels that have not opened.

SERVES FOUR TO SIX

INGREDIENTS
1kg/2¼lb live mussels
2 lemon grass stalks
4 shallots, chopped
4 kaffir lime leaves, roughly torn
1–2 fresh red chillies, seeded
  and sliced
15ml/1 tbsp Thai fish sauce
  (*nam pla*)
30ml/2 tbsp lime juice
2 spring onions (scallions), chopped,
  to garnish
coriander (cilantro) leaves,
  to garnish

1 Scrub the mussels and remove the beards, discarding any mussels that are damaged or that fail to close when tapped with a knife. Place in a large heavy pan.

4 Using a slotted spoon, transfer the cooked mussels to a serving dish, along with any liquid that has been produced. Garnish with chopped spring onions and coriander leaves. Serve immediately.

SPICY SHELLFISH WONTONS

THESE TASTY WONTONS LOOK A BIT LIKE TORTELLINI BUT THE TASTE IS MORE THAI THAN
TRIESTE. WATER CHESTNUTS ADD A LIGHT CRUNCH TO THE CRAB AND CHILLI FILLING.

SERVES FOUR

INGREDIENTS

225g/8oz raw prawns (shrimp),
  peeled and deveined
115g/4oz white crab meat,
  picked over
4 drained canned water chestnuts,
  finely diced
1 spring onion (scallion), chopped
1 small fresh green chilli, seeded and
  finely chopped
1.5ml/¼ tsp grated (shredded) fresh
  root ginger
1 egg, separated
20–24 wonton wrappers
salt and ground black pepper
coriander (cilantro) leaves, to garnish

For the dressing
30ml/2 tbsp rice vinegar
15ml/1 tbsp chopped pickled ginger
90ml/6 tbsp olive oil
15ml1/ tbsp soy sauce
45ml/3 tbsp chopped
  coriander (cilantro)
30ml/2 tbsp diced red (bell) pepper

1 Finely dice the prawns and place
them in a bowl. Stir in the next
5 ingredients and the egg white. Season
with salt and pepper and mix well.

2 Place a wonton wrapper on a board.
Put about 5ml/1 tsp of the filling just
above the centre of the wrapper. With a
pastry brush, moisten the edges of the
wrapper with a little of the egg yolk.
Bring the bottom of the wrapper up over
the filling. Press gently to expel any air,
then seal neatly in a triangle.

3 For a more elaborate shape, bring the
2 side points up over the filling, overlap
the points and pinch the ends firmly
together. Space the filled wontons on a
large baking sheet lined with
greaseproof (waxed) paper, so that they
do not stick together.

4 Half-fill a large pan with water. Bring
to simmering point. Add the filled
wontons, a few at a time, and simmer
for 2–3 minutes. The wontons will float
to the surface and when they are
cooked and ready to remove, the
wrappers will be translucent and the
filling cooked. Remove the wontons with
a large slotted spoon, drain them briefly,
then spread them on trays. Keep warm
while cooking the remaining wontons.

5 Make the dressing by whisking all the
ingredients together in a bowl. Divide
the warm wontons among 4 serving
dishes, drizzle with the spicy dressing
and serve garnished with a handful of
coriander leaves.

CAJUN "POPCORN"

*CORNMEAL-COATED SPICY SEAFOOD RESEMBLES POPCORN WHEN MADE, HENCE THE NAME
FOR THIS TASTY CAJUN SNACK SERVED WITH A DELICIOUS BASIL MAYONNAISE.*

SERVES 8

INGREDIENTS
　　900g/2lb raw crayfish tails, peeled,
　　　or small prawns (shrimp),
　　　peeled and deveined
　　2 eggs
　　250ml/8fl oz/1 cup dry white wine
　　50g/2oz/⅓ cup fine cornmeal (or plain
　　　(all-purpose) flour, if not available)
　　50g/2oz/½ cup plain (all purpose) flour
　　15ml/1 tbsp chopped fresh chives
　　1 garlic clove, crushed
　　2.5ml/½ tsp fresh thyme leaves
　　1.5ml/¼ tsp salt
　　1.5ml/¼ tsp cayenne pepper
　　1.5ml/½ tsp ground black pepper
　　oil, for deep-frying

For the mayonnaise
　　1 egg yolk
　　10ml/2 tsp Dijon mustard
　　15ml/1 tbsp white wine vinegar
　　250ml/8fl oz/1 cup olive or vegetable oil
　　15g/½ oz/½ cup fresh basil
　　　leaves, chopped
　　salt and ground black pepper

1 Rinse the crayfish tails or prawns in
cold water. Drain well and set aside in
a cool place.

2 Mix together the eggs and wine in a
small bowl.

3 In a mixing bowl, combine the
cornmeal and/or flour, chives, garlic,
thyme, salt, cayenne and pepper.
Gradually whisk in the egg mixture,
blending well. Cover the batter and
stand for 1 hour at room temperature.

4 For the mayonnaise, combine the egg
yolk, mustard and vinegar in a mixing
bowl and add salt and pepper to taste.
Add the oil in a thin stream, beating
vigorously with a wire whisk. When the
mixture is thick and smooth, stir in
the basil. Cover and chill until ready
to serve.

5 Heat 7.5cm/3in of oil in a large frying
pan or deep-fryer to a temperature of
180°C/350°F. Dip the seafood into the
batter and fry in small batches for
2–3 minutes, until golden brown.
Turn as necessary for even colouring.
Remove with a slotted spoon and drain
the "popcorn" on kitchen paper. Serve
hot, with the basil mayonnaise.

CHILLIED MONKFISH PARCELS

HOT RED CHILLI, GARLIC AND LEMON RIND ADD TANGY FLAVOUR TO MONKFISH IN THESE
TASTY AND APPEALING LITTLE PARCELS.

SERVES 4

INGREDIENTS

175g/6oz/1½ cups strong white
  bread flour
2 eggs
115g/4oz skinless monkfish
  fillet, diced
grated rind of 1 lemon
1 garlic clove, chopped
1 small red chilli, seeded
  and sliced
45ml/3 tbsp chopped
  fresh parsley
30ml/2 tbsp single (light) cream

For the tomato oil
2 tomatoes, peeled, seeded and
  finely diced
45ml/3 tbsp extra virgin olive oil
30ml/1 tbsp fresh lemon juice
salt and ground black pepper

1 Place the flour, eggs and 2.5ml/½ tsp salt in a food processor; pulse to form a soft dough. Knead for 2–3 minutes, then wrap in clear film (plastic wrap). Chill for 20 minutes.

2 Place the monkfish, lemon rind, garlic, chilli and parsley in the clean food processor; process until very finely chopped. Add the cream, with plenty of salt and pepper and process again to form a very thick purée.

3 Make the tomato oil by stirring the diced tomato with the olive oil and lemon juice in a bowl. Add salt to taste. Cover and chill.

4 Roll out the dough on a lightly floured surface and cut out 32 rounds, using a 4cm/1½in plain cutter. Divide the filling among half the rounds, then cover with the remaining rounds. Pinch the edges tightly to seal, trying to exclude as much air as possible.

5 Bring a large pan of water to simmering point and poach the parcels, in batches, for 2–3 minutes, or until they rise to the surface. Drain and serve hot, drizzled with the tomato oil.

CEVICHE OF FISH WITH CITRUS FRUITS

FRESH FISH IS "COOKED" BY BEING MARINATED IN A MIXTURE OF MANGO, LIME JUICE AND CHILLIES. THE RESULT IS AN APPETIZER WITH A WONDERFULLY FRESH FLAVOUR.

SERVES SIX

INGREDIENTS

350g/12oz medium cooked
   prawns (shrimp)
350g/12oz scallops, removed from
   their shells, with corals intact
2 tomatoes, about 175g/6oz
1 red onion, finely chopped
1 small mango
350g/12oz salmon fillet
1 fresh red chilli
12 limes
30ml/2 tbsp caster (superfine) sugar
2 pink grapefruit
3 oranges
salt and ground black pepper
lime slices, to garnish (optional)

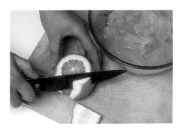

3 Skin the salmon, if necessary, then cut it into small pieces. Slit the chilli and scrape out and discard the seeds. Dice the flesh. Add the tomatoes, mango, salmon, chilli and onion to the shellfish in the bowl.

4 Squeeze 8 of the limes and add the juice to the bowl, with the sugar and seasoning. Stir, cover and leave the ceviche to marinate for 3 hours in the refrigerator.

5 Segment the grapefruit, oranges and remaining limes. Drain off as much excess lime juice as possible from the marinated fish and gently fold in the fruit segments. Season to taste and arrange on a platter. Garnish with lime slices, if you like. Serve immediately.

COOK'S TIP

Take very special care in choosing the fish for this dish; it must be very fresh and served on the day it is prepared.

1 Peel the prawns and place them in a large bowl. Cut the scallop meat into 1cm/½in dice. Add it to the bowl.

2 Dice the tomatoes. Peel the mango and cut off a thick slice close to the flat side of the stone (pit). Repeat on the other side. Score the flesh with criss-cross lines, then fold the slices inside out so the dice stand proud of the skin. Slice these off the skin and into a bowl.

THAI-STYLE MARINATED SALMON

THIS IS A WONDERFUL WAY OF PREPARING SALMON, SIMILAR TO THE SCANDINAVIAN SPECIALITY,
GRAVLAX. START THE PREPARATION TWO TO FIVE DAYS BEFORE YOU INTEND TO EAT IT.

SERVES FOUR TO SIX

INGREDIENTS

tail piece of 1 salmon, about
  675g/1½lb, cleaned and prepared
  (see below)
20ml/4 tsp coarse sea salt
20ml/4 tsp granulated sugar
2.5cm/1in piece fresh root
  ginger, grated (shredded)
2 lemon grass stalks
4 kaffir lime leaves, finely chopped
  or shredded
grated (shredded) rind of
  1 kaffir lime
1 fresh red chilli, seeded and chopped
5ml/1 tsp black peppercorns,
  coarsely crushed
30ml/2 tbsp chopped fresh coriander
  (cilantro), plus sprigs to garnish
wedges of kaffir lime, to garnish

For the dressing
150ml/¼ pint/⅔ cup mayonnaise
juice of ½ lime
10ml/2 tsp chopped fresh
  coriander (cilantro)

1 Ask your fishmonger to scale the fish and remove the skin, splitting the fish lengthways to remove it from the backbone in 2 matching fillets. Use tweezers to remove all the bones from the salmon.

2 In a bowl, mix together the salt, sugar and ginger. Remove the outer leaves from the lemon grass and slice the inner portion finely. Add to the bowl, with the lime leaves, lime rind, chilli, peppercorns and coriander.

3 Place one-quarter of the spice mixture in a shallow dish. Place one salmon fillet, skin-side down, on top of the spices. Spread two-thirds of the remaining mixture over the flesh then place the remaining fillet on top, flesh-side down. Arrange the rest of the spice mixture over the fish.

COOK'S TIP
Kaffir lime leaves and the rind of the fruit are very aromatic and a distinctive feature of Thai cooking. They should be available from Asian food stores. If not, substitute ordinary limes.

4 Cover the fish with foil, then place a board on top. Add some weights, such as clean cans of food. Chill for 2–5 days, turning the fish each day in the spicy marinade to ensure that the flavour permeates all parts of the fish.

5 Make the dressing by mixing the mayonnaise, lime juice and chopped coriander in a bowl.

6 Scrape the spices off the fish. Slice it as thinly as possible. Serve with the lime dressing, garnished with fresh coriander and wedges of kaffir lime.

SINGAPORE CRABS

EAT THESE CRABS WITH THE FINGERS. GIVE GUESTS CRAB CRACKERS FOR THE CLAWS AND
HAVE SOME FINGER BOWLS OR HOT TOWELS TO HAND AS THE MEAL WILL BE MESSY!

SERVES FOUR

INGREDIENTS
  2 cooked crabs, each about
    675g/1½lb
  90ml/6 tbsp sunflower oil
  2.5cm/1in piece fresh root ginger,
    peeled and chopped
  2–3 garlic cloves, crushed
  1–2 fresh red chillies, seeded and
    pounded to a paste
  175ml/6fl oz/¾ cup tomato ketchup
  30ml/2 tbsp soft light brown sugar
  15ml/1 tbsp light soy sauce
  120ml/4fl oz/½ cup boiling water
  salt
  hot toast and cucumber chunks,
    to serve

1 Prepare each crab in turn. Twist off the large claws, then turn the crab on its back with its mouth and eyes facing away from you. Using both of your thumbs, push the body, with the small legs attached, upwards from beneath the flap, separating the body from the main shell in the process. Discard the stomach sac and grey spongy lungs.

2 Using a teaspoon, scrape the brown creamy meat from the large shell into a small bowl. Twist the legs from the body. Cut the body section in half. Pick out the white meat and add it to the bowl. Pick out the meat from the legs, or leave it for guests to remove at the table.

3 Heat the oil in a wok and gently fry the ginger, garlic and fresh chilli paste for 1–2 minutes without browning. Stir in the ketchup, sugar and soy sauce, with salt to taste and heat gently.

4 Stir in all the crab meat. Pour in the boiling water, stir well and heat through over a high heat. Pile on serving plates. If the crab claws were left intact, add them to the plate, with the cucumber. Serve immediately, with pieces of toast.

PORK SATAY STICKS

THERE ARE FEW DISHES AS DELICIOUS AS SATAY. THE SKEWERS OF SPICED MEAT CAN BE SERVED
AS SNACKS, AS PART OF A BARBECUE OR AS A LIGHT MEAL.

SERVES EIGHT TO TWELVE

INGREDIENTS
  450g/1lb pork fillet (tenderloin)
  15ml/1 tbsp soft light brown sugar
  1cm/½in cube shrimp paste
  1–2 lemon grass stalks, trimmed
  30ml/2 tbsp coriander
    seeds, dry-fried
  6 macadamia nuts or blanched almonds
  2 onions, roughly chopped
  3–6 fresh red chillies, seeded and
    roughly chopped
  2.5ml/½ tsp ground turmeric
  300ml/½ pint/1¼ cups canned
    coconut milk
  30ml/2 tbsp groundnut (peanut) oil
    or sunflower oil
  salt

COOK'S TIP
How many chillies you use for the marinade depends on their strength.

1 Soak 8–12 bamboo skewers in water for at least 1 hour to prevent them from scorching when they are placed under the grill (broiler).

2 Cut the pork into small chunks, then spread it out in a single layer in a shallow dish. Sprinkle with the sugar to help release the juices. Wrap the shrimp paste in foil and heat it briefly in a dry frying pan or warm it on a skewer held over a gas flame.

3 Cut off the lower 5cm/2in of the lemon grass stalks and chop finely. Process the dry-fried coriander seeds to a powder in a food processor. Add the nuts and chopped lemon grass, process briefly, then add the onions, chillies, shrimp paste, turmeric and a little salt; process to a fine paste. Pour in the coconut milk and oil. Switch the machine on very briefly to mix.

4 Pour the mixture over the pork, stir well, cover and leave to marinate for 1–2 hours.

5 Preheat the grill or prepare the barbecue. Drain the bamboo skewers and thread 3–4 pieces of marinated pork on each. Cook the skewered meat for 8–10 minutes, turning often until tender and basting frequently with the remaining marinade. Serve as soon as they are cooked.

SAN FRANCISCO CHICKEN WINGS

SERVES 4

INGREDIENTS
    75ml/5 tbsp soy sauce
    15ml/1 tbsp light brown sugar
    15ml/1 tbsp rice vinegar
    30ml/2 tbsp dry sherry
    juice of 1 orange
    5cm/2in strip of orange rind
    1 star anise
    5ml/1 tsp cornflour (cornstarch)
    50ml/2fl oz/¼ cup water
    15ml/1 tbsp chopped fresh
      root ginger
    5ml/1 tsp chilli-garlic sauce, to taste
    1.5kg/3–3½lb chicken wings,
      tips removed

1 Preheat the oven to 200°C/400°F/
Gas 6. Mix the soy sauce, sugar,
vinegar, sherry, orange juice and rind
and anise in a pan. Bring to the boil.

2 Combine the cornflour and water in a
small bowl and stir until blended. Add
to the boiling soy sauce mixture, stirring
well until it has dissolved. Boil for
another minute, stirring constantly.

3 Remove the soy sauce mixture from
the heat and stir in the ginger and
chilli-garlic sauce.

4 Arrange the chicken wings, in one
layer, in a large ovenproof dish. Pour
over the soy sauce mixture and stir to
coat the wings evenly.

5 Bake in the centre of the oven for
30–40 minutes, until the chicken wings
are tender and browned, basting
occasionally. Serve the chicken wings
either hot or warm.

CHICKEN SATAY

CONCERTINAS OF TENDER CHICKEN, SERVED WITH A CHILLI-FLAVOURED PEANUT SAUCE, ARE IRRESISTIBLE. GARNISH WITH SLICED FRESH RED CHILLIES FOR EXTRA FIRE.

SERVES FOUR

INGREDIENTS

    4 boneless, skinless chicken breasts
    10ml/2 tsp soft light brown sugar

For the marinade
    5ml/1 tsp cumin seeds
    5ml/1 tsp fennel seeds
    7.5ml/1½ tsp coriander seeds
    6 small onions, chopped
    1 garlic clove, crushed
    1 lemon grass stalk, trimmed
    3 macadamia nuts or 6 cashew nuts
    2.5ml/½ tsp ground turmeric

For the peanut sauce
    4 small onions, sliced
    2 garlic cloves, crushed
    1cm/½in cube shrimp paste
    6 cashew nuts or almonds
    2 lemon grass stalks, trimmed
    45ml/3 tbsp sunflower oil, plus extra
    5–10ml/1–2 tsp chilli powder
    400ml/14fl oz can coconut milk
    60–75ml/4–5 tbsp tamarind water or
        30ml/2 tbsp tamarind concentrate
        mixed with 45ml/3 tbsp water
    15ml/1 tbsp soft light brown sugar
    175g/6oz/½ cup crunchy peanut butter

1 Cut the chicken into 16 thin strips, sprinkle with the sugar and set aside.

2 Make the marinade. Dry-fry the spices, then grind to a powder in a food processor. Set aside. Add the onions and garlic to the processor. Chop the lower 5cm/2in of the lemon grass and add with the nuts, spices and turmeric. Grind to a paste; scrape into a bowl.

3 Add the chicken and stir well until coated. Cover loosely with clear film (plastic wrap) and leave to marinate for at least 4 hours. Soak 16 bamboo skewers for 1 hour in a bowl of warm water before use to prevent scorching.

4 Prepare the sauce. Pound or process the onions with the garlic and shrimp paste. Slice the lower parts of the lemon grass stalks and add with the nuts. Process to a fine purée. Heat the oil in a wok and fry the purée for 2–3 minutes. Add the chilli powder and cook for 2 minutes more.

5 Stir in the coconut milk and bring slowly to the boil. Reduce the heat and stir in the tamarind water and brown sugar. Add the peanut butter and cook over a low heat, stirring gently, until fairly thick. Keep warm. Prepare the barbecue or preheat the grill (broiler).

6 Thread the chicken on to the bamboo skewers. Cook on the barbecue or under the grill for about 5 minutes or until golden and tender, brushing with oil occasionally. Serve with the hot peanut sauce handed around in a separate bowl.

MIXED TOSTADAS

LIKE LITTLE EDIBLE PLATES, THESE FRIED TORTILLAS CAN SUPPORT ANYTHING THAT IS NOT TOO JUICY.

MAKES 14

INGREDIENTS
  oil, for shallow frying
  14 freshly prepared unbaked
    corn tortillas
  225g/8oz/1 cup mashed red kidney
    or pinto beans
  1 iceberg lettuce, shredded
  oil and vinegar dressing (optional)
  2 cooked chicken breast portions,
    skinned and thinly sliced
  225g/8oz Guacamole
  115g/4oz/1 cup coarsely grated
    Cheddar cheese
  pickled jalapeño chillies, seeded and
    sliced, to taste

1 Heat the oil in a frying pan and fry the tortillas until golden brown on both sides and crisp but not hard.

2 Spread each tortilla with a layer of beans. Put a layer of shredded lettuce (which can be left plain or lightly tossed with a little dressing) over the beans.

3 Arrange pieces of chicken in a layer on top of the lettuce. Carefully spread over a layer of the guacamole and finally, sprinkle over a layer of the grated cheese.

4 Arrange the mixed tostadas on a large platter. Serve on individual plates but eat using your hands.

TORTILLA TURNOVERS

THESE DELICIOUS FILLED AND DEEP-FRIED TORTILLA TURNOVERS MAKE A POPULAR SNACK AND SMALLER VERSIONS MAKE EXCELLENT CANAPÉS.

MAKES 14

INGREDIENTS
  14 freshly prepared unbaked tortillas

For the filling
  225g/8oz/2 cups finely chopped or
    grated Cheddar cheese
  3 jalapeño chillies, seeded and cut
    into strips
  salt
  oil, for shallow frying

1 Have the tortillas ready, covered with a clean cloth. Combine the cheese and chilli strips in a bowl. Season with salt. Set aside.

2 Heat the oil in a frying pan, then holding an unbaked tortilla on your palm, put a spoonful of filling along the centre, avoiding the edges.

COOK'S TIP
For other stuffing ideas try leftover beans with chillies, or chopped chorizo sausage fried with a little chopped onion.

3 Fold the tortilla and seal the edges by pressing or crimping well together. Fry in hot oil, on both sides, until golden brown and crisp.

4 Using a metal spatula, lift out the turnover and drain it on kitchen paper. Transfer to a plate and keep warm while frying the remaining tortillas. Serve hot.

CHICKEN TORTILLAS <u>WITH</u> FRESNO CHILLI SALSA

CRISP FRIED TORTILLAS WITH A CHICKEN AND CHEESE FILLING MAKE A DELICIOUS LIGHT MEAL, ESPECIALLY WHEN SERVED WITH A SPICY TOMATO SALSA.

MAKES TWELVE

INGREDIENTS
　2 skinless, boneless chicken
　　breast portions
　15ml/1 tbsp vegetable oil
　1 onion, chopped
　2 garlic cloves, crushed
　90g/3½oz/generous ½ cup crumbled
　　feta cheese
　12 corn tortillas
　oil, for frying
　salt and ground black pepper

For the salsa
　3 tomatoes, peeled seeded
　　and chopped
　juice of ½ lime
　small bunch of fresh coriander
　　(cilantro), chopped
　½ small onion, finely chopped
　3 fresh green fresno chillies,
　　seeded and chopped

1 Start by making the salsa. Mix the chopped tomatoes, lime juice, chopped coriander, onion and chillies in a bowl. Season with salt to taste, cover and chill until needed.

2 Put the chicken portions in a large pan, add water to cover and bring to the boil. Reduce the heat and simmer for 15–20 minutes or until the chicken is cooked. Remove the chicken from the pan and let it cool a little. Using 2 forks, shred the chicken into small pieces. Set it aside.

3 Heat the oil in a frying pan and fry the onion and garlic over a low heat for about 5 minutes, or until the onion has softened but not coloured. Add the shredded chicken, with salt and pepper to taste. Mix well, remove from the heat and stir in the feta.

4 Before attempting to roll the tortillas, soften 3 or 4 at a time by steaming them on a plate over boiling water. Alternatively, wrap them in microwave-safe clear film (plastic wrap) and then heat them in a microwave oven on full power for about 30 seconds.

5 Place a teaspoonful of the chicken filling on one of the tortillas. Roll the tortilla tightly around the filling to make a neat cylinder. Secure with a cocktail stick or toothpick. Immediately cover the roll with clear film to prevent the tortilla from drying out and splitting. Fill and roll the remaining tortillas in exactly the same way, covering them each time with clear film.

6 Pour oil into a frying pan to a depth of 2.5cm/1in. Heat it until a small cube of day-old bread, added to the oil, rises to the surface and bubbles at the edges before turning golden. Remove the cocktail sticks or toothpicks, then add the flutes to the pan, a few at a time.

7 Fry the flutes for 2–3 minutes until golden, turning frequently. Drain on kitchen paper and serve at once, with the spicy tomato salsa.

COOK'S TIP
You might find it easier to keep the cocktail sticks or toothpicks in place until after the flutes have been fried. Remove them before serving.

CHICKEN NAAN POCKETS

THIS QUICK-AND-EASY DISH IS IDEAL FOR A SNACK LUNCH OR SUPPER.

SERVES 4

INGREDIENTS
    4 naan
    45ml/3 tbsp natural (plain) yogurt
    7.5ml/1½ tsp garam masala
    5ml/1 tsp chilli powder
    5ml/1 tsp salt
    45ml/3 tbsp lemon juice
    15ml/1 tbsp chopped fresh
        coriander (cilantro)
    1 fresh green chilli, chopped
    450g/1lb chicken, skinned, boned
        and cubed
    15ml/1 tbsp vegetable oil
    8 onion rings
    2 tomatoes, quartered
    ½ white cabbage, shredded
    lemon wedges, 2 small tomatoes,
        halved, mixed salad leaves and
        fresh coriander, to garnish

1 Using a small, sharp knife, carefully cut into the middle of each naan to make a pocket, then set them aside until needed.

2 In a bowl, mix together the natural yogurt, garam masala, chilli powder, salt, lemon juice, fresh coriander and chopped fresh green chilli. Pour this marinade over the chicken pieces and leave to marinate for about 1 hour.

3 After 1 hour preheat the grill (broiler) to very hot, then lower the heat to medium. Place the marinated chicken pieces in a flameproof dish and grill (broil) for about 15–20 minutes, until they are tender and cooked through, turning the chicken pieces at least twice. Baste with the vegetable oil occasionally while cooking.

4 Remove the dish from the heat and fill each naan with the chicken and then with the onion rings, tomatoes and shredded cabbage. Serve garnished with lemon, tomatoes, salad leaves and coriander.

CHICKEN TIKKA

GINGER, GARLIC AND CHILLI POWDER ADD A CHARACTERISTIC SPICY TASTE TO THIS POPULAR INDIAN APPETIZER, WHICH IS QUICK AND EASY TO COOK.

SERVES 6

INGREDIENTS
    450g/1lb chicken, skinned, boned and
        cubed
    5ml/1 tsp ginger pulp
    5ml/1 tsp garlic pulp
    5ml/1 tsp chilli powder
    1.5ml/¼ tsp ground turmeric
    5ml/1 tsp salt
    150ml/¼ pint/⅔ cup natural
        (plain) yogurt
    60ml/4 tbsp lemon juice
    15ml/1 tbsp chopped fresh
        coriander (cilantro)
    15ml/1 tbsp vegetable oil
    1 small onion, cut into rings, lime
        wedges, mixed salad and fresh
        coriander, to garnish

1 In a medium mixing bowl, combine the chicken pieces, ginger and garlic pulp, chilli powder, turmeric, salt, yogurt, lemon juice and fresh coriander and leave to marinate for at least 2 hours.

2 Place the marinated chicken on a grill (broiler) tray or in a flameproof dish lined with foil and baste with the vegetable oil.

3 Preheat the grill to medium. Grill (broil) the chicken for 15–20 minutes, until cooked, turning and basting 2–3 times. Serve garnished with onion, lime, salad and coriander.

COOK'S TIP
Chicken tikka can be served with naan or chapatis, pickles and salad as a main dish for four people.

Chorizo Sausage ᴵᴺ Olive Oil

Spanish chorizo sausage has a deliciously pungent chilli taste. Frying chorizo with onions and olive oil is one of its simplest and most delicious uses.

SERVES FOUR

INGREDIENTS
75ml/5 tbsp extra virgin
olive oil
350g/12oz chorizo, sliced
1 large onion, thinly sliced
fresh flat leaf parsley, to garnish
warm crusty bread, to serve

1 Heat the olive oil in a medium frying pan and fry the sliced chorizo sausage over a high heat until beginning to colour around the edges. Remove the sausage from the pan with a slotted spoon and set aside.

COOK'S TIPS
• The robust seasoning of garlic, chilli and paprika used in chorizo flavours the ingredients it is cooked with, so there is no need to add extra flavouring.
• A mezzaluna is a handy alternative to a knife and is used with a seesaw motion.

2 Add the thinly sliced onion to the pan and fry for about 10–15 minutes until softened and golden brown.

3 Return the chorizo sausage slices to the frying pan and cook for 1 minute more to heat them through thoroughly.

4 Roughly chop the fresh parsley using a sharp knife or mezzaluna.

5 Tip the mixture into a warmed, shallow serving dish and sprinkle over the chopped flat leaf parsley. Serve at once while they are hot, with warm crusty bread.

VARIATION
Chorizo is usually available in large supermarkets or delicatessens. Other similarly rich, spicy sausages can be used instead.

Chilli ᴬᴺᴰ Garlic Prawns

For this simple Spanish tapas dish, you really need fresh shellfish that will absorb the flavour of the garlic and chilli while being fried.

SERVES FOUR

INGREDIENTS
350–450g/12oz–1lb raw king prawns
(jumbo shrimp)
2 fresh red fresno or serrano chillies
75ml/5 tbsp olive oil
3 garlic cloves, crushed
salt and ground black pepper
crusty bread, to serve

1 Remove the heads and shells from the prawns, leaving the tails intact.

COOK'S TIP
Have everything ready for last minute cooking so that it is served still sizzling.

2 Cut each fresno or serrano chilli in half lengthways. Scrape out and discard all the seeds. Heat the olive oil in a flameproof dish, suitable for serving. (Alternatively, use a frying pan and have a warmed serving dish ready in a preheated oven.)

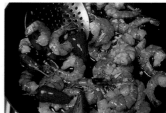

3 Add all the prawns, chillies and crushed garlic to the pan and cook over a high heat for about 3 minutes, stirring until the prawns turn pink. Season lightly with salt and pepper and serve immediately with crusty bread to mop up the juices.

STUFFED ROLLS <u>WITH</u> SPICY SALSA

MEXICAN STREET TRADERS SELL THIS TASTY SNACK WITH A CHUNKY SALSA, SPIKED WITH CHILLIES.

SERVES FOUR

INGREDIENTS
    4 crusty finger rolls
    50g/2oz/¼ cup butter, softened
    225g/8oz/1⅓ cups canned
      refried beans
    30ml/2 tbsp chopped bottled pickled
      jalapeño chillies
    150g/5oz/1¼ cups grated (shredded)
      medium Cheddar cheese
    green salad leaves, to garnish
    120ml/4fl oz/½ cup tomato salsa,
      to serve

1 Preheat the grill (broiler). Cut the rolls in half, then take a sliver off the base so that they lie flat. Remove a little of the crumb. Spread them lightly with butter.

2 Arrange the rolls on a baking sheet and grill (broil) for about 5 minutes, or until they are crisp and golden.

3 Meanwhile, heat the refried beans over a low heat in a small pan, stirring occasionally to avoid them sticking. Add the pickled jalapeño chillies.

4 Scoop the beans on to the rolls, then sprinkle the grated cheese on top. Place them back under the grill until the cheese melts. Garnish with salad leaves and serve with the tomato salsa. If the salsa is not very spicy, add a seeded and finely chopped chilli to enhance the flavour.

EGGS <u>WITH</u> TORTILLAS <u>AND</u> BEANS

A TASTY AND FILLING SNACK, TORTILLAS ARE TOPPED WITH BEANS, FRIED EGG AND HOT CHILLI SAUCES.

SERVES FOUR

INGREDIENTS
    225g/8oz/generous 1 cup black
      beans, soaked overnight in water
    1 small onion, finely chopped
    2 garlic cloves, crushed
    small bunch of fresh coriander
      (cilantro), chopped
    150g/5oz/1 cup frozen peas
    4 corn tortillas
    30ml/2 tbsp oil
    4 eggs
    150g/5oz cooked ham, diced
    60ml/4 tbsp hot chilli sauce
    75g/3oz/generous ½ cup feta
      cheese, crumbled
    salt and ground black pepper
    tomato salsa, to serve

1 Drain the beans, rinse them under cold water and drain again. Put them in a pan, add the onion and garlic with water to cover. Bring to the boil, then simmer for 40 minutes. Stir in the coriander, season to taste, and keep hot.

2 Cook the peas in a small pan of boiling water until they are just tender. Drain and set aside. Heat the tortillas, following the instructions on the packet.

3 Heat the oil in a frying pan and fry the eggs until the whites are set. Lift them on to a plate and keep them warm while you quickly heat the ham and peas in the oil remaining in the pan.

COOK'S TIP
When frying eggs, crack them into a saucer first, to avoid breaking the yolk. Then slide into the pan.

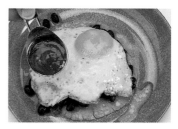

4 Place the tortillas on warmed plates and top each one with some beans. Place an egg on each tortilla, spoon over 15ml/1 tbsp hot chilli sauce, then surround each egg with some peas and ham. Sprinkle feta over the peas and serve at once, with salsa on the side.

VARIATIONS
Tortillas with a foundation of black beans and feta cheese can be covered with a variety of toppings. Try them with a dab of salsa and sliced radishes. Or try courgettes (zucchini), guacamole and spring onions (scallions).

ROLLS WITH REFRIED BEANS AND CHILLI

FILLED ROLLS WITH A DIFFERENCE, TORTAS ARE LIKE EDIBLE TREASURE CHESTS, WITH MEAT, CHEESE, CHILLIES AND TOMATOES PILED ON TOP OF REFRIED BEANS.

SERVES TWO

INGREDIENTS
2 fresh jalapeño chillies
juice of ½ lime
2 French bread rolls or 2 pieces of
   French bread
115g/4oz/⅔ cup home-made or
   canned refried beans
150g/5oz roast pork
2 small tomatoes, sliced
115g/4oz Cheddar cheese, sliced
small bunch of fresh
   coriander (cilantro)
30ml/2 tbsp crème fraîche

VARIATIONS
The essential ingredients of a *torta* are refried beans and chillies. Everything else is subject to change. Ham, chicken or turkey could all be used instead of pork, or another kind of cheese, and lettuce is often added.

1 Cut the chillies in half, scrape out the seeds, then cut the flesh into thin strips. Put it in a bowl, pour over the lime juice and leave to stand.

2 If using rolls, slice them in half and remove some of the crumb so that they are slightly hollowed. If using French bread, slice each piece in half lengthways and hollow likewise. Set the tops aside and spread the bottom halves with the refried beans.

3 Cut the pork into thin shreds and put these on top of the refried beans. Top with the tomato slices. Drain the jalapeño strips and put them on top of the tomato slices. Add the cheese and sprinkle with coriander leaves.

4 Turn the top halves of the bread or rolls over, so that the cut sides are uppermost, and spread these with crème fraîche. Sandwich back together again and serve.

SPRING ROLLS WITH FIERY CHILLI SAUCE

THIS POPULAR SNACK COMES FROM SOUTH-EAST ASIA. THE SAUCE IS TRADITIONALLY MADE WITH HOT CHILLIES, BUT SUBSTITUTE MILDER ONES, IF YOU PREFER.

MAKES FIFTEEN

INGREDIENTS

25g/1oz cellophane noodles soaked
  for 10 minutes in hot water to cover
6–8 dried wood ears, soaked for
  30 minutes in warm water to cover
225g/8oz minced (ground) pork
225g/8oz fresh or canned crab meat
4 spring onions (scallions), chopped
5ml/1 tsp Thai fish sauce (*nam pla*)
250g/9oz packet spring roll wrappers
flour and water paste, to seal
vegetable oil, for deep-frying
salt and ground black pepper

For the sauce
2 fresh red chillies, seeded
2 garlic cloves, chopped
15ml/1 tbsp granulated sugar
45ml/3 tbsp Thai fish sauce
  (*nam pla*)
juice of 1 lime or ½ lemon

2 Mix the noodles and the wood ears with the pork and set aside. Remove any cartilage from the crab meat and add to the pork mixture with the spring onions and Thai fish sauce. Season to taste, mixing well.

3 Place a spring roll wrapper in front of you, diamond-fashion. Spoon some mixture just below the centre, across the width, fold over the nearest point and roll once.

4 Fold in the sides to enclose the mixture, then brush the edges with flour paste and roll up to seal. Repeat with the remaining spring roll wrappers and filling mixture.

5 Heat the oil in a wok or deep-fryer to 190°C/375°F. Deep-fry the rolls in batches for 8–10 minutes or until they are cooked through. Drain them well on kitchen paper and serve hot. To eat, dip the rolls in the fiery chilli sauce.

1 Make the sauce by pounding the chillies and garlic to a paste. Scrape into a bowl and mix in the sugar and fish sauce, with citrus juice to taste. Drain the noodles and snip them into 2.5cm/1in lengths. Drain the wood ears, trim away any rough stems and slice the caps finely. Mix with the noodles.

COOK'S TIPS

• Wood ears (Chinese black fungus) is a gelatinous species collected and cultivated in China.
• Serve the rolls Vietnamese-style by wrapping each one in a lettuce leaf with a few sprigs of fresh mint and coriander (cilantro) and a stick of cucumber.

FIRECRACKERS

IT'S EASY TO SEE HOW THESE PASTRY-WRAPPED PRAWN SNACKS GOT THEIR NAME (KRATHAK IN THAI) — AS WELL AS RESEMBLING FIREWORKS, THEIR CONTENTS EXPLODE WITH FLAVOUR.

3 Place a wonton wrapper on the work surface at an angle so that it forms a diamond shape, then fold the top corner over so that the point is in the centre. Place a prawn, slits down, on the wrapper, with the tail projecting from the folded end, then fold the bottom corner over the other end of the prawn.

4 Fold each side of the wrapper over in turn to make a tightly folded roll. Tie a noodle in a bow around the roll and set it aside. Repeat with the remaining prawns and wrappers.

5 Heat the oil in a deep-fryer or wok to 190°C/375°F or until a cube of bread, added to the oil, browns in 45 seconds. Fry the prawns, a few at a time, for 5–8 minutes, until golden brown and cooked through. Drain well on kitchen paper and keep hot while you cook the remaining batches.

COOK'S TIP
Soak the fine egg noodles used as ties for the prawn rolls in a bowl of boiling water for 2–3 minutes, until softened, then drain, refresh under cold running water and drain well again.

MAKES SIXTEEN

INGREDIENTS
  16 large, raw king prawns (jumbo
    shrimp), heads and shells removed
    but tails left on
  5ml/1 tsp red curry paste
  15ml/1 tbsp Thai fish sauce
  16 small wonton wrappers, about
    8cm/3¼in square, thawed if frozen
  16 fine egg noodles, soaked
    (see Cook's Tip)
  oil, for deep-frying

1 Place the prawns on their sides and cut two slits through the underbelly of each, one about 1cm/½in from the head end and the other about 1cm/½in from the first cut, cutting across the prawn. This will prevent the prawns from curling when they are cooked.

2 Mix the curry paste with the fish sauce in a shallow dish. Add the prawns and turn them in the mixture until they are well coated. Cover and leave to marinate for 10 minutes.

CHILLI CRAB CLAWS

CRAB CLAWS ARE READILY AVAILABLE FROM THE FREEZER CABINET OF MANY ASIAN STORES AND SUPERMARKETS. THAW THEM THOROUGHLY AND DRY ON KITCHEN PAPER BEFORE COATING THEM.

SERVES FOUR

INGREDIENTS
50g/2oz/⅓ cup rice flour
15ml/1 tbsp cornflour (cornstarch)
2.5ml/½ tsp granulated sugar
1 egg
60ml/4 tbsp cold water
1 lemon grass stalk, root trimmed
2 garlic cloves, finely chopped
15ml/1 tbsp chopped fresh coriander (cilantro)
1–2 fresh red chillies, seeded and finely chopped
5ml/1 tsp Thai fish sauce
vegetable oil, for deep-frying
12 half-shelled crab claws
ground black pepper

For the chilli vinegar dip
45ml/3 tbsp granulated sugar
120ml/4fl oz/½ cup water
120ml/4fl oz/½ cup red wine vinegar
15ml/1 tbsp Thai fish sauce
2–4 fresh red chillies, seeded and chopped

1 First make the chilli vinegar dip. Mix the sugar and water in a pan. Heat gently, stirring until the sugar has dissolved, then bring to the boil. Lower the heat and simmer for 5–7 minutes. Stir in the rest of the ingredients, pour into a serving bowl and set aside.

2 Combine the rice flour, cornflour and sugar in a bowl. Beat the egg with the cold water, then stir the egg and water mixture into the flour mixture and beat well until it forms a light batter.

3 Cut off the lower 5cm/2in of the lemon grass stalk and chop it finely. Add the lemon grass to the batter, with the garlic, coriander, red chillies and fish sauce. Stir in pepper to taste.

4 Heat the oil in a deep-fryer or wok to 190°C/375°F or until a cube of bread browns in 45 seconds. Dip the crab claws into the batter, then fry, in batches, until golden. Serve with the dip.

Fresh fish is popular all over the world so fire up your fish with red hot chillies or chilli paste, pickle it with jalapeño chillies or turn it into a curry with aromatic warm spices. Although chillies have a reputation for robust flavour, they can also be surprisingly subtle, a fact that creative cooks have capitalized on for centuries. If it's fiery fish you're after, try Cajun Blackened Fish with Papaya Salsa or Balinese Fish Curry. Or step into calmer waters to savour Salmon with Tequila Cream Sauce or Seared Tuna with Red Onion Salsa.

Fiery Fish
and Seafood

SALT AND PEPPER PRAWNS

THIS SPICY DISH FLAVOURED WITH CHILLIES, GINGER AND FRIED SALT AND PEPPERCORNS
MAKES A DELICIOUS SUPPERTIME TREAT. SERVE WITH CRUSTY WARM BREAD.

2 Carefully remove and discard the heads and legs from the raw prawns. Leave the body shells and the tails in place. Pat the prepared prawns dry with kitchen paper.

3 Heat the oil for deep-frying to 190°C/375°F or until a cube of day-old bread, added to the oil, browns in 30–45 seconds. Fry the prawns for 1 minute, then lift them out and drain thoroughly on kitchen paper. Spoon 30ml/2 tbsp of the hot oil into a large frying pan, leaving the rest of the oil to one side to cool.

4 Heat the oil in the frying pan. Add the fried salt, with the finely chopped onion, garlic, ginger, chillies and sugar. Toss together for 1 minute, then add the prawns and toss them over the heat for 1 minute more until they are coated and the shells are impregnated with the seasonings. Serve at once, garnished with the spring onions.

SERVES THREE TO FOUR

INGREDIENTS
    15–18 large raw prawns (shrimp),
        in the shell, about 450g/1lb
    vegetable oil, for deep-frying
    1 small onion, finely chopped
    2 garlic cloves, crushed
    1cm/½in piece fresh root ginger,
        peeled and very finely grated
    2 fresh red chillies, seeded and sliced
    2.5ml/½ tsp granulated sugar
    3–4 spring onions (scallions), sliced,
        to garnish

For the fried salt
    10ml/2 tsp salt
    5ml/1 tsp Sichuan peppercorns

1 Make the fried salt by dry-frying the salt and peppercorns in a heavy frying pan over a medium heat until the peppercorns begin to release their aroma. Cool the mixture, then tip into a mortar and crush with a pestle or process in a blender.

COOK'S TIPS
• These succulent prawns beg to be eaten with the fingers, so provide finger bowls or hot cloths for your guests.
• "Fried salt" is also known as "Cantonese salt" or simply "salt and pepper mix". It is widely used as a table condiment or as a dip for deep-fried or roasted food, but can also be an ingredient, as here. It is best when freshly prepared.
• Black or white peppercorns can be substituted for the Sichuan peppercorns.

SPICY PRAWNS WITH OKRA

SERVES 4–6

INGREDIENTS

60–90ml/4–6 tbsp oil
225g/8oz okra, washed, dried and
  left whole
4 garlic cloves, crushed
5cm/2in piece of fresh root
  ginger, chopped
4–6 green chillies, cut diagonally
2.5ml/½ tsp ground turmeric
4–6 curry leaves
5ml/1 tsp cumin seeds
450g/1lb raw king prawns (jumbo
  shrimp), peeled and deveined
10ml/2 tsp brown sugar
juice of 2 lemons
salt, to taste

1 Heat the oil in a frying pan and cook the okra on a fairly high heat until they are slightly crisp and browned on all sides. Remove from the oil and keep aside on a piece of kitchen paper.

2 In the same oil, gently cook the garlic, ginger, chillies, turmeric, curry leaves and cumin seeds for 2–3 minutes. Add the prawns and mix well. Cook until the prawns are tender.

3 Add the salt, sugar, lemon juice and cooked okra. Increase the heat and quickly cook for a further 5 minutes, stirring gently to prevent the okra from breaking. Adjust the seasoning, if necessary. Serve hot.

COOK'S TIP
Okra should be cooked rapidly to prevent the pods from breaking up and releasing their distinctive thick, sticky liquid. Try to buy firm brightly coloured pods – larger pods may be tough or fibrous.

PRAWNS <u>IN</u> SPICED COCONUT SAUCE

SPICES, CHILLIES AND HERBS MAKE A FRAGRANT SAUCE FOR THIS DISH.

SERVES 4

INGREDIENTS
    24–30 large raw prawns (shrimp)
    spice seasoning, for dusting
    juice of 1 lemon
    30ml/2 tbsp butter or margarine
    1 onion, chopped
    2 garlic cloves, crushed
    30ml/2 tbsp tomato purée (paste)
    2.5ml/½ tsp dried thyme
    2.5ml/½ tsp ground cinnamon
    15ml/1 tbsp chopped coriander (cilantro)
    ½ hot chilli pepper, chopped
    175g/6oz/1 cup frozen or
        canned corn
    300ml/½ pint/1¼ cups
        coconut milk
    chopped fresh coriander,
        to garnish

1 Sprinkle the prawns with spice seasoning and lemon juice and marinate in a cool place for an hour.

2 Melt the butter or margarine in a pan, cook the onion and garlic for 5 minutes, until slightly softened. Add the prawns and cook for a few minutes, stirring occasionally until cooked through and pink.

3 Transfer the prawns, onion and garlic to a bowl, leaving behind some of the buttery liquid. Add the tomato purée to the pan and cook over a low heat, stirring thoroughly. Add the thyme, cinnamon, coriander and hot pepper and stir well.

4 Blend the corn (reserving 15ml/ 1 tbsp) in a blender or food processor with the coconut milk. Add to the pan and simmer until reduced. Add the prawns and reserved corn, and simmer for 5 minutes. Serve hot, garnished with coriander.

COOK'S TIP
If you use raw king prawns (jumbo shrimp), make a stock from the shells and use in place of some of the coconut milk.

CURRIED PRAWNS <u>AND</u> SALTFISH

SHRIMP PASTE AND SPICES ADD TASTY FLAVOUR TO THIS FISH DISH.

SERVES 4

INGREDIENTS
    450g/1 lb raw prawns
        (shrimp), peeled
    15ml/1 tbsp spice seasoning
    25g/1oz/2 tbsp butter
        or margarine
    15ml/1 tbsp olive oil
    2 shallots, finely chopped
    1 garlic clove, crushed
    350g/12oz okra, trimmed and cut
        into 2.5cm/1 in lengths
    5ml/1 tsp curry powder
    10ml/2 tsp shrimp paste
    15ml/1 tbsp chopped fresh
        coriander (cilantro)
    15ml/1 tbsp lemon juice
    175g/6oz prepared saltfish (see
        Cook's Tip), shredded

1 Season the prawns with the spice seasoning and leave to marinate in a cool place for about 1 hour.

2 Heat the butter or margarine and olive oil in a large frying pan or wok over a medium heat and stir-fry the shallots and garlic for 5 minutes. Add the okra, curry powder and shrimp paste, stir well and cook for about 10 minutes, until the okra is tender.

3 Add 30ml/2 tbsp water, coriander, lemon juice, prawns and saltfish, and cook gently for 5–10 minutes. Adjust the seasoning and serve hot.

COOK'S TIP
Soak the saltfish for 12 hours, changing the water two or three times. Rinse, bring to the boil in fresh water, then cool.

STIR-FRIED PRAWNS WITH TAMARIND

THE SOUR, TANGY FLAVOUR THAT IS CHARACTERISTIC OF MANY THAI DISHES COMES FROM TAMARIND. FRESH TAMARIND PODS CAN SOMETIMES BE BOUGHT, BUT PREPARING THEM IS A LABORIOUS PROCESS. THE THAIS PREFER TO USE COMPRESSED BLOCKS OF TAMARIND PASTE, WHICH IS SIMPLY SOAKED IN WARM WATER AND THEN STRAINED.

SERVES 4–6

INGREDIENTS

50g/2oz tamarind paste
150ml/¼ pint/⅔ cup boiling water
30ml/2 tbsp vegetable oil
30ml/2 tbsp chopped onion
30ml/2 tbsp palm sugar
30ml/2 tbsp chicken stock or water
15ml/1 tbsp fish sauce
6 dried red chillies, fried
450g/1lb raw shelled
  prawns (shrimp)
15ml/1 tbsp fried chopped garlic
30ml/2 tbsp fried sliced shallots
2 spring onions (scallions), chopped,
  to garnish

1 Put the tamarind paste in a small bowl, pour over the boiling water and stir well to break up any lumps. Leave to stand for 30 minutes. Strain, pushing as much of the juice through as possible. Measure 90ml/6 tbsp of the tamarind juice, the amount needed, and store the remainder in the refrigerator. Heat the oil in a wok. Add the chopped onion and cook until golden brown.

2 Add the sugar, stock, fish sauce, dried chillies and the tamarind juice, stirring well until the sugar dissolves. Bring to the boil.

3 Add the prawns, garlic and shallots. Stir-fry until the prawns are cooked, about 3–4 minutes. Garnish with the spring onions.

SPICY PRAWNS WITH CORNMEAL

THESE CRISPY FRIED PRAWNS WITH A CORNMEAL COATING AND A CHEESE TOPPING ARE
DELICIOUS WHEN SERVED WITH A SPICY TOMATO SALSA AND LIME WEDGES TO EASE THE HEAT.

SERVES 4

INGREDIENTS
115g/4oz/¾ cup cornmeal
5–10ml/1–2 tsp
  cayenne pepper
2.5ml/½ tsp ground cumin
5ml/1 tsp salt
30ml/2 tbsp chopped
  fresh coriander (cilantro)
  or parsley
900g/2lb large raw prawns (shrimp),
  peeled and deveined
flour, for dredging
¼ cup vegetable oil
115g/4oz/1 cup grated
  Cheddar cheese
lime wedges and tomato salsa,
  to serve

1 Preheat the grill (broiler). In a mixing bowl, combine the cornmeal, cayenne, cumin, salt and coriander or parsley.

COOK'S TIP
Fresh prawns (shrimp) should be eaten as soon as possible after purchase. All fresh raw prawns should have crisp, firm shells and a fresh smell. Do not buy them if they smell of ammonia.

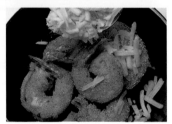

2 Coat the prawns lightly in flour, then dip them in water and roll them in the cornmeal mixture to coat.

3 Heat the oil in a non-stick frying pan. When hot, add the prawns, in batches if necessary. Cook them until they are opaque throughout, for about 2–3 minutes on each side. Drain on kitchen paper.

4 Place the prawns in a large ovenproof dish, or in individual dishes. Sprinkle the cheese evenly over the top. Grill (broil) about 8cm/3in from the heat until the cheese melts, for about 2–3 minutes. Serve immediately, with lime wedges and tomato salsa.

PINEAPPLE CURRY WITH PRAWNS AND MUSSELS

THE DELICATE SWEET AND SOUR FLAVOUR OF THIS CURRY COMES FROM THE PINEAPPLE AND ALTHOUGH IT SEEMS AN ODD COMBINATION, IT IS RATHER DELICIOUS. USE THE VERY FRESHEST SHELLFISH THAT YOU CAN FIND.

SERVES 4–6

INGREDIENTS

600ml/1 pint/2½ cups coconut milk
30ml/2 tbsp red curry paste
30ml/2 tbsp fish sauce
15ml/1 tbsp granulated sugar
225g/8oz king prawns (jumbo
  shrimp), peeled and deveined
450g/1lb mussels, scrubbed and
  beards removed
175g/6oz fresh pineapple, finely
  crushed or chopped
5 kaffir lime leaves, torn
2 red chillies, chopped, and
  coriander (cilantro) leaves,
  to garnish

1 In a large pan, bring half the coconut milk to the boil and heat, stirring, until it separates.

2 Add the red curry paste and cook until fragrant. Add the fish sauce and sugar and continue to cook for a few moments.

3 Stir in the rest of the coconut milk and bring back to the boil. Add the king prawns, mussels, pineapple and kaffir lime leaves.

4 Reheat until boiling and then simmer for 3–5 minutes, until the prawns are cooked and the mussels have opened. Remove any mussels that have not opened and discard. Serve garnished with chopped red chillies and coriander leaves.

CURRIED PRAWNS IN COCONUT MILK

A CURRY-LIKE DISH WHERE THE PRAWNS ARE COOKED IN A SPICY COCONUT GRAVY.

SERVES 4–6

INGREDIENTS

600ml/1 pint/2½ cups coconut milk
30ml/2 tbsp yellow curry paste (see
  Cook's Tip)
15ml/1 tbsp fish sauce
2.5ml/½ tsp salt
5ml/1 tsp granulated sugar
450g/1lb king prawns (jumbo
  shrimp), peeled, tails left intact
  and deveined
225g/8oz cherry tomatoes
juice of ½ lime, to serve
2 red chillies, cut into strips, and
  coriander (cilantro) leaves,
  to garnish

1 Put half the coconut milk into a pan or wok and bring to the boil.

2 Add the yellow curry paste to the coconut milk, stir until it disperses, then simmer for about 10 minutes.

3 Add the fish sauce, salt, sugar and remaining coconut milk. Simmer for another 5 minutes.

4 Add the prawns and cherry tomatoes. Simmer very gently for about 5 minutes, until the prawns are pink and tender.

5 Serve the curried prawns sprinkled with lime juice and garnish the dish with chillies and coriander.

COOK'S TIP
To make yellow curry paste, process together 6–8 yellow chillies, 1 chopped lemon grass stalk, 4 peeled shallots, 4 garlic cloves, 15ml/1 tbsp peeled chopped fresh root ginger, 5ml/1 tsp coriander seeds, 5ml/1 tsp mustard powder, 5ml/1 tsp salt, 2.5ml/½ tsp ground cinnamon, 15ml/1 tbsp light brown sugar and 30ml/2 tbsp oil in a blender or food procesor. When a paste has formed, transfer to a glass jar and keep in the refrigerator.

PRAWNS WITH CHAYOTE IN TURMERIC SAUCE

GALANGAL, RED CHILLIES AND TURMERIC ADD DISTINCTIVE HOT AND SPICY FLAVOURS TO THIS TASTY INDONESIAN DISH.

SERVES 4

INGREDIENTS

1–2 chayotes or 2–3
  courgettes (zucchini)
2 fresh red chillies, seeded
1 onion, quartered
5mm/½ in fresh galangal, peeled
1 lemon grass stalk, lower 5cm/2in
  sliced, top bruised
2.5cm/1in fresh turmeric, peeled
200ml/7fl oz/scant 1 cup water
lemon juice
400ml/14fl oz can coconut milk
450g/1 lb cooked peeled
  prawns (shrimp)
salt
red chilli shreds, to
  garnish (optional)
boiled rice, to serve

1 Peel the chayotes, remove the seeds and cut into strips. If using courgettes, cut into 5cm/2in strips.

2 Grind the fresh red chillies, onion, sliced galangal, sliced lemon grass and the fresh turmeric to a paste in a food processor or with a mortar and pestle. Add the water to the paste mixture, with a squeeze of lemon juice and salt to taste.

3 Pour into a pan. Add the top of the lemon grass stalk. Bring to the boil and cook for 1–2 minutes. Add the chayote or courgette pieces and cook for 2 minutes. Stir in the coconut milk. Taste and adjust the seasoning.

4 Stir in the prawns and cook gently for 2–3 minutes. Remove the lemon grass stalk. Garnish with shreds of chilli, if using, and serve with rice.

INDONESIAN SPICY FISH

FISH IS GIVEN A HOT, PIQUANT TWIST IN THIS FLAVOURFUL DISH.

SERVES 6–8

INGREDIENTS

1 kg/2¼ lb fresh mackerel
  fillets, skinned
30ml/2 tbsp tamarind pulp,
  soaked in 200ml/7fl oz/scant
  1 cup water
1 onion
1cm/½ in fresh galangal, peeled
2 garlic cloves
1–2 fresh red chillies, seeded, or
  5ml/1 tsp chilli powder
5ml/1 tsp ground coriander
5ml/1 tsp ground turmeric
2.5ml/½ tsp ground
  fennel seeds
15ml/1 tbsp dark
  brown sugar
90–105ml/6–7 tbsp oil
200ml/7fl oz/scant 1 cup
  coconut cream
salt and ground black pepper
fresh chilli shreds, to garnish

1 Rinse the fish fillets in cold water and dry them well on kitchen paper. Put into a shallow dish and sprinkle with a little salt. Strain the tamarind and pour the juice over the fish fillets. Leave for 30 minutes.

2 Quarter the onion, peel and slice the galangal and peel the garlic. Grind the onion, galangal, garlic and chillies or chilli powder to a paste in a food processor. Add the ground coriander, turmeric, fennel seeds and sugar.

3 Heat half of the oil in a frying pan. Drain the fish fillets and cook for 5 minutes, or until tender. Set aside.

4 Wipe the pan and heat the remaining oil. Fry the spice paste, stirring constantly, until it gives off a spicy aroma. Do not let it brown. Add the coconut cream and simmer gently for a few minutes. Add the fish fillets and gently heat through.

5 Taste for seasoning and serve the mackerel sprinkled with shredded chilli.

FLASH-FRIED SQUID WITH PAPRIKA AND GARLIC

THESE QUICK-FRIED SQUID ARE GOOD SERVED WITH A DRY SHERRY AS AN APPETIZER OR AS PART OF MIXED TAPAS. SERVE THEM ON A BED OF SALAD LEAVES.

SERVES FOUR TO SIX

INGREDIENTS
500g/1¼lb very small squid, cleaned
90ml/6 tbsp olive oil
1 fresh red chilli, seeded and
 finely chopped
10ml/2 tsp Spanish mild smoked
 paprika (*pimentón dulce*)
30ml/2 tbsp plain (all-purpose) flour
2 garlic cloves, finely chopped
15ml/1 tbsp sherry vinegar
5ml/1 tsp shredded lemon rind
30–45ml/2–3 tbsp finely chopped
 fresh parsley
salt and ground black pepper
salad leaves, to serve (optional)

1 Choose small squid that are no longer than 10cm/4in. Cut the body sacs into rings and cut the tentacles into bitesize pieces.

2 Place the squid in a bowl and add 30ml/2 tbsp of the oil, half the chilli and the paprika. Season with a little salt and some pepper, cover and marinate for 2–4 hours in the refrigerator.

COOK'S TIPS
• Make sure the wok or pan is very hot, as the squid should cook for only 1–2 minutes: any longer and it will begin to toughen.
• Smoked paprika, known as *pimentón dulce* in Spain, has a wonderful smoky flavour. If you cannot find it, use mild paprika, which should be described as such on the packet.

3 Heat the remaining oil in a preheated wok or fairly deep frying pan over a high heat until very hot. Toss the squid in the flour and divide it into 2 batches. Add the first batch of squid to the wok or frying pan and stir-fry quickly, turning the squid constantly for 1–2 minutes, or until the squid rings become opaque and the tentacles have curled.

4 Sprinkle in half the garlic. Stir to mix then turn out on to a plate and keep warm. Repeat the stir-frying with the second batch of squid and garlic.

5 Sprinkle the sherry vinegar, lemon rind, remaining chilli and parsley over the squid. Taste for seasoning and serve hot or cool, on a bed of salad leaves, if you like.

CARIBBEAN CHILLI CRAB CAKES

CRAB MEAT MAKES WONDERFUL FISH CAKES, AS EVIDENCED WITH THESE GUTSY MORSELS.
THE RICH, SPICY TOMATO DIP IS DELICIOUS, AND YOU CAN SUBSTITUTE FRESH TOMATOES.

MAKES ABOUT FIFTEEN

INGREDIENTS
- 225g/8oz white crab meat (fresh, frozen or canned)
- 115g/4oz cooked floury potatoes, mashed
- 30ml/2 tbsp fresh herb seasoning
- 2.5ml/½ tsp mild mustard
- 2.5ml/½ tsp ground black pepper
- ½ fresh hot chilli, seeded and finely chopped
- 5ml/1 tsp chopped fresh oregano
- 1 egg, beaten
- plain (all-purpose) flour, for dredging
- vegetable oil, for frying
- lime wedges, coriander (cilantro) sprigs and fresh whole chillies, to garnish

For the tomato dip
- 15g/½oz/1 tbsp butter
- ½ onion, finely chopped
- 2 drained canned plum tomatoes, chopped
- 1 garlic clove, crushed
- 150ml/¼ pint/⅔ cup water
- 5–10ml/1–2 tsp malt vinegar
- 15ml/1 tbsp chopped fresh coriander (cilantro)
- ½ fresh chilli, seeded and chopped

1 To make the crab cakes, mix the crab meat, potatoes, herb seasoning, mustard, pepper, chilli, oregano and egg in a large bowl. Chill the mixture in the bowl for at least 30 minutes.

COOK'S TIP
Use French Dijon mustard for this dish as it is not as overpowering as English.

2 Meanwhile, make the tomato dip. Melt the butter in a small pan and sauté the onion, tomatoes and garlic for about 5 minutes until the onion is tender. Add the water, vinegar, coriander and fresh chilli. Bring to the boil, then reduce the heat and simmer for 10 minutes.

3 Pour the mixture into a blender or food processor and blend to a smooth purée. Scrape into a pan or bowl. Keep warm or chill.

4 Preheat the oven. Using a spoon, shape the crab mixture into rounds and dredge with flour, shaking off the excess. Heat a little oil in a frying pan and fry, a few at a time, for 2–3 minutes on each side. Drain the crab cakes on kitchen paper and keep warm in a low oven while cooking the remainder.

5 Garnish with lime wedges, coriander sprigs and whole chillies. Serve with the tomato dip.

CHILLI CRABS

THERE ARE VARIATIONS ON THIS RECIPE ALL OVER ASIA, BUT ALL ARE HOT AND SPICY. THIS DELICIOUS DISH OWES ITS SPICINESS AND FLAVOUR TO CHILLIES, GINGER AND SHRIMP PASTE.

SERVES 4

INGREDIENTS

- 2 cooked crabs, about 675g/1½lb
- 1cm/½in cube shrimp paste
- 2 garlic cloves
- 2 fresh red chillies, seeded, or 5ml/1 tsp chopped chilli from a jar
- 1cm/½in fresh root ginger, peeled and sliced
- 60ml/4 tbsp sunflower oil
- 300ml/½ pint/1¼ cups tomato ketchup
- 15ml/1 tbsp dark brown sugar
- 150ml/¼ pint/⅔ cup warm water
- 4 spring onions (scallions), chopped, to garnish
- cucumber chunks and hot toast, to serve (optional)

1 Remove the large claws of one crab and turn on to its back, with the head facing away from you. Use your thumbs to push the body up from the main shell. Discard the stomach sac and "dead men's fingers", i.e. lungs and any green matter. Leave the creamy brown meat in the shell and cut the shell in half, with a cleaver or strong knife. Cut the body section in half and crack the claws with a sharp blow from a hammer or cleaver. Avoid splintering the claws. Repeat with the other crab.

2 Grind the shrimp paste, garlic, chillies and root ginger to a paste with a mortar and pestle.

3 Heat a work and add the oil. Fry the spice paste, stirring it all the time, without browning.

4 Stir in the tomato ketchup, sugar and water and mix the sauce well. When just boiling, add all the crab pieces and toss in the sauce until well-coated and hot. Serve in a large bowl, sprinkled with the spring onions. Place in the centre of the table for everyone to help themselves. Accompany this finger-licking dish with cool cucumber chunks and hot toast for mopping up the sauce, if you like.

FIVE-SPICE SQUID WITH CHILLI AND BLACK BEAN SAUCE

SQUID IS PERFECT FOR STIR-FRYING AS IT BENEFITS FROM BEING FAST COOKING. THE SPICY SAUCE MAKES THE IDEAL ACCOMPANIMENT AND CAN BE MADE VERY QUICKLY.

SERVES SIX

INGREDIENTS
- 450g/1lb small prepared squid
- 45ml/3 tbsp oil
- 2.5cm/1in piece fresh root ginger, grated (shredded)
- 1 garlic clove, crushed
- 8 spring onions (scallions), cut diagonally into 2.5cm/1in lengths
- 1 red (bell) pepper, seeded and cut into strips
- 1 fresh green chilli, seeded and thinly sliced
- 6 mushrooms, sliced
- 5ml/1 tsp five-spice powder
- 30ml/2 tbsp black bean sauce
- 30ml/2 tbsp soy sauce
- 5ml/1 tsp granulated sugar
- 15ml/1 tbsp rice wine or dry sherry

2 Heat a wok briefly and add the oil. When it is hot, stir-fry the squid quickly. Remove the squid strips from the wok with a slotted spoon and set aside. Add the ginger, garlic, spring onions, red pepper, chilli and mushrooms to the oil in the wok and stir-fry for 2 minutes.

3 Return the partially cooked squid to the wok and stir in the five-spice powder. Stir in the black bean sauce, soy sauce, sugar and rice wine or sherry. Bring to the boil and cook, stirring, for 1 minute. Serve immediately in warmed bowls.

1 Rinse the squid and pull away the outer skin. Dry on kitchen paper. Make a lengthways slit down the body of each squid, then open out the body flat. Score the outside of the bodies in a criss-cross pattern with the tip of a sharp knife. Cut the squid into strips.

CHARGRILLED SQUID <u>WITH</u> CHILLIES

IF YOU LIKE YOUR FOOD HOT, USE THE CHILLI SEEDS WITH THE FLESH. IF NOT, SLIT THE CHILLIES IN HALF LENGTHWAYS, AND SCRAPE OUT THE SEEDS AND DISCARD THEM.

SERVES TWO

INGREDIENTS
2 whole prepared squid,
  with tentacles
75ml/5 tbsp olive oil
30ml/2 tbsp balsamic vinegar
250g/9 oz/1¼ cups hot cooked rice
2 fresh red chillies, finely chopped
60ml/4 tbsp dry white wine
salt and ground black pepper
sprigs of fresh parsley, to garnish

1 Rinse the squid and pull away the outer skin. Dry on kitchen paper. Make a lengthways cut down the body of each squid, and open out flat. Score the flesh on both sides of the bodies in a criss-cross pattern. Chop the tentacles. Place all the squid in a china or glass dish. Whisk the oil and vinegar in a small bowl, season to taste and pour over the squid. Cover and marinate for about 1 hour.

2 Heat a ridged cast-iron pan. When hot, add 1 squid body. Cook over a medium heat for 2–3 minutes, pressing with a spatula to keep it flat. Repeat on the other side. Cook the other squid body in the same way.

3 Cut the squid bodies into diagonal strips. Pile the rice into the centre of 2 heated soup plates and top with the squid, arranging them criss-cross fashion. Keep hot either in the oven or over pans of simmering water while you cook the tentacles and chillies.

4 Heat a pan. Add the marinated chopped tentacles and the finely chopped chillies to the pan and toss over a medium heat for 2 minutes. Stir in the marinade and wine, then drizzle the mixture over the squid and rice. Garnish with the parsley and serve.

STEAMED FISH <u>WITH</u> CHILLI SAUCE

CHILLIES CAN BE USED IN MANY DIFFERENT WAYS. HERE THEY FLAVOUR A WHOLE FISH SIMPLY BY BEING STREWN OVER DURING STEAMING. AN EXTRA KICK COMES FROM THE HOT SAUCE.

SERVES FOUR

INGREDIENTS

1 large, firm fish such as bass or
   grouper, scaled and cleaned
1 fresh banana leaf or piece of foil
2 lemon grass stalks, trimmed
30ml/2 tbsp rice wine
3 fresh red chillies, seeded and
   finely sliced
2 garlic cloves, finely chopped
2cm/¾in piece fresh root ginger,
   finely shredded
2 spring onions (scallions), chopped
30ml/2 tbsp Thai fish sauce (*nam pla*)
juice of 1 lime

For the hot chilli sauce
10 fresh red chillies, seeded and
   roughly chopped
4 garlic cloves, halved
60ml/4 tbsp Thai fish sauce (*nam pla*)
15ml/1 tbsp granulated sugar
75ml/5 tbsp lime juice

1 Rinse the fish under cold running water. Pat dry with kitchen paper. With a sharp knife, slash the skin of the fish a few times on both sides.

2 Place the fish on a banana leaf or a piece of foil. Cut off the lower 5cm/2in of the lemon grass and chop it finely. Put it in a bowl, stir in all the remaining ingredients and spoon the mixture over the fish.

COOK'S TIP

Ten chillies may seem a lot for the sauce, but bear in mind that the mixture is meant to be used sparingly.

3 Place a rack or a small upturned plate in the base of a wok and pour in boiling water to a depth of 5cm/2in. Lift the banana leaf or piece of foil holding the fish, and place on the rack or plate (the water should not come into contact with the fish). Cover with a lid and steam for about 10–15 minutes or until the fish is cooked.

4 Place all the chilli sauce ingredients in a food processor and process until smooth. You may need to add a little cold water. Scrape into a bowl.

5 Serve the fish hot, on the banana leaf if you like, with the chilli sauce to spoon sparingly over the top. This dish goes very well with boiled rice or potatoes.

SPICED SCALLOPS IN THEIR SHELLS

SCALLOPS ARE EXCELLENT STEAMED. WHEN SERVED WITH THIS SPICY GINGER AND CHILLI SAUCE, THEY MAKE A DELICIOUS APPETIZER.

SERVES FOUR

INGREDIENTS

    8 scallops, shelled (ask the fishmonger
      to reserve the cupped side of 4 shells)
    2 slices fresh root ginger, shredded
    1 garlic clove, shredded
    2 spring onions (scallions), green
      parts only, shredded
    salt and ground black pepper

For the sauce
    1 garlic clove, crushed
    15ml/1 tbsp grated (shredded) fresh
      root ginger
    2 spring onions (scallions), white
      parts only, chopped
    1–2 fresh green chillies, seeded and
      finely chopped
    15ml/1 tbsp light soy sauce
    15ml/1 tbsp dark soy sauce
    10ml/2 tsp sesame oil

1 Remove the dark beard-like fringe and tough muscle from the scallops. Leave the corals attached.

COOK'S TIPS
• When the fishmonger is preparing the scallops, ask for the gills and mantle to use in soup or stock.
• If you do not have a bamboo steamer, you can use a flat-based stainless steel steamer or flour sifter.

2 Place 2 scallops in each shell. Season lightly with salt and pepper, then sprinkle the ginger, garlic and spring onion green on top. Place the shells in a bamboo steamer and steam for about 6 minutes until the scallops look opaque (you may do this in batches).

3 Meanwhile, make the sauce. Mix the garlic and ginger in a bowl and stir in the white parts of the spring onions. Add the chillies, both soy sauces and the sesame oil. Stir well and set aside.

4 Carefully remove each shell from the steamer, taking care not to spill the juices, and arrange them on a serving plate with the sauce bowl in the centre. Serve immediately.

MUSSELS IN CHILLI AND BLACK BEAN SAUCE

THE LARGE GREEN-SHELLED MUSSELS FROM NEW ZEALAND ARE PERFECT FOR THIS DELICIOUS DISH. BUY THE COOKED MUSSELS ON THE HALF-SHELL.

2 Remove the sauce from the heat and stir in the sesame oil and soy sauce. Mix thoroughly.

3 Have ready a bamboo steamer or a pan holding 5cm/2in of simmering water, and fitted with a metal trivet. Place the mussels in a single layer on a heatproof plate that will fit inside the steamer or pan. Spoon over the sauce.

SERVES FOUR

INGREDIENTS

- 15ml/1 tbsp vegetable oil
- 2.5cm/1in piece of fresh root ginger, finely chopped
- 2 garlic clove, finely chopped
- 1 fresh red chilli, seeded and chopped
- 15ml/1 tbsp black bean sauce
- 15ml/1 tbsp dry sherry
- 5ml/1 tsp granulated sugar
- 5ml/1 tsp sesame oil
- 10ml/2 tsp dark soy sauce
- 20 cooked New Zealand green-shelled mussels
- 2 spring onions (scallions), 1 shredded and 1 cut into fine rings

1 Heat the vegetable oil in a pan or wok. Fry the ginger, garlic and chilli with the black bean sauce for a few seconds, then add the sherry and sugar and cook for 30 seconds more, stirring with cooking chopsticks or a wooden spoon to ensure the sugar is dissolved.

4 Sprinkle all the spring onions over the mussels. Place in the steamer or cover the plate tightly with foil and place it on the trivet in the pan. It should be just above the level of the water. Cover and steam over a high heat for about 10 minutes or until the mussels have heated through. Serve immediately.

PRAWNS <u>IN</u> SPICY TOMATO SAUCE

*CUMIN AND CINNAMON ADD SUBTLE SPICINESS TO THIS DELICIOUS, SIMPLE-TO-MAKE
SPICY PRAWN RECIPE, WHICH COMES FROM THE MIDDLE EAST.*

SERVES 4

INGREDIENTS

30ml/2 tbsp oil
2 onions, finely chopped
2–3 garlic cloves, crushed
5–6 tomatoes, peeled
  and chopped
30ml/2 tbsp tomato
  purée (paste)
120ml/4fl oz/½ cup fish stock
  or water
2.5ml/½ tsp ground cumin
2.5ml/½ tsp ground cinnamon
450g/1 lb raw, peeled Mediterranean
  prawns (shrimp)
juice of 1 lemon
salt and ground black pepper
fresh parsley, to garnish
rice, to serve

1 Heat the oil in a large frying pan and cook the onions for 3–4 minutes, until golden. Add the garlic, cook for about 1 minute, and then stir in the tomatoes.

2 Blend the tomato purée with the stock or water and stir into the pan with the cumin, cinnamon and seasoning. Simmer, covered, over a low heat for 15 minutes, stirring occasionally. Do not allow to boil.

3 Add the prawns and lemon juice and simmer the sauce for a further 10–15 minutes over a low to medium heat until the prawns are cooked and the stock is reduced by about half.

4 Serve with plain rice or in a decorative ring of Persian Rice, garnished with sprigs of fresh parsley.

SPICED FISH KEBABS

MARINATING ADDS SPICY FLAVOUR TO THESE DELICIOUS KEBABS.

SERVES 4–6

900g/2lb swordfish steaks
45ml/3 tbsp olive oil
juice of ½ lemon
1 garlic clove, crushed
5ml/1 tsp cayenne pepper
3 tomatoes, quartered
2 onions, cut into wedges
salt and ground black pepper
salad and pitta bread, to serve

1 Cut the fish into large cubes and place in a dish.

2 Blend together the oil, lemon juice, garlic, paprika and seasoning in a small mixing bowl and pour over the fish. Cover loosely with clear film (plastic wrap) and leave to marinate in a cool place for up to 2 hours.

3 Thread the fish cubes on to skewers alternating the fish with pieces of tomato and onion.

4 Grill the kebabs over hot charcoal for 5–10 minutes, basting frequently with the remaining marinade and turning occasionally. Serve with salad and pitta bread.

THREE-COLOUR FISH KEBABS

FOR FOOD TO BE APPETIZING, IT NEEDS TO LOOK AS WELL AS TASTE GOOD, AND THIS DISH,
WITH ITS SWEET TOMATO AND CHILLI SALSA, SCORES ON BOTH COUNTS.

SERVES FOUR

INGREDIENTS
   120ml/4fl oz/½ cup olive oil
   finely grated (shredded) rind and
      juice of 1 large lemon
   5ml/1 tsp crushed chilli flakes
   350g/12oz monkfish fillet, cubed
   350g/12oz swordfish fillet, cubed
   350g/12oz thick salmon fillet or
      steak, cubed
   2 red, yellow or orange (bell)
      peppers, cored, seeded and cut
      into squares
   30ml/2 tbsp finely chopped fresh flat
      leaf parsley
   salt and ground black pepper

For the salsa
   2 ripe tomatoes, finely chopped
   1 garlic clove, crushed
   1 fresh red chilli, seeded and chopped
   45ml/3 tbsp extra virgin olive oil
   15ml/1 tbsp lemon juice
   15ml/1 tbsp finely chopped fresh flat
      leaf parsley
   pinch of granulated sugar

1 Put the oil in a shallow glass or china bowl and add the lemon rind and juice, the chilli flakes and pepper to taste. Whisk to combine, then add the fish chunks. Turn to coat evenly.

2 Add the pepper squares, stir, then cover and marinate in a cool place for 1 hour, turning occasionally. Preheat the grill (broiler) or prepare the barbecue.

COOK'S TIP
Don't let the fish marinate for more than an hour. The lemon juice will start to break down the fibres of the fish after this time and it will be quickly overcooked.

3 Drain the fish and peppers, reserving the marinade, then thread them on to 8 oiled metal skewers. Barbecue or grill (broil) the skewered fish for 5–8 minutes, turning once to ensure even cooking.

4 Meanwhile, make the salsa by mixing all the ingredients in a bowl, seasoning to taste with salt and pepper. Heat the reserved marinade in a small pan, remove from the heat and stir in the parsley, with salt and pepper to taste. Serve the fish kebabs hot, with the marinade spooned over, accompanied by the tomato and chilli salsa.

SEARED TUNA <u>WITH</u> RED ONION SALSA

*A FRUITY CHILLI SUCH AS ITALIA WOULD BE GOOD IN THIS SALSA, AS WOULD A
PEACHY POBLANO CHILLI. THE SALSA MAKES A FINE ACCOMPANIMENT FOR THE TUNA.*

SERVES FOUR

INGREDIENTS

    4 tuna loin steaks, each weighing
      about 175–200g/6–7oz
    5ml/1 tsp cumin seeds, toasted
      and crushed
    pinch of dried red chilli flakes
    grated (shredded) rind and juice
      of 1 lime
    45–60ml/3–4 tbsp extra virgin olive oil
    salt and ground black pepper
    lime wedges and coriander (cilantro)
      sprigs, to garnish

For the salsa

    1 small red onion, finely chopped
    6 red or yellow cherry tomatoes,
      roughly chopped
    1 avocado, peeled, stoned (pitted)
      and chopped
    2 kiwi fruit, peeled and chopped
    1 fresh red or green chilli, seeded
      and finely chopped
    60ml/4 tbsp chopped fresh
      coriander (cilantro)
    leaves from 6 fresh mint sprigs,
      finely chopped
    5–10ml/1–2 tsp Thai fish sauce
      (*nam pla*)
    about 5ml/1 tsp muscovado
      (molasses) sugar

1 Wash the tuna steaks and pat them dry with kitchen paper. Sprinkle with half the crushed cumin seeds, the dried chilli flakes, a little salt and freshly ground black pepper and half the lime rind and juice. Rub in 30ml/ 2 tbsp of the olive oil and set aside in a glass or china dish for 30 minutes.

2 Meanwhile, make the salsa: mix the onion, tomatoes, avocado, kiwi fruit, fresh chilli, chopped coriander and mint in a bowl. Add the remaining crushed cumin, the rest of the lime rind and half the remaining lime juice. Add Thai fish sauce and sugar to taste. Set aside for 15–20 minutes for the flavours to develop, then add a further seasoning of Thai fish sauce, lime juice and extra virgin olive oil to taste.

3 Heat a ridged, cast-iron grill (broiling) pan for at least 5 minutes. Cook the tuna, allowing about 3 minutes on each side if you like it rare or a little longer for a medium result.

4 Serve the tuna steaks immediately, garnished with lime wedges and coriander sprigs. Serve the salsa separately or spoon some or all of it on the plates with the tuna.

BRAISED FISH <u>IN</u> CHILLI <u>AND</u> GARLIC SAUCE

SERVES 4–6

INGREDIENTS

1 bream or trout, 675g/
   1½ lb, cleaned
15ml/1 tbsp light soy sauce
15ml/1 tbsp Chinese rice wine
vegetable oil, for deep-frying

For the sauce
2 garlic cloves, finely chopped
2–3 spring onions (scallions),
   finely chopped
5ml/1 tsp chopped fresh root ginger
30ml/2 tbsp chilli bean sauce
15ml/1 tbsp tomato purée (paste)
10ml/2 tsp light brown sugar
15ml/1 tbsp rice vinegar
about 120ml/4fl oz/½ cup fish stock
15ml/1 tbsp cornflour
   (cornstarch) paste
few drops sesame oil

1 Rinse and dry the fish well. Using a sharp knife, score both sides of the fish as far down as the bone with diagonal cuts about 2.5cm/1in apart.

2 Rub the whole fish with soy sauce and wine on both sides, then leave to marinate for 10–15 minutes.

3 In a wok, deep-fry the fish in hot oil for about 3–4 minutes on both sides until golden brown.

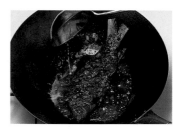

4 Pour off the excess oil, leaving a thin layer in the wok. Push the fish to one side of the wok and add the garlic, the white part of the spring onions, fresh ginger, chilli bean sauce, tomato purée, brown sugar, rice vinegar and stock. Bring to the boil and braise the fish in the sauce for about 4–5 minutes, turning it over once. Add the green part of the chopped spring onions. Thicken the sauce with the cornflour paste, sprinkle with the sesame oil and place on a dish to serve immediately.

VARIATION
Any whole fish is suitable for this dish; try sea bass, grouper or grey mullet, if you like. If you can't find Chinese wine, use dry sherry instead.

SALT COD <u>IN</u> MILD CHILLI SAUCE

SERVES 6

INGREDIENTS
  900g/2lb dried salt cod
  1 onion, chopped
  2 garlic cloves, chopped

For the sauce
  6 dried ancho chillies
  1 onion, chopped
  2.5ml/½ tsp dried oregano
  2.5ml/½ tsp ground coriander
  1 serrano chilli, seeded
    and chopped
  45ml/3 tbsp corn oil
  750ml/1½ pints/3 cups
    good-quality fish or
    chicken stock
  salt

For the garnish
  1 fresh green chilli, sliced

COOK'S TIP
Dried salt cod is a great favourite in
Spain and Portugal and throughout Latin
America. Look for it in Spanish and
Portuguese markets.

1 Soak the cod in cold water for several hours, depending on how hard and salty it is. Change the water once or twice during soaking.

2 Drain the fish and transfer it to a pan. Pour in water to cover. Bring to a gentle simmer and cook for about 15 minutes, until the fish is tender. Drain, reserving the stock. Remove any skin or bones from the fish and cut it into 4cm/ 1½ in pieces.

3 Make the sauce. Remove the stems and shake out the seeds from the ancho chillies. Tear the pods into pieces, put in a bowl of warm water and soak until they are soft.

4 Drain the soaked chillies and put them into a food processor with the onion, oregano, coriander and serrano chilli. Process to a purée.

5 Heat the oil in a frying pan and cook the purée, stirring, for about 5 minutes. Stir in the fish or chicken stock and simmer for 3–4 minutes.

6 Add the prepared cod and simmer for a few minutes longer to heat the fish through and blend the flavours. Serve garnished with the sliced chilli.

BAKED OR GRILLED SPICED WHOLE FISH

SERVES 6

INGREDIENTS

1 kg/2¼ lb bream, carp or pomfret,
  cleaned and scaled if necessary
1 fresh red chilli, seeded and ground,
  or 5ml/1 tsp chopped chilli
  from a jar
4 garlic cloves, crushed
2.5cm/1 in fresh root ginger, peeled
  and sliced
4 spring onions (scallions), chopped
juice of ½ lemon
30ml/2 tbsp sunflower oil
salt

1 Rinse the fish and dry it well inside
and out with absorbent kitchen paper.
Slash two or three times through the
fleshy part on each side of the fish.

2 Place the chilli, garlic, ginger and
spring onions in a food processor and
blend to a paste, or grind the mixture
together with a mortar and pestle.
Add the lemon juice and salt, then stir
in the oil.

COOK'S TIP
Almost any kind of firm fish can be
used for this recipe.

3 Spoon a little of the mixture inside
the fish and pour the rest over the top.
Turn the fish to coat it completely in the
spice mixture and leave to marinate for
at least 1 hour.

4 Preheat the grill (broiler). Place a long
strip of double foil under the fish to
support it and to make turning it over
easier. Put on a rack in a grill pan and cook
under the hot grill for 5 minutes on one
side and 8 minutes on the second side,
basting with the marinade during
cooking. Serve with boiled rice.

VINEGAR CHILLI FISH

SERVES 2–3

INGREDIENTS

2–3 mackerel, filleted
2–3 fresh red chillies, seeded
4 macadamia nuts or 8 almonds
1 red onion, quartered
2 garlic cloves, crushed
1 cm/½ in fresh root ginger, peeled
  and sliced
5ml/1 tsp ground turmeric
45ml/3 tbsp coconut or vegetable oil
45ml/3 tbsp wine vinegar
150ml/¼ pint/⅔ cup water
salt
deep-fried onions, to garnish
finely chopped fresh chilli, to garnish

1 Rinse the fish fillets in cold water and
then dry them well on kitchen paper.
Set aside.

2 Grind the chillies, nuts, onion, garlic,
ginger, turmeric and 15ml/1 tbsp of the
oil to a paste in a food processor or with
a mortar and pestle. Heat the remaining
oil in a frying pan and cook the paste
for 1–2 minutes, without browning. Stir
in the vinegar and water. Add salt to
taste. Bring to the boil, then reduce
to a simmer.

3 Place the fish fillets in the sauce.
Cover and cook for 6–8 minutes, or
until the fish is tender.

4 Lift the fish on to a plate and keep
warm. Reduce the sauce by boiling
rapidly for 1 minute. Pour over the fish
and serve. Garnish with deep-fried
onions and chopped chilli.

MEXICAN SPICY FISH

THIS IS A TYPICAL MEXICAN SUPPER DISH, POPULAR AS IT CAN BE LEFT TO MARINATE.

SERVES 6

INGREDIENTS
  1.5kg/3 – 3½lb striped bass or any
    non-oily white fish, cut into 6 steaks
  120ml/4fl oz/½ cup corn oil
  1 large onion, thinly sliced
  2 garlic cloves, chopped
  350g/12oz tomatoes, sliced
  2 drained canned jalapeño chillies,
    rinsed and sliced

For the marinade
  4 garlic cloves, crushed
  5ml/1 tsp black peppercorns
  5ml/1 tsp dried oregano
  2.5ml/½ tsp ground cumin
  5ml/1 tsp ground annatto
  2.5ml/½ tsp ground cinnamon
  120ml/4fl oz/½ cup mild white vinegar
  salt
  flat leaf parsley, to garnish

1 Arrange the fish steaks in a single layer in a shallow dish. Make the marinade. Using a pestle, grind the garlic and black peppercorns in a mortar. Add the dried oregano, cumin, annatto and cinnamon and mix to a paste with the vinegar. Add salt to taste and spread the marinade on both sides of each of the fish steaks. Cover and leave in a cool place for 1 hour.

2 Select a flameproof dish large enough to hold the fish in a single layer and pour in enough of the oil to coat the base. Arrange the fish in the dish with any remaining marinade.

3 Top the fish with the onion, garlic, tomatoes and chillies and pour the rest of the oil over the top.

4 Cover the dish and cook over a low heat on top of the stove for 15–20 minutes, or until the fish is no longer translucent. Serve immediately garnished with flat leaf parsley.

CITRUS FISH WITH CHILLIES

SERVES 4

INGREDIENTS
    4 halibut or cod steaks,
       175g/6oz each
    juice of 1 lemon
    5ml/1 tsp garlic granules
    5ml/1 tsp paprika
    5ml/1 tsp ground cumin
    4ml/¾ tsp dried tarragon
    about 60ml/4 tbsp olive oil
    flour, for dusting
    300ml/½ pint/1¼ cups fish stock
    2 red chillies, seeded and
       finely chopped
    30ml/2 tbsp chopped fresh
       coriander (cilantro)
    1 red onion, cut into rings
    salt and ground black pepper

1 Place the fish in a shallow bowl and mix together the lemon juice, garlic, paprika, cumin, tarragon and a little salt and pepper. Spoon over the lemon mixture, cover loosely with clear film (plastic wrap) and marinate for a few hours or overnight in the refrigerator.

3 Pour the fish stock around the fish, and simmer, covered for about 5 minutes, until the fish is thoroughly cooked through.

5 Transfer the fish and sauce to a serving plate and keep warm.

2 Gently heat all of the oil in a large non-stick frying pan, dust the fish with flour and then fry the fish for a few minutes each side, until golden brown all over.

4 Add the chopped red chillies and 15ml/1 tbsp of the coriander to the pan. Simmer for 5 minutes.

6 Wipe the pan, heat some olive oil and stir-fry the onion rings until speckled brown. Sprinkle over the fish with the remaining chopped coriander and serve immediately.

SAFFRON FISH

SERVES 4

INGREDIENTS
 2–3 saffron threads
 2 egg yolks
 1 garlic clove, crushed
 4 salmon trout steaks
 oil for deep-frying
 salt and ground black pepper
 green salad, to serve

1 Soak the saffron in 15ml/1 tbsp boiling water and then beat the mixture into the egg yolks. Season to taste with garlic, salt and pepper.

COOK'S TIP
Any type of fish can be used in this recipe. Try a combination of plain and smoked for a delicious change, such as smoked and unsmoked cod or haddock.

2 Place the fish steaks in a shallow dish and coat with the egg mixture. Cover with clear film (plastic wrap). and marinate for up to 1 hour.

3 Heat the oil in a deep-fryer until it is very hot, then fry the fish, one steak at a time, for about 10 minutes, until golden brown. Drain each steak on kitchen paper. Serve with a green salad.

PAN-FRIED SPICY SARDINES

THIS DELICIOUS FISH RECIPE IS A FAVOURITE IN MANY ARAB COUNTRIES.

SERVES 4

INGREDIENTS
 10g/¼oz fresh parsley
 3–4 garlic cloves, crushed
 8–12 sardines, prepared
 30ml/2 tbsp lemon juice
 50g/2oz/½ cup plain
  (all-purpose) flour
 2.5ml/½ tsp ground cumin
 60ml/4 tbsp vegetable oil
 salt and ground black pepper
 naan bread and salad, to serve

COOK'S TIP
If you don't have a garlic crusher, then crush the garlic using the flat side of a large knife blade instead.

1 Finely chop the parsley and mix in a small bowl with the garlic.

2 Pat the parsley and garlic mixture all over the outsides and insides of the sardines. Sprinkle them with the lemon juice and set aside, covered, in a cool place for about 2 hours to absorb the flavours.

3 Place the flour on a large plate and season with cumin, salt and pepper. Roll the sardines in the flour, taking care to coat each fish throughly.

4 Heat the oil in a large frying pan and fry the fish, in batches, for 5 minutes on each side, until crisp. Keep warm in the oven while cooking the remaining fish and then serve with naan bread and salad.

FRIED CATFISH FILLETS <u>WITH</u> PIQUANT SAUCE

SPICY FILLETS OF CATFISH ARE FRIED IN A HERBED BATTER AND SERVED WITH
A WONDERFULLY TASTY SAUCE TO CREATE THIS EXCELLENT SUPPER DISH.

SERVES 4

INGREDIENTS
 1 egg
 50ml/2fl oz/¼ cup olive oil
 squeeze of lemon juice
 2.5ml/½ tsp chopped fresh dill
 4 catfish fillets
 50g/2oz/½ cup flour
 25g/1 oz/2 tbsp butter or margarine
 salt and ground black pepper

For the sauce
 1 egg yolk
 30ml/2 tbsp Dijon mustard
 30ml/2 tbsp white wine vinegar
 10ml/2 tsp paprika
 300ml/½ pint/1¼ cups olive or
   vegetable oil
 30ml/2 tbsp prepared horseradish
 2.5ml/½ tsp chopped garlic
 1 celery stick, chopped
 30ml/2 tbsp tomato ketchup
 2.5ml/½ tsp ground black pepper
 2.5ml/½ tsp salt

1 For the sauce, combine the egg yolk mustard, vinegar and paprika in a mixing bowl. Add the oil in a thin stream, beating vigorously with a wire whisk to blend it in.

2 When the mixture is smooth and thick, beat in all the other sauce ingredients. Cover and chill until ready to serve.

3 Combine the egg, 15ml/1 tbsp olive oil, the lemon juice, dill and a little salt and pepper in a shallow dish. Beat until all is well combined.

4 Dip both sides of each catfish fillet in the egg and herb mixture, then coat lightly with flour, shaking off any excess flour from it.

5 Heat the butter or margarine with the remaining olive oil in a large, heavy frying pan. Add the fish fillets and fry until they are golden brown on both sides and cooked, about 8–10 minutes. To test they are done, insert the point of a sharp knife into the fish: the flesh should be opaque in the centre.

6 Serve the fried catfish fillets hot, accompanied by the piquant sauce in a dish.

COOK'S TIP
If you can't find catfish, you can use any firm fish fillets instead. Cod or haddock fillets would both make good substitutes.

RED SNAPPER, VERACRUZ-STYLE

THIS IS MEXICO'S BEST-KNOWN FISH DISH. IN VERACRUZ RED SNAPPER IS ALWAYS USED BUT FILLETS OF ANY FIRM-FLESHED WHITE FISH CAN BE SUBSTITUTED SUCCESSFULLY.

SERVES 4

INGREDIENTS

4 large red snapper fillets
30ml/2 tbsp freshly squeezed lime
 or lemon juice
120ml/4fl oz/½ cup olive oil
1 onion, finely chopped
2 garlic cloves, chopped
675g/1½ lb tomatoes, peeled
 and chopped
1 bay leaf, plus a few sprigs
 to garnish
1.5ml/¼ tsp dried oregano
30ml/2 tbsp large capers, plus extra
 to serve (optional)
16 pitted green olives, halved
2 drained canned jalapeño chillies,
 seeded and cut into strips
butter, for frying
3 slices firm white bread, cut
 into triangles
salt and ground black pepper

1 Arrange the fish fillets in a single layer in a shallow dish. Season with salt and pepper, drizzle with the lime or lemon juice and set aside.

2 Heat the oil in a large frying pan and sauté the onion and garlic until the onion is soft. Add the tomatoes and cook for about 10 minutes, until the mixture is thick and flavoursome. Stir the mixture from time to time.

3 Stir in the bay leaf, oregano, capers, olives and chillies. Add the fish and cook over a very low heat for about 10 minutes, or until tender.

COOK'S TIP
This dish can also be made with a whole fish, weighing about 1.5kg/3–3½lb. Bake together with the sauce, in a preheated oven at 160°C/325°F/Gas 3. Allow 10 minutes cooking time for every 2.5cm/1in thickness of the fish.

4 While the fish is cooking, heat the butter in a small frying pan and sauté the bread triangles until they are golden brown on both sides.

5 Transfer the fish to a heated platter, pour over the sauce and surround with the fried bread triangles. Garnish with bay leaves and serve with extra capers, if you like.

RED SNAPPER WITH CHILLI, GIN AND GINGER SAUCE

CHILLIES, GINGER AND GIN ADD SPICE AND PIQUANCY TO A COLOURFUL OVEN-BAKED DISH THAT TASTES EVERY BIT AS GOOD AS IT LOOKS.

SERVES FOUR

INGREDIENTS

1 red snapper, about
   1.6kg/3½lb, cleaned
30ml/2 tbsp sunflower oil
1 onion, chopped
2 garlic cloves, crushed
50g/2oz/½ cup sliced button
   (white) mushrooms
5ml/1 tsp ground coriander
15ml/1 tbsp chopped fresh parsley
30ml/2 tbsp grated (shredded) fresh
   root ginger
2 fresh red chillies, seeded and sliced
15ml/1 tbsp cornflour (cornstarch)
45ml/3 tbsp gin
300ml/½ pint/1¼ cups chicken or
   vegetable stock
salt and ground black pepper

For the garnish
   15ml/1 tbsp sunflower oil
   6 garlic cloves, sliced
   1 lettuce heart, finely shredded
   1 bunch fresh coriander (cilantro),
      tied with red raffia

1 Preheat the oven to 190ºC/375ºF/
Gas 5. Grease a flameproof dish that is
large enough to hold the fish. Make
several diagonal cuts on one side of
the fish.

2 Heat the oil in a frying pan and
gently fry the onion, garlic and sliced
mushrooms for 2–3 minutes. Stir in
the ground coriander and the chopped
parsley. Season with salt and pepper
to taste.

3 Spoon the filling into the cavity of the
fish, then lift the snapper into the dish.
Pour in enough cold water to cover the
base of the dish. Sprinkle the ginger
and chillies over, then cover and bake
for 30–40 minutes, basting from time to
time. Remove the cover for the last
10 minutes.

4 Carefully lift the snapper on to a
serving dish, cover with foil and keep
hot. Tip the cooking juices from the
dish into a pan.

5 Mix the cornflour and gin in a cup
and stir into the cooking juices. Pour in
the stock. Bring to the boil and cook
gently for 3–4 minutes or until
thickened, stirring. Taste for seasoning,
then pour into a bowl.

6 Make the garnish. Heat the oil in a
small pan and stir-fry the garlic and
lettuce over a high heat until crisp.
Spoon alongside the snapper. Place the
coriander bouquet on the other side.
Serve with the sauce.

SPICED FISH WITH CHILLIES, LEMON AND RED ONIONS

SOMETIMES IT'S THE SIMPLEST DISHES THAT MAKE THE MOST IMPACT. THIS DISH NOT ONLY LOOKS PRETTY, IT ALSO TASTES GOOD, WITH PAPRIKA AND FRESH RED CHILLIES.

SERVES FOUR

INGREDIENTS

4 halibut or cod steaks or cutlets, about 175g/6oz each
juice of 1 lemon
5ml/1 tsp crushed garlic
5ml/1 tsp paprika
5ml/1 tsp ground cumin
4ml/¾ tsp dried tarragon
about 60ml/4 tbsp olive oil, plus extra for frying the onion
flour, for dusting
300ml/½ pint/1¼ cups fish stock
2 fresh red chillies, seeded and finely chopped
30ml/2 tbsp chopped fresh coriander (cilantro)
1 red onion, cut into rings
salt and ground black pepper

1 Place the fish in a single layer in a shallow dish. Mix together the lemon juice, garlic, paprika, cumin, tarragon and a little salt and pepper. Spoon over the fish, cover loosely with clear film (plastic wrap) and marinate for a few hours or overnight in the refrigerator. The longer the fish is left to marinate, the stronger the flavour will be.

2 Gently heat the olive oil in a large non-stick frying pan. Drain the fish, dust the pieces with flour, then fry for a few minutes on each side, until golden brown all over.

3 Pour the fish stock around the fish, and simmer, covered, for about 5 minutes until the fish is thoroughly cooked through.

4 Add the chopped red chillies and 15ml/1 tbsp of the coriander to the pan. Simmer for 5 minutes.

5 Transfer the fish and sauce to a serving plate and keep warm.

6 Wipe the pan, heat some extra olive oil and stir-fry the onion rings until speckled brown. Arrange them over the fish, with the remaining chopped coriander and serve at once.

CAJUN BLACKENED FISH WITH PAPAYA SALSA

THIS IS AN EXCELLENT WAY OF COOKING FILLETS OF SNAPPER OR COD, LEAVING IT MOIST IN THE MIDDLE AND CRISP AND SPICY ON THE OUTSIDE.

SERVES FOUR

INGREDIENTS
5ml/1 tsp black peppercorns
5ml/1 tsp cumin seeds
5ml/1 tsp white mustard seeds
10ml/2 tsp paprika
5ml/1 tsp chilli powder
5ml/1 tsp dried oregano
10ml/2 tsp dried thyme
4 skinned fish fillets, 225g/8oz each
50g/2oz/¼ cup butter, melted
salt
lime wedges and coriander (cilantro)
    sprigs, to garnish

For the papaya salsa
1 papaya
1 fresh red chilli
½ small red onion, diced
45ml/3 tbsp chopped fresh
    coriander (cilantro)
grated rind and juice of 1 lime

1 Start by making the salsa. Cut the papaya in half and scoop out the seeds. Remove the skin, cut the flesh into small dice and place it in a bowl. Slit the chilli, remove and discard the seeds and finely chop the flesh.

2 Add the onion, chilli, coriander, lime rind and juice to the papaya. Season with salt to taste. Mix well and set aside.

3 Dry-fry the peppercorns, cumin and mustard seeds in a pan, then grind them to a fine powder. Add the paprika, chilli powder, oregano, thyme and 5ml/1 tsp salt. Grind again and spread on a plate.

4 Preheat a heavy frying pan over a medium heat for about 10 minutes. Brush the fish fillets with the melted butter then dip them in the spices until well coated.

5 Place the fish in the hot pan and cook for 1–2 minutes on each side until blackened. Garnish with lime and coriander, and serve with the salsa.

COOK'S TIP
Cooking fish in this way can be a smoky affair, so make sure the kitchen is well ventilated or use an extractor fan.

CARIBBEAN FISH STEAKS

THIS QUICK AND EASY RECIPE IS A GOOD EXAMPLE OF HOW CHILLIES, CAYENNE AND ALLSPICE CAN ADD AN EXOTIC ACCENT TO A TOMATO SAUCE FOR FISH.

SERVES FOUR

INGREDIENTS
4 cod steaks
5ml/1 tsp muscovado (molasses) sugar
10ml/2 tsp angostura bitters
salt
steamed okra or green beans,
    to serve

For the tomato sauce
45ml/3 tbsp oil
6 shallots, finely chopped
1 garlic clove, crushed
1 fresh green chilli, seeded and
    finely chopped
400g/14oz can chopped tomatoes
2 bay leaves
1.5ml/¼ tsp cayenne pepper
5ml/1 tsp crushed allspice
juice of 2 limes

1 First make the tomato sauce. Heat the oil in a frying pan and fry the shallots, until soft. Add the garlic and chilli, and cook for 2 minutes. Stir in tomatoes, bay, cayenne, allspice and lime juice, with salt to taste.

VARIATION
Almost any robust fish steaks or fillets can be cooked in this way.

2 Cook gently for 15 minutes, then add the cod steaks and baste with the tomato sauce. Cover and cook for 10 minutes or until the cod steaks are cooked. Keep hot in a warmed dish.

3 Stir the sugar and angostura bitters into the sauce, simmer for 2 minutes, then pour it over the fish. Serve with steamed okra or green beans.

KING PRAWNS IN CURRY SAUCE

SERVES 4

INGREDIENTS
    450g/1lb raw king prawns
       (jumbo shrimp)
    600ml/1 pint/2½ cups water
    3 thin slices fresh root ginger
    10ml/2 tsp curry powder
    2 garlic cloves, crushed
    15g/½oz/1 tbsp butter or margarine
    60ml/4 tbsp ground almonds
    1 green chilli, seeded and
       finely chopped
    45ml/3 tbsp single (light) cream
    salt and ground black pepper

For the vegetables
    15ml/1 tbsp mustard oil
    15ml/1 tbsp vegetable oil
    1 onion, sliced
    ½ red (bell) pepper, seeded and
       thinly sliced
    ½ green (bell) pepper, seeded and
       thinly sliced
    1 christophene, peeled, stoned
       (pitted) and cut into strips
    salt and ground black pepper

1 Peel the prawns and place the shells in a pan with the water and ginger. Simmer, uncovered, for 15 minutes, until reduced by half. Strain into a jug (pitcher) and discard the shells.

2 Devein the prawns, place in a bowl and season with the curry powder, garlic and salt and pepper and set aside.

3 Heat the mustard and vegetable oils in a large frying pan, add all the vegetables and stir-fry for 5 minutes. Season with salt and pepper, spoon into a serving dish and keep warm.

4 Wipe out the frying pan, then melt the butter or margarine and sauté the prawns for about 5 minutes, until pink. Spoon over the bed of vegetables, cover and keep warm.

5 Add the ground almonds and chilli to the pan, stir-fry for a few seconds and then add the reserved stock and bring to the boil. Reduce the heat, stir in the cream and simmer for a few minutes, without boiling.

6 Pour the sauce over the vegetables and prawns before serving.

FRIED FISH IN GREEN CHILLI SAUCE

SERVES 4

INGREDIENTS
    4 medium pomfret
    juice of 1 lemon
    5ml/1 tsp garlic granules
    salt and ground black pepper
    vegetable oil, for shallow frying

For the coconut sauce
    450ml/¾ pint/scant 2 cups water
    2 thin slices fresh root ginger
    25–40g/1–1½oz creamed coconut
       or 120–175ml/4–6fl oz/½–¾ cup
       coconut cream
    30ml/2 tbsp vegetable oil
    1 red onion, sliced
    2 garlic cloves, crushed
    1 green chilli, seeded and
       thinly sliced
    15ml/1 tbsp chopped fresh coriander
    salt and ground black pepper

1 Cut the fish in half and sprinkle inside and out with the lemon juice. Season with the garlic granules and salt and pepper and set aside to marinate for a few hours.

2 Heat a little oil in a large frying pan. Pat away the excess lemon juice from the fish, cook in the oil for 10 minutes, turning once. Set aside

3 To make the sauce, place the water in a pan with the slices of ginger, bring to the boil and simmer until the liquid is reduced to just over 300ml/½ pint/ 1½ cups. Take out the ginger and reserve, then add the creamed coconut to the pan and stir until the coconut has melted.

4 Heat the oil in a wok or large pan and cook the onion and garlic for 2–3 minutes. Add the reserved ginger and coconut stock, the chilli and coriander, stir well and then gently add the fish. Simmer for 10 minutes, until the fish is cooked through. Transfer the fish to a warmed serving plate, adjust the seasoning for the sauce and pour over the fish. Serve immediately.

COCONUT SALMON

*CHILLIES AND COCONUT MILK HAVE A SPECIAL AFFINITY, THE FORMER FURNISHING
FIRE WHILE THE LATTER IS COOL AND CREAMY.*

SERVES FOUR

INGREDIENTS
    10ml/2 tsp ground cumin
    10ml/2 tsp chilli powder
    2.5ml/½ tsp ground turmeric
    30ml/2 tbsp white wine vinegar
    1.5ml/¼ tsp salt
    4 salmon steaks, about
      175g/6oz each
    45ml/3 tbsp oil
    1 onion, chopped
    2 fresh green chillies, seeded
      and chopped
    2 garlic cloves, crushed
    2.5cm/1in piece root ginger,
      grated (shredded)
    5ml/1 tsp ground coriander
    175ml/6fl oz/¾ cup coconut milk
    spring onion (scallion) rice, to serve
    fresh coriander (cilantro) sprigs,
      to garnish

1 In a small bowl, mix half the cumin
with the chilli powder, turmeric, vinegar
and salt. Place the salmon in a single
layer in a non-metallic dish and rub all
over with the paste. Cover and leave to
marinate for 15 minutes.

COOK'S TIP
Make coconut milk by dissolving grated
(shredded) creamed coconut (coconut
cream) in boiling water, then strain.

2 Heat the oil in a wide, deep-sided
frying pan and fry the onion, chillies,
garlic and ginger for 5–6 minutes.
Scrape the mixture into a food
processor or blender and process to
a paste. Use a hand-held blender if
you prefer.

3 Return the paste to the pan. Add the
coriander and remaining cumin, then
pour in the coconut milk, stirring
constantly. Bring to the boil, then
simmer for 5 minutes.

4 Add the salmon steaks and spoon the
sauce over them. Cover and cook for
15 minutes until the fish is tender.
Serve with spring onion rice and garnish
with coriander sprigs.

SALMON WITH TEQUILA CREAM SAUCE

ROASTED JALAPEÑO CHILLIES AND LIGHTLY AGED REPOSADA TEQUILA ARE A WINNING COMBINATION IN THIS EXCITING AND UNUSUAL DINNER-PARTY FISH DISH.

SERVES FOUR

INGREDIENTS

3 fresh green jalapeño chillies
45ml/3 tbsp olive oil
1 small onion, finely chopped
150ml/¼ pint/⅔ cup fish stock
grated (shredded) rind and juice
 of 1 lime
120ml/4fl oz/½ cup single
 (light) cream
30ml/2 tbsp reposada tequila
1 firm avocado
4 salmon fillets
salt and ground white pepper
strips of green (bell) pepper and
 fresh flat leaf parsley, to garnish

3 Stir the cream into the onion and stock mixture. Slice the chilli flesh into strips and add to the pan. Cook over a gentle heat, stirring constantly, for 2–3 minutes. Season to taste with salt and white pepper.

4 Stir the tequila into the onion and chilli mixture. Leave the pan over a very low heat. Peel the avocado, remove the stone (pit) and slice the flesh. Brush the salmon fillets on one side with a little of the remaining oil.

5 Heat a frying pan or ridged griddle pan until very hot and add the salmon, oiled side down. Cook for 2–3 minutes, until the underside is golden, then brush the top with oil, turn each fillet over and cook the other side until the fish is cooked and flakes easily when tested with the tip of a sharp knife.

6 Serve on a pool of sauce, with the avocado slices. Garnish with strips of green pepper and fresh parsley. This dish is good with fried potatoes.

1 Roast the chillies in a frying pan until the skins are blistered but not burnt. Put them in a strong plastic bag and tie the top to keep the steam in. Set aside.

2 Heat 15ml/1 tbsp of the oil in a pan. Add the onion and fry for 3–4 minutes, then pour in the stock with the lime rind and juice. Cook for 10 minutes, until the stock starts to reduce. Remove the chillies from the bag. Peel them, then slit and scrape out the seeds.

SWORDFISH TACOS

COOKED CORRECTLY, SWORDFISH IS MOIST AND MEATY, AND SUFFICIENTLY ROBUST
TO MORE THAN HOLD ITS OWN WHEN MIXED WITH CHILLIES.

SERVES SIX

INGREDIENTS
   3 swordfish steaks
   30ml/2 tbsp vegetable oil
   2 garlic cloves, crushed
   1 small onion, chopped
   3 fresh green chillies, seeded
      and chopped
   3 tomatoes
   small bunch of fresh coriander
      (cilantro), chopped
   6 fresh corn tortillas
   ½ Iceberg lettuce, shredded
   salt and ground black pepper
   lemon wedges, to serve (optional)

1 Preheat the grill (broiler). Put the
swordfish on an oiled rack over a grill
(broiling) pan and grill (broil) for no
longer than 2–3 minutes on each side.
When cool, remove the skin and flake
the fish into a bowl.

2 Heat the oil in a pan and gently fry
the crushed garlic, and chopped onion
and chillies for 5 minutes or until the
onion is soft.

3 Cut a cross in the base of each
tomato. Put them in a heatproof bowl
and pour over boiling water. After
30 seconds, plunge into cold water.
Drain and remove the skins. Cut them
in half and squeeze out the seeds and
dice the flesh.

4 Add the tomatoes and swordfish to
the onion mixture. Cook for 5 minutes
over a low heat. Add the coriander and
cook for 1–2 minutes. Season to taste
with salt and pepper.

5 Wrap the tortillas in foil and steam on
a plate over boiling water until pliable.
Place some shredded lettuce and fish
mixture on each tortilla. Fold in half and
serve immediately, with lemon wedges
if you like.

SWORDFISH WITH CHILLI AND LIME SAUCE

SWORDFISH IS A PRIME CANDIDATE FOR THE BARBECUE, AS LONG AS IT IS NOT OVERCOOKED.
IT TASTES WONDERFUL WITH A SPICY SAUCE WHOSE FIRE IS TEMPERED WITH CRÈME FRAÎCHE.

SERVES FOUR

INGREDIENTS
   2 fresh serrano chillies
   4 tomatoes
   45ml/3 tbsp olive oil
   grated (shredded) rind and juice
      of 1 lime
   4 swordfish steaks
   2.5ml/½ tsp salt
   2.5ml/½ tsp ground black pepper
   175ml/6fl oz/¾ cup crème fraîche
   fresh flat leaf parsley, to garnish

1 Roast the chillies in a dry griddle pan
until the skins are blistered. Put in a
plastic bag and tie the top. Set aside for
20 minutes, then peel off the skins. Cut
off the stalks, then slit the chillies, scrape
out the seeds and slice the flesh.

2 Cut a cross in the base of each
tomato. Place them in a heatproof bowl
and pour over boiling water to cover.
After 30 seconds, lift the tomatoes out
on a slotted spoon and plunge them
into a bowl of cold water. Drain. The
skins will have begun to peel back from
the crosses. Remove the skin from the
tomatoes, then cut them in half and
squeeze out the seeds. Chop the flesh
into 1cm/½in pieces.

3 Heat 15ml/1 tbsp of the oil in a
small pan and add the strips of chilli,
with the lime rind and juice. Cook for
2–3 minutes, then stir in the tomatoes.
Cook for 10 minutes, stirring the
mixture occasionally, until the tomato
is pulpy. Preheat the grill (broiler) or
prepare the barbecue.

4 Brush the swordfish steaks with olive
oil and season. Barbecue or grill (broil)
for 3–4 minutes or until just cooked,
turning once. Meanwhile, stir the crème
fraîche into the sauce and heat it
through gently. Pour over the swordfish
steaks. Serve garnished with fresh
parsley. This is delicious served with
chargrilled vegetables.

COD WITH CHILLI AND MUSTARD SEEDS

SERVES 4

INGREDIENTS
30ml/2 tbsp olive oil
5ml/1 tsp mustard seeds
1 large potato, cubed
2 slices of Serrano ham, shredded
1 onion, thinly sliced
2 garlic cloves, thinly sliced
1 red chilli, seeded and sliced
115g/4oz skinless, boneless
   cod, cubed
120ml/4fl oz/½ cup vegetable stock
50g/2oz/½ cup grated tasty cheese,
   such as Manchego or Cheddar
salt and ground black pepper

COOK'S TIP
For a crisp topping, replace half
the grated cheese with wholemeal
(whole-wheat) breadcrumbs.

1 Heat the oil in a heavy frying pan.
Add the mustard seeds. Cook for
1–2 minutes, until the seeds begin to
pop and splutter, then add the potato,
ham and onion.

2 Cook, stirring regularly for about
10–15 minutes, until the potatoes are
brown and almost tender.

3 Add the garlic and chilli and cook for
2 minutes more.

4 Stir in the cod cubes and cook for
2–3 minutes, until white, then add the
stock and plenty of salt and pepper.
Cover the pan and cook for 5 minutes,
until the fish is just cooked and the
potatoes are tender.

5 Transfer the mixture to a flame-proof
dish. Sprinkle over the grated cheese
and place under a hot grill (broiler) for
about 2–3 minutes, until the cheese is
golden and bubbling.

CARIBBEAN SPICED FISH

*THIS DISH IS OF SPANISH ORIGIN AND IS POPULAR THROUGHOUT THE CARIBBEAN. THERE
ARE AS MANY VARIATIONS ON THE NAME OF THE DISH AS THERE ARE WAYS OF PREPARING IT.*

SERVES 4–6

INGREDIENTS

900g/2lb cod fillet
½ lemon
15ml/1 tbsp spice seasoning
flour, for dusting
oil, for frying
lemon wedges, to garnish

For the sauce

30ml/2 tbsp vegetable oil
1 onion, sliced
½ red pepper, sliced
½ chayote, peeled and stoned (pitted),
   cut into small pieces
2 garlic cloves, crushed
120ml/4fl oz/½ cup malt vinegar
75ml/5 tbsp water
2.5ml/½ tsp ground allspice
1 bay leaf
1 small Scotch Bonnet chilli, chopped
15ml/1 tbsp soft brown sugar
salt and ground black pepper

1 Place the fish in a shallow dish,
squeeze over the lemon, then sprinkle
with the spice seasoning and pat into
the fish. Leave to marinate in a cool
place for at least 1 hour.

2 Cut the fish into 7.5cm/3in pieces
and dust with a little flour, shaking off
any excess flour.

3 Heat the oil in a heavy frying pan and
cook the fish pieces for 2–3 minutes,
until golden brown and crisp, turning
occasionally. To make the sauce, heat
the oil in a heavy frying pan and cook
the onion until soft.

4 Add the pepper, chayote and garlic
and stir-fry for 2 minutes. Pour in
the vinegar, then add the remaining
ingredients and simmer gently for
5 minutes. Leave to stand for
10 minutes, then pour over the fish.
Serve hot, garnished with lemon.

COOK'S TIP
In the Caribbean, whole red snapper or
red mullet are used for this dish.

CURRIED SEAFOOD WITH COCONUT MILK

THIS CURRY IS BASED ON A THAI CLASSIC. THE LOVELY GREEN COLOUR IS IMPARTED
BY THE FINELY CHOPPED CHILLI AND FRESH HERBS.

SERVES FOUR

INGREDIENTS

225g/8oz small ready-prepared squid
225g/8oz raw tiger prawns
    (jumbo shrimp)
400ml/14fl oz/1⅔ cups coconut milk
2 kaffir lime leaves, finely shredded
30ml/2 tbsp Thai fish sauce
450g/1lb firm white fish fillets,
    skinned, boned and cut into chunks
2 fresh green chillies, seeded and
    finely chopped
30ml/2 tbsp torn fresh basil or
    coriander (cilantro) leaves
squeeze of fresh lime juice
cooked Thai jasmine rice, to serve

For the curry paste
6 spring onions (scallions),
    coarsely chopped
4 fresh coriander (cilantro) stems,
    coarsely chopped, plus 45ml/3 tbsp
    chopped fresh coriander (cilantro)
4 kaffir lime leaves, shredded
8 fresh green chillies, seeded and
    coarsely chopped
1 lemon grass stalk,
    coarsely chopped
2.5cm/1in piece fresh root ginger,
    peeled and coarsely chopped
45ml/3 tbsp chopped fresh basil
15ml/1 tbsp vegetable oil

1 Make the curry paste. Put all the ingredients, except the oil, in a food processor and process to a paste. Alternatively, pound together in a mortar with a pestle. Stir in the oil.

2 Rinse the squid and pat dry with kitchen paper. Cut the bodies into rings and halve the tentacles, if necessary.

3 Heat a wok until hot, add the prawns and stir-fry, without any oil, for about 4 minutes, until they turn pink.

4 Remove the prawns from the wok and leave to cool slightly, then peel off the shells, saving a few with shells on for the garnish. Make a slit along the back of each one and remove the black vein.

5 Pour the coconut milk into the wok, then bring to the boil over a medium heat, stirring constantly. Add 30ml/ 2 tbsp of curry paste, the shredded lime leaves and fish sauce and stir well to mix. Reduce the heat to low and simmer gently for about 10 minutes.

6 Add the squid, prawns and chunks of fish and cook for about 2 minutes, until the seafood is tender. Take care not to overcook the squid as it will become tough very quickly.

7 Just before serving, stir in the chillies and basil or coriander. Taste and adjust the flavour with a squeeze of lime juice. Garnish with prawns in their shells, and serve with Thai jasmine rice.

VARIATIONS
• You can use any firm-fleshed white fish for this curry, such as monkfish, cod, haddock or John Dory.
• If you prefer, you could substitute shelled scallops for the squid. Slice them in half horizontally and add them with the prawns (shrimp). As with the squid, be careful not to overcook them.

COCONUT FISH CURRY

THIS IS A VERY POPULAR SOUTH-EAST ASIAN FISH CURRY IN A COCONUT SAUCE. CHOOSE A FIRM-TEXTURED FISH SO THAT THE PIECES STAY INTACT DURING THE BRIEF COOKING PROCESS.

SERVES FOUR

INGREDIENTS
500g/1¼lb firm-textured fish fillets, skinned and cut into 2.5cm/ 1in cubes
2.5ml/½ tsp salt
50g/2oz/⅔ cup desiccated (dry unsweetened shredded) coconut
6 shallots or small onions, roughly chopped
6 blanched almonds
2–3 garlic cloves, roughly chopped
2.5cm/1in piece fresh root ginger, peeled and sliced
2 lemon grass stalks, trimmed
10ml/2 tsp ground turmeric
45ml/3 tbsp vegetable oil
2 × 400ml/14fl oz cans coconut milk
1–3 fresh red or green chillies, seeded and sliced
salt and ground black pepper
fresh chives, to garnish
boiled long grain rice, to serve

1 Spread out the pieces of fish in a shallow dish and sprinkle them with the salt. Dry-fry the coconut in a wok over medium to low heat, turning all the time until it is crisp and golden (see Cook's Tip below).

2 Tip the dry-fried coconut into a food processor and process until you have an oily paste. Scrape into a bowl and reserve.

3 Add the shallots or onions, almonds, garlic and ginger to the food processor. Cut off the lower 5cm/2in of the lemon grass stalks, chop them roughly and add to the other ingredients in the processor. Process the mixture to a paste. Bruise the remaining lemon grass and set the stalks aside.

4 Add the ground turmeric to the mixture in the processor and process briefly to mix.

5 Heat the oil in the clean wok. Add the onion mixture and cook for a few minutes without browning. Stir in the coconut milk and bring to the boil, stirring constantly to prevent the mixture from curdling.

6 Add the cubes of fish, most of the sliced chillies and the bruised lemon grass stalks. Cook for 3–4 minutes. Stir in the coconut paste (moistened with some of the sauce if necessary) and cook for a further 2–3 minutes only. Do not overcook the fish. Taste and adjust the seasoning.

7 Remove the lemon grass stalks. Spoon the moolie on to a hot serving dish and sprinkle with the remaining slices of chilli. Garnish with chopped and whole chives and serve with boiled long grain rice.

COOK'S TIP
Dry-frying is a feature of Malay cooking that demands the cook's close attention. The coconut must be constantly on the move so that it becomes crisp and uniformly golden in colour.

BALINESE FISH CURRY

*A SIMPLE FISH CURRY IS THE IDEAL DISH TO PREPARE WHEN YOU ARE IN A HURRY. THE
CURRY SAUCE CAN BE MADE IN ADVANCE, AND THE FISH TAKES ONLY MINUTES TO COOK.*

SERVES FOUR TO SIX

INGREDIENTS

675g/1½lb cod or haddock fillet
celery leaves or chopped fresh chilli,
  to garnish
boiled rice, to serve

For the sauce

1cm/½in cube shrimp paste
2 red or white onions
2.5cm/1in fresh root ginger, peeled
  and sliced
1cm/½in fresh galangal, peeled
  and sliced
2 garlic cloves
2 fresh red chillies, seeded and sliced
90ml/6 tbsp sunflower oil
15ml/1 tbsp dark soy sauce
5ml/1 tsp tamarind pulp, soaked in
  30ml/2 tbsp warm water
  then strained
250ml/8fl oz/1 cup water

3 Heat 30ml/2 tbsp of the oil in a pan
and fry the spices, stirring, for about
2 minutes. Add the soy sauce and the
tamarind liquid, with the water. Cook for
2–3 minutes, stirring.

4 Heat the remaining oil in a separate
pan and fry the fish for 2–3 minutes.
Turn once only so that the pieces stay
whole. Lift out with a slotted spoon and
put into the sauce.

5 Cook the fish in the sauce for
3 minutes, until cooked through. Spoon
on to a serving dish, garnish with
feathery celery leaves or a little chopped
fresh chilli and serve with the rice.

COOK'S TIPS

• Save time by asking the fishmonger
to skin the fish for you.
• Tamarind has a refreshing acid taste.

1 Skin the fish, remove any bones with
a pair of tweezers, and then cut the
flesh into bitesize pieces. Pat dry with
kitchen paper and set aside.

2 Grind the shrimp paste, onions,
ginger, galangal, garlic and fresh chillies
to a paste in a food processor or with a
mortar and pestle.

VARIATIONS
• Use 450g/1lb cooked tiger prawns
(jumbo shrimp) instead of fish. Add
them 3 minutes before the end of the
cooking time.
• If you don't have any fresh chillies,
use 5–10ml/1–2 tsp chilli powder.

Chillies crop up across the globe, featuring in delectable

dishes from places as far apart as Thailand and Tobago.

This chapter chooses some of the best, from a classic

Mexican mole to a sweet and spicy Moroccan tagine.

Peanuts are partnered with chillies in a Caribbean

chicken dish, while China's choice is the famous Sichuan

Chicken with Kung Po Sauce. The collection includes

dishes that would do you proud at dinner parties, but

also features such family favourites as Tandoori Chicken

and Hot Pepperoni and Chilli Pizza.

Sizzling Poultry
and Meat Dishes

SPICY FRIED CHICKEN

THIS CRISPY CHICKEN IS SUPERB HOT OR COLD. SERVED WITH A SALAD OR VEGETABLES, IT
MAKES A DELICIOUS LUNCH AND IS IDEAL FOR PICNICS OR SNACKS TOO.

SERVES 4–6

INGREDIENTS
    4 chicken drumsticks
    4 chicken thighs
    10ml/2 tsp curry powder
    2.5ml/½ tsp garlic granules
    2.5ml/½ tsp ground black pepper
    2.5ml/½ tsp paprika
    about 300ml/½ pint/1¼ cups milk
    oil, for deep frying
    50g/2oz/4 tbsp plain
      (all-purpose) flour
    salt
    salad leaves, to serve

1 Place the chicken pieces in a large bowl and sprinkle with the curry powder, garlic granules, black pepper, paprika and salt. Rub the spices well into the chicken, then cover and leave to marinate in a cool place for at least 2 hours, or overnight in the refrigerator.

2 Preheat the oven to 180°C/350°F/ Gas 4. Pour enough milk into the bowl to cover the chicken and leave to stand for a further 15 minutes.

3 Heat the oil in a large pan or deep-fat fryer and tip the flour on to a plate. Shake off excess milk, dip each piece of chicken in flour and fry two or three pieces at a time until golden, but not cooked through. Continue until all the chicken pieces are fried.

4 Remove with a slotted spoon, place the chicken pieces on a baking sheet, and bake for about 30 minutes. Serve hot or cold with salad.

CHICKEN WITH COCONUT

TRADITIONALLY, THE CHICKEN PIECES FOR THIS INDONESIAN DISH ARE PART-COOKED BY FRYING, BUT ROASTING IN THE OVEN IS JUST AS SUCCESSFUL. THIS RECIPE IS UNUSUAL IN THAT IT DOES NOT CONTAIN ANY CHILLIES OR TURMERIC, BUT GALANGAL, LEMON GRASS, CORIANDER AND LIME LEAVES ADD A SPICY FLAVOUR.

SERVES 4–6

INGREDIENTS

1.5kg/3–3½lb chicken or
  4 chicken quarters
4 garlic cloves
1 onion, sliced
4 macadamia nuts or
  8 almonds
15ml/1 tbsp coriander seeds,
  dry-fried, or 5ml/1 tsp
  ground coriander
45ml/3 tbsp oil
2.5cm/1in fresh galangal,
  peeled and bruised
2 lemon grass stalks, fleshy
  part bruised
3 lime leaves
2 bay leaves
5ml/1 tsp sugar
600ml/1 pint/2½ cups
  coconut milk
salt
boiled rice and deep-fried onions,
  to serve

1 Preheat the oven to 190°C/375°F/ Gas 5. Cut the chicken into four or eight pieces. Season with salt. Put in an oiled roasting pan and cook in the oven for 25–30 minutes. Meanwhile prepare the sauce.

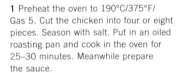

2 Grind the garlic, onion, nuts and coriander to a fine paste in a food processor or with a mortar and pestle. Heat the oil and fry the paste to bring out the flavour. Do not allow it to brown.

3 Add the part-cooked chicken pieces to a wok together with the galangal, lemon grass, lime and bay leaves, sugar, coconut milk and salt to taste. Mix well to coat in the sauce.

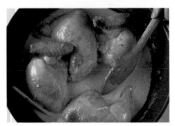

4 Bring to the boil and then reduce the heat and simmer gently for 30–40 minutes, uncovered, until the chicken is tender and the coconut sauce is reduced and thickened. Stir the mixture occasionally during cooking.

5 Just before serving, remove the bruised galangal and lemon grass. Serve with boiled rice sprinkled with crisp deep-fried onions.

CHICKEN SAUCE PIQUANTE

RED CHILLI PEPPERS ADD HEAT TO THIS CAJUN RECIPE. SAUCE PIQUANTE IS COMMONLY USED IN MANY RECIPES TO LIVEN UP MEAT AND FISH. SHALLOTS CAN BE SUBSTITUTED FOR THE ONION, AND PICKLED GHERKINS WILL ADD EXTRA FLAVOUR AND ZEST.

SERVES 4

INGREDIENTS

4 chicken legs or 2 legs and
  2 breast portions
75ml/5 tbsp oil
50g/2oz/½ cup plain
  (all-purpose) flour
1 onion, chopped
2 celery sticks, sliced
1 green (bell) pepper, seeded
  and diced
2 garlic cloves, crushed
1 bay leaf
2.5ml/½ tsp dried thyme
2.5ml/½ tsp dried oregano
1–2 red chillies, seeded and
  finely chopped
400g/14oz can tomatoes, chopped,
  with their juice
300ml/½ pint/1¼ cups chicken stock
salt and ground black pepper
watercress, to garnish
boiled potatoes, to serve

VARIATION

This recipe also brings spice and flavour to leftovers of festive turkey. Simmer the vegetables for 25 minutes in step 6 before adding the turkey.

1 Halve the chicken legs through the joint, or the breast portions across the middle, to give eight pieces.

2 In a heavy frying pan, cook the chicken pieces in the oil until brown on all sides, lifting them out and setting them aside as they are done.

3 Strain the oil from the pan into a heavy flameproof casserole. Heat it and stir in the flour. Stir constantly over a low heat until the roux is the colour of peanut butter.

4 As soon as the roux reaches the right stage, tip in the onion, celery and pepper and stir over the heat for 2–3 minutes.

5 Add the garlic, bay leaf, thyme, oregano and chilli or chillies. Stir for 1 minute, then turn down the heat and stir in the tomatoes with their juice.

6 Return the casserole to the heat and gradually stir in the stock. Add the chicken pieces, cover and simmer for 45 minutes, until the chicken is tender.

7 If there is too much sauce or it is too runny, remove the lid for the last 10–15 minutes of the cooking time and raise the heat a little.

8 Check the seasoning and serve garnished with watercress and accompanied by boiled potatoes, or perhaps rice or pasta, and a green vegetable or salad of your choice.

COOK'S TIP

If you prefer to err on the side of caution with chilli heat, use just 1 chilli and hot up the seasoning at the end with a dash or two of Tabasco sauce.

VARIATION

Any kind of meat, poultry or fish can be served with Sauce Piquante. Just cook the meat or fish first, then serve it with plenty of the sauce.

CHICKEN <u>WITH</u> CHIPOTLE CHILLI SAUCE

THIS IS AN EASY RECIPE FOR ENTERTAINING, WITH JUST A FEW KEY INGREDIENTS, INCLUDING DRIED CHILLIES. IT IS COOKED IN THE OVEN AND NEEDS NO LAST-MINUTE ATTENTION.

SERVES SIX

INGREDIENTS
6 chipotle chillies
chicken stock (see method
  for quantity)
3 onions
45ml/3 tbsp vegetable oil
6 skinless, boneless chicken
  breast portions
salt and ground black pepper
fresh oregano, to garnish
boiled rice, to serve

1 Put the dried chillies in a bowl and pour over hot water to cover. Leave to stand for at least 20 minutes, until very soft. Drain, reserving the soaking water in a liquid measure. Cut off the stalk from each chilli, then slit them lengthways and scrape out the seeds with a small sharp knife.

2 Preheat the oven to 180°C/350°F/ Gas 4. Chop the flesh of the chillies roughly and put it in a food processor or blender. Add enough chicken stock to the soaking water to make it up to 400ml/14fl oz/1⅔ cups. Pour it into the processor and process until smooth.

3 Peel the onions. Using a sharp knife, cut them in half, then slice them thinly. Separate the slices.

4 Heat the oil in a large frying pan, add the onions and cook over a low to moderate heat for about 5 minutes, or until they have softened but not coloured, stirring occasionally.

5 Using a slotted spoon, transfer the onion slices to a casserole that is large enough to hold all the chicken breast portions in a single layer. Sprinkle the onion slices with a little salt and ground black pepper.

COOK'S TIPS
• It is important to seek out chipotle chillies, as they impart a wonderfully rich and smoky flavour to the chicken.
• Dried chillies of various types can be bought by mail order, as well as from specialist food stores.
• The chilli purée can be prepared ahead of time.
• If tears come to your eyes when peeling onions, peel them under water. Then pat dry with kitchen paper before slicing.

6 Arrange the chicken on top of the onion slices. Sprinkle with a little salt and several grindings of pepper.

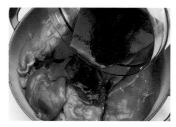

7 Pour the chipotle purée over the chicken, making sure that each piece is evenly coated.

8 Bake in the oven for 45–60 minutes or until the chicken is cooked through, but is still moist and tender. Garnish with fresh oregano and serve with boiled white rice.

VARIATION
Prepare the chipotles as in the main method. Put them in a stainless steel pan along with the soaking water; 2 peeled tomatoes, cut in wedges; ½ a sweet onion, chopped; 4 garlic cloves and 75ml/5 tbsp chopped fresh coriander (cilantro). Add water if needed to just cover. Simmer for 30 minutes. Dry-fry 15ml/1 tbsp cumin seeds, grind in a mortar or process in a blender and add to the chilli mixture. Cook for 5 minutes, season with salt, and purée. Refrigerated, it will keep for 1 week.

B L A

SERVES 6

INGRED
6 skin
    brea
75g/3
5ml/1
10ml/
5ml/1
10ml/
7.5m
2.5m
5ml/1
1.5m
5ml/1

1 Slice e
half hori
about th
slightly

2 Melt t
small pa

3 Comb
in a sha
Brush th
with me
sprinkle
seasoni

RED CHICKEN CURRY <u>WITH</u> BAMBOO SHOOTS

THE CHILLI PASTE THAT IS THE BASIS OF THIS DISH HAS A SUPERB FLAVOUR, USEFUL IN ALL SORTS OF SPICY DISHES, SO IT IS WORTH MAKING IT IN QUANTITY.

SERVES FOUR TO SIX

INGREDIENTS

1 litre/1¾ pints/4 cups coconut milk
450g/1lb skinless, boneless chicken
   breast portions, diced
30ml/2 tbsp Thai fish sauce (*nam pla*)
15ml/1 tbsp granulated sugar
225g/8oz canned bamboo shoots,
   rinsed and sliced
5 kaffir lime leaves, torn
salt and ground black pepper
2 fresh red chillies, chopped, 10–12
   fresh basil leaves, 10–12 fresh mint
   leaves, to garnish

For the red curry paste

12–15 fresh red chillies, seeded
4 shallots, thinly sliced
2 garlic cloves, chopped
15ml/1 tbsp chopped fresh galangal
2 lemon grass stalks, tender
   portions chopped
3 kaffir lime leaves, chopped
4 coriander (cilantro) roots
10 black peppercorns
5ml/1 tsp coriander seeds
2.5ml/½ tsp cumin seeds
good pinch of ground cinnamon
5ml/1 tsp ground turmeric
2.5ml/½ tsp shrimp paste
30ml/2 tbsp oil

1 Make the red curry paste. Combine all the ingredients except for the oil in a mortar. Add 5ml/1 tsp salt. Pound with a pestle, or process in a food processor, until smooth. If you are using a pestle and mortar, you might need to pound the ingredients in batches and then combine them.

2 Add the oil to the paste a little at a time and blend in well. If you are using a food processor or blender, add it slowly through the feeder tube. Scrape the paste into a jar and store in the refrigerator until ready to use.

3 Pour half the coconut milk into a large heavy pan. Gently bring to the boil, stirring all the time until the milk separates, then reduce the heat.

4 Add 30ml/2 tbsp of the red curry paste, stir to mix, and cook for a few minutes to allow the flavours to develop. The sauce should begin to thicken and may need to be stirred frequently to prevent it from sticking to the pan. Add a little more coconut milk if necessary.

5 Add the chicken, fish sauce and sugar. Fry for 3–5 minutes until the chicken changes colour, stirring constantly to prevent it from sticking.

6 Add the rest of the coconut milk, with the bamboo shoots and kaffir lime leaves. Bring back to the boil. Stir in salt and pepper to taste. Serve garnished with the chillies, basil and mint leaves.

COOK'S TIPS

• The surplus curry paste can be stored in a sealed jar in the refrigerator for 3–4 weeks. Alternatively, freeze it in small tubs, each containing about 30ml/2 tbsp.

• Young bamboo shoots are cultivated in China for the table. The preparation is laborious, so the canned shoots are used in the West. They provide a crunchy texture, and are a useful contrast to other ingredients.

• The roots of coriander have a deep earthy fragrance and are used widely in Thai cooking. They can be frozen for storage until you need them. Simply cut the roots off and wrap in clear film (plastic wrap).

HOT CHICKEN CURRY

*THIS CURRY HAS A NICE THICK SAUCE, AND USING RED AND GREEN PEPPERS GIVES
IT EXTRA COLOUR. SERVE WITH WHOLEMEAL CHAPATIS OR PLAIN BOILED RICE.*

SERVES 4

INGREDIENTS
  30ml/2 tbsp corn oil
  1.5ml/¼ tsp fenugreek seeds
  1.5ml/¼ tsp onion seeds
  2 onions, chopped
  2.5ml/½ tsp garlic pulp
  2.5ml/½ tsp ginger pulp
  5ml/1 tsp ground coriander
  5ml/1 tsp chilli powder
  5ml/1 tsp salt
  400g/14oz/1¾ cups canned tomatoes
  30ml/2 tbsp lemon juice
  350g/12oz/2½ cups skinned, boned
    and cubed chicken
  30ml/2 tbsp chopped
    coriander (cilantro)
  3 fresh green chillies, chopped
  ½ red (bell) pepper, cut into chunks
  ½ green (bell) pepper, cut
    into chunks
  fresh coriander sprigs

3 Meanwhile, in a separate bowl, mix
together the ground coriander, chilli
powder, salt, canned tomatoes and
lemon juice.

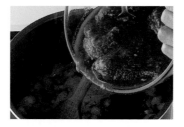

4 Pour this mixture into the pan and
turn up the heat to medium. Stir-fry for
about 3 minutes.

6 Add the fresh coriander, green chillies
and the red and green peppers. Lower
the heat, cover the pan and simmer
for about 10 minutes, until the chicken
is cooked.

7 Serve hot, garnished with fresh
coriander sprigs.

1 In a medium pan, heat the oil and fry
the fenugreek and onion seeds until
they turn a shade darker.

2 Add the chopped onions, garlic and
ginger and cook for about 5 minutes,
until the onions turn golden brown. Turn
the heat to very low.

5 Add the chicken pieces and stir-fry for
5–7 minutes until golden-brown all over.

VARIATION
This recipe also works well with turkey or
pork fillet. Increase the cooking time, if
necessary, to ensure that the meat is
cooked through.

COOK'S TIP
Cucumber raita is a wonderfully
refreshing dish to serve with anything
spicy. To make it, dice 1 cucumber and
place it in a bowl. Stir in 300ml/½ pint/
1¼ cups natural (plain) yogurt, 1.5ml/
¼ tsp salt and 1.5ml/¼ tsp ground cumin.
A chopped fresh green chilli can be added
if you like, or top the raita with a dusting
of chilli powder and a fresh mint sprig.

CRISPY AND AROMATIC DUCK

AS THIS DISH IS OFTEN SERVED WITH PANCAKES, SPRING ONIONS, CUCUMBER AND DUCK SAUCE (A SWEET BEAN PASTE), MANY PEOPLE MISTAKE IT FOR PEKING DUCK. THIS RECIPE, HOWEVER, USES A DIFFERENT COOKING METHOD. THE RESULT IS JUST AS CRISPY BUT THE DELIGHTFUL AROMA MAKES THIS DISH PARTICULARLY DISTINCTIVE.

SERVES 6–8

INGREDIENTS
  1 oven-ready duckling,
    about 2.25kg/5–5¼lb
  10ml/2 tsp salt
  5–6 whole star anise
  15ml/1 tbsp Sichuan peppercorns
  5ml/1 tsp cloves
  2–3 cinnamon sticks
  3–4 spring onions (scallions)
  3–4 slices fresh root ginger, unpeeled
  75–90ml/5–6 tbsp Chinese rice wine
  vegetable oil, for deep-frying
  lettuce leaves, to garnish

To serve
  Chinese pancakes
  duck sauce
  spring onions, shredded
  cucumber, diced

2 Marinate the duck with the spices, onions, ginger and wine for 4–6 hours.

3 Vigorously steam the duck with the marinade for 3–4 hours (or for longer if possible). Carefully remove the steamed duck from the cooking liquid and leave to cool for at least 5–6 hours. The duck must be cold and dry or the skin will not be crisp.

4 Heat the vegetable oil in a wok until it is just smoking, then place the duck pieces in the oil, skin side down. Deep-fry the duck for about 5–6 minutes, or until it becomes crisp and brown. Turn the duck just once at the very last moment.

5 Remove the fried duck, drain it well and place it on a bed of lettuce leaves.

6 To serve, scrape the meat off the bone and wrap a portion in each pancake with a little duck sauce, shredded spring onions and cucumber. Eat with your fingers.

1 Remove the wings from the duck and split the body in half down the backbone. Rub salt all over the two duck halves, taking care to work it all in thoroughly.

VARIATION
For those following a wheat-free diet, crispy and aromatic duck is also delicious served with fresh lettuce leaves or steamed rice pancakes.

COOK'S TIP
Small pancakes suitable for this dish can be found in most Chinese supermarkets. They can be frozen and will keep for up to 3 months in the freezer.

TURKEY STEW <u>WITH</u> SPICY CHOCOLATE SAUCE

A MOLE IS A RICH STEW, SERVED ON FESTIVE OCCASIONS IN MEXICO. TOASTED NUTS, FRUIT AND CHOCOLATE ARE AMONG THE CLASSIC INGREDIENTS.

SERVES FOUR

INGREDIENTS
    1 ancho chilli, seeded
    1 guajillo chilli, seeded
    115g/4oz/¾ cup sesame seeds
    50g/2oz/½ cup whole
        blanched almonds
    50g/2oz/½ cup shelled unsalted
        peanuts, skinned
    50g/2oz/¼ cup lard (shortening) or
        60ml/4 tbsp vegetable oil
    1 small onion, finely chopped
    2 garlic cloves, crushed
    50g/2oz/¼ cup canned tomatoes in
        tomato juice
    1 ripe plaintain
    50g/2oz/⅓ cup raisins
    75g/3oz/½ cup ready-to-eat
        pitted prunes
    5ml/1 tsp dried oregano
    2.5ml/½ tsp ground cloves
    2.5ml/½ tsp crushed allspice berries
    5ml/1 tsp ground cinnamon
    25g/1oz/¼ cup cocoa powder
    4 turkey breast steaks
    chopped fresh oregano, to garnish

1 Soak both types of dried chilli in a bowl of hot water for 20–30 minutes, then lift them out and chop them roughly. Reserve 250ml/8fl oz/1 cup of the soaking liquid.

COOK'S TIPS
• It is important to use good-quality cocoa powder, which is unsweetened.
• Mexican-style cocoa powder is available from specialist food stores and by mail order.

2 Spread out the sesame seeds in a heavy frying pan. Toast them over a moderate heat, shaking the pan lightly so that they turn golden all over. Do not let them burn, or the sauce will taste bitter. Set aside 45ml/3 tbsp of the toasted seeds for the garnish and tip the rest into a bowl. Toast the blanched almonds and skinned peanuts in the same way and add them to the bowl with the sesame seeds.

3 Heat half the lard or oil in a frying pan, sauté the chopped onion and garlic for 2–3 minutes, then add the chillies and tomatoes. Cook gently for 10 minutes.

4 Peel the plantain and slice it into short diagonal slices. Add it to the onion mixture with the raisins, prunes, dried oregano, spices and cocoa. Stir in the 250ml/8fl oz/1 cup of the reserved water in which the chillies were soaked. Bring to the boil, stirring, then add the toasted sesame seeds, almonds and peanuts. Cook gently for 10 minutes, stirring frequently; do not let the sauce stick to the pan and burn. Remove from the heat and leave to cool slightly.

5 Blend the sauce in batches in a food processor or blender until smooth. The sauce should be fairly thick, but a little water can be added if you think it is necessary.

6 Heat the remaining lard or oil in a flameproof casserole. Add the turkey and brown over a medium heat.

7 Pour the sauce over the steaks and cover the casserole with foil and a tight-fitting lid. Simmer over a gentle heat for 20–25 minutes or until the turkey is cooked, and the sauce has thickened. Sprinkle with the reserved sesame seeds and the chopped fresh oregano. Turkey *Mole* is traditionally served with a rice dish and warm tortillas.

MEXICAN TURKEY MOLE

MOLE POBLANO DE GUAJOLOTE IS THE GREAT FESTIVE DISH OF MEXICO. IT IS SERVED AT
ANY SPECIAL OCCASION, BE IT A BIRTHDAY, WEDDING, OR FAMILY GET-TOGETHER. RICE, BEANS,
TORTILLAS AND GUACAMOLE ARE THE TRADITIONAL ACCOMPANIMENTS.

SERVES 6–8

INGREDIENTS
2.75–3.6kg/6–8lb turkey, cut into
  serving pieces
1 onion, chopped
1 garlic clove, chopped
90ml/6 tbsp lard or corn oil
salt
fresh coriander (cilantro) and 30ml/2 tbsp
  toasted sesame seeds, to garnish

For the sauce
6 dried ancho chillies
4 dried pasilla chillies
4 dried mulato chillies
1 drained canned chipotle chilli,
  seeded and chopped (optional)
2 onions, chopped
2 garlic cloves, chopped
450g/1lb tomatoes, peeled
  and chopped
1 stale tortilla, torn into pieces
50g/2oz/⅓ cup seedless raisins
115g/4oz/1 cup ground almonds
45ml/3 tbsp sesame seeds, ground
2.5ml/½ tsp coriander seeds, ground
5ml/1 tsp ground cinnamon
2.5ml/½ tsp ground anise
1.5ml/¼ tsp ground black peppercorns
60ml/4 tbsp lard or corn oil
40g/1½oz unsweetened (bitter)
  chocolate, broken into squares
15ml/1 tbsp sugar
salt and ground pepper

COOK'S TIP
Roasting the dried chillies lightly, taking
care not to burn them, brings out the
flavour and is worth the extra effort.

1 Put the turkey pieces into a pan or
flameproof casserole large enough to
hold them in one layer comfortably. Add
the onion and garlic, and enough cold
water to cover. Season with salt, bring to
a gentle simmer, cover and cook for about
1 hour, or until the turkey is tender.

2 Meanwhile, put the ancho, pasilla and
mulato chillies in a dry frying pan over a
low heat and roast them for a few
minutes, shaking the pan frequently.
Remove the stems and shake out the
seeds. Tear the pods into pieces and
put these into a small bowl. Add
sufficient warm water to just cover
and soak, turning occasionally, for
30 minutes until soft.

3 Lift out the turkey pieces and pat
them dry with kitchen paper. Reserve
the stock in a measuring jug (pitcher).
Heat the lard or oil in a large frying pan
and sauté the turkey pieces until lightly
browned all over. Transfer to a plate and
set aside. Reserve the oil that is left in
the frying pan.

4 Tip the chillies, with the water in
which they have been soaked, into a
food processor. Add the chipotle chilli, if
using, with the onions, garlic, tomatoes,
tortilla, raisins, ground almonds and
spices. Process to a purée. Do this in
batches if necessary.

5 Add the lard or oil to the fat
remaining in the frying pan used for
sautéing the turkey. Heat the mixture,
then add the chilli and spice paste.
Cook, stirring, for 5 minutes.

6 Transfer the mixture to the pan or
casserole in which the turkey was
originally cooked. Stir in 475ml/16fl oz/
2 cups of the turkey stock (make it up
with water if necessary). Add the
chocolate and season with salt and
pepper. Cook over a low heat until the
chocolate has melted. Stir in the sugar.
Add the turkey and more stock if
needed. Cover the pan and simmer very
gently for 30 minutes. Serve, garnished
with fresh coriander and sprinkled with
the sesame seeds.

DEEP-FRIED SPARERIBS WITH SPICY SALT AND PEPPER

IF YOU WANT THESE SPARERIBS TO BE HOTTER, JUST INCREASE THE AMOUNT OF CHILLI SAUCE.

SERVES 4–6

INGREDIENTS

10–12 finger ribs, in total about
675g/1½ lb, with excess fat and
gristle trimmed
about 30–45ml/2–3 tbsp flour
vegetable oil, for deep-frying

For the marinade
1 garlic clove, crushed and chopped
15ml/1 tbsp light brown sugar
15ml/1 tbsp dark soy sauce
30ml/2 tbsp Chinese rice wine or
dry sherry
2.5ml/½ tsp chilli sauce
few drops sesame oil

1 Chop each rib into 3–4 pieces.
Combine all the marinade ingredients in
a bowl, add the spareribs and leave to
marinate for at least 2–3 hours.

2 Coat the spareribs with flour and
deep-fry them in medium-hot oil for
4–5 minutes, stirring to separate.
Remove and drain.

3 Heat the oil to high and deep-fry
the spareribs once more for about
1 minute, or until the colour is an even
dark brown. Remove and drain, then
serve hot.

SPICY SALT AND PEPPER
To make Spicy Salt and Pepper, mix
15ml/1 tbsp salt with 10ml/2 tsp ground
Sichuan peppercorns and 5ml/1 tsp
fivespice powder. Heat together in a
preheated dry pan for about 2 minutes
over a low heat, stirring constantly.
This quantity is sufficient for at least
six servings.

PORK WITH CHILLIES AND PINEAPPLE

SERVES 6

INGREDIENTS

30ml/2 tbsp corn oil
900g/2lb boneless pork shoulder or
  loin, cut into 5cm/2in cubes
1 onion, finely chopped
1 large red (bell) pepper, seeded and
  finely chopped
1 or more jalapeño chillies, seeded
  and finely chopped
450g/1lb fresh pineapple chunks
8 fresh mint leaves, chopped
250ml/8fl oz/1 cup chicken stock
salt and ground black pepper
fresh mint sprig, to garnish
rice, to serve

1 Heat the oil in a large frying pan and
sauté the pork, in batches, until the
cubes are lightly coloured. Transfer the
pork to a flameproof casserole, leaving
the oil behind in the pan.

2 Add the finely chopped onion, finely
chopped red pepper and the chilli(es)
to the oil remaining in the pan. Sauté
until the onion is tender, then add to
the casserole with the pineapple. Stir
to mix all together.

3 Add the mint, then cover and simmer
gently for about 2 hours, or until the
pork is tender. Garnish with fresh mint
and serve with rice.

COOK'S TIP
If fresh pineapple is not available, use
pineapple canned in its own juice.

PORK CASSEROLE <u>WITH</u> CHILLIES <u>AND</u> DRIED FRUIT

USING A TECHNIQUE TAKEN FROM SOUTH AMERICAN COOKING, THIS CASSEROLE IS BASED ON A RICH PASTE OF CHILLIES, SHALLOTS AND NUTS. SERVE WITH PLAIN BOILED RICE.

SERVES SIX

INGREDIENTS
   25ml/5 tsp plain (all-purpose) flour
   1kg/2¼lb shoulder or leg of pork, cut
      into 5cm/2in cubes
   45–60ml/3–4 tbsp olive oil
   2 large onions, chopped
   2 garlic cloves, finely chopped
   600ml/1 pint/2½ cups fruity
      white wine
   105ml/7 tbsp water
   115g/4oz/⅔ cup ready-to-eat prunes
   115g/4oz/⅔ cup ready-to-eat
      dried apricots
   grated (shredded) rind and juice of
      1 small orange
   pinch of soft light brown sugar
   30ml/2 tbsp chopped fresh parsley
   ½–1 fresh red chilli, seeded and
      finely chopped
   salt and ground black pepper

For the paste
   3 ancho chillies
   2 pasilla chillies
   30ml/2 tbsp olive oil
   2 shallots, chopped
   2 garlic cloves, chopped
   1 fresh green chilli, seeded
      and chopped
   10ml/2 tsp ground coriander
   5ml/1 tsp mild Spanish paprika
      or *pimentón dulce*
   50g/2oz/½ cup blanched
      almonds, toasted
   15ml/1 tbsp chopped fresh oregano
      or 7.5ml/1½ tsp dried oregano
   plain boiled rice, to serve

1 Make the paste first. Toast the dried chillies in a dry frying pan over a low heat for 1–2 minutes, until they are aromatic, then soak them in a bowl of warm water for 20–30 minutes.

2 Drain the chillies, reserving the soaking water, and discard their stalks and seeds. Preheat the oven to 160°C/325°F/Gas 3.

3 Heat the oil in a small frying pan. Add the shallots, garlic, fresh chilli and ground coriander, and fry over a very low heat for 5 minutes.

4 Transfer the mixture to a food processor or blender and add the drained chillies, paprika or *pimentón dulce*, almonds and oregano. Process the mixture, adding 45–60ml/3–4 tbsp of the chilli soaking liquid to make a smooth workable paste.

5 Season the flour generously with salt and black pepper, then use to coat the pork. Heat 45ml/3 tbsp of the olive oil in a large, heavy pan and fry the pork, stirring frequently, until sealed on all sides. Transfer the pork cubes to a flameproof casserole.

6 If necessary, add the remaining oil to the pan. When it is hot, fry the onions and garlic gently for 8–10 minutes.

COOK'S TIP
A Californian Chardonnay would be a suitably fruity wine to use.

7 Add the wine and water to the pan. Bring up to the boil, reduce the heat and cook for 2 minutes. Stir in half the paste, bring back to the boil and bubble for a few seconds before pouring over the pork.

8 Season lightly with salt and pepper, stir to mix, then cover and cook in the oven for 1½ hours. Increase the oven temperature to 180°C/350°F/Gas 4.

9 Add the prunes, apricots and orange juice to the casserole. Taste the sauce and add more salt and pepper if needed and a pinch of brown sugar if the orange juice has made the sauce a bit tart. Stir, cover, return to the oven and cook for a further 30–45 minutes.

10 Place the casserole over a direct heat and stir in the remaining paste. Simmer, stirring once or twice, for 5 minutes. Sprinkle with the orange rind, chopped parsley and fresh chilli. Serve with boiled rice.

LAMB MASALA

WHOLE SPICES ARE USED IN THIS CURRY SO REMOVE THEM BEFORE SERVING OR WARN THE DINERS OF THEIR PRESENCE IN ADVANCE! LAMB MASALA IS DELICIOUS SERVED WITH FRESHLY BAKED NAAN BREAD OR WITH A RICE ACCOMPANIMENT AND A COOL CUCUMBER RAITA. THIS DISH IS BEST MADE WITH GOOD-QUALITY SPRING LAMB.

SERVES 4

INGREDIENTS
    75ml/5 tbsp corn oil
    2 onions, chopped
    5ml/1 tsp shredded ginger
    6 whole dried red chillies
    3 cardamom pods
    2 cinnamon sticks
    6 black peppercorns
    3 cloves
    2.5ml/½ tsp salt
    450g/1lb boned leg of
      lamb, cubed
    600ml/1 pint/2½
      cups water
    2 fresh green chillies, sliced
    30ml/2 tbsp chopped fresh
      coriander (cilantro)
    rice or naan bread, to serve

4 Add the lamb and cook over a medium heat. Stir constantly with a semi-circular movement, using a wooden spoon to scrape the base of the pan. Continue in this way for about 5 minutes.

5 Pour in the water, cover the stew with a lid and cook it over a medium-low heat for 35–40 minutes, or until the water has evaporated and the meat is tender.

7 Continue to stir over the heat until you see some free oil on the sides of the pan.

8 Transfer to a serving dish and serve immediately with fresh naan bread or boiled rice.

COOK'S TIP
The action of stirring the meat and spices together using a semi-circular motion, as described in step 4, is called bhoono-ing. It makes sure that the meat becomes well-coated and combined with the spice mixture before the cooking liquid is added.

1 Heat the oil in a large pan. Lower the heat slightly and cook the onions until they are lightly browned.

2 Add half the ginger and half the garlic and stir well.

3 Throw in half the red chillies, the cardamoms, cinnamon, peppercorns, cloves and salt.

6 Add the rest of the shredded ginger, sliced garlic and the whole dried red chillies, along with the sliced fresh green chillies and the chopped fresh coriander.

VARIATION
Replace the lamb with cubes of braising or stewing beef for a hearty warming winter dish all the family will enjoy.

SPICY LAMB STEW

*THIS STEW IS KNOWN AS ESTOFADO DE CARNERO IN MEXICO. THE RECIPE FOR THIS
DISH HAS AN INTERESTING MIX OF CHILLIES — THE MILD, FULL-FLAVOURED ANCHO, AND
THE PIQUANT JALAPEÑO WHICH GIVES EXTRA "BITE". THE HEAT OF THE CHILLIES IS MELLOWED
BY THE ADDITION OF GROUND CINNAMON AND CLOVES. BONELESS NECK FILLET IS VERY GOOD
FOR THIS DISH; IT IS LEAN, TENDER, FLAVOURSOME AND INEXPENSIVE.*

SERVES 4

INGREDIENTS

3 dried ancho chillies
30ml/2 tbsp olive oil
1 jalapeño chilli, seeded
  and chopped
1 onion, finely chopped
2 garlic cloves, chopped
450g/1lb tomatoes, peeled
  and chopped
50g/2oz/⅓ cup seedless raisins
1.5ml/¼ tsp ground cinnamon
1.5ml/¼ tsp ground cloves
900g/2lb boneless lamb, cut into
  5cm/2in cubes
250ml/8fl oz/1 cup lamb stock
  or water
salt and ground black pepper
a few sprigs of fresh coriander
  (cilantro), to garnish
coriander rice, to serve

COOK'S TIP

To make coriander (cilantro) rice, simply
heat 30ml/2 tbsp corn oil in a large
frying pan and gently cook 1 finely
chopped onion for about 8 minutes, or
until soft but not brown. Stir in enough
cooked, long grain rice for four and stir
gently over a medium heat until heated
through. Sprinkle over 30–45ml/
2–3 tbsp chopped fresh coriander and
stir in thoroughly.

1 Roast the ancho chillies lightly in a
dry frying pan over a low heat to bring
out the flavour.

2 Remove the stems, shake out the
seeds and tear the pods into pieces,
then put them into a bowl. Pour in
enough warm water to just cover. Leave
to soak for 30 minutes.

3 Heat the olive oil in a frying pan and
sauté the jalapeño chilli together with
the onion and garlic until the onion
is tender.

4 Add the chopped tomatoes to the pan
and cook until the mixture is thick and
well blended. Stir in the raisins, ground
cinnamon and cloves, and season to
taste with salt and pepper. Transfer the
mixture to a flameproof casserole.

5 Tip the ancho chillies and their
soaking water into a food processor and
process to a smooth purée. Add the
chilli purée to the tomato mixture in
the casserole.

6 Add the lamb cubes to the casserole,
stir to mix and pour in enough of the
lamb stock or water to just cover
the meat.

7 Bring to a simmer, then cover the
casserole and cook over a low heat for
about 2 hours, or until the lamb is
tender. Garnish with fresh coriander and
serve with coriander rice.

VARIATION

Replace some of the fresh tomatoes with
sun-dried tomatoes for a rich stew with a
delicious sauce

FIRE FRY

HERE'S ONE FOR LOVERS OF HOT, SPICY FOOD. TENDER STRIPS OF LAMB, MARINATED IN SPICES AND STIR-FRIED WITH A TOP-DRESSING OF CHILLIES, REALLY HITS THE HOT SPOT.

SERVES FOUR

INGREDIENTS
225g/8oz lean lamb fillet (tenderloin)
120ml/4fl oz/½ cup natural
   (plain) yogurt
1.5ml/¼ tsp ground cardamom
5ml/1 tsp grated (shredded) fresh
   root ginger
5ml/1 tsp crushed garlic
5ml/1 tsp hot chilli powder
5ml/1 tsp garam masala
5ml/1 tsp salt
15ml/1 tbsp corn oil
2 onions, chopped
1 bay leaf
300ml/½ pint/1¼ cups water
2 fresh red chillies, seeded and
   sliced in strips
2 fresh green chillies, seeded and
   sliced in strips
30ml/2 tbsp fresh coriander
   (cilantro) leaves

1 Using a sharp knife, cut the lamb into 7.5–10cm/3–4in pieces, then into strips.

2 In a bowl, whisk the yogurt with the cardamom, ginger, garlic, chilli powder, garam masala and salt. Add the lamb strips and stir to coat them in the mixture. Cover and marinate in a cool place for about 1 hour.

COOK'S TIP
This is a useful recipe for a family divided into those who love chillies and those who don't. Serve the doubters before adding the chillies, or perhaps top their portions with strips of a sweet mild chilli or even a peeled red or green (bell) pepper.

3 Heat the oil in a wok or frying pan and fry the onions for 3–5 minutes, or until they are tender and golden brown.

4 Add the bay leaf and then add the marinated lamb with the yogurt and spices, and toss over a medium heat for about 2–3 minutes.

5 Pour over the water, stir well, then cover and cook for 15–20 minutes over a low heat, stirring occasionally. Once the water has evaporated, stir-fry the mixture for 1 minute.

6 Strew the red and green chillies over the stir-fry, with the fresh coriander. Serve hot. Offer a cooling yogurt dip, if you like.

CARIBBEAN LAMB CURRY

THIS POPULAR NATIONAL DISH OF JAMAICA IS KNOWN AS CURRY GOAT ALTHOUGH GOAT MEAT OR LAMB CAN BE USED TO MAKE IT.

SERVES 4–6

INGREDIENTS

900g/2lb boned leg of lamb
60ml/4 tbsp curry powder
3 garlic cloves, crushed
1 large onion, chopped
4 thyme sprigs or 1 teaspoon dried thyme
3 bay leaves
5ml/1 tsp ground allspice
30ml/2 tbsp vegetable oil
50g/2oz/¼ cup butter or margarine
900ml/1½ pints/3¾ cups stock
  or water
1 fresh hot chilli, chopped
cooked rice, to serve
coriander (cilantro) sprigs, to garnish

1 Cut the meat into 5cm/2in cubes, discarding any excess fat and gristle.

2 Place the lamb, curry powder, garlic, onion, thyme, bay leaves, allspice and oil in a large bowl and mix. Marinate the meat in the refrigerator for at least 3 hours or overnight.

3 Melt the butter or margarine in a large heavy pan, add the seasoned lamb and cook over a medium heat for about 10 minutes, turning the meat frequently.

4 Stir in the stock and chilli and bring to the boil. Reduce the heat, cover the pan and simmer for 1½ hours, or until the meat is tender. Serve with rice, garnish with coriander.

COOK'S TIP
Try goat, or mutton, if you can and enjoy a robust curry.

SPICY MEAT FRITTERS

MAKES 30

INGREDIENTS
450g/1lb potatoes, boiled
  and drained
450g/1lb lean minced (ground) beef
1 onion, quartered
1 bunch spring onions
  (scallions), chopped
3 garlic cloves, crushed
5ml/1 tsp ground nutmeg
15ml/1 tbsp coriander seeds,
  dry-fried and ground
10ml/2 tsp cumin seeds, dry-fried
  and ground
4 eggs, beaten
oil, for shallow frying
salt and ground black pepper

1 While the potatoes are still warm, mash them in the pan until they are well broken up. Add to the minced beef and mix well together.

2 Finely chop the onion, spring onions and garlic. Add to the meat with the ground nutmeg, coriander and cumin. Stir in enough beaten egg to give a soft consistency which can be formed into fritters. Season with salt and pepper to taste.

3 Heat the oil in a large frying pan. Using a dessertspoon, scoop out 6–8 oval-shaped fritters and drop them into the hot oil. Leave to set, so that they keep their shape (this will take about 3 minutes) and then turn over and cook for a further minute.

4 Drain well on kitchen paper and keep them warm while cooking the remaining fritters.

BARBECUE PORK SPARERIBS

SERVES 4

INGREDIENTS
1kg/2¼lb pork spareribs
1 onion
2 garlic cloves
2.5cm/1in fresh root ginger
75ml/3fl oz/⅓ cup dark soy sauce
1–2 fresh red chillies, seeded
  and chopped
5ml/1 tsp tamarind pulp, soaked in
  75ml/5 tbsp water
15–30ml/1–2 tbsp dark brown sugar
30ml/2 tbsp groundnut (peanut) oil
salt and ground black pepper

1 Wipe the pork spareribs and place them in a wok, wide frying pan or large flameproof casserole.

2 Finely chop the onion, crush the garlic and peel and slice the ginger. Blend the soy sauce, onion, garlic, ginger and chopped chillies together to a paste in a food processor or with a mortar and pestle. Strain the tamarind and reserve the juice. Add the tamarind juice, brown sugar, oil and seasoning to taste to the onion mixture and mix well together.

3 Pour the sauce over the ribs and toss well to coat. Bring to the boil and then simmer, uncovered and stirring frequently, for 30 minutes. Add extra water if necessary.

4 Put the ribs on a rack in a roasting tin, place under a preheated grill (broiler), on a barbecue or in the oven at 200°C/400°F/Gas 6 and continue cooking until the ribs are tender, about 20 minutes, depending on the thickness of the ribs. Baste the ribs with the sauce and turn them over occasionally.

INDONESIAN BEEF PATTIES

THESE SPICY LITTLE MEATBALLS COME FROM INDONESIA. SERVE THEM WITH BROAD EGG NOODLES AND FIERY CHILLI SAMBAL AS A DIPPING SAUCE.

SERVES FOUR TO SIX

INGREDIENTS
  1cm/½in cube shrimp paste
  1 large onion, roughly chopped
  1–2 fresh red chillies, seeded
    and chopped
  2 garlic cloves, crushed
  15ml/1 tbsp coriander seeds
  5ml/1 tsp cumin seeds
  450g/1lb lean minced (ground) beef
  10ml/2 tsp dark soy sauce
  5ml/1 tsp soft dark brown sugar
  juice of 1½ lemons
  a little beaten egg
  vegetable oil, for shallow frying
  salt and ground black pepper
  1 fresh green and 1–2 fresh red
    chillies, to garnish
  Chilli Sambal (below), to serve

1 Wrap the shrimp paste in a piece of foil and gently warm it in a dry frying pan for 5 minutes, turning a few times. Unwrap the paste and put in a food processor or blender.

COOK'S TIP
When processing the shrimp paste, onion, chillies and garlic, do not run the machine for too long, or the onion will become too wet and spoil the consistency of the meatballs.

2 Add the onion, chillies and garlic to the food processor and process until finely chopped. Set aside. Dry-fry the coriander and cumin seeds in a hot frying pan for 1 minute, to release the aroma. Tip the seeds into a mortar and grind with a pestle.

3 Put the meat in a large bowl. Stir in the onion mixture. Add the ground spices, soy sauce, brown sugar, lemon juice and beaten egg. Season to taste.

4 Shape the meat mixture into small, even-size balls, and chill these for 5–10 minutes to firm them up.

5 Heat the oil in a wok or large frying pan and fry the meatballs for 4–5 minutes, turning often, until cooked through and browned. You may have to do this in batches.

6 Drain the meatballs on kitchen paper, and then pile them on to a warm serving platter or into a large serving bowl. Finely slice the green chilli and one of the red chillies, and sprinkle over the meatballs. Garnish with a whole red chilli, if you like. Serve with the sambal, spooned into a small dish.

VARIATION
Beef is traditionally used for this dish, but minced (ground) pork, lamb – or even turkey – would also be good.

CHILLI SAMBAL

THIS FIERCE CONDIMENT IS BOTTLED AS SAMBAL OELEK, BUT IT IS EASY TO PREPARE AND WILL KEEP FOR SEVERAL WEEKS IN A WELL-SEALED JAR IN THE REFRIGERATOR.

MAKES 450G/1LB

INGREDIENTS
  450g/1lb fresh red chillies, seeded
  10ml/2 tsp salt

COOK'S TIP
If any sambal drips on your fingers, wash well in soapy water *immediately*.

1 Bring a pan of water to the boil, add the seeded chillies and cook them for 5–8 minutes.

2 Drain the chillies and chop roughly. Grind the chillies in a food processor or blender, without making the paste too smooth. If you like, you can do this in batches.

3 Scrape into a screw-topped glass jar, stir in the salt and cover with a piece of greaseproof (waxed) paper or clear film (plastic wrap). Screw on the lid and store in the refrigerator. Wash all implements in soapy water. Spoon into dishes using a stainless-steel or plastic spoon. Serve as an accompaniment, as suggested in recipes.

HOT AND SPICY ENCHILADAS

SERVES 4

INGREDIENTS

900g/2lb braising steak
15ml/1 tbsp vegetable oil, plus extra
  for frying
5ml/1 tsp salt
5ml/1 tsp dried oregano
2.5ml/½ tsp ground cumin
1 onion, quartered
2 garlic cloves, crushed
1 litre/1¾ pints/4 cups enchilada sauce
12 corn tortillas
115g/4oz/1 cup grated cheese
chopped spring onions (scallions),
  to garnish
sour cream, to serve

1 Preheat the oven to 160°C/325°F/
Gas 3. Place the meat on a sheet of foil
and rub it all over with the oil. Sprinkle
both sides with the salt, oregano and
cumin and rub in well. Add the onion
and garlic.

2 Top with another sheet of
foil and roll up to seal the edges,
leaving room for some steam expansion
during cooking.

3 Place in an ovenproof dish and bake
for 3 hours, until the meat is tender
enough to shred. Remove from the foil
and shred the meat using two forks.

4 Stir 120ml/4fl oz/½ cup of the
enchilada sauce into the beef. Spoon a
thin layer of enchilada sauce on the
base of a rectangular ovenproof dish, or
in four individual dishes.

5 Place the remaining sauce in a frying
pan and warm gently.

6 Put a 1cm/½in layer of vegetable oil
in a second frying pan and heat until
hot but not smoking. With tongs, lower
a tortilla into the oil; the temperature is
correct if it just sizzles. Cook for
2 seconds, then turn and cook the
other side for 2 seconds. Lift out, drain
over the pan and then transfer to the
pan with the sauce. Dip in the sauce
just to coat both sides.

7 Transfer the softened tortilla
immediately to a plate. Spread about
2–3 spoonfuls of the beef mixture down
the centre of the tortilla. Roll it up and
place the filled tortilla, seam side down,
in the prepared dish. Repeat this
process for all the remaining tortillas.

8 Spoon the remaining sauce from the
frying pan over the beef enchiladas,
spreading it right down to the ends.
Sprinkle the grated cheese down the
centre of the enchiladas.

9 Bake the enchiladas until the cheese
topping just melts, for about 10–15
minutes. Sprinkle with chopped spring
onions and serve immediately, with sour
cream on the side.

COOK'S TIP
For a quicker recipe, use minced
(ground) beef. Cook in a little oil with
chopped onion and garlic, until browned
all over. Continue the recipe from step 3.

CHILLI CON CARNE

*THIS FAMOUS TEX-MEX STEW HAS BECOME AN INTERNATIONAL FAVOURITE. SERVE IT
WITH RICE OR BAKED POTATOES AND A HEARTY GREEN SALAD.*

SERVES EIGHT

INGREDIENTS
    1.2kg/2½lb lean braising steak
    30ml/2 tbsp sunflower oil
    1 large onion, chopped
    2 garlic cloves, finely chopped
    15ml/1 tbsp plain (all-purpose) flour
    300ml/½ pint/1¼ cups red wine
    300ml/½ pint/1¼ cups beef stock
    30ml/2 tbsp tomato purée (paste)
    salt and ground black pepper

For the beans
    30ml/2 tbsp olive oil
    1 onion, chopped
    1 fresh red chilli, seeded
        and chopped
    2 × 400g/14oz cans red kidney
        beans, drained and rinsed
    400g/14oz can chopped tomatoes

For the topping
    6 tomatoes, peeled and chopped
    1 fresh green chilli, seeded
        and chopped
    30ml/2 tbsp chopped fresh chives
    30ml/2 tbsp chopped fresh
        coriander (cilantro), plus sprigs
        to garnish
    150ml/¼ pint/⅔ cup sour cream

2 Use a slotted spoon to remove the onion from the pan, then add the floured beef and cook over a high heat until browned on all sides. Remove from the pan and set aside, then flour and brown another batch of meat.

3 When the last batch of meat has been browned, return the reserved meat and the onion to the pan. Stir in the wine, stock and tomato purée. Bring to the boil, reduce the heat and simmer for 45 minutes, or until the beef is tender.

4 Meanwhile, for the beans, heat the olive oil in a frying pan and cook the onion and chilli until softened. Stir in the kidney beans and tomatoes, and simmer gently for 20–25 minutes, or until thickened and reduced.

5 Mix the tomatoes, chilli, chives and coriander for the topping. Ladle the meat mixture on to warmed plates. Add a layer of bean mixture and tomato topping. Finish with sour cream and garnish with coriander leaves.

1 Cut the meat into thick strips, then cut it crossways into small cubes. Heat the oil in a large, flameproof casserole. Add the chopped onion and garlic, and cook until softened but not coloured. Season the flour and place it on a plate, then toss a batch of meat in it.

MEATBALLS WITH SPAGHETTI

FOR A GREAT INTRODUCTION TO THE CHARM OF CHILLIES, THIS SIMPLE PASTA DISH IS HARD TO BEAT. CHILDREN LOVE THE GENTLE HEAT OF THE TOMATO SAUCE.

SERVES SIX TO EIGHT

INGREDIENTS
 350g/12oz minced (ground) beef
 1 egg
 60ml/4 tbsp roughly chopped fresh
  flat leaf parsley
 2.5ml/½ tsp crushed dried
  red chillies
 1 thick slice white bread,
  crusts removed
 30ml/2 tbsp milk
 about 30ml/2 tbsp olive oil
 300ml/½ pint/1¼ cups passata
  (bottled strained tomatoes)
 400ml/14fl oz/1⅔ cups
  vegetable stock
 5ml/1 tsp granulated sugar
 350–450g/12oz–1lb fresh or
  dried spaghetti
 salt and ground black pepper
 shavings of Parmesan cheese,
  to serve

1 Put the beef in a large bowl. Add the egg, with half the parsley and half the crushed chillies. Season with plenty of salt and pepper.

2 Tear the bread into small pieces and place these in a small bowl. Moisten with the milk. Leave to soak for a few minutes, then squeeze out the excess milk and crumble the bread over the meat mixture. Mix everything together with a wooden spoon, then use your hands to squeeze and knead the mixture so that it becomes smooth and quite sticky.

3 Wash your hands, rinse them under the cold tap, then pick up small pieces of the mixture and roll them between your palms to make about 40–60 small balls. Place the meatballs on a tray and chill for 30 minutes.

4 Heat the oil in a large non-stick frying pan. Cook the meatballs in batches until browned on all sides. Pour the passata and stock into a large pan. Heat gently, then add the remaining chillies and the sugar, and season. Add the meatballs and bring to the boil. Reduce the heat, and simmer for 20 minutes.

5 Bring a large pan of lightly salted water to the boil and cook the pasta until it is just tender, following the instructions on the packet. Drain and tip it into a large heated bowl. Pour over the sauce and toss gently. Sprinkle with the remaining parsley and shavings of Parmesan cheese. Serve immediately.

MUSSAMAN BEEF CURRY

*THIS DISH IS TRADITIONALLY BASED ON BEEF, BUT CHICKEN, LAMB OR TOFU CAN BE USED
INSTEAD. IT HAS A RICH, SWEET AND SPICY FLAVOUR AND IS BEST SERVED WITH BOILED RICE.
MUSSAMAN CURRY PASTE IS AVAILABLE FROM SPECIALIST STORES.*

4 Return the coconut cream and curry paste mixture to the pan with the beef and stir until thoroughly blended. Simmer for a further 4–5 minutes, stirring occasionally.

5 Stir the fish sauce, sugar, tamarind juice, cardamom pods, cinnamon stick, potato chunks and onion wedges into the beef curry. Continue to simmer for a further 15–20 minutes, or until the potato is cooked and tender.

6 Add the roasted peanuts to the pan and mix well to combine. Cook for about 5 minutes more, then transfer to warmed individual serving bowls and serve immediately.

COOK'S TIP

To make Mussaman curry paste, halve 12 large dried chillies and discard the seeds, then soak the chillies in hot water for about 15 minutes. Remove the chillies from the water and chop finely. Place the chopped chillies in a mortar or food processor and pound or process with 60ml/4 tbsp chopped shallots, 5 garlic cloves, the base of 1 lemon grass stalk and 30ml/2 tbsp chopped fresh galangal. Dry-fry 5ml/1 tsp cumin seeds, 15ml/1 tbsp coriander seeds, 2 cloves and 6 black peppercorns over a low heat for 1–2 minutes. Grind the toasted spices to a powder, then combine with 5ml/1 tsp shrimp paste, 5ml/1 tsp salt, 5ml/1 tsp granulated sugar and 30ml/2 tbsp vegetable oil. Add the shallot mixture to the spice mixture and stir well to make a paste.

SERVES FOUR TO SIX

INGREDIENTS
675g/1½lb stewing steak
600ml/1 pint/2½ cups coconut milk
250ml/8fl oz/1 cup coconut cream
45ml/3 tbsp Mussaman curry paste
30ml/2 tbsp Thai fish sauce
15ml/1 tbsp palm sugar or light
  muscovado (brown) sugar
60ml/4 tbsp tamarind juice (tamarind
  paste mixed with warm water)
6 green cardamom pods
1 cinnamon stick
1 large potato, about 225g/8oz,
  cut into even chunks
1 onion, cut into wedges
50g/2oz/½ cup roasted peanuts

1 Trim off any excess fat from the stewing steak, then, using a sharp knife, cut it into 2.5cm/1in chunks.

2 Pour the coconut milk into a large, heavy pan and bring to the boil over a medium heat. Add the chunks of beef, reduce the heat to low, partially cover the pan and simmer gently for about 40 minutes, or until tender.

3 Transfer the coconut cream to a separate pan. Cook over a medium heat, stirring constantly, for about 5 minutes, or until it separates. Stir in the Mussaman curry paste and cook rapidly for 2–3 minutes, until fragrant and thoroughly blended.

CHILLI BEEF WITH BASIL

THIS IS A VERY EASY DISH THAT CHILLI LOVERS WILL ENJOY COOKING AND EATING. USE BIRD'S EYE CHILLIES IF YOU CAN AND FRAGRANT THAI JASMINE RICE TO SERVE.

SERVES TWO

INGREDIENTS

16–20 large fresh basil leaves, plus
    30ml/2 tbsp finely chopped basil
about 90ml/6 tbsp groundnut
    (peanut) oil
275g/10oz rump (round) steak
30ml/2 tbsp Thai fish sauce
    (*nam pla*)
5ml/1 tsp soft dark brown sugar
2 fresh red chillies, sliced into rings
3 garlic cloves, chopped
5ml/1 tsp chopped fresh root ginger
1 shallot, thinly sliced
squeeze of lemon juice
salt and ground black pepper
Thai jasmine rice, to serve

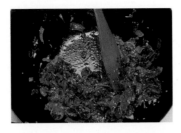

3 Reheat the oil until hot, add the chillies, garlic, ginger and shallot, and stir-fry for 30 seconds. Add the beef and chopped basil, and stir-fry for about 3 minutes more. Flavour with lemon juice and add salt and pepper to taste.

4 Transfer to a warmed serving platter, arrange the fried basil leaves over the top and serve immediately with rice. Good accompaniments would be lightly steamed green vegetables or a crisp green salad to provide contrast.

1 Dry the basil leaves thoroughly, if necessary. Heat the oil in a wok. When it is hot, add the basil leaves and fry for about 1 minute until crisp and golden. Scoop out and drain on kitchen paper. Remove the wok from the heat and carefully pour off all but 30ml/2 tbsp of the oil.

2 Cut the steak across the grain into thin strips. In a bowl, mix together the fish sauce and sugar. Add the beef, mix well, then cover and set aside to marinate for about 30 minutes.

COOK'S TIP

Groundnut oil is widely used in Chinese cooking. Its ability to be heated to a high temperature without burning makes it ideal for stir-frying. It has a mild, pleasant taste.

Pasta, noodles and rice lend themselves to flavouring with mild or hot spices. Give a new twist to traditional pasta dishes in a spicy Penne with Tomato and Chilli Sauce or Spaghetti with Garlic, Chilli and Oil. Try tongue-tingling noodle dishes from China and Thailand as Spicy Sichuan Noodles and Thai Fried Noodles are enlivened with chillies, limes and coriander. Savour the flavour of fish and rice with an Aromatic Mussel Risotto or Japanese Sushi with breathtaking wasabi paste.

Flame-filled Pasta, Noodle and Rice Main Dishes

PENNE WITH CHILLI AND BROCCOLI

SERVES 4

INGREDIENTS

  450g/1lb/3 cups penne
  450g/1lb small broccoli florets
  30ml/2 tbsp stock
  1 garlic clove, crushed
  1 small red chilli, sliced, or
    2.5ml/½ tsp chilli sauce
  60ml/4 tbsp natural (plain) yogurt
  30ml/2 tbsp toasted pine nuts
    or cashews
salt and ground black pepper

1 Add the pasta to a large pan of lightly salted, boiling water and return to the boil. Place the broccoli in a steamer basket over the top. Cover and cook for 8–10 minutes, until both the pasta and the brocolli are just tender. Drain.

VARIATION
Green chillies can be used instead of red chillies and toasted almonds make a good substitute for pine nuts.

2 Heat the stock to simmering point and add the crushed garlic and the sliced chilli or chilli sauce. Stir over a low heat for 2–3 minutes.

3 Stir in the broccoli, pasta and yogurt. Adjust the seasoning, sprinkle with toasted pine nuts or cashew nuts and serve hot.

FIVE-SPICE VEG[...]

THE MELLOW WARMTH OF FIVE-SPICE [...]
TO THE RAW HEAT OF THE CHILLIES IN[...]

SERVES TWO TO THREE

INGREDIENTS
    225g/8oz dried egg noodles
    30ml/2 tbsp sesame oil
    2 carrots
    1 celery stick
    1 small fennel bulb
    2 fresh red chillies
    2 courgettes (zucchini), halved
      and sliced
    2.5cm/1in piece of fresh root ginger,
      peeled and grated (shredded)
    1 garlic clove, crushed
    7.5ml/1½ tsp Chinese
      five-spice powder
    2.5ml/½ tsp ground cinnamon
    4 spring onions (scallions), sliced
    60ml/4 tbsp warm water

BLACK PASTA WITH SQUID SAUCE

ANOTHER SHELLFISH DISH WITH A SUBTLE, RATHER THAN A STRIDENT, CHILLI FLAVOUR.
DON'T BE TEMPTED TO OMIT THE CHILLI FLAKES.

SERVES FOUR

INGREDIENTS
    105ml/7 tbsp olive oil
    2 shallots, finely chopped
    3 garlic cloves, crushed
    45ml/3 tbsp chopped fresh parsley
    675g/1½lb cleaned squid, cut into
      rings and rinsed
    150ml/¼ pint/⅔ cup dry white wine
    400g/14oz can chopped tomatoes
    2.5ml/½ tsp dried chilli flakes
      or powder
    450g/1lb squid ink tagliatelle
    salt and ground black pepper

1 Heat the oil in a pan and cook the shallots until pale golden, then add the garlic. When the garlic colours a little, add 30ml/2 tbsp of the parsley, stir, then add the squid and stir again. Cook for 3–4 minutes, then pour in the dry white wine.

2 Simmer for a few seconds, then add the tomatoes and chilli flakes. Season with salt and pepper. Cover and simmer gently for about 1 hour, until the squid is tender. Add more water during the cooking time if necessary.

3 Bring a large pan of lightly salted water to the boil and cook the squid ink tagliatelle, following the instructions on the packet, or until it is *al dente*. Drain and return the pasta to the pan. Add the squid sauce and mix well to coat the tagliatelle evenly. Serve in warmed dishes, sprinkling each portion with the remaining chopped parsley.

COOK'S TIPS
• Tagliatelle flavoured with squid ink looks amazing and tastes deliciously of the sea. Look for it in good Italian delicatessens and better supermarkets.
• If you make your own pasta, you can buy sachets of squid ink from delicatessens.
• If you prepare the squid yourself, you will find the ink sac in the innards.

PENNE WITH TO

IN ITS NATIVE ITALY, THIS PASTA

SERVES FOUR

INGREDIENTS
25g/1oz/½ cup dried
  porcini mushrooms
90g/3½oz/7 tbsp butter
150g/5oz pancetta or rindless
  smoked streaky (fatty) bacon, diced
1–2 dried red chillies
2 garlic cloves, crushed
8 ripe Italian plum tomatoes, peeled
  and chopped
a few fresh basil leaves, torn, plus
  extra to garnish
350g/12oz/3 cups fresh or
  dried penne
50g/2oz/⅔ cup freshly grated
  (shredded) Parmesan cheese
25g/1oz/⅓ cup freshly grated
  (shredded) Pecorino cheese
salt

TOMATO NOODLES WITH FRIED EGG

SERVES 4

INGREDIENTS
350g/12oz medium-thick
  dried noodles
60ml/4 tbsp vegetable oil
2 garlic cloves, very
  finely chopped
4 shallots, chopped
2.5ml/½ tsp chilli powder
5ml/1 tsp paprika
2 carrots, finely diced
115g/4oz button (white)
  mushrooms, quartered
50g/2oz/½ cup peas
15ml/1 tbsp tomato ketchup
10ml/2 tsp tomato purée (paste)
salt and ground black pepper
butter, for frying
4 eggs

1 Cook the noodles in a pan of boiling water until just tender. Drain, rinse under cold running water and drain well.

2 Heat the oil in a wok or large frying pan. Add the garlic, shallots, chilli powder and paprika. Stir-fry for about 1 minute, then add the carrots, mushrooms and peas. Continue to stir-fry until the vegetables are cooked.

3 Stir the tomato ketchup and purée into the vegetable mixture. Add the noodles and cook over a medium heat until the noodles are heated through.

4 Meanwhile, melt the butter in a frying pan and fry the eggs. Season the noodle mixture, divide it among four serving plates and top each portion with a fried egg.

CURRY FRIED NOODLES

SERVES 4

INGREDIENTS
60ml/4 tbsp vegetable oil
30–45ml/2–3 tbsp curry paste
225g/8oz smoked tofu, cut into
  2.5cm/1in cubes
225g/8oz/1½ cups green beans, cut
  into 2.5cm/1in lengths
1 red (bell) pepper, seeded and cut
  into fine strips
350g/12oz rice vermicelli, soaked in
  warm water until soft
15ml/1 tbsp soy sauce
salt and ground black pepper
2 spring onions (scallions), finely
  sliced, 2 red chillies, seeded and
  chopped, and 1 lime, cut into
  wedges, to garnish

1 Heat half the oil in a wok or large frying pan. Add the curry paste and stir-fry for a few minutes, then add the tofu and continue to stir-fry until golden brown. Using a slotted spoon remove the cubes from the pan and set aside until required.

2 Add the remaining oil to the wok or pan. When hot, add the green beans and red pepper. Stir-fry until the vegetables are cooked. You may need to moisten them with a little water.

3 Drain the noodles and add them to the wok or frying pan. Continue to stir-fry until the noodles are heated through, then return the curried tofu to the wok. Season with soy sauce, salt and pepper.

4 Transfer the mixture to a serving dish. Sprinkle with the spring onions and chillies and serve the lime wedges on the side.

VARIATION
All kinds of thinly sliced smoked chicken, turkey or venison or flaked lightly smoked fish would combine well with this noodle dish.

TOSSED NOODLES WITH SEAFOOD

SERVES 4–6

INGREDIENTS
    350g/12oz thick egg noodles
    60ml/4 tbsp vegetable oil
    3 slices fresh root ginger, grated
    2 garlic cloves, finely chopped
    225g/8oz mussels or clams
    225g/8oz raw prawns
        (shrimp), peeled
    225g/8oz squid, cut into rings
    115g/4oz Asian fried fish cake, sliced
    1 red (bell) pepper, seeded and cut
        into rings
    50g/2oz sugar snap peas, trimmed
    30ml/2 tbsp soy sauce
    2.5ml/½ tsp sugar
    120ml/4fl oz/½ cup stock or water
    15ml/1 tbsp cornflour (cornstarch)
    5–10ml/1–2 tsp sesame oil
    salt and ground black pepper
    2 spring onions (scallions), chopped,
        and 2 red chillies, seeded and
        chopped, to garnish

1 Cook the noodles in a large pan of boiling water until just tender. Drain, rinse under cold water and drain well.

2 Heat the oil in a wok or large frying pan. Fry the ginger and garlic for 30 seconds. Add the mussels or clams, prawns and squid and stir-fry for about 4–5 minutes, until the seafood changes colour. Add the fish cake slices, red pepper rings and sugar snap peas and stir well.

3 In a bowl, mix the soy sauce, sugar, stock or water and cornflour.

4 Stir into the seafood and bring to the boil. Add the noodles and cook until they are heated through thoroughly.

5 Add the sesame oil to the wok or pan and season with salt and pepper to taste. Serve immediately, garnished with the spring onions and red chillies.

NOODLES WITH SPICY MEAT SAUCE

SERVES 4–6

INGREDIENTS
    30ml/2 tbsp vegetable oil
    2 dried red chillies, chopped
    5ml/1 tsp grated fresh root ginger
    2 garlic cloves, finely chopped
    15ml/1 tbsp chilli bean paste
    450g/1lb minced (ground) pork
        or beef
    450g/1lb broad flat egg noodles
    15ml/1 tbsp sesame oil
    2 spring onions (scallions), chopped,
        to garnish

For the sauce
    1.25ml/¼ tsp salt
    5ml/1 tsp sugar
    15ml/1 tbsp soy sauce
    5ml/1 tsp mushroom ketchup
    15ml/1 tbsp cornflour (cornstarch)
    250ml/8fl oz/1 cup chicken stock
    5ml/1 tsp Chinese rice wine or
        dry sherry

1 Heat the vegetable oil in a large pan. Add the dried chillies, ginger and garlic. Cook until the garlic starts to colour, then gradually stir in the chilli bean paste.

2 Add the minced pork or beef, breaking it up with a spatula or wooden spoon. Cook over a high heat until the minced meat changes colour and any liquid has evaporated.

3 Mix all the sauce ingredients in a jug (pitcher). Make a well in the centre of the pork mixture. Pour in the sauce mixture and stir together. Simmer for 10–15 minutes, until tender.

4 Meanwhile, cook the noodles in a large pan of boiling water for 5–7 minutes, until just tender. Drain well and toss with the sesame oil. Serve, topped with meat sauce and garnished with spring onions.

SPICY SICHUAN NOODLES

SERVES 4

INGREDIENTS
  350g/12oz thick noodles
  175g/6oz cooked chicken, shredded
  50g/2oz/½ cup roasted
    cashew nuts

For the dressing
  4 spring onions (scallions), chopped
  30ml/2 tbsp chopped
    coriander (cilantro)
  2 garlic cloves, chopped
  30ml/2 tbsp smooth peanut butter
  30ml/2 tbsp sweet chilli sauce
  15ml/1 tbsp soy sauce
  15ml/1 tbsp sherry vinegar
  15ml/1 tbsp sesame oil
  30ml/2 tbsp olive oil
  30ml/2 tbsp chicken stock
    or water
  10 toasted Sichuan
    peppercorns, ground

1 Cook the noodles in a pan of boiling water until just tender, following the directions on the packet. Drain, rinse under cold running water and drain well.

2 While the noodles are cooking combine all the ingredients for the dressing in a large bowl and whisk together well.

3 Add the noodles, chicken and nuts to the dressing, toss gently to coat and season to taste. Serve immediately.

SESAME NOODLES WITH SPRING ONIONS

THIS SIMPLE BUT TASTY WARM SALAD CAN BE PREPARED AND COOKED IN JUST A FEW MINUTES.

SERVES 4

INGREDIENTS
  2 garlic cloves, peeled and
    coarsely chopped
  30ml/2 tbsp Chinese
    sesame paste
  15ml/1 tbsp dark
    sesame oil
  30ml/2 tbsp soy sauce
  30ml/2 tbsp rice wine
  15ml/1 tbsp honey
  pinch of five-spice powder
  350g/12oz soba or
    buckwheat noodles
  4 spring onions (scallions),
    finely sliced diagonally
  50g/2oz/1 cup beansprouts
  7.5cm/3in piece of cucumber,
    cut into batons
  toasted sesame seeds
  salt and ground black pepper

1 Process the garlic, sesame paste, oil, soy sauce, rice wine, honey and five-spice powder with a pinch each of salt and pepper in a blender or food processor until smooth.

2 Cook the noodles in a pan of boiling water until just tender, following the directions on the packet. Drain the noodles immediately and tip them into a bowl.

3 Toss the hot noodles with the dressing and the spring onions. Top with the beansprouts, cucumber and sesame seeds and serve.

COOK'S TIP
If you can't find Chinese sesame paste, then use either tahini paste or smooth peanut butter instead.

CHINESE CHILLI NOODLES

*THERE ARE PLENTY OF CONTRASTING TEXTURES IN THIS SPICY STIR-FRY. CRISP GREEN BEANS
AND BEANSPROUTS VERSUS NOODLES AND OMELETTE STRIPS MAKE AN INTERESTING DISH.*

SERVES FOUR

INGREDIENTS
2 eggs
5ml/1 tsp chilli powder
5ml/1 tsp ground turmeric
60ml/4 tbsp vegetable oil
1 large onion, finely sliced
2 fresh red chillies, seeded and
   finely sliced
15ml/1 tbsp soy sauce
2 large cooked potatoes, cut into
   small cubes
6 pieces fried beancurd
   (tofu), sliced
225g/8oz/4 cups beansprouts
115g/4oz green beans, blanched
350g/12oz fresh thick
   egg noodles
salt and ground black pepper
sliced spring onions (scallions),
   to garnish

1 Beat the eggs lightly, then strain them through a fine sieve into a bowl. Heat a lightly greased omelette pan. Pour in half of the beaten egg and tilt the pan quickly to cover the base thinly. When the egg is just set, turn the omelette over, using chopsticks or a spatula, and fry the other side.

2 Slide the omelette on to a plate, blot with kitchen paper, roll up and cut into narrow strips. Make a second omelette in the same way and slice. Set the omelette strips aside for the garnish.

3 In a cup, mix together the chilli powder and turmeric. Form a paste by stirring in a little water.

4 Heat the oil in a wok or frying pan. Fry the onion until soft. Reduce the heat and stir in the chilli paste, chillies and soy sauce. Fry for 2 minutes.

5 Add the potatoes and fry for about 2 minutes, mixing well with the chillies. Add the beancurd, the beansprouts, green beans and noodles.

6 Gently stir-fry until the noodles are evenly coated and heated through. Take care not to break up the potatoes or the beancurd. Season with salt and pepper. Serve hot, garnished with the reserved omelette strips and spring onion slices.

COOK'S TIPS
• When making this dish for non-vegetarians, or for vegetarians who eat fish, add a piece of shrimp paste. A small chunk about the size of a stock (bouillon) cube, mashed with the chilli paste, will add a rich, aromatic flavour.
• Most chilli powder we buy is actually a blended mixture of ground dried red chillies, cumin, oregano and salt, often with a little garlic powder mixed in. For a pure powder, you'll need to find a specialist food store or order by mail.

TRADITIONAL INDONESIAN NOODLES

THIS FRIED NOODLE DISH IS WONDERFULLY ACCOMMODATING. TO THE BASIC RECIPE YOU CAN ADD OTHER VEGETABLES, SUCH AS MUSHROOMS, TINY PIECES OF CHAYOTE, BROCCOLI, LEEKS OR BEANSPROUTS. AS WITH FRIED RICE, YOU CAN USE WHATEVER YOU HAVE TO HAND, BEARING IN MIND THE NEED TO ACHIEVE A BALANCE OF COLOURS, FLAVOURS AND TEXTURES.

SERVES 6–8

INGREDIENTS

450g/1lb dried egg noodles
1 boneless, skinless chicken
   breast portion
115g/4oz pork fillet (tenderloin)
115g/4oz calf's liver (optional)
2 eggs, beaten
90ml/6 tbsp oil
25g/1oz/2 tbsp butter or margarine
2 garlic cloves, crushed
115g/4oz/1 cup cooked, peeled
   prawns (shrimp)
115g/4oz spinach or Chinese leaves
   (Chinese cabbage)
2 celery sticks, finely sliced
4 spring onions (scallions), shredded
about 60ml/4 tbsp chicken stock
dark soy sauce and light soy sauce
salt and ground black pepper
deep-fried onions and celery leaves,
   to garnish

1 Cook the noodles in salted, boiling water for 3–4 minutes. Drain, rinse with cold water and drain again. Set aside until required.

2 Finely slice the chicken, pork fillet and calf's liver, if using.

3 Season the eggs. Heat 5ml/1 tsp oil with the butter or margarine in a small pan until melted and then stir in the eggs and keep stirring until scrambled. Set aside.

4 Heat the remaining oil in a wok and cook the garlic with the chicken, pork and liver for 2–3 minutes, until they have changed colour. Add the prawns, spinach or Chinese leaves, celery and spring onions, tossing well.

5 Add the cooked and drained noodles and toss well again so that all the ingredients are well mixed. Add enough stock just to moisten and dark and light soy sauce to taste. Finally, stir in the scrambled eggs.

6 Serve, garnished with deep-fried onions and celery leaves.

COOK'S TIP
You could substitute turkey and bacon for the chicken and pork for a change.

INDIAN PILAU RICE

<u>SERVES 4</u>

INGREDIENTS
225g/8oz/generous 1 cup basmati
  rice, rinsed well
30ml/2 tbsp vegetable oil
1 small onion, finely chopped
1 garlic clove, crushed
5ml/1 tsp fennel seeds
15ml/1 tbsp sesame seeds
2.5ml/½ tsp ground turmeric
5ml/1 tsp ground cumin
1.5ml/½ tsp salt
2 whole cloves
4 green cardamom pods,
  lightly crushed
5 black peppercorns
450ml/¾ pint/scant 2 cups
  vegetable stock
15ml/1 tbsp ground almonds
coriander (cilantro) sprigs,
  to garnish

1 Soak the basmati rice in a pan of cold water for 30 minutes. Heat the vegetable oil in a pan, and then add the chopped onion and crushed garlic, and cook all together gently for 5–6 minutes, stirring occasionally, until softened.

2 Stir in the fennel and sesame seeds, the turmeric, cumin, salt, cloves, cardamom pods and peppercorns and cook for about 1 minute.

3 Drain the rice well, add it to the pan and stir-fry for a further 3 minutes.

4 Pour in the vegetable stock. Bring to the boil, then cover the pan, reduce the heat to very low and simmer very gently for 20 minutes, without removing the lid, until all the liquid has been absorbed.

5 Remove from the heat and leave to stand for 2–3 minutes. Fork up the rice and stir in the ground almonds. Garnish the rice with coriander sprigs.

OKRA FRIED RICE

SLICED OKRA PROVIDES A WONDERFUL CREAMY TEXTURE TO THIS DELICIOUS, SIMPLE DISH.

<u>SERVES 3–4</u>

INGREDIENTS
30ml/2 tbsp vegetable oil
15ml/1 tbsp butter or margarine
1 garlic clove, crushed
½ red onion, finely chopped
115g/4oz okra, trimmed
30ml/2 tbsp diced green and red
  (bell) peppers
2.5ml/½ tsp dried thyme
2 green chillies, finely chopped
2.5ml/½ tsp five-spice powder
1 vegetable stock (bouillon) cube
30ml/2 tbsp soy sauce
15ml/1 tbsp chopped coriander (cilantro)
225g/8oz/3 cups cooked rice
salt and ground black pepper
coriander (cilantro) sprigs,
  to garnish

1 Heat the oil and the butter or margarine in a frying pan, add the garlic and onion and cook over a medium heat for 5 minutes, until soft.

2 Thinly slice the okra, add to the frying pan and stir-fry gently for a further 6–7 minutes.

3 Add the green and red peppers, thyme, chillies and five-spice powder and cook for 3 minutes, then crumble in the stock cube.

4 Add the soy sauce, coriander and rice and heat through, stirring. Season with salt and pepper. Serve hot, garnished with coriander sprigs.

CHILLI CHIVE RICE WITH MUSHROOMS

*WHILE COOKING, THIS RICE DISH DEVELOPS A WONDERFUL AROMA, WHICH IS MATCHED
BY THE COMPLEMENTARY FLAVOURS OF CHILLI, GARLIC CHIVES AND FRESH CORIANDER.*

3 Add the rice to the onions and fry over a low heat, stirring frequently, for 4–5 minutes. Pour in the stock mixture, then stir in the salt and a good grinding of black pepper.

4 Bring to the boil, stir and reduce the heat to very low. Cover tightly and cook for 15–20 minutes, until the rice has absorbed all the liquid.

5 Remove from the heat. Lay a clean, folded dishtowel over the open pan and press on the lid, jamming it firmly in place. Leave to stand for 10 minutes. The towel will absorb the steam while the rice becomes completely tender.

SERVES FOUR

INGREDIENTS
    350g/12oz/1¾ cups long grain rice
    60ml/4 tbsp groundnut (peanut) oil
    1 small onion, finely chopped
    2 fresh green chillies, seeded and
      finely chopped
    a handful of garlic chives, chopped
    15g/½oz/¼ cup fresh
      coriander (cilantro)
    600ml/1 pint/2½ cups vegetable or
      mushroom stock
    5ml/1 tsp salt
    250g/9oz/3–3½ cups mixed
      mushrooms, thickly sliced
    50g/2oz/½ cup cashew nuts, fried in
      15ml/1 tbsp oil until golden brown
    ground black pepper

1 Wash and drain the rice. Heat half the oil in a pan and cook the onion and chillies over a low heat, stirring occasionally, for 10–12 minutes, until soft, but not browned.

2 Set half the garlic chives aside. Cut the stalks off the coriander and set the leaves aside. Purée the remaining chives and the coriander stalks with the stock in a blender or food processor.

COOK'S TIP
Wild mushrooms are often expensive, but they do have distinctive flavours. Mixing them with cultivated mushrooms is an economical way of using them. Look for ceps, chanterelles, oyster, morels and horse mushrooms.

6 Meanwhile, heat the remaining oil in a frying pan and cook the mushrooms for 5–6 minutes, until tender and browned. Add the remaining chives and cook for a further 1–2 minutes.

7 Stir the mixed, sliced mushrooms and chopped fresh coriander leaves into the cooked rice. Adjust the seasoning, transfer to a warmed serving dish and serve immediately, sprinkled with the cashew nuts.

BROWN RICE WITH LIME AND LEMON GRASS

IT IS UNUSUAL TO FIND BROWN RICE GIVEN THE THAI TREATMENT, BUT THE NUTTY FLAVOUR OF THE GRAINS IS HERE ENHANCED BY THE FRAGRANCE OF LIMES AND LEMON GRASS.

SERVES FOUR

INGREDIENTS

2 limes
1 lemon grass stalk
225g/8oz/generous 1 cup brown long grain rice
15ml/1 tbsp olive oil
1 onion, chopped
2.5cm/1in piece fresh root ginger, peeled and finely chopped
7.5ml/1½ tsp coriander seeds
7.5ml/1½ tsp cumin seeds
750ml/1¼ pints/3 cups vegetable stock
60ml/4 tbsp chopped fresh coriander (cilantro)
spring onion (scallion) green and toasted coconut strips, to garnish
lime wedges, to serve

1 Pare the limes, using a cannelle knife (zester) or fine grater, taking care to avoid cutting the bitter pith. Set the rind aside. Finely chop the lower portion of the lemon grass stalk and set it aside.

2 Rinse the rice in plenty of cold water until the water runs clear. Tip it into a sieve and drain thoroughly.

3 Heat the oil in a large pan. Add the onion, ginger, coriander and cumin seeds, lemon grass and lime rind and cook over a low heat for 2–3 minutes.

4 Add the rice to the pan and cook, stirring constantly, for 1 minute, then pour in the stock and bring to the boil. Reduce the heat to very low and cover the pan. Cook gently for 30 minutes, then check the rice. If it is still crunchy, cover the pan and cook for 3–5 minutes more. Remove from the heat.

5 Stir in the fresh coriander, fluff up the rice grains with a fork, cover the pan and leave to stand for 10 minutes. Transfer to a warmed dish, garnish with spring onion green and toasted coconut strips, and serve with lime wedges.

CARIBBEAN RED BEAN CHILLI

WHEN PULSES PARTNER CHILLIES, THE HEAT SEEMS TO BE MODERATED SLIGHTLY, SO THIS LENTIL AND BEAN MIXTURE IS GOOD FOR A HABANERO OR SCOTCH BONNET CHILLI.

3 Add the lentils, thyme, cumin, soy sauce, chilli, mixed spice and vegetarian oyster sauce, if using.

4 Cover and simmer for 40 minutes or until the lentils are cooked, stirring occasionally and adding more water if the lentils begin to dry out.

5 Stir in the red kidney beans and sugar and continue cooking for 10 minutes, adding a little extra stock or water if necessary. Season to taste with salt. Serve the chilli hot with boiled rice and sweetcorn.

SERVES FOUR

INGREDIENTS
30ml/2 tbsp vegetable oil
1 onion, chopped
400g/14oz can chopped tomatoes
2 garlic cloves, crushed
300ml/½ pint/1¼ cups white wine
about 300ml/½ pint/1¼ cups stock
115g/4oz/½ cup red lentils
5ml/1 tsp dried thyme
10ml/2 tsp ground cumin
45ml/3 tbsp dark soy sauce
½–1 habanero or Scotch bonnet
  chilli, seeded and finely chopped
5ml/1 tsp mixed (pumpkin pie) spice
15ml/1 tbsp vegetarian oyster
  sauce (optional)
225g/8oz can red kidney
  beans, drained
10ml/2 tsp granulated sugar
salt
boiled rice and sweetcorn, to serve

1 Heat the oil in a large pan and fry the onion over a medium heat for a few minutes until slightly softened.

2 Add the tomatoes and garlic, cook for 10 minutes, then stir in the white wine and stock.

COOK'S TIP
It's a good idea to cut any surplus chillies in half, wrap the halves separately, and freeze them.

VARIATION
You could substitute a can of black beans for the red kidney beans.

SAVOURY SPICY RICE

SERVES 6

INGREDIENTS

350g/12oz/1¾ cups long grain white rice
1 onion, chopped
2 garlic cloves, chopped
450g/1lb tomatoes, peeled, seeded
   and coarsely chopped
60ml/4 tbsp corn or groundnut
   (peanut) oil
900ml/1½ pints/3¾ cups chicken stock
4–6 small red chillies
175g/6oz/1 cup cooked green peas
salt and ground black pepper
fresh coriander (cilantro) sprigs,
   to garnish

1 Soak the rice in a bowl of hot water for 15 minutes. Drain, rinse well under cold running water, drain again and set aside.

2 Combine the onion, garlic and tomatoes in a food processor and process to a purée.

3 Heat the oil in a large frying pan. Add the drained rice and sauté until it is golden brown. Using a slotted spoon, transfer the rice to a pan.

4 Reheat the oil remaining in the pan and cook the tomato purée for 2–3 minutes. Tip it into the rice pan and pour in the stock. Season to taste. Bring to the boil, reduce the heat to the lowest possible setting, cover the pan and cook for 15–20 minutes, until almost all the liquid has been absorbed. Slice the red chillies from tip to stem end into four or five sections. Place in a bowl of iced water until they curl back to form flowers, then drain.

5 Stir the peas into the rice mixture and cook, uncovered, until the liquid has been absorbed and the rice is tender. Stir the mixture occasionally.

6 Transfer the rice to a serving dish and garnish with the drained chilli flowers and sprigs of coriander. Warn the diners that these elaborate chilli "flowers" are hot and should be approached with caution.

SPICY RICE CAKES

MAKES 16 CAKES

INGREDIENTS
1 garlic clove, crushed
1cm/½ in piece fresh root ginger,
  peeled and finely chopped
1.5ml/¼ tsp ground turmeric
5ml/1 tsp sugar
2.5ml/½ tsp salt
5ml/1 tsp chilli sauce
10ml/2 tsp fish or soy sauce
30ml/2 tbsp chopped fresh
  coriander (cilantro)
juice of ½ lime
115g/4oz/generous ½ cup dry weight
  long grain rice, cooked
peanuts, chopped
150ml/¼ pint/⅔ cup vegetable oil,
  for deep-frying
coriander sprigs, to garnish

1 In a food processor, process the garlic, ginger and turmeric. Add the sugar, salt, chilli and fish or soy sauce, coriander and lime juice.

2 Add three-quarters of the cooked rice and process until smooth and sticky. Transfer to a mixing bowl and stir in the remainder of the rice. Wet your hands and shape into thumb-size balls.

3 Roll the balls in chopped peanuts to coat evenly. Then set aside until ready to cook and serve.

VARIATION
Replace the chilli sauce with a small red chilli, but you would be wise to avoid incendiary varieties like habanero or Scotch bonnet. Red serranos or a mild red wax chilli would be suitable.

4 Heat the vegetable oil in a deep frying pan. Prepare a tray lined with kitchen paper to drain the rice cakes. Deep-fry three cakes at a time until crisp and golden, remove with a slotted spoon, then drain on the kitchen paper before serving hot.

RED RICE RISSOLES

SERVES 6

INGREDIENTS
1 large red onion, chopped
1 red (bell) pepper, chopped
2 garlic cloves, crushed
1 red chilli, finely chopped
30ml/2 tbsp olive oil
25g/1oz/2 tbsp butter
225g/8oz/generous 1 cup risotto rice
1 litre/1¾ pints/4 cups stock
4 sun-dried tomatoes, chopped
30ml/2 tbsp tomato purée (paste)
10ml/2 tsp dried oregano
45ml/3 tbsp chopped fresh parsley
150g/6oz cheese, e.g. red Leicester
  or smoked Cheddar
1 egg, beaten
115g/4oz/1 cup dried breadcrumbs
oil, for deep-frying
salt and ground black pepper

1 Cook the onion, pepper, garlic and chilli in the oil and butter for 5 minutes. Stir in the rice and cook for a further 2 minutes.

2 Pour in the stock and add the sun-dried tomatoes, purée, oregano and seasoning. Bring to the boil, stirring occasionally, then cover and simmer for 20 minutes.

3 Stir in the parsley, then turn into a shallow dish and chill until firm. When cold, divide into 12 and shape into equal-sized balls.

4 Cut the cheese into 12 pieces and press a nugget into the centre of each rice rissole.

5 Put the beaten egg in one bowl and the breadcrumbs into another. Dip the rissoles first into the egg, then into the breadcrumbs, coating each of them evenly and completely.

6 Place the rissoles on a plate and chill again for 30 minutes. Fill a deep frying pan one-third full of oil and heat until a cube of day-old bread browns in under a minute.

7 Fry the rissoles, in batches, for about 3–4 minutes, reheating the oil in between. Drain on kitchen paper and keep warm, uncovered. Serve with a side salad.

SQUID AND CHILLI RISOTTO

SQUID NEEDS TO BE COOKED VERY QUICKLY OR VERY SLOWLY. HERE THE SQUID IS MARINATED IN LIME AND KIWI FRUIT – A POPULAR METHOD IN NEW ZEALAND FOR TENDERIZING SQUID.

SERVES THREE TO FOUR

INGREDIENTS
   about 450g/1lb squid
   about 45ml/3 tbsp olive oil
   15g/½oz/1 tbsp butter
   1 onion, finely chopped
   2 garlic cloves, crushed
   1 fresh red chilli, seeded and
      finely sliced
   275g/10oz/1½ cups risotto rice
   175ml/6fl oz/¾ cup dry white wine
   1 litre/1¾ pints/4 cups simmering
      fish stock
   30ml/2 tbsp chopped fresh
      coriander (cilantro)
   salt and ground black pepper

For the marinade
   2 ripe kiwi fruit, chopped
      and mashed
   1 fresh red chilli, seeded and sliced
   30ml/2 tbsp lime juice

1 If not already cleaned, prepare the squid by cutting off the tentacles at the base and pulling to remove the quill. Discard the quill and intestines, if necessary, and pull away the thin outer skin. Rinse the body and cut into thin strips: cut the tentacles into short pieces, discarding both the beak and the eyes.

2 Put the kiwi fruit for the marinade in a bowl, then stir in the chilli and lime juice. Add the squid, stirring to coat all the strips in the mixture. Season with salt and pepper, cover with clear film (plastic wrap) and set aside in the refrigerator for 4 hours or overnight.

3 Drain the squid. Heat 15ml/1 tbsp of the olive oil in a frying pan and cook the strips, in batches if necessary, for about 30–60 seconds over a high heat. It is important that the squid cooks very quickly to keep it tender.

4 Transfer the cooked squid to a plate and set aside. Don't worry if some of the marinade clings to the squid, but if too much juice accumulates in the pan, pour this into a jug and add more olive oil when cooking the next batch, so that the squid fries rather than simmers. Reserve the accumulated juices in a jug.

5 Heat the remaining oil with the butter in a large pan and gently fry the onion and garlic for 5–6 minutes until soft. Add the sliced chilli to the pan and fry for 1 minute more.

COOK'S TIPS
• You can only make a true risotto with Italian risotto rice. Names to look for are Arborio, Carnaroli, Roma and Baldo. These are the rices that give the right kind of creamy texture.
• As in this recipe, always use a well-flavoured stock.

6 Add the rice. Cook for a few minutes, stirring, until the rice is coated with oil and is slightly translucent, then stir in the wine until it has been absorbed.

7 Gradually add the hot stock and the reserved cooking liquid from the squid, a ladleful at a time, stirring the rice constantly and waiting until each quantity of stock has been absorbed before adding the next.

8 When the rice is about three-quarters cooked, stir in the squid and continue cooking the risotto until all the stock has been absorbed and the rice is tender, but retains a bit of "bite". Stir in the chopped coriander, cover with the lid or a dishtowel, and leave to rest for a few minutes before serving.

VARIATIONS
• Use a long hot chilli, such as cayenne, for this dish, or try a milder variety, such as a red fresno.
• You can use a habanero if you like, but one-quarter or half will probably be sufficient, and remember to wear gloves when you handle it.

SPICY FISH AND RICE

THIS ARABIC FISH DISH, SAYADICH, IS ESPECIALLY POPULAR IN LEBANON.

SERVES 4–6

INGREDIENTS
juice of 1 lemon
45ml/3 tbsp oil
900g/2lb cod steaks
4 large onions, chopped
5ml/1 tsp ground cumin
2–3 saffron threads
1 litre/1¾ pints/4 cups fish stock
450g/1lb/generous 2¼ cups basmati or
  long grain rice
50g/2oz/½ cup pine nuts,
  lightly toasted
salt and ground black pepper
fresh parsley, to garnish

1 Blend the lemon juice and 15ml/
1 tbsp of oil in a shallow dish. Add the
fish, turn to coat thoroughly, then cover
and marinate for 30 minutes.

2 Heat the remaining oil in a large pan
and cook the onions for 5–6 minutes,
stirring occasionally.

3 Drain the fish, reserving the
marinade, and add to the pan. Cook for
1–2 minutes each side, until lightly
golden, then add the cumin, saffron
threads and a little salt and pepper.

4 Pour in the fish stock and the
reserved marinade, bring to the boil
and then simmer for 5–10 minutes, or
until the fish is nearly done.

5 Transfer the fish to a plate and add
the rice to the stock. Bring to the boil,
reduce the heat and simmer gently for
15 minutes, until nearly all the stock
has been absorbed.

6 Arrange the fish on top of the rice
and cover the pan. Steam over a low
heat for 15–20 minutes.

7 Transfer the fish to a plate, then
spoon the rice on to a large flat dish
and arrange the fish on top. Sprinkle
with toasted pine nuts and garnish with
fresh parsley.

MASALA PRAWNS AND RICE

SERVES 4–6

INGREDIENTS
2 large onions, sliced and deep-fried
300ml/½ pint/1¼ cups natural
  (plain) yogurt
30ml/2 tbsp tomato purée (paste)
60ml/4 tbsp green masala paste
30ml/2 tbsp lemon juice
5ml/1 tsp black cumin seeds
5cm/2in cinnamon stick
4 green cardamom pods
450g/1lb fresh king prawns (jumbo
  shrimp), peeled and deveined
225g/8oz/3 cups button (white)
  mushrooms
225g/8oz/2 cups frozen peas, thawed
450g/1lb/generous 2¼ cups basmati
  rice soaked for 5 minutes in boiled
  water and drained
300ml/½ pint/1¼ cups water
1 sachet saffron powder mixed in
  90ml/6 tbsp milk
30ml/2 tbsp ghee or unsalted (sweet)
  butter
salt

1 Mix the onions, yogurt, tomato purée,
green masala paste, lemon juice, black
cumin seeds, cinnamon stick and
cardamom pods together with salt to
taste. Mix the prawns, mushrooms and
peas into the marinade and leave for
about 2 hours.

2 Grease the base of a heavy pan and
add the prawns, vegetables and any
marinade juices. Cover with the
drained rice and smooth the surface
gently until you have an even layer.

3 Pour the water all over the surface
of the rice. Make random holes through
the rice with the handle of a spoon and
pour in the saffron milk.

4 Dot the ghee or butter on the surface
and place a circular piece of foil
directly on top of the rice. Cover and
steam over a low heat for 45–50
minutes, until the rice is cooked. Gently
toss the rice, prawns and vegetables
together and serve hot.

LOUISIANA SHELLFISH GUMBO

GUMBO IS A SOUP, BUT IS SERVED OVER RICE AS A MAIN COURSE. IN THIS VERSION, CHILLI IS ADDED TO THE "HOLY TRINITY" OF ONION, CELERY AND SWEET PEPPER.

SERVES SIX

INGREDIENTS
450g/1lb fresh mussels
450g/1lb raw prawns (shrimp),
  in the shell
1 cooked crab, about 1kg/2¼lb
small bunch of parsley, leaves
  chopped and stalks reserved
150ml/¼ pint/⅔ cup vegetable oil
115g/4oz/1 cup plain
  (all-purpose) flour
1 green (bell) pepper, seeded
  and chopped
1 large onion, chopped
2 celery sticks, sliced
1 fresh green chilli, seeded
  and chopped
3 garlic cloves, finely chopped
75g/3oz smoked spiced sausage,
  skinned and sliced
275g/10oz/1½ cups white long
  grain rice
6 spring onions (scallions), sliced
Tabasco sauce, to taste
salt

1 Wash the mussels in several changes of cold water, pulling away the black "beards". Discard broken mussels or any that do not close when tapped firmly.

2 Bring 250ml/8fl oz/1 cup water to the boil in a deep pan. Add the prepared mussels, cover the pan tightly and cook over a high heat, shaking frequently, for 3 minutes. As the mussels open, lift them out with tongs into a sieve set over a bowl. Discard any that fail to open. Shell the mussels, discarding most of the shells but reserving a few.

3 Peel the prawns and set them aside, reserving a few for the garnish. Put the shells and heads into the pan.

4 Remove all the meat from the crab, separating the brown and white meat. Add all the pieces of shell to the pan and stir in 5ml/1 tsp salt.

5 Return the mussel liquid from the bowl to the pan and make it up to 2 litres/3½ pints/8 cups with water. Bring the shellfish stock to the boil, skimming it regularly. When there is no more froth on the surface, add the parsley stalks and simmer for 15 minutes. Cool the reduced stock, then strain into a liquid measure and make it up to 2 litres/3½ pints/8 cups with water.

6 Heat the oil in a heavy pan and stir in the flour. Stir constantly over a medium heat with a wooden spoon or whisk until the roux reaches a golden-brown colour. Immediately add the pepper, onion, celery, chilli and garlic. Continue cooking for about 3 minutes until the onion is soft. Stir in the sausage. Reheat the stock.

7 Stir the brown crab meat into the roux, then ladle in the hot stock a little at a time, stirring constantly until it has all been smoothly incorporated. Bring to a low boil, partially cover the pan, then simmer for 30 minutes.

8 Meanwhile, cook the rice in plenty of lightly salted boiling water until the grains are tender.

9 Add the prawns, mussels, white crab meat and spring onions to the gumbo. Return to the boil and season with salt if necessary. Taste and add a dash or two of Tabasco sauce to heighten the heat generated by the chilli. Simmer for a further minute, then add the chopped parsley leaves. Serve immediately, ladling the soup over the hot rice in soup plates.

COOK'S TIP
It is vital to stir constantly to darken the roux without burning. Should black specks occur at any stage of cooking, discard the roux and start again. Have the pepper, onion, celery, chilli and garlic ready to add to the roux the minute it reaches the correct golden-brown stage, as this stops it from becoming too dark.

SEAFOOD AND RICE

<u>SERVES 4</u>

INGREDIENTS
30ml/2 tbsp oil
115g/4oz smoked bacon, rind
  removed, diced
1 onion, chopped
2 celery sticks, chopped
2 large garlic cloves, chopped
10ml/2 tsp cayenne pepper
2 bay leaves
5ml/1 tsp dried oregano
2.5ml/½ tsp dried thyme
4 tomatoes, peeled and chopped
150ml/¼ pint/⅔ cup tomato sauce
350g/12oz/1¾ cups long grain rice
475ml/16fl oz/2 cups fish stock
175g/6oz cod, or haddock, skinned,
  boned and cubed
115g/4oz/1 cup cooked, peeled
  prawns (shrimp)
salt and ground black pepper
2 spring onions (scallions), chopped,
  to garnish

1 Preheat the oven to 180°C/350°F/
Gas 4. Heat the oil in a large pan and
fry the bacon until crisp. Add the onion
and celery and stir until beginning to
stick to the pan.

2 Add the garlic, cayenne pepper,
herbs, tomatoes and seasoning and
mix well. Stir in the tomato sauce, rice
and stock and bring to the boil.

3 Gently stir in the fish and transfer
to an ovenproof dish. Cover tightly with
foil and bake for 20–30 minutes, until
the rice is just tender. Stir in the prawns
and heat through. Serve sprinkled with
the spring onions.

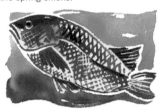

CHICKEN JAMBALAYA

<u>SERVES 10</u>

INGREDIENTS
2 × 1.5kg/3–3½ lb chickens
450g/1lb raw smoked gammon
  (cured ham)
50g/2oz/4 tbsp lard or bacon fat
50g/2oz/½ cup plain
  (all-purpose) flour
3 onions, finely sliced
2 green (bell) peppers, seeded
  and sliced
675g/1½ lb tomatoes, chopped
2–3 garlic cloves, crushed
10ml/2 tsp chopped fresh thyme or
  5ml/1 tsp dried thyme
24 Mediterranean prawns
  (shrimp), peeled
500g/1¼ lb/scant 3 cups long
  grain rice
2–3 dashes Tabasco sauce
6 spring onions (scallions),
  finely chopped
45ml/3 tbsp chopped fresh parsley
salt and ground black pepper

1 Cut each chicken into 10 pieces and
season. Dice the gammon, discarding
the rind and fat.

2 In a large casserole, melt the lard
or bacon fat and brown the chicken
pieces all over, lifting them out and
setting them aside as they are done.

3 Turn the heat down, sprinkle the flour
on to the fat in the pan and stir until
the roux turns golden brown.

4 Return the chicken pieces to the pan,
add the diced gammon, onions, green
peppers, tomatoes, garlic and thyme
and cook, stirring regularly, for
10 minutes, then stir in the prawns.

5 Stir the rice into the pan with one-
and-a-half times the rice's volume
in cold water. Season with salt, pepper
and Tabasco sauce. Bring to the boil
and cook over a low heat until the rice
is tender and the liquid absorbed. Add
a little extra boiling water if the rice
dries out before it is cooked.

6 Mix the spring onions and parsley
into the finished dish, reserving a little
of the mixture to sprinkle over the
jambalaya. Serve hot.

VARIATION
A traditional Creole dish, Jambalaya
is served with almost any kind of meat,
poultry or shellfish, according to the
taste of the individual cook.

COCONUT RICE

THIS IS A VERY POPULAR WAY OF COOKING RICE THROUGHOUT THE WHOLE OF SOUTH-EAST ASIA. IT MAKES A WONDERFUL ACCOMPANIMENT TO ANY DISH, ESPECIALLY FISH, CHICKEN AND PORK.

SERVES 4–6

INGREDIENTS

350g/12oz/1¾ cups Thai
   fragrant rice
400ml/14fl oz can coconut milk
300ml/½ pint/1¼ cups water
2.5ml/½ tsp ground coriander
1 cinnamon stick
1 lemon grass stalk, bruised
1 *pandan* or bay leaf (optional)
salt
deep-fried onions, to garnish

1 Wash the rice in several changes of water and then put in a pan with the coconut milk, water, coriander, cinnamon stick, lemon grass and *pandan* or bay leaf, if using, and salt. Bring to the boil, stirring to prevent the rice from settling on the base of the pan. Cover and cook over a very low heat for 12–15 minutes, or until all the coconut milk has been absorbed.

2 Fork the rice through carefully and remove the cinnamon stick, lemon grass and *pandan* or bay leaf. Cover the pan with a tight-fitting lid and then cook over the lowest possible heat for a further 3–5 minutes.

3 Pile the rice on to a warm serving dish and serve garnished with the crisp deep-fried onions.

SPICY RICE WITH CHICKEN

THIS IS A DISH THAT IS POPULAR ALL OVER THE EAST, IN COUNTRIES SUCH AS INDONESIA. IT IS OFTEN SERVED AS SUSTAINING BREAKFAST FARE FOR HEARTY EATERS.

SERVES 6

INGREDIENTS

1kg/2¼ lb chicken, cut in 4 pieces or
   4 chicken quarters
1.75 litres/3 pints/7½ cups water
1 large onion, quartered
2.5cm/1in fresh root ginger, peeled,
   halved and bruised
350g/12oz/1¾ cups Thai fragrant
   rice, rinsed
salt and ground black pepper
cooked prawns (shrimp), deep-fried
   onions, chopped garlic, strips of fresh
   red and green chilli, fried eggs and
   celery leaves, to garnish (optional)

1 Place the chicken pieces in a large pan with the water, onion and ginger. Add seasoning, bring to the boil and simmer for 45–50 minutes, until tender. Remove from the heat and reserve the stock.

2 Lift out the chicken, remove the meat and discard the skin and bones. Cut the chicken into bite-size pieces.

3 Strain the chicken stock into a clean pan and make it up to 1.75 litres/ 3 pints/7½ cups with water.

4 Add the rinsed rice to the chicken stock and stir constantly until it comes to the boil, to prevent the rice from settling on the base of the pan.

5 Simmer gently for 20 minutes, without a lid. Stir, cover and cook for a further 20 minutes, stirring occasionally, until the rice is soft and rather like a creamy risotto.

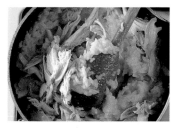

6 Stir the chicken pieces into the mixture and heat through for 5 minutes. Serve as it is, or with any of the garnishes and accompaniments.

MADRAS CURRY WITH SPICY RICE

CHILLIES ARE AN INDISPENSABLE INGREDIENT OF A HOT MADRAS CURRY. AFTER LONG, GENTLE SIMMERING, THEY MERGE WITH THE OTHER FLAVOURINGS TO GIVE A DELECTABLE RESULT.

SERVES FOUR

INGREDIENTS

    30ml/2 tbsp vegetable oil
    25g/1oz/2 tbsp ghee or butter
    675g/1½lb stewing beef, cut into
      bitesize cubes
    1 onion, chopped
    3 green cardamom pods
    2 fresh green chillies, seeded and
      finely chopped
    2.5cm/1in piece of fresh root
      ginger, grated (shredded)
    2 garlic cloves, crushed
    15ml/1 tbsp Madras curry paste
    5ml/1 tsp ground cumin
    5ml/1 tsp ground coriander
    150ml/¼ pint/⅔ cup beef stock
    salt

For the rice

    225g/8oz/generous 1 cup basmati rice
    15ml/1 tbsp sunflower oil
    25g/1oz/2 tbsp ghee or butter
    1 onion, finely chopped
    1 garlic clove, crushed
    5ml/1 tsp ground cumin
    2.5ml/½ tsp ground coriander
    4 green cardamom pods
    1 cinnamon stick
    1 small red (bell) pepper, seeded
      and diced
    1 small green (bell) pepper, seeded
      and diced
    300ml/½ pint/1¼ cups chicken stock

1 Heat half the oil with half the ghee or butter in a large, shallow pan. Fry the meat, in batches if necessary, until browned on all sides. Transfer to a plate and set aside.

2 Heat the remaining oil and ghee or butter and fry the onion for about 3–4 minutes until softened. Add the cardamom pods and fry for 1 minute, then stir in the chillies, ginger and garlic, and fry for 2 minutes more.

3 Stir in the curry paste, ground cumin and coriander, then return the meat to the pan. Stir in the stock. Season with salt, bring to the boil, then reduce the heat and simmer very gently for 1–1½ hours, until the meat is tender.

4 When the curry is almost ready, prepare the rice. Put it in a bowl and pour over boiling water to cover. Set aside for 10 minutes, then drain, rinse under cold water and drain again. The rice will still be uncooked but should have lost its brittleness.

VARIATION

If you like, you can serve plain boiled rice with this curry. Put the rice in a sieve and rinse it under cold water. Place in a pan with 5ml/1 tsp salt, and add water to come 5cm/2in above the level of the rice. Bring to the boil and simmer for 9–12 minutes. Drain and serve.

5 Heat the oil and ghee or butter in a flameproof casserole and fry the onion and garlic gently for 3–4 minutes until softened and lightly browned.

6 Stir in the ground cumin and coriander, green cardamom pods and cinnamon stick. Fry for 1 minute, then add the diced peppers.

7 Add the rice, stirring to coat the grains in the spice mixture, and pour in the chicken stock. Bring to the boil, then reduce the heat, cover the pan tightly and simmer for about 8–10 minutes, or until the rice is tender and the stock has been absorbed. Spoon into a bowl and serve with the curry.

COOK'S TIPS

• The curry should be fairly dry, but take care that it does not catch on the base of the pan. If you want to leave it unattended, cook it in a heavy pan. Alternatively, cook it in a flameproof casserole, in an oven preheated to 180°C/350°F/Gas 4.
• Offer a little mango chutney, if you like, and if you want to cool the heat, a bowl of yogurt raita.

Get into the habit of buying fresh chillies whenever you see them on sale, and you'll be surprised how often you'll use them in cooking, not necessarily as the principal ingredient, but for pungent punctuation. Chillies are great for highlighting other flavours, and nowhere is this more apparent than when they are added to vegetable and vegetarian dishes. Try Mushrooms with Chipotle Chillies, Peppers Filled with Spiced Vegetables or Jalapeño and Onion Quiche.

Vibrant Vegetarian and Side Dishes

MUSHROOMS <u>WITH</u> CHIPOTLE CHILLIES

CHIPOTLE CHILLIES ARE JALAPEÑOS THAT HAVE BEEN SMOKE-DRIED. THEIR SMOKY FLAVOUR IS THE PERFECT FOIL FOR THE MUSHROOMS IN THIS SIMPLE SALAD.

SERVES SIX

INGREDIENTS
  2 chipotle chillies
  450g/1lb/6 cups button
    (white) mushrooms
  60ml/4 tbsp vegetable oil
  1 onion, finely chopped
  2 garlic cloves, crushed or chopped
  salt
  small bunch of fresh coriander
    (cilantro), to garnish

VARIATION
Use cascabel instead of chipotle chillies. The name "cascabel" means "little rattle" and accurately describes the sound they make when shaken. Cascabel's nutty flavour is best appreciated when the skin is removed. Soak as for chipotle chillies, scoop out the flesh and add it to the onion and garlic.

1 Put the dried chillies in a heatproof bowl and pour over hot (not boiling) water to cover. Leave to stand for 20–30 minutes until they have softened. Drain, cut off the stalks, then slit the chillies and scrape out the seeds. Chop the flesh finely.

2 Trim the mushrooms, then clean them with a damp cloth or kitchen paper. If they are large, cut them in half.

3 Heat the oil in a large frying pan. Add the onion, garlic, chillies and mushrooms, and stir until evenly coated in the oil. Fry for 6–8 minutes, stirring occasionally, until the onion and mushrooms are tender.

4 Season with salt and spoon into a serving dish. Chop some of the coriander, leaving some whole leaves, and use to garnish. Serve hot.

RED HOT CAULIFLOWER

VEGETABLES ARE SELDOM SERVED PLAIN IN MEXICO. THE CAULIFLOWER HERE IS
FLAVOURED WITH A SIMPLE SERRANO AND TOMATO SALSA AND FRESH CHEESE.

SERVES SIX

INGREDIENTS

1 small onion
1 lime
1 medium cauliflower
400g/14oz can chopped tomatoes
4 fresh serrano chillies, seeded and
    finely chopped
1.5ml/¼ tsp granulated sugar
75g/3oz feta cheese, crumbled
salt
chopped fresh flat leaf parsley,
    to garnish

1 Chop the onion very finely and place in a bowl. With a zester or sharp knife, peel away the zest of the lime in thin strips. Add the lime zest to the finely chopped onion.

2 Cut the lime in half and use a reamer or citrus squeezer to extract the juice from each half in turn, adding it to the onion and lime zest mixture. Set aside for the lime juice to soften the onion.

COOK'S TIP
A zester enables you to pare off tiny strips of lime rind with no pith.

3 Cut the cauliflower into florets. Tip the tomatoes into a pan and add the chillies and sugar. Heat gently. Meanwhile, bring a pan of water to the boil, add the cauliflower florets and cook gently for 5–8 minutes until tender.

4 Add the chopped onion mixture to the tomato salsa, with salt to taste. Stir and heat through, then spoon about one-third of the salsa into a serving dish.

5 Arrange the drained cauliflower florets on top of the salsa and spoon the remaining salsa on top.

6 Sprinkle with the feta, which should soften a little on contact. Serve immediately, sprinkled with chopped fresh flat leaf parsley.

BEANS IN HOT SAUCE

A TASTY DISH OF NUTRITIOUS BEANS WITH A TOMATO AND CHILLI SAUCE.

SERVES 4

INGREDIENTS

450g/1lb green lima or broad (fava)
  beans, thawed if frozen
30ml/2 tbsp olive oil
1 onion, finely chopped
2 garlic cloves, chopped
350g/12oz tomatoes, peeled, seeded
  and chopped
1 or 2 drained canned jalapeño
  chillies, seeded and chopped
salt
chopped fresh coriander (cilantro)
  sprigs, to garnish

1 Cook the beans in a pan of boiling water for 15–20 minutes, until tender. Drain and keep hot, to one side, in the covered pan.

2 Heat the olive oil in a frying pan and sauté the onion and garlic until the onion is soft but not brown. Add the tomatoes and cook until the mixture is thick and flavoursome.

3 Add the jalapeños and cook for 1–2 minutes. Season with salt.

4 Pour the mixture over the reserved beans and check that they are hot. If not, return everything to the frying pan and cook over a low heat for just long enough to heat through. Put into a warm serving dish, garnish with the coriander and serve.

BROAD BEAN AND CAULIFLOWER CURRY

THIS IS A HOT AND SPICY VEGETABLE CURRY, IDEAL WHEN SERVED WITH BROWN BASMATI RICE, SMALL POPPADUMS AND MAYBE A COOLING CUCUMBER RAITA AS WELL.

SERVES 4

INGREDIENTS

2 garlic cloves, chopped
2.5cm/1 in cube fresh root ginger
1 fresh green chilli, seeded
  and chopped
15ml/1 tbsp oil
1 onion, sliced
1 large potato, chopped
30ml/2 tbsp ghee or softened butter
15ml/1 tbsp curry powder, mild
  or hot
1 cauliflower, cut into small florets
600ml/1 pint/2½ cups stock
30ml/2 tbsp creamed coconut or
  coconut cream
275g/10oz can broad (fava) beans
juice of ½ lemon (optional)
salt and ground black pepper
fresh coriander (cilantro), chopped,
  to garnish

1 Blend the garlic, ginger, chilli and oil in a food processor or blender until they form a smooth paste.

2 In a large pan, cook the onion and potato in the ghee or butter for 5 minutes, then stir in the spice paste and curry powder. Cook for 1 minute.

VARIATION
Try using broccoli florets instead of cauliflower in this recipe. Top with toasted pine nuts to add flavour and contrast to the dish.

3 Add the cauliflower florets and stir well into the spicy mixture, then pour in the stock. Bring to the boil and mix in the coconut, stirring until it melts and is combined.

4 Season well, then cover and simmer for 10 minutes. Add the beans and their can juices and cook, uncovered, for a further 10 minutes.

5 Check the seasoning and add a good squeeze of lemon juice, if you like. Serve hot, garnished with chopped coriander.

THAI ASPARAGUS

THIS IS AN EXCITINGLY DIFFERENT WAY OF COOKING ASPARAGUS. THE FLAVOUR IS COMPLEMENTED BY THE ADDITION OF GALANGAL AND CHILLI.

SERVES FOUR

INGREDIENTS
    350g/12oz asparagus stalks
    30ml/2 tbsp vegetable oil
    1 garlic clove, crushed
    15ml/1 tbsp sesame seeds, toasted
    2.5cm/1in piece fresh galangal,
      finely shredded
    1 fresh red chilli, seeded and
      finely chopped
    15ml/1 tbsp Thai fish sauce
    15ml/1 tbsp light soy sauce
    45ml/3 tbsp water
    5ml/1 tsp palm sugar or light
      muscovado (brown) sugar

VARIATIONS
Try this with broccoli or pak choi (bok choy). The sauce also works very well with green beans.

1 Snap the asparagus stalks. They will break naturally at the junction between the woody base and the more tender portion of the stalk. Discard the woody parts of the stems.

2 Heat the oil in a wok and stir-fry the garlic, sesame seeds and galangal for 3–4 seconds, until the garlic is just beginning to turn golden.

3 Add the asparagus stalks and chilli, toss to mix, then add the fish sauce, soy sauce, water and sugar. Using two spoons, toss over the heat for a further 2 minutes, or until the asparagus just begins to soften and the liquid is reduced by half.

4 Carefully transfer to a warmed platter and serve immediately.

SPRING ONIONS WITH ROMESCO SAUCE

SPRING ONIONS (CALÇOT) HAVE THEIR OWN FESTIVAL IN THE SPANISH PROVINCE OF TARRAGONA. IT IS A DAY TO MARK THE RETURN OF BETTER WEATHER, AND IN THE PAST LARGE SPRING ONIONS WERE BARBECUED IN THE FIELDS.

SERVES SIX

INGREDIENTS
  3 bunches of plump spring onions
    (scallions), or Chinese green onions,
    about 2.5cm/1in across the bulb
  olive oil, for brushing

For the romesco sauce
  2–3 *ñoras* or other mild dried red
    chillies, such as Mexican
    anchos or *guajillos*
  1 large red (bell) pepper, halved
    and seeded
  2 large tomatoes, halved and seeded
  4–6 large garlic cloves, unpeeled
  75–90ml/5–6 tbsp olive oil
  25g/1oz/¼ cup hazelnuts, blanched
  4 slices French bread, each about
    2cm/¾in thick
  15ml/1 tbsp sherry vinegar
  squeeze of lemon juice (optional)
  chopped fresh parsley, to garnish

1 Prepare the sauce. Soak the dried chillies in hot water for about 30 minutes. Preheat the oven to 220°C/425°F/Gas 7.

2 Place the pepper, tomatoes and garlic on a baking sheet and drizzle with 15ml/1 tbsp olive oil. Roast, uncovered, for 30–40 minutes, until the pepper is blistered and blackened and the garlic is soft. Cool slightly, then peel the pepper, tomatoes and garlic.

COOK'S TIP
This piquant romesco sauce is a variation on the classic, roasting the vegetables rather than frying them.

3 Heat the remaining oil in a small frying pan and fry the hazelnuts until lightly browned, then transfer them to a plate. Fry the bread in the same oil until light brown on both sides, then transfer to the plate with the nuts and leave to cool. Reserve the oil from cooking.

4 Drain the chillies, discard as many of their seeds as you can, then place the chillies in a food processor. Add the red pepper halves, tomatoes, garlic, hazelnuts and bread chunks together with the reserved olive oil. Add the vinegar and process to a paste. Check the seasoning and thin the sauce with a little more oil or lemon juice, if necessary. Set aside.

5 Trim the roots from the spring onions or trim the Chinese onion leaves so that they are about 15–18cm/6–7in long. Brush with oil.

6 Heat an oiled ridged grill pan and cook the onions for about 2 minutes on each side, turning once and brushing with oil. (Alternatively, place under a preheated grill (broiler) 10cm/4in away from the heat and cook for 3 minutes on each side, brushing with more oil when turned; roast in a preheated oven at 200°C/400°F/Gas 6 for 5–6 minutes; or barbecue over grey charcoal for 3–4 minutes on each side, brushing with oil as needed.) Serve immediately with the sauce.

MASALA MASHED POTATOES

THESE POTATOES ARE HERBY, HOT AND SPICY AND WILL PERK UP ANY MEAL.

SERVES 4

INGREDIENTS
3 potatoes
15ml/1 tbsp chopped fresh mint
  and coriander (cilantro), mixed
5ml/1 tsp mango powder
5ml/1 tsp salt
5ml/1 tsp crushed black peppercorns
1 fresh red chilli, chopped
1 fresh green chilli, chopped
50g/2oz/4 tbsp margarine

1 Boil the potatoes until soft enough to be mashed. Mash the potatoes down using a masher.

2 Blend together the chopped herbs, mango powder, salt, pepper, chillies and margarine to form a paste.

3 Stir the mixture into the mashed potatoes and mix together thoroughly with a fork. Serve warm as an accompaniment.

VARIATION
Instead of potatoes, try sweet potatoes. Cook them until tender, mash and continue from step 2.

SPICY CABBAGE

AN EXCELLENT VEGETABLE ACCOMPANIMENT, THIS IS A VERY VERSATILE SPICY DISH THAT CAN ALSO BE SERVED AS A WARM SIDE SALAD. IT'S SO QUICK TO MAKE THAT IT CAN BE A HANDY LAST MINUTE ADDITION TO ANY MEAL.

SERVES 4

INGREDIENTS
50g/2oz/4 tbsp margarine
2.5ml/½ tsp white cumin seeds
3–8 dried red chillies, to taste
1 small onion, sliced
225g/8oz/2½ cups
  cabbage
2 carrots, grated
2.5ml/½ tsp salt
30ml/2 tbsp lemon juice

1 Melt the margarine in a pan and stir-fry the white cumin seeds and dried red chillies for about 30 seconds.

2 Add the sliced onion and cook for about 2 minutes. Add the cabbage and carrots and stir-fry for a further 5 minutes, until the cabbage is soft.

3 Finally, stir in the salt and lemon juice and serve.

SPICY CARROTS

ADDING SPICES TO THE CARROTS BEFORE LEAVING THEM TO COOL INFUSES THEM
WITH FLAVOUR — AN IDEAL DISH TO SERVE COLD THE NEXT DAY.

SERVES 4

INGREDIENTS
  450g/1lb carrots
  475ml/16fl oz/2 cups water
  2.5ml/½ tsp salt
  5ml/1 tsp cumin seeds
  ½–1 red chilli (to taste)
  1 large garlic clove, crushed
  30ml/2 tbsp olive oil
  5ml/1 tsp paprika
  juice of 1 lemon
  flat leaf parsley, to garnish

VARIATION
For a more mellow variation try the juice
of a small blood-orange in place of the
juice of a lemon.

1 Cut the carrots into slices about
5mm/¼in thick. Bring the water to the
boil and add the salt and carrot slices.
Simmer for about 8 minutes, or until the
carrots are just tender, without allowing
them to get too soft. Drain the carrots,
put them into a bowl and set aside.

2 Grind or crush the cumin to a powder.
Remove the seeds from the chilli and
chop the chilli finely. Take care when
handling as they can irritate the skin
and eyes.

3 Gently heat the oil in a pan and toss
in the garlic and the chilli. Stir over a
medium heat for about a minute,
without allowing the garlic to brown. Stir
in the paprika and the lemon juice.

4 Pour the warm mixture over the
carrots, tossing them well so they are
coated with the spices. Spoon into a
serving dish and garnish with a sprig of
flat leaf parsley.

FIERY VEGETABLES IN COCONUT MILK

EIGHT CHILLIES MAY SEEM A BIT EXCESSIVE, ESPECIALLY IF YOU CHOOSE A SUPER-HOT VARIETY SUCH AS BIRD'S EYES, BUT REMEMBER THAT THE COCONUT MILK WILL PACIFY YOUR PALATE SOMEWHAT.

SERVES FOUR TO SIX

INGREDIENTS

450g/1lb mixed vegetables, such as
aubergines (eggplant), baby
sweetcorn, carrots, green beans,
asparagus and patty pan squash
8 fresh red chillies, seeded
2 lemon grass stalks, tender
portions chopped
4 kaffir lime leaves, torn
30ml/2 tbsp vegetable oil
250ml/8fl oz/1 cup coconut milk
30ml/2 tbsp Thai fish sauce
(*nam pla*)
salt (optional)
15–20 fresh holy basil leaves,
to garnish

COOK'S TIP
If you are unsure about the heat, use
fewer chillies or mix hot with mild
Anaheims or sweet (bell) peppers.

1 Trim the vegetables, then, using a sharp knife, cut them into pieces. They should all be more or less the same shape and thickness. Set aside.

2 Chop the fresh red chillies roughly and put them in a mortar. Add the lemon grass and kaffir lime leaves and grind to a paste. This can be done using a small blender, if you have one, or in the small bowl attachment of a food processor.

3 Heat the oil in a wok or large deep frying pan. Add the chilli mixture and fry over a medium heat for 2–3 minutes, stirring continuously.

4 Stir in the coconut milk and bring to the boil. Add the vegetables and cook for about 5 minutes or until they are all crisp-tender. Season with the fish sauce, and salt if needed. Spoon on to heated plates, garnish with holy basil leaves, and serve.

SICHUAN SIZZLER

THIS DISH IS ALSO KNOWN AS FISH-FRAGRANT AUBERGINE, AS THE FLAVOURINGS OFTEN ACCOMPANY FISH. IF YOU USE TINY AUBERGINES, OMIT THE SALTING PROCESS.

SERVES FOUR

INGREDIENTS
2 medium aubergines (eggplant)
5ml/1 tsp salt
3 dried red chillies
groundnut (peanut) oil, for
    deep-frying
3–4 garlic cloves, finely chopped
1cm/½in piece fresh root ginger,
    finely chopped
4 spring onions (scallions), cut into
    2.5cm/1in lengths (white and green
    parts kept separate)
15ml/1 tbsp Chinese rice wine or
    medium-dry sherry
15ml/1 tbsp light soy sauce
5ml/1 tsp granulated sugar
1.5ml/¼ tsp ground roasted
    Sichuan peppercorns
15ml/1 tbsp Chinese rice vinegar
5ml/1 tsp sesame oil

1 Trim the aubergines and cut them into strips, about 4cm/1½in wide and 7.5cm/3in long. Place the aubergines in a colander and sprinkle over the salt. Leave for 30 minutes, then rinse them thoroughly under cold running water. Pat dry with kitchen paper.

2 Meanwhile, soak the chillies in a bowl of warm water for 20–30 minutes. Then drain and pat dry with kitchen paper.

3 Cut each chilli into 3–4 pieces, discarding the seeds.

4 Half-fill a wok with oil and heat to 180°C/350°F. Deep-fry the aubergine pieces until golden brown. Drain on kitchen paper. Pour off most of the oil from the wok.

5 Reheat the oil left in the wok and add the garlic, ginger, chillies and the white spring onion. Stir-fry for 30 seconds.

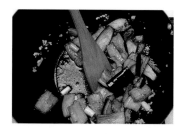

6 Add the aubergine and toss over the heat for 1–2 minutes. Stir in the rice wine or sherry, soy sauce, sugar, ground peppercorns and rice vinegar. Stir-fry for 1–2 minutes. Sprinkle over the sesame oil and green spring onion, and serve.

STEAMED VEGETABLES WITH THAI SPICY DIP

IN THAILAND, STEAMED VEGETABLES ARE OFTEN PARTNERED WITH RAW ONES TO CREATE THE CONTRASTING TEXTURES THAT ARE SUCH A FEATURE OF THE NATIONAL CUISINE. BY HAPPY COINCIDENCE, IT IS AN EXTREMELY HEALTHY WAY TO SERVE THEM.

SERVES FOUR

INGREDIENTS
1 head broccoli, divided into florets
130g/4½oz 1 cup green
   beans, trimmed
130g/4½oz asparagus, trimmed
½ head cauliflower, divided
   into florets
8 baby corn cobs
130g/4½oz mangetouts (snow peas)
   or sugar snap peas
salt

For the dip
1 fresh green chilli, seeded
4 garlic cloves, peeled
4 shallots, peeled
2 tomatoes, halved
5 pea aubergines (eggplant)
30ml/2 tbsp lemon juice
30ml/2 tbsp soy sauce
2.5ml/½ tsp salt
5ml/1 tsp granulated sugar

COOK'S TIP
Cauliflower varieties with pale green curds have a more delicate flavour than those with white curds.

1 Place the broccoli, green beans, asparagus and cauliflower in a steamer and steam over boiling water for about 4 minutes, until just tender but still with a "bite". Transfer them to a bowl and add the corn cobs and mangetouts or sugar snap peas. Season to taste with a little salt. Toss to mix, then set aside.

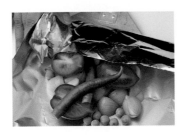

2 Make the dip. Preheat the grill (broiler). Wrap the chilli, garlic cloves, shallots, tomatoes and aubergines in a foil package. Grill (broil) for 10 minutes, until the vegetables have softened, turning the package over once or twice.

3 Unwrap the foil and tip its contents into a mortar or food processor. Add the lemon juice, soy sauce, salt and sugar. Pound with a pestle or process to a fairly liquid paste.

4 Scrape the dip into a serving bowl or four individual bowls. Serve, surrounded by the steamed and raw vegetables.

VARIATIONS
You can use a combination of other vegetables if you like. Use pak choi (bok choy) instead of the cauliflower or substitute raw baby carrots for the corn cobs and mushrooms in place of the mangetouts (snow peas).

PANCAKES STUFFED WITH LIGHTLY SPICED SQUASH

IN ORDER TO APPRECIATE THE INDIVIDUAL FLAVOURS OF THE BUTTERNUT SQUASH, LEEKS AND CHICORY IN THESE PANCAKES, IT IS IMPORTANT NOT TO OVERDO THE CHILLI.

SERVES FOUR

INGREDIENTS

   115g/4oz/1 cup plain (all-purpose) flour
   50g/2oz ⅓ cup yellow corn meal
   2.5ml/½ tsp salt
   2.5ml/½ tsp chilli powder
   2 large (US extra large) eggs
   450ml/¾ pint/scant 2 cups milk
   65g/2½oz/5 tbsp butter
   vegetable oil, for greasing
   25g/1oz/⅓ cup freshly grated
     (shredded) Parmesan cheese

For the filling

   30ml/2 tbsp olive oil
   450g/1lb butternut squash (peeled
     weight), seeded
   large pinch of dried red chilli flakes
   2 large leeks, thickly sliced
   2.5ml/½ tsp chopped fresh or
     dried thyme
   3 chicory (Belgian endive) heads,
     thickly sliced
   115g/4oz full-flavoured goat's
     cheese, cut into cubes
   90g/3½oz/scant 1 cup walnuts or
     pecan nuts, roughly chopped
   30ml/2 tbsp chopped fresh flat
     leaf parsley
   salt and ground black pepper

2 When ready to cook the pancakes, melt 25g/1oz/2 tbsp of the butter and stir it into the batter. Heat a lightly greased 18cm/7in heavy frying pan or crêpe pan. Pour about 60ml/4 tbsp of the batter into the pan, tilt it so that the batter forms a pancake and cook for 2–3 minutes, until set and lightly browned underneath. Turn and cook the pancake on the other side for 2–3 minutes. Lightly grease the pan after every second pancake.

3 Make the filling. Heat the oil in a large pan. Add the squash and cook, stirring frequently, for 10 minutes, until almost tender. Add the chilli flakes and cook, stirring, for a further 1–2 minutes. Stir in the leeks and thyme, and cook for 4–5 minutes more.

5 Preheat the oven to 200°C/400°F/ Gas 6. Lightly grease an ovenproof dish. Either layer the pancakes with the filling to make a stack in the dish or stuff each pancake with 30–45ml/2–3 tbsp filling. Roll or fold the pancakes to enclose the filling and place in the dish.

6 Sprinkle the grated Parmesan over the pancakes. Melt the remaining butter and drizzle it over the layered or filled pancakes. Bake for 10–15 minutes, until the cheese is bubbling and the pancakes are piping hot. Serve immediately.

COOK'S TIP
This can all be prepared in advance, but make sure the filling is cold before adding to the pancakes.

VARIATIONS
• Fennel could be used instead of chicory, and pumpkin, other varieties of winter squash or courgette (zucchini) instead of butternut squash.
• If you like, you can add a fresh chilli, but make it a mild one, such as Anaheim. Roast and peel it first.

1 Sift the flour, corn meal, salt and chilli powder into a bowl. Make a well in the centre. Add the eggs and a little of the milk. Whisk the eggs and milk, gradually incorporating the dry ingredients and adding more milk to make a batter with a consistency like that of thick cream.

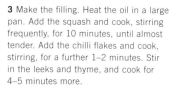

4 Add the chicory and cook, stirring frequently, for 4–5 minutes, until the leeks are cooked and the chicory is hot, but still with some bite to its texture. Cool slightly, then stir in the cheese, nuts and parsley. Season the mixture well with salt and pepper.

CHILLI AND PAK CHOI OMELETTE PARCELS

COLOURFUL STIR-FRIED VEGETABLES AND CORIANDER IN BLACK BEAN SAUCE MAKE
A REMARKABLY GOOD OMELETTE FILLING, WHICH IS QUICK AND EASY TO PREPARE.

SERVES FOUR

INGREDIENTS

130g/4½oz broccoli, cut into
 small florets
30ml/2 tbsp groundnut (peanut) oil
1cm/½in piece fresh root ginger,
 finely grated (shredded)
1 large garlic clove, crushed
2 fresh red chillies, seeded and
 finely sliced
4 spring onions (scallions),
 diagonally sliced
175g/6oz/3 cups pak choi
 (bok choy), shredded
50g/2oz/2 cups fresh coriander
 (cilantro) leaves, plus extra
 to garnish
115g/4oz/2 cups beansprouts
45ml/3 tbsp black bean sauce
4 eggs
salt and ground black pepper

1 Bring a pan of lightly salted water to the boil and blanch the broccoli for 2 minutes. Drain, then refresh under cold running water, and drain again.

2 Heat 15ml/1 tbsp of the oil in a frying pan and stir-fry the ginger, garlic and half the chilli for 1 minute. Add the spring onions, broccoli and pak choi, and toss the mixture over the heat for 2 minutes more.

3 Chop three-quarters of the coriander and add to the frying pan. Add the beansprouts and stir-fry for 1 minute, then add the black bean sauce and heat through for 1 minute more. Remove the pan from the heat and keep warm.

4 Mix the eggs lightly with a fork and season well. Heat a little of the remaining oil in a small frying pan and add one-quarter of the beaten egg. Tilt the pan so that the egg covers the base, then sprinkle over one-quarter of the reserved coriander leaves. Cook until set, then turn out the omelette on to a plate and keep warm while you make 3 more omelettes.

5 Spoon one-quarter of the stir-fry on to each omelette and roll up. Cut in half crossways and serve, garnished with coriander leaves and chilli slices.

COOK'S TIP
If you overdo the chilli, don't reach for a glass of water. Drinking it will simply spread the discomfort. Instead, eat something starchy, such as a piece of bread, or try a spoonful of yogurt.

SPICY ROOT VEGETABLE GRATIN

SUBTLY SPICED WITH CURRY POWDER, TURMERIC, CORIANDER AND MILD CHILLI POWDER, THIS RICH GRATIN IS SUBSTANTIAL ENOUGH TO SERVE ON ITS OWN.

2 Preheat the oven to 180°C/350°F/Gas 4. Heat half the butter in a heavy pan, and add the curry powder, turmeric and coriander. Stir in half the chilli powder. Cook for 2 minutes, then put aside to cool slightly.

3 Drain the vegetable slices, then pat them dry with kitchen paper. Place in a bowl, add the spice mixture and the shallots, and mix well.

4 Arrange the vegetables in a gratin dish, adding salt and pepper to each layer. Mix together the cream and milk, pour the mixture over the vegetables, then sprinkle the remaining chilli powder on top

SERVES FOUR

INGREDIENTS
    2 large potatoes, total weight
        about 450g/1lb
    2 sweet potatoes, total weight
        about 275g/10oz
    175g/6oz celeriac
    15ml/1 tbsp unsalted
        (sweet) butter
    5ml/1 tsp curry powder
    5ml/1 tsp ground turmeric
    2.5ml/½ tsp ground coriander
    5ml/1 tsp mild chilli powder
    3 shallots, chopped
    150ml/¼ pint/⅔ cup single
        (light) cream
    150ml/¼ pint/⅔ cup milk
    salt and ground black pepper
    chopped fresh flat leaf parsley,
        to garnish

1 Thinly slice the potatoes, sweet potatoes and celeriac, using a sharp knife or the slicing attachment in a food processor. Immediately place the slices in a bowl of cold water to prevent discolouring. Set aside.

VARIATION
Substitute parsnips or carrots for the sweet potatoes, and turnips for the celeriac.

5 Cover with baking parchment and bake for about 45 minutes. Remove the parchment, dot with the remaining butter and bake for 50 minutes more until the top is golden. Serve garnished with the chopped fresh parsley.

COOK'S TIP
A salad of mixed leaves could be served separately with the gratin then some fresh fruit, such as mango, to follow.

CHILLI COURGETTES

CALABACITAS IS AN EXTREMELY EASY RECIPE TO MAKE. IF THE COOKING TIME SEEMS UNDULY LONG, THIS IS BECAUSE THE ACID PRESENT IN THE TOMATOES SLOWS DOWN THE COOKING OF THE COURGETTES. USE YOUNG TENDER COURGETTES.

SERVES 4

INGREDIENTS
    30ml/2 tbsp corn oil
    450g/1lb young courgettes
      (zucchini), sliced
    1 onion, finely chopped
    2 garlic cloves, chopped
    450g/1lb tomatoes, peeled, seeded
      and chopped
    2 drained canned jalapeño chillies,
      rinsed, seeded and chopped
    15ml/1 tbsp chopped fresh
      coriander (cilantro)
    salt
    fresh coriander, to garnish

1 Heat the oil in a flameproof casserole and add all the remaining ingredients, except the salt.

2 Bring to simmering point, cover and cook over a low heat for about 30 minutes, until the courgettes are tender, checking from time to time that the dish is not drying out. If it is, add a little tomato juice, stock or water.

3 Season with salt and serve the Mexican way as a separate course. Alternatively, serve accompanied by any plainly cooked meat or poultry. Garnish with fresh coriander.

REFRIED BEANS

THERE IS MUCH DISAGREEMENT ABOUT THE TRANSLATION OF THE TERM REFRITO. IT MEANS, LITERALLY, TWICE FRIED. SOME COOKS SAY THIS IMPLIES THE BEANS MUST BE REALLY WELL FRIED, OTHERS THAT IT MEANS TWICE COOKED.

SERVES 6–8

INGREDIENTS
    90–120ml/6–8 tbsp lard or corn oil
    1 onion, finely chopped
    1 quantity Hot Chilli Beans
      (cooked beans)

To garnish
    freshly grated Parmesan cheese or
      crumbled cottage cheese
    crisp fried corn tortillas, cut
      into quarters

COOK'S TIP
Lard is the traditional (and best tasting) fat for the beans but many people prefer to use corn oil. Avoid using olive oil, which is too strongly flavoured and distinctive.

1 Heat 30ml/2 tbsp of the lard or oil in a large, heavy frying pan and sauté the onion until it is soft. Add about 225ml/8fl oz/1 cup of the Hot Chilli Beans (cooked beans).

2 Mash the beans with a potato masher, gradually adding more beans and melted lard or oil. The beans will form a heavy paste. Use extra lard or oil if necessary.

3 Tip out on to a warmed platter, piling the mixture up in a roll. Garnish with the cheese. Spike with the tortilla quarters, at intervals along the length of the roll.

GREEN CHILLI DHAL

THIS DHAL (TARKA DHAL) IS PROBABLY THE MOST POPULAR OF LENTIL DISHES AND IS FOUND IN MOST INDIAN AND PAKISTANI RESTAURANTS.

SERVES 4

INGREDIENTS
115g/4oz/½ cup masoor dhal (split red lentils)
50g/2oz/¼ cup moong dhal (small split yellow lentils)
600ml/1 pint/2½ cups water
5ml/1 tsp ginger pulp
5ml/1 tsp garlic pulp
1.5ml/¼ tsp ground turmeric
2 fresh green chillies, chopped
7.5ml/1½ tsp salt

For the tarka
30ml/2 tbsp oil
1 onion, sliced
1.5ml/¼ tsp mixed mustard and onion seeds
4 dried red chillies
1 tomato, sliced

To garnish
15ml/1 tbsp chopped fresh coriander (cilantro)
1–2 fresh green chillies, seeded and sliced
15ml/1 tbsp chopped fresh mint

COOK'S TIP
Dried red chillies are available in many different sizes. If the ones you have are large, or if you want a less spicy flavour, reduce the quantity specified to 1–2.

1 Pick over the lentils for any stones before washing them.

2 Boil the lentils in the water with the ginger, garlic, turmeric and chopped green chillies for about 15–20 minutes, until soft.

3 Mash the lentil mixture down. The consistency of the mashed lentils should be similar to that of a creamy chicken soup.

4 If the mixture looks too dry, just add some more water. Season with the salt.

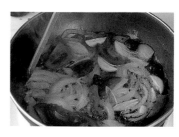

5 To prepare the tarka, heat the oil and cook the onion with the mustard and onion seeds, dried red chillies and sliced tomato for 2 minutes.

6 Pour the tarka over the dhal and garnish with fresh coriander, green chillies and mint.

VARIATION
In India, the term 'dhal' refers to any of almost 60 varieties of dried pulses, including mung beans, peas and all sorts of lentils. including red, yellow and brown. Adapt the recipe according to the contents of your store cupboard.

COUSCOUS WITH EGGS AND SPICY RELISH

A RICHLY FLAVOURED ROASTED TOMATO SAUCE, SPIKED WITH CHILLI, IS AN IDEAL TOPPING FOR LIGHTLY COOKED EGGS IN A SAVOURY COUSCOUS NEST.

SERVES FOUR

INGREDIENTS
    675g/1½lb plum tomatoes,
        roughly chopped
    4 garlic cloves, chopped
    75ml/5 tbsp olive oil
    ½ fresh red chilli, seeded
        and chopped
    10ml/2 tsp soft light
        brown sugar
    4 eggs
    1 large onion, chopped
    2 celery sticks, finely sliced
    50g/2oz/⅓ cup sultanas
        (golden raisins)
    200g/7oz/generous 1 cup ready-to-
        use couscous
    about 350ml/12fl oz/1½ cups hot
        vegetable stock
    salt and ground black pepper

1 Preheat the oven to 200°C/400°F/ Gas 6. Put the tomatoes and garlic in a roasting pan, drizzle with 30ml/2 tbsp of the oil, sprinkle with chopped chilli, sugar and salt and pepper, and roast for 20 minutes until soft.

VARIATION
Add a drained bottled pimiento or two to the tomato mixture before sieving it.

2 Lower the eggs carefully into boiling water and boil them for 4 minutes, then plunge them straight into cold water. When cold, shell them carefully.

3 Remove the tomatoes from the oven and push them through a sieve. Add 15ml/1 tbsp boiling water and 15ml/ 1 tbsp olive oil to the puréed tomatoes and blend to give a smooth, rich sauce. Season to taste with salt and pepper. Keep the sauce hot while you prepare the couscous.

4 Put 15–30ml/1–2 tbsp of the remaining olive oil in a large pan and gently fry the onion and celery until softened. Add the sultanas, couscous and hot stock, and set aside until all the liquid has been absorbed. This will take about 7 minutes. Stir gently, add extra hot stock if necessary and season to taste.

5 Spread out the couscous on to a large heated serving dish, half bury the eggs in it and spoon a little tomato sauce over the top of each egg. Serve immediately, with the rest of the sauce handed separately.

PARSNIPS AND CHICKPEAS IN A CHILLI PASTE

THE SWEET FLAVOUR OF PARSNIPS GOES VERY WELL WITH THE SPICES IN THIS INDIAN-STYLE VEGETABLE STEW. SERVE IT WITH PLAIN YOGURT AND OFFER INDIAN BREADS TO MOP UP THE SAUCE.

SERVES FOUR

INGREDIENTS

200g/7oz/scant 1 cup dried
   chickpeas, soaked overnight in
   cold water, then drained
7 garlic cloves, finely chopped
1 small onion, chopped
5cm/2in piece fresh root
   ginger, chopped
2 fresh green chillies, such as
   jalapeños or serranos, seeded and
   finely chopped
550ml/18fl oz/2½ cups water
60ml/4 tbsp groundnut (peanut) oil
5ml/1 tsp cumin seeds
10ml/2 tsp ground coriander seeds
5ml/1 tsp ground turmeric
2.5–5ml/½–1 tsp mild chilli powder
50g/2oz/½ cup cashew nuts, toasted
   and ground
250g/9oz tomatoes, peeled
   and chopped
900g/2lb parsnips, cut into chunks
5ml/1 tsp ground toasted
   cumin seeds
juice of ½–1 lime
salt and ground black pepper

To serve
   fresh coriander (cilantro) leaves
   a few cashew nuts, toasted

1 Put the chickpeas in a pan, cover with cold water and bring to the boil. Boil vigorously for 10 minutes, then reduce the heat so that the water boils steadily and cook for 1–1½ hours, or until tender. The cooking time will depend on how long the chickpeas have been stored.

2 Meanwhile, for the sauce, set 10ml/ 2 tsp of the garlic aside, and place the remainder in a food processor or blender. Add the onion, ginger and half the chillies. Pour in 75ml/5 tbsp of the water and process to a smooth paste.

COOK'S TIP
For a milder result, use Anaheim chillies and mild paprika instead of chilli powder.

3 Heat the oil in a large, deep frying pan and cook the cumin seeds for 30 seconds. Stir in the coriander seeds, turmeric, chilli powder and ground cashew nuts. Add the ginger and chilli paste and cook, stirring frequently, until the water begins to evaporate. Add the tomatoes and stir-fry until the mixture begins to turn red-brown in colour.

4 Drain the chickpeas and add them to the pan, with the parsnips and remaining water. Season with 5ml/1 tsp salt and plenty of black pepper. Bring to the boil, stir, then simmer, uncovered, for 15–20 minutes, until the parsnips are completely tender.

5 Reduce the liquid, if necessary, by boiling fiercely until the sauce is thick. Add the ground toasted cumin with lime juice to taste. Stir in the reserved garlic and chilli, and cook for a final 1–2 minutes. Sprinkle the coriander leaves and toasted cashew nuts over and serve immediately.

VARIATIONS
Substitute red kidney beans for chickpeas or use carrots and butter (lima) beans.

Chillies taste great in all sorts of salads, from a simple

mixture of spinach and serranos to the colourful

combination of fruit and vegetables that is known as

Gado-gado, served here with a peanut and chilli sauce.

Not surprisingly, they have a great affinity for sweet

peppers, but also work well with shellfish, especially

squid. Some fresh chillies are tender enough to use as

they are, seeded and sliced, but others benefit from being

roasted so that the flesh takes on a smoky flavour. Do

this over a flame or under the grill, or use a culinary

blow torch so that only the outer skin is charred.

Piquant Salads

TOMATO AND ONION SALAD

A REFRESHING SALAD, WHICH CAN BE MADE AHEAD; IT IMPROVES IF WELL CHILLED BEFORE SERVING. USE FIRM, SLIGHTLY UNDER-RIPE TOMATOES TO MAKE FIRM DICE.

SERVES 6

INGREDIENTS
    1 cucumber
    45ml/3 tbsp white wine vinegar
    10ml/2 tsp sugar
    1 tomato, peeled, seeded and diced
    1 small onion, finely sliced
    1 fresh red chilli, seeded
      and chopped
    salt

1 Trim the ends from the cucumber. Peel it lengthways but leave some of the skin on to make the salad look more attractive. Cut it in thin slices and lay them out on a large plate. Sprinkle with a little salt and leave for about 15 minutes. Rinse well and dry.

2 Mix the vinegar, sugar and a pinch of salt together. Arrange all the vegetables in a bowl and pour over the vinegar, sugar and salt mixture. Cover the salad and chill before serving.

COCONUT AND PEANUT RELISH

THE AROMA OF TOASTED COCONUT IS WONDERFUL AND IMMEDIATELY WILL HAVE YOU DREAMING OF WARMER CLIMES! SERUDENG IS SERVED AS AN ACCOMPANIMENT TO MANY INDONESIAN DISHES; ANY LEFTOVERS CAN BE STORED IN AN AIRTIGHT BOX.

SERVES 6-8

INGREDIENTS
    115g/4oz/1⅓ cups grated fresh
      coconut, or desiccated (dry
      unsweetened shredded) coconut
    175g/6oz salted peanuts
    5mm/¼ in cube shrimp paste
    1 small onion, quartered
    2–3 garlic cloves, crushed
    45ml/3 tbsp oil
    2.5ml/½ tsp tamarind pulp, soaked in
      30ml/2 tbsp warm water
    5ml/1 tsp coriander seeds, dry-fried
      and ground
    2.5ml/½ tsp cumin seeds, dry-fried
      and ground
    5ml/1 tsp dark brown sugar

1 Dry-fry the coconut in a wok or large frying pan over a medium heat, turning constantly, until crisp and a rich, golden colour. Leave to cool and add half to the peanuts. Toss together to mix.

2 Grind the shrimp paste, with the onion and garlic, to a paste in a food processor or with a mortar and pestle. Stir-fry in hot oil, without browning.

3 Strain the tamarind and reserve the juice. Add the coriander, cumin, tamarind juice and brown sugar to the fried paste. Stir constantly and cook for 2–3 minutes.

4 Stir in the remaining toasted coconut and leave to cool. When quite cold, mix with the peanut and coconut mixture.

VINEGARED CHILLI CABBAGE

A HOT CABBAGE DISH THAT WILL CERTAINLY ADD A BIT OF SPICE TO EVERY MEAL.
THE ADDITION OF VINEGAR AT THE END GIVES THIS DISH ITS DISTINCT FLAVOUR.

SERVES 4–6

INGREDIENTS

1 fresh red chilli, halved, seeded
   and shredded
25g/1oz/2 tbsp lard or butter
2 garlic cloves, crushed (optional)
1 white cabbage, cored
   and shredded
10ml/2 tsp cider vinegar
5ml/1 tsp cayenne pepper
salt

1 Put the chilli with the lard or butter into a large pan and cook over a medium heat until the chilli sizzles and curls at the edges.

2 Add the garlic and cabbage and stir, over the heat, until the cabbage is coated and warm. Add salt to taste and 75ml/5 tbsp water. Bring to the boil, cover and lower the heat.

3 Cook, shaking the pan regularly, for 3–4 minutes, until the cabbage wilts. Remove the lid, raise the heat and cook off the liquid. Check the seasoning and sprinkle with vinegar and cayenne pepper.

VARIATION
For a very savoury dish, replace the white cabbage with 450g/1lb sauerkraut. Rinse the sauerkraut well before use and take care not to add too much salt.

COOK'S TIP
A wok with a domed lid is good for this part-frying, part-steaming method of cooking cabbage.

COLESLAW IN TRIPLE-HOT DRESSING

THE TRIPLE HOTNESS IN THIS COLESLAW IS SUPPLIED BY MUSTARD, HORSERADISH AND TABASCO.

SERVES 6

INGREDIENTS

½ white cabbage, cored and
   shredded
2 celery sticks, finely sliced
1 green (bell) pepper, seeded and
   finely sliced
4 spring onions (scallions), shredded
30ml/2 tbsp chopped fresh dill
cayenne pepper

For the dressing

15ml/1 tbsp Dijon mustard
10ml/2 tsp creamed horseradish
5ml/1 tsp Tabasco sauce
30ml/2 tbsp red wine vinegar
75ml/5 tbsp olive oil
salt and ground black pepper

1 Mix the cabbage, celery, pepper and spring onions in a salad bowl.

2 Mix the mustard, horseradish and Tabasco sauce, then gradually stir in the vinegar with a fork and finally beat in the oil and seasoning. Toss the salad in the dressing and leave to stand, if possible, for at least 1 hour, turning it once or twice.

3 Immediately before serving, season the salad if necessary, toss again and sprinkle with dill and cayenne.

COOK'S TIP
This is a good salad for a buffet table or picnic as it improves after standing in its dressing (it could be left overnight in the refrigerator) and travels well in a covered plastic bowl or box.

KACHUMBALI SALAD

THIS IS A PEPPERY RELISH FROM TANZANIA, WHERE IT IS SERVED WITH GRILLED POULTRY, MEAT OR FISH DISHES, TOGETHER WITH RICE — THIS SALAD USES THE SAME COMBINATION OF VEGETABLES AND FLAVOURS.

SERVES 4–6

INGREDIENTS

  2 red onions
  4 tomatoes
  1 green chilli
  ½ cucumber
  1 carrot
  juice of 1 lemon
  salt and ground black pepper

1 Slice the onions and tomatoes very thinly and place in a bowl.

2 Slice the chilli lengthways, discard the seeds, then chop very finely. Peel and slice the cucumber and carrot and add to the onions and tomatoes.

COOK'S TIP
Traditional *Kachumbali* is made by very finely chopping the onions, tomatoes, cucumber and carrot. This produces a very moist, sauce-like mixture, which is good when served inside chapatis and eaten as a snack.

3 Squeeze the lemon juice over the salad. Season with salt and freshly ground black pepper and toss together to mix. Serve as an accompaniment, salad or relish.

COCONUT CHILLI RELISH

THIS SIMPLE BUT DELICIOUS RELISH IS WIDELY MADE IN TANZANIA. ONLY THE WHITE PART OF THE COCONUT FLESH IS USED — EITHER SHRED IT FAIRLY COARSELY, OR GRATE IT FINELY FOR A MOISTER RESULT.

MAKES ABOUT 50G/2OZ

INGREDIENTS

  50g/2oz fresh or desiccated
    (dry unsweetened
    shredded) coconut
  10ml/2 tsp lemon juice
  1.5ml/¼ tsp salt
  10ml/2 tsp water
  1.5ml/¼ tsp finely chopped
    red chilli

1 Grate the coconut and place in a mixing bowl. If using desiccated coconut, add just enough water to moisten it.

2 Add the lemon juice, salt, water and chilli. Stir thoroughly and serve as a relish with meats or as an accompaniment to a main dish.

VEGETABLES IN PEANUT AND CHILLI SAUCE

SERVES 4

INGREDIENTS

    15ml/1 tbsp palm or vegetable oil
    1 onion, chopped
    2 garlic cloves, crushed
    400g/14oz can tomatoes, puréed
    45ml/3 tbsp smooth peanut butter,
      preferably unsalted
    750ml/1¼ pint/3⅔ cups water
    5ml/1 tsp dried thyme
    1 green chilli, seeded and chopped
    1 vegetable stock (bouillon) cube
    2.5ml/½ tsp ground allspice
    2 carrots
    115g/4oz white cabbage
    175g/6oz okra
    ½ red (bell) pepper
    150ml/¼ pint/⅔ cup vegetable stock
    salt

1 Heat the oil in a large pan and cook the onion and garlic over a medium heat for 5 minutes, stirring frequently, until they are golden brown but not scorched. Add the tomatoes and peanut butter and stir well.

2 Stir in the water, thyme, chilli, stock cube, allspice and a little salt. Bring to the boil, lower the heat and then simmer gently, uncovered for about 35 minutes.

3 Cut the carrots into sticks, slice the cabbage, trim the okra and seed and slice the red pepper.

4 Place the vegetables in a pan with the stock, bring to the boil and cook until tender but still with a little "bite".

5 Drain the vegetables and place in a warmed serving dish. Pour the sauce over the top and serve.

MARINATED VEGETABLES ON SKEWERS

THESE KEBABS ARE A DELIGHTFUL MAIN DISH FOR VEGETARIANS, OR SERVE THEM AS A VEGETABLE SIDE DISH.

SERVES 4

INGREDIENTS
115g/4oz pumpkin
1 red onion
1 small courgette (zucchini)
1 ripe plantain
1 aubergine (eggplant)
½ red (bell) pepper, seeded
½ green (bell) pepper, seeded
12 button (white) mushrooms
25g/1oz/2 tbsp butter or margarine
300ml/½ pint/1¼ cups vegetable stock

For the marinade
60ml/4 tbsp lemon juice
60ml/4 tbsp olive or sunflower oil
45–60ml/3–4 tbsp soy sauce
150ml/¼ pint/⅔ cup tomato juice
1 green chilli, seeded and chopped
½ onion, grated
3 garlic cloves, crushed
7.5ml/1½ tsp dried tarragon, crushed
4ml/¾ tsp dried basil
4ml/¾ tsp dried thyme
4ml/¾ tsp ground cinnamon
ground black pepper

1 Peel and cube the pumpkin, place in a small bowl and cover with boiling water. Blanch for 2–3 minutes, then drain and refresh under cold water.

2 Cut the onion into wedges, slice the courgette and plantain and cut the aubergine and red and green peppers into chunks. Trim the mushrooms. Place the vegetables, including the pumpkin, in a large bowl.

3 Mix the marinade ingredients together and pour over the vegetables. Toss together and marinate for a few hours.

4 Thread the vegetables on to eight skewers. Preheat the grill (broiler).

5 Grill (broil) the skewers under a low heat for about 15 minutes, turning frequently, until golden brown, basting with the marinade to keep moist.

6 Place the remaining marinade, butter or margarine and stock in a pan and simmer for 10 minutes to cook the onion and reduce the sauce.

7 Pour the sauce into a serving jug (pitcher) and arrange the skewers on a plate. Serve with a rice dish or salad.

SWEET POTATO, PEPPER AND CHILLI SALAD

THIS SALAD IS COMPOSED OF A DELICIOUS BLEND OF INGREDIENTS AND HAS A TRULY TROPICAL TASTE. IT IS IDEAL SERVED WITH ASIAN OR CARIBBEAN DISHES.

2 Meanwhile, mix the dressing ingredients together in a bowl and season to taste.

3 Put the red pepper in a large bowl and add the celery and onion. Tip in the finely chopped chilli and mix with a wooden spoon.

4 Remove the sweet potatoes from the oven. When they are cool enough to handle, peel them. Cut them into cubes and add them to the large bowl. Drizzle the dressing over and toss carefully. Season again to taste and serve, garnished with fresh coriander.

SERVES FOUR TO SIX

INGREDIENTS
1kg/2¼lb sweet potatoes
1 red (bell) pepper, seeded and diced
3 celery sticks, finely diced
¼ red skinned onion, finely chopped
1 fresh red chilli, finely chopped
salt and ground black pepper

For the dressing
45ml/3 tbsp chopped fresh coriander
    (cilantro), plus extra to garnish
juice of 1 lime
150ml/¼ pint/⅔ cup natural
    (plain) yogurt

1 Preheat the oven to 200°C/400°F/ Gas 6. Wash the potatoes and pat dry with kitchen paper, pierce them all over and bake in the oven for 40 minutes or until tender.

VARIATION
This would work well with potatoes.

GADO-GADO <u>WITH</u> PEANUT <u>AND</u> CHILLI SAUCE

A BANANA LEAF, WHICH CAN BE BOUGHT FROM ASIAN FOOD STORES, CAN BE USED AS WELL AS THE MIXED SALAD LEAVES TO LINE THE PLATTER FOR A SPECIAL OCCASION.

SERVES SIX

INGREDIENTS
½ cucumber
2 pears (not too ripe) or 175g/6oz
  wedge of yam bean (jicama)
1–2 eating apples
juice of ½ lemon
mixed salad leaves
6 small tomatoes, cut in wedges
3 slices fresh pineapple, cored and
  cut in wedges
3 eggs, hard-boiled (hard-cooked)
  and shelled
175g/6oz egg noodles, cooked,
  cooled and chopped
deep-fried onions, to garnish

For the peanut sauce
2–4 fresh red chillies, seeded and
  ground, or 15ml/1 tbsp chilli sambal
300ml/½ pint/1¼ cups coconut milk
350g/12oz/1¼ cups crunchy
  peanut butter
15ml/1 tbsp dark soy sauce or soft
  dark brown sugar
5ml/1 tsp tamarind pulp, soaked in
  45ml/3 tbsp warm water
coarsely crushed peanuts
salt

2 Simmer gently until the sauce thickens, then stir in the soy sauce or sugar. Strain in the tamarind juice, add salt to taste and stir well. Spoon into a bowl and sprinkle with a few coarsely crushed peanuts.

VARIATION
Quail's eggs can be used instead of hen's eggs and look very attractive in this dish. Hard-boil for 3 minutes, shell, then halve or leave whole.

3 To make the salad, core the cucumber and peel the pears or yam bean. Cut them into matchsticks. Finely shred the apples and sprinkle them with the lemon juice. Spread a bed of salad leaves on a flat platter, then pile the fruit and vegetables on top.

4 Add the sliced or quartered hard-boiled eggs, the chopped noodles and the deep-fried onions. Serve at once, with the sauce.

1 Make the peanut sauce. Put the chillies or chilli sambal in a pan. Pour in the coconut milk. Stir in the peanut butter. Heat gently, stirring, until mixed.

COOK'S TIP
To make your own peanut butter, process roasted peanuts in a food processor, slowly adding vegetable oil to achieve the right texture. Add salt to taste.

HOT HOT CAJUN POTATO SALAD

IN CAJUN COUNTRY, WHERE TABASCO ORIGINATES, HOT MEANS REALLY HOT, SO
YOU CAN GO TO TOWN WITH THIS SALAD IF YOU THINK YOU CAN TAKE IT!

SERVES SIX TO EIGHT

INGREDIENTS
  8 waxy potatoes
  1 green (bell) pepper, seeded
  and diced
  1 large gherkin, chopped
  4 spring onions (scallions), shredded
  3 eggs, hard-boiled (hard-cooked),
  shelled and chopped
  250ml/8fl oz/1 cup mayonnaise
  15ml/1 tbsp Dijon mustard
  Tabasco sauce, to taste
  pinch or 2 of cayenne
  salt and ground black pepper
  fanned, sliced gherkin, to garnish
  salad leaves, to serve

1 Put the unpeeled potatoes in a pan of cold salted water, bring to the boil and cook for 20–30 minutes, until tender. Drain. When the potatoes are cool enough to handle, peel them and cut into large chunks.

2 Place the potatoes in a large bowl and add the green pepper, gherkin, spring onions and eggs. Mix gently.

3 In a separate bowl, mix the mayonnaise with the mustard and season with salt, black pepper and Tabasco sauce to taste.

4 Add the dressing to the potato mixture, toss gently to coat, then sprinkle a pinch or 2 of cayenne on top. Garnish with fanned, sliced gherkin.

COOK'S TIP
To hard-boil eggs, pierce the round end so air can escape to prevent cracking. Place in boiling water for 8 minutes. Remove into cold water, then peel.

CHAYOTE SALAD

COOL AND REFRESHING, THIS SALAD IS IDEAL ON ITS OWN OR WITH FISH OR CHICKEN DISHES.
THE SOFT FLESH OF THE CHAYOTES ABSORBS THE FLAVOUR OF THE DRESSING.

SERVES FOUR

INGREDIENTS
  2 *chayotes*, peeled, halved and seeded
  2 firm tomatoes
  1 small onion, finely chopped
  finely sliced strips of fresh red and
    green chilli, to garnish

For the dressing
  2.5ml/½ tsp Dijon mustard
  2.5ml/½ tsp ground anise
  90ml/6 tbsp white wine vinegar
  60ml/4 tbsp olive oil
  salt and ground black pepper

1 Bring a pan of water to the boil. Add the *chayotes* to the boiling water. Lower the heat and simmer for 20 minutes or until the *chayotes* are tender. Drain and set them aside to cool.

2 Meanwhile, peel the tomatoes. Cut a cross in the base of each tomato. Place them in a heatproof bowl and pour over boiling water to cover. After 3 minutes, lift the tomatoes out on a slotted spoon and plunge them into a bowl of cold water. Drain. The skins will have begun to peel back from the crosses. Remove the skins completely and cut the tomatoes into wedges.

3 Make the dressing by combining all the ingredients in a screw top jar. Close the lid tightly and shake the jar vigorously.

4 Cut the *chayotes* into wedges and place in a bowl with the tomato and onion. Pour over the dressing and serve garnished with strips of fresh red and green chilli.

BALTI POTATOES

BALTI IS A TRADITIONAL WAY OF COOKING INDIAN CURRIES IN A KARAHI COOKING PAN.

<u>SERVES 4</u>

INGREDIENTS
75ml/3 tbsp corn oil
2.5ml/½ tsp white cumin seeds
3 curry leaves
5ml/1 tsp crushed dried red chillies
2.5ml/½ tsp mixed onion, mustard and
  fenugreek seeds
2.5ml/½ tsp fennel seeds
3 garlic cloves
2.5ml/½ tsp shredded ginger
2 onions, sliced
6 new potatoes, sliced thinly
15ml/1 tbsp chopped fresh
  coriander (cilantro)
1 fresh red chilli, seeded and sliced
1 fresh green chilli, seeded
  and sliced

1 Heat the oil in a deep round-based frying pan or a karahi. Lower the heat slightly and add the cumin seeds, curry leaves, dried red chillies, mixed onion, mustard and fenugreek seeds, fennel seeds, garlic cloves and ginger. Cook for 1 minute, then add the onions and cook for a further 5 minutes, or until the onions are golden brown.

2 Add the potatoes, fresh coriander and fresh red and green chillies and mix well. Cover the pan tightly with a lid or foil, making sure the foil does not touch the food. Cook over a very low heat for about 7 minutes, or until the potatoes are tender.

3 Remove the pan from the heat, take off the foil and serve hot.

OKRA <u>WITH</u> GREEN MANGO <u>AND</u> LENTILS

IF YOU LIKE OKRA, YOU'LL LOVE THIS SPICY TANGY DISH.

<u>SERVES 4</u>

INGREDIENTS
115g/4oz/½ cup yellow lentils
45ml/3 tbsp corn oil
2.5ml/½ tsp onion seeds
2 onions, sliced
2.5ml/½ tsp ground fenugreek
5ml/1 tsp ginger pulp
5ml/1 tsp garlic pulp
7.5ml/1½ tsp chilli powder
1.5ml/¼ tsp ground turmeric
5ml/1 tsp ground coriander
1 green mango, peeled and sliced
450g/1lb okra, cut into
  1cm/½in pieces
7.5ml/1½ tsp salt
2 fresh red chillies, seeded
  and sliced
30ml/2 tbsp chopped fresh
  coriander (cilantro)
1 tomato, sliced

1 Wash the lentils thoroughly and put in a pan with enough water to cover. Bring to the boil and cook until soft but not mushy. Drain and set to one side.

2 Heat the oil in a deep round-based frying pan or a karahi and cook the onion seeds until they begin to pop. Add the onions and cook until golden brown. Lower the heat and add the ground fenugreek, ginger, garlic, chilli powder, turmeric and ground coriander.

3 Throw in the mango slices and the okra. Stir well and add the salt, red chillies and fresh coriander. Stir-fry for about 3 minutes, or until the okra is well cooked.

4 Finally, add the cooked lentils and sliced tomato and cook for a further 3 minutes. Serve hot.

PIQUANT PRAWN SALAD

THE FISH SAUCE DRESSING ADDS A SUPERB FLAVOUR TO THE NOODLES AND PRAWNS.
THIS DELICIOUS SALAD CAN BE ENJOYED WARM OR COLD.

SERVES FOUR

INGREDIENTS
  200g/7oz rice vermicelli
  8 baby corn cobs, halved
  150g/5oz mangetouts (snow peas)
  15ml/1 tbsp vegetable oil
  2 garlic cloves, finely chopped
  2.5cm/1in piece fresh root ginger,
    peeled and finely chopped
  1 fresh red or green chilli, seeded
    and finely chopped
  450g/1lb raw peeled tiger prawns
    (jumbo shrimp)
  4 spring onions (scallions), sliced
  15ml/1 tbsp sesame seeds, toasted
  1 lemon grass stalk, thinly shredded

For the dressing
  15ml/1 tbsp chopped fresh chives
  15ml/1 tbsp Thai fish sauce
  5ml/1 tsp soy sauce
  45ml/3 tbsp groundnut (peanut) oil
  5ml/1 tsp sesame oil
  30ml/2 tbsp rice vinegar

1 Put the rice vermicelli in a wide heatproof bowl, pour over boiling water and leave to soak for 10 minutes. Drain, refresh under cold water and drain well again. Tip into a large serving bowl and set aside until required.

2 Boil or steam the corn cobs and mangetouts for about 3 minutes, until tender but still crunchy. Refresh under cold running water and drain. Make the dressing by mixing all the ingredients in a screw-top jar. Close tightly and shake vigorously to combine.

3 Heat the oil in a large frying pan or wok. Add the garlic, ginger and red or green chilli and cook for 1 minute. Add the tiger prawns and toss over the heat for about 3 minutes, until they have just turned pink. Stir in the spring onions, corn cobs, mangetouts and sesame seeds, and toss lightly to mix.

4 Tip the contents of the pan or wok over the rice vermicelli. Pour the dressing on top and toss well. Sprinkle with lemon grass and serve, or chill for 1 hour before serving.

PINK AND GREEN SALAD

THERE'S JUST ENOUGH CHILLI IN THIS STUNNING SALAD TO BRING A ROSY BLUSH TO YOUR CHEEKS.

SERVES FOUR

INGREDIENTS
225g/8oz/2 cups dried farfalle or
  other pasta shapes
juice of ½ lemon
1 small fresh red chilli, seeded and
  very finely chopped
60ml/4 tbsp chopped fresh basil
30ml/2 tbsp chopped fresh
  coriander (cilantro)
60ml/4 tbsp extra virgin olive oil
15ml/1 tbsp mayonnaise
250g/9oz peeled cooked
  prawns (shrimp)
1 avocado
salt and ground black pepper

1 Bring a large pan of lightly salted water to the boil and cook the pasta for 10–12 minutes, folllowing the packet instructions, or until it is *al dente*.

2 Meanwhile, put the lemon juice and chilli in a bowl with half the basil and coriander. Add salt and pepper to taste. Whisk well to mix, then whisk in the oil and mayonnaise until thick. Add the prawns and stir to coat in the dressing.

3 Drain the pasta in a colander, and rinse under cold running water until cold. Leave to drain and dry, shaking the colander occasionally.

4 Halve, stone (pit) and peel the avocado, then cut the flesh into dice. Add to the prawns and dressing with the pasta, toss well to mix and taste for seasoning. Serve immediately, sprinkled with the remaining basil and coriander.

COOK'S TIP
Keep a few chillies in the freezer and you'll never need to worry about getting fresh supplies just when you want them.

THAI SHELLFISH SALAD WITH CHILLI DRESSING AND FRIZZLED SHALLOTS

IN THIS INTENSELY FLAVOURED SALAD, SWEET PRAWNS AND MANGO ARE PARTNERED WITH A SWEET-SOUR GARLIC DRESSING HEIGHTENED WITH THE HOT TASTE OF CHILLI.

SERVES FOUR TO SIX

INGREDIENTS
  675g/1½lb raw prawns (shrimp),
    shelled and deveined, with
    tails on
  finely shredded rind of 1 lime
  ½ fresh red chilli, seeded and
    finely chopped
  30ml/2 tbsp olive oil, plus extra
    for brushing
  1 ripe but firm mango
  2 carrots, cut into long
    thin shreds
  10cm/4in piece cucumber, sliced
  1 small red onion, halved and
    thinly sliced
  45ml/3 tbsp roasted peanuts,
    roughly chopped
  salt and ground black pepper

For the dressing
  1 large garlic clove, chopped
  10–15ml/2–3 tsp granulated sugar
  juice of 1½–2 limes
  15–30ml/1–2 tbsp Thai fish sauce
    (*nam pla*)
  1 fresh red chilli, seeded
  5–10ml/1–2 tsp light rice vinegar

For the frizzled shallots
  30ml/2 tbsp groundnut
    (peanut) oil
  4 large shallots, thinly sliced

COOK'S TIPS
• For an authentic flavour, use Pacific shrimp, which are a wonderful brownish blue when raw. If they are frozen, make sure they are thawed before using.
• When searing the prawns, make sure that they have all turned pink, as undercooked prawns are unpleasant to eat and may be harmful. However, do not overcook, which spoils the texture.
• Mangoes vary considerably. Some are ripe when the skin is green flushed with red; others when they are red-gold or yellow. Ripe mangoes give gently when squeezed lightly in the palm of the hand.

1 Place the prawns in a glass or china dish and add the lime rind and chilli. Season with salt and pepper, and spoon the oil over. Toss to mix, cover and leave to marinate for 30–40 minutes.

2 Make the dressing. Place the garlic in a mortar with 10ml/2 tsp sugar. Pound until smooth, then work in the juice of 1½ limes and 15ml/1 tbsp of the fish sauce.

3 Transfer the dressing to a jug (pitcher). Finely chop half the fresh red chilli, and add it to the dressing. Taste the mixture and add more sugar, lime juice, fish sauce and the rice vinegar to taste.

4 Cut through the mango lengthwise 1cm/½in from each side of the centre to free the stone (pit). Remove all the peel and cut the flesh away from the stone. Cut all the flesh into fine strips. Set the mango aside. Make the frizzled shallots by heating the oil in a wok or frying pan and frying them until crisp. Drain on kitchen paper and set aside.

5 In a bowl, toss the mango, carrots, cucumber and onion with half the dressing. Arrange the salad on individual plates or in bowls.

6 Heat a ridged, cast-iron griddle pan or heavy frying pan until very hot. Brush the prawns with a little oil, then sear them for 2–3 minutes on each side, until they turn pink and are patched with brown on the outside. Arrange the prawns on the salads.

7 Sprinkle the remaining dressing over the salads. Finely shred the remaining chilli and sprinkle it over the salads with the crisp-fried shallots. Serve, with the peanuts handed around separately.

VARIATIONS
• Use scallops or chicken breast portions instead of prawns.
• Chop cashew nuts in place of peanuts.
• Substitute finely sliced baby leeks for the shallots.
• Make into a more substantial meal by mixing with cooked pasta shapes.

SCALLOP CONCHIGLIE

SCALLOPS, PASTA AND ROCKET ARE FLAVOURED WITH PEPPER, CHILLI AND BALSAMIC VINEGAR.

2 Make the vinaigrette. Put the vinegar in a bowl and stir in the honey until dissolved. Add the chopped pepper, chillies and garlic, then whisk in the oil.

3 Bring a large pan of lightly salted water to the boil and cook the pasta for 10–12 minutes, or until *al dente*.

4 Meanwhile, heat the oil and butter in a frying pan until sizzling. Add half the scallops and toss over a high heat for 2 minutes. Remove with a slotted spoon and keep warm. Cook the remaining scallops in the same way.

5 Add the wine to the liquid remaining in the pan and stir over a high heat until the mixture has reduced to a few tablespoons. Remove from the heat and keep warm.

6 Drain the pasta and tip it into a warmed bowl. Add the rocket, scallops, the reduced cooking juices and the vinaigrette, and toss well to combine.

SERVES FOUR

INGREDIENTS
    8 large fresh scallops
    300g/11oz/2¾ cups dried conchiglie
        or other pasta shapes
    15ml/1 tbsp olive oil
    15g/½oz/1 tbsp butter
    120ml/4fl oz/½ cup dry white wine
    90g/3½oz/1½–2 cups rocket
        (arugula) leaves, stalks trimmed
    salt and ground black pepper

For the vinaigrette
    15ml/1 tbsp balsamic vinegar
    5–10ml/1–2 tsp clear honey, to taste
    1 piece bottled roasted (bell) pepper,
        drained and finely chopped
    1–2 fresh red chillies, seeded
        and chopped
    1 garlic clove, crushed
    60ml/4 tbsp extra virgin olive oil

1 Unless the fishmonger has already done so, remove the dark beard-like fringe and tough muscle from the scallops. Cut each of the scallops into 2–3 pieces. If the corals are attached, pull them off and cut each piece in half. Season with salt and pepper.

VARIATION
Use prawns (shrimp) instead of scallops.

COOK'S TIP
This is best prepared using fresh scallops, which look creamy-grey. If pure white they will have been frozen.

SPICY SQUID SALAD

THIS COLOURFUL SALAD IS A REFRESHING WAY OF SERVING SQUID. THE GINGER AND CHILLI
DRESSING IS ADDED WHILE THE SQUID IS STILL HOT, AND FLAVOURS THE SHELLFISH AND BEANS.

SERVES FOUR

INGREDIENTS
  450g/1lb squid
  300ml/½ pint/1¼ cups fish stock
  175g/6oz green beans, trimmed
    and halved
  45ml/3 tbsp fresh coriander
    (cilantro) leaves
  10ml/2 tsp granulated sugar
  30ml/2 tbsp rice vinegar
  5ml/1 tsp sesame oil
  15ml/1 tbsp light soy sauce
  15ml/1 tbsp vegetable oil
  2 garlic cloves, finely chopped
  10ml/2 tbsp finely chopped fresh
    root ginger
  1 fresh chilli, seeded and chopped
  salt

3 Bring the fish stock to the boil in a
wok or pan. Add all the squid pieces,
then lower the heat and cook for about
2 minutes until they are tender and
have curled. Drain.

4 Bring a pan of lightly salted water to
the boil, add the beans and cook them
for 3–5 minutes, until they are crisp-
tender. Drain, refresh under cold water
or turn into a bowl of iced water, then
drain again. Mix the squid and beans in
a serving bowl.

5 In a bowl, mix the coriander leaves,
sugar, rice vinegar, sesame oil and soy
sauce. Pour the mixture over the squid
and beans, and toss lightly, using a
spoon, to coat.

6 Heat the vegetable oil in a wok or
small pan. When it is very hot, stir-fry
the garlic, ginger and chilli for a few
seconds, then pour the dressing over
the squid mixture. Toss gently and leave
for at least 5 minutes. Add salt to taste
and serve warm or cold.

1 Prepare the squid. Holding the body
in one hand, gently pull away the head
and tentacles. Discard the head then
trim and reserve the tentacles. Remove
the transparent "quill" from inside the
body of the squid and peel off the
purplish skin on the outside.

2 Cut the body of the squid open
lengthways and wash thoroughly. Score
criss-cross patterns on the inside,
taking care not to cut through the flesh
completely, then cut into 7.5 × 5cm/
3 × 2in pieces.

COOK'S TIPS
• If you hold your knife at an angle when
scoring the squid, there is less of a risk
of cutting right through it.
• Always make sure your knives are kept
sharp to make cutting easier.

CHILLI CHICKEN SALAD

ANYONE WHO HAS TRAVELLED THROUGH NORTH-EAST THAILAND WILL HAVE ENCOUNTERED THIS TRADITIONAL DISH, IN WHICH CHICKEN IS COATED IN A HOT AND SHARP CHILLI SAUCE.

SERVES FOUR TO SIX

INGREDIENTS
450g/1lb minced (ground) chicken
1 lemon grass stalk, trimmed
3 kaffir lime leaves, finely chopped
4 fresh red chillies, seeded
   and chopped
60ml/4 tbsp lime juice
30ml/2 tbsp Thai fish sauce
   (*nam pla*)
15ml/1 tbsp roasted ground rice
   (see Cook's Tip)
2 spring onions (scallions), chopped
30ml/2 tbsp fresh coriander
   (cilantro) leaves
thinly sliced kaffir lime leaves, mixed
   salad leaves and fresh mint sprigs,
   to garnish

1 Heat a large non-stick frying pan. Add the chicken and moisten with a little water. Stir constantly over a medium heat for 7–10 minutes until it is cooked.

2 While the chicken is cooking, cut off the lower 5cm/2in of the lemon grass stalk and chop finely.

3 Transfer the cooked chicken to a bowl and add the chopped lemon grass, lime leaves, chillies, lime juice, fish sauce, ground rice, spring onions and coriander leaves. Mix thoroughly.

4 Spoon the chicken mixture into a salad bowl. Sprinkle sliced kaffir lime leaves over the top and garnish with salad leaves and sprigs of mint.

COOK'S TIP
Use glutinous rice (a short to medium grain rice) for the roasted ground rice. Put in a frying pan and dry-roast it until golden brown. Remove and grind to a powder, using a mortar and pestle or a food processor. When the rice is cold, store it in a glass jar in a cool, dry place.

THAI BEEF SALAD

A HEARTY MAIN MEAL SALAD, THIS COMBINES TENDER STRIPS OF STEAK WITH A WONDERFUL CHILLI AND LIME DRESSING. SERVE IT WITH WARM CRUSTY BREAD OR A BOWL OF RICE.

SERVES FOUR

INGREDIENTS
oil, for frying
2 sirloin steaks, each
   about 225g/8oz
1 lemon grass stalk, trimmed
1 red onion, finely sliced
½–1 fresh red chilli,
   finely chopped
½ cucumber, cut into strips
30ml/2 tbsp chopped spring
   onion (scallion)
juice of 2 limes
15–30ml/1–2 tbsp Thai fish sauce
   (*nam pla*)
Chinese mustard cress, or fresh
   herbs, to garnish

COOK'S TIP
Look out for gui chai leaves in Thai groceries. These look like very thin spring onions and are often used as a substitute for the more familiar vegetable.

1 Heat a large frying pan until hot, add a little oil and pan-fry the steaks for 6–8 minutes for medium-rare. If you prefer, cook the steaks under a preheated medium grill (broiler). Allow to rest for 10–15 minutes.

2 Cut off the lower 5cm/2in of the lemon grass stalk and chop it finely.

3 When the meat is cool, slice it thinly on a cutting board and put the slices in a large bowl.

4 Add the sliced onion, chilli, cucumber, lemon grass and chopped spring onion to the meat slices.

5 Toss the salad and flavour with the lime juice and fish sauce. Transfer to a serving bowl or plate and serve at room temperature or chilled, garnished with Chinese mustard cress or fresh herbs.

VARIATION
Instead of beef, use pork, chicken or meaty tuna steaks.

Warm spices, such as nutmeg, ginger, cinnamon and cardamom, enliven fresh fruit salads, ice creams, pastries, hot puddings and cakes. Indulge yourself with Fresh Pineapple with Ginger and wickedly sweet spicy Baklava from Persia. Give your friends a dessert to remember with an Egyptian version of Spiced Bread Pudding, scented with rose-water and flavoured with chopped pistachio nuts, almonds and hazelnuts.

Sweet and
Spicy Dishes

CARAMEL RICE PUDDING

THIS RICE PUDDING IS DELICIOUS SERVED WITH CRUNCHY FRESH FRUIT.

SERVES 4

INGREDIENTS
  50g/2oz/4 tbsp short grain rice
  75ml/5 tbsp demerara (raw) sugar
  5ml/1 tsp ground cinnamon
  400g/14oz can evaporated (unsweetened
    condensed) milk made up to
    600ml/1 pint/2½ cups with water
  knob (pat) of butter
  1 small fresh pineapple
  2 crisp eating apples
  10ml/2 tsp lemon juice

1 Preheat the oven to 150°C/300°F/ Gas 2. Put the rice in a sieve and wash thoroughly under cold water. Drain well and put into a lightly greased soufflé dish.

2 Add 30ml/2 tbsp sugar and the cinnamon to the dish. Add the diluted milk and stir gently.

3 Dot the surface of the rice with butter and bake for 2 hours, then leave to cool for 30 minutes.

4 Meanwhile, peel, core and slice the pineapple and apples and then cut the pineapple into chunks. Toss the fruit in lemon juice and set aside.

5 Preheat the grill (broiler) and sprinkle the remaining sugar over the rice. Grill (broil) for 5 minutes, or until the sugar has caramelized. Leave the rice to stand for 5 minutes to allow the caramel to harden, then serve with the fresh fruit.

SPICED RICE PUDDING

BOTH MUSLIM AND HINDU COMMUNITIES PREPARE THIS TRADITIONAL PUDDING.

SERVES 4–6

INGREDIENTS
  15ml/1 tbsp ghee or melted unsalted
    (sweet) butter
  5cm/2in piece cinnamon stick
  225g/8oz/1 cup soft brown sugar
  115g/4oz/½ cup ground rice
  1.2 litres/2 pints/5 cups milk
  5ml/1 tsp ground cardamom seeds
  50g/2oz/scant ½ cup sultanas
    (golden raisins)
  25g/1oz/¼ cup slivered almonds
  2.5ml/½ tsp grated nutmeg, to serve

1 In a heavy pan, heat the ghee or butter and cook the cinnamon and sugar. Keep cooking until the sugar begins to caramelize. Reduce the heat immediately when this happens.

2 Add the rice and half of the milk. Bring to the boil, stirring constantly to avoid the milk boiling over. Reduce the heat and simmer until the rice is cooked, stirring frequently.

3 Add the remaining milk, cardamom, sultanas and almonds and leave to simmer, but keep stirring to prevent the rice from sticking to the base of the pan. When the mixture has thickened, serve hot or cold, sprinkled with the grated nutmeg.

BAKLAVA

THIS IS THE QUEEN OF ALL PASTRIES WITH ITS EXOTIC FLAVOURS AND IS USUALLY SERVED FOR THE PERSIAN NEW YEAR ON 21 MARCH, CELEBRATING THE FIRST DAY OF SPRING.

SERVES 6–8

INGREDIENTS
350g/12oz/3 cups ground
  pistachio nuts
150g/5oz/1¼ cups icing
  (confectioners') sugar
15ml/1 tbsp ground cardamom
150g/5oz/⅔ cup unsalted (sweet)
  butter, melted
450g/1lb filo pastry

For the syrup
450g/1lb/2 cups granulated sugar
300ml/½ pint/1¼ cups water
30ml/2 tbsp rose-water

1 First make the syrup: place the sugar and water in a pan, bring to the boil and then simmer for 10 minutes, until syrupy. Stir in the rose-water and leave to cool.

2 Mix together the nuts, icing sugar and cardamom. Preheat the oven to 160°C/325°F/Gas 3 and brush a large rectangular baking tin (pan) with a little melted butter.

3 Taking one sheet of filo pastry at a time, and keeping the remainder covered with a damp cloth, brush with melted butter and lay on the base of the tin. Continue until yoy have six buttered layers in the tin. Spread half of the nut mixture over, pressing down with a spoon.

4 Take another six sheets of filo pastry, brush with butter and lay over the nut mixture. Sprinkle over the remaining nuts and top with a final layer of six filo sheets brushed again with butter. Cut the pastry diagonally into small lozenge shapes using a sharp knife. Pour the remaining melted butter over the top.

5 Bake for 20 minutes, then increase the heat to 200°C/400°F/Gas 6 and bake for 15 minutes, until light golden in colour and puffed.

6 Remove from the oven and drizzle about three-quarters of the syrup over the pastry, reserving the remainder for serving. Arrange the baklava lozenges on a large glass dish and serve with extra syrup.

SPICED BREAD PUDDING

HERE'S A SPICY EGYPTIAN VERSION OF BREAD AND BUTTER PUDDING.

SERVES 4

INGREDIENTS
  10–12 sheets filo pastry
  600ml/1 pint/2½ cups milk
  250ml/8fl oz/1 cup double (heavy) cream
  1 egg, beaten
  30ml/2 tbsp rose-water
  50g/2oz/½ cup each chopped
    pistachio nuts, almonds and hazelnuts
  115g/4oz/⅔ cup raisins
  15ml/1 tbsp ground cinnamon
  single (light) cream, to serve

1 Preheat the oven to 160°C/325°F/
Gas 3. Bake the filo pastry, on a
baking sheet, for 15–20 minutes,
until crisp. Remove the sheet from
the oven and raise the temperature
to 200°C/400°F/Gas 6.

2 Scald the milk and cream by pouring
into a pan and heating the mixture
very gently until it is hot but not
boiling. Gradually add the beaten egg
and the rose-water. Cook over a very
low heat until the mixture begins to
thicken, stirring constantly.

3 Crumble the pastry using your hands
and then spread in layers with the nuts
and raisins into the base of a shallow
ovenproof dish.

4 Pour the custard mixture over the
nut and pastry base and bake in the
oven for 20 minutes, until golden.
Sprinkle with cinnamon and serve with
single cream.

DATE AND NUT PASTRIES

MAKES 35–40

INGREDIENTS
  450g/1lb/4 cups plain
    (all-purpose) flour
  225g/8oz/1 cup unsalted (sweet)
    butter, cut into cubes
  45ml/3 tbsp rose-water
  60–75ml/4–5 tbsp milk
  icing (confectioners') sugar,
    for sprinkling

For the filling
  225g/8oz/1¼ cups dates, pitted
    and chopped
  175g/6oz/1½ cups walnuts,
    finely chopped
  115g/4oz/1 cup blanched
    almonds, chopped
  50g/2oz/½ cup pistachio
    nuts, chopped
  120ml/4fl oz/½ cup water
  115g/4oz/½ cup sugar
  10ml/2 tsp ground cinnamon

1 Preheat the oven to 160°C/325°F/
Gas 3. First make the filling: place the
dates, walnuts, almonds, pistachios,
water, sugar and cinnamon in a small
pan and cook over a low heat until
the dates are soft and the water has
been absorbed.

2 Place the flour in a large bowl and
add the butter, working it into the flour
with your fingertips.

3 Add the rose-water and milk and
knead the dough until it's soft.

4 Take walnut-size lumps of dough. Roll
each into a ball and hollow with your
thumb. Pinch the sides.

5 Place a spoonful of date mixture in
the hollow and then press the dough
back over the filling to seal.

6 Arrange the pastries on a large
baking sheet. Press to flatten them
slightly. Make little dents with a fork
on the pastry. Bake in the oven for
20 minutes. Do not let them change
colour or the pastry will become hard.
Cool slightly and then sprinkle with icing
sugar and serve.

CINNAMON BALLS

GROUND ALMONDS OR HAZELNUTS FORM THE BASIS OF MOST PASSOVER CAKES AND BISCUITS.
THESE BALLS SHOULD BE SOFT INSIDE, WITH A VERY STRONG CINNAMON FLAVOUR. THEY HARDEN
WITH KEEPING, SO FREEZE SOME AND ONLY USE THEM WHEN REQUIRED.

MAKES ABOUT 15

INGREDIENTS
    175g/6oz/1½ cups ground almonds
    75g/3oz/scant ½ cup caster
      (superfine) sugar
    15ml/1 tbsp ground cinnamon
    2 egg whites
    oil, for greasing
    icing (confectioners') sugar,
      for dredging

1 Preheat the oven to 180°C/350°F/Gas
4. Grease a large baking sheet with oil.

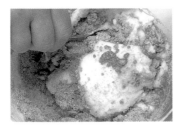

2 Mix together the ground almonds,
sugar and cinnamon.

3 Whisk the egg whites until they
begin to stiffen and fold enough egg
white into the almonds to make a
fairly firm mixture.

4 Wet your hands with cold water and
roll small spoonfuls of the mixture into
balls. Place these at intervals on the
baking sheet. Bake for about 15 minutes
in the centre of the oven. They should
be slightly soft inside – too much
cooking will make them hard and tough.

5 Slide a spatula under the balls to
release them from the baking sheet and
leave to cool. Sift a little icing sugar on
to a plate and when the balls are cold
slide them on to the plate. Shake gently
to cover the balls in sugar and store in
an airtight container or in the freezer.

APPLE AND CINNAMON CRUMBLE CAKE

THIS SCRUMPTIOUS CAKE HAS LAYERS OF SPICY FRUIT AND CRUMBLE AND IS QUITE
DELICIOUS SERVED WARM WITH FRESH CREAM.

MAKES 1 CAKE

INGREDIENTS
  3 large cooking apples
  2.5ml/½ tsp ground cinnamon
  250g/9oz/1 cup butter
  250g/9oz/1¼ cups caster (superfine)
    sugar
  4 eggs
  450g/1lb/4 cups self-raising
    (self-rising) flour

For the crumble topping
  175g/6oz/¾ cup demerara (raw) sugar
  125g/4¼ oz/generous 1 cup plain
    (all-purpose) flour
  5ml/1 tsp ground cinnamon
  65g/2½ oz/about 4½ tbsp desiccated
    (dry unsweetened shredded) coconut
  115g/4oz/½ cup butter

1 Preheat the oven to 180°C/350°F/
Gas 4. Grease a 25cm/10in round
cake tin (pan) and line the base with
greaseproof (waxed) paper. To make
the crumble topping, mix together the
sugar, flour, cinnamon and coconut in a
bowl, then rub in the butter with your
fingertips and set aside.

2 Peel and core the apples, then
grate them coarsely. Place them in a
bowl, sprinkle with the cinnamon and
set aside.

3 Cream the butter and sugar in a bowl
with an electric mixer, until light and
fluffy. Beat in the eggs, one at a time,
beating well after each addition.

4 Sift in half the flour, mix well, then
add the remaining flour and stir
until smooth.

5 Spread half the cake mixture evenly
over the base of the prepared tin.
Spoon the apples on top and sprinkle
over half the crumble topping.

6 Spread the remaining cake mixture
over the crumble and finally top with
the remaining crumble topping.

7 Bake for 1 hour 10 minutes – 1 hour
20 minutes, covering the cake with foil
if it browns too quickly. Leave in the tin
for about 5 minutes, before turning out
on to a wire rack. Once cool, cut into
slices to serve.

COOK'S TIP
To make the topping in a food processor,
add all the ingredients and process for a
few seconds until the mixture resembles
bread-crumbs. You can also grate the
apples using the grating disc. If you
don't have a 25cm/10in round tin, you
can use a 20cm/8in square cake tin.

MEXICAN BREAD PUDDING

MEXICAN COOKS BELIEVE IN MAKING GOOD USE OF EVERYTHING AVAILABLE TO THEM.
THIS PUDDING WAS INVENTED AS A WAY OF USING UP FOOD BEFORE THE LENTEN FAST,
BUT IS NOW EATEN AT OTHER TIMES TOO.

SERVES SIX

INGREDIENTS
1 small French stick, a few days old
75–115g/3–4oz/⅓–½ cup butter,
    softened, plus extra for greasing
200g/7oz/scant 1 cup soft dark
    brown sugar
1 cinnamon stick, about 15cm/
    6in long
400ml/14fl oz/1⅔ cups water
45ml/3 tbsp dry sherry
75g/3oz/¾ cup flaked almonds, plus
    extra, to decorate
75g/3oz/½ cup raisins
115g/4oz/1 cup grated Monterey Jack
    or mild Cheddar cheese
single cream, for pouring

1 Slice the bread into about 30 rounds,
each 1cm/½in thick. Lightly butter on
both sides. Cook in batches in a warm
frying pan until browned, turning over
once. Set the slices aside.

2 Place the sugar, cinnamon stick and
water in a saucepan. Heat gently,
stirring all the time, until the sugar has
dissolved. Bring to the boil, then lower
the heat and simmer for 15 minutes
without stirring. Remove the cinnamon
stick, then stir in the sherry.

COOK'S TIP
This recipe works well with older bread
that is quite dry. If you only have fresh
bread, slice it and dry it out for a few
minutes in a low oven.

3 Preheat the oven to 180°C/350°F/
Gas 4. Grease a 20cm/8in square
baking dish with butter. Layer the bread
rounds, almonds, raisins and cheese in
the dish, pour the syrup over, letting it
soak into the bread. Bake the pudding
for about 30 minutes until golden brown.

4 Remove from the oven, leave to stand
for 5 minutes, then cut into squares.
Serve cold, with single cream poured
over and decorated with the extra
flaked almonds.

DRUNKEN PLANTAIN

MEXICANS ENJOY THEIR NATIVE FRUITS AND UNTIL THEIR CUISINE WAS INFLUENCED BY
THE SPANISH AND THE FRENCH, THEY HAD NO PASTRIES OR CAKES, PREFERRING TO END
THEIR MEALS WITH FRUIT. THIS DELICIOUS DESSERT IS QUICK AND EASY TO PREPARE.

SERVES SIX

INGREDIENTS
3 ripe plantains
50g/2oz/¼ cup butter, diced
45ml/3 tbsp rum
grated rind and juice of
    1 small orange
5ml/1 tsp ground cinnamon
50g/2oz/¼ cup soft dark brown sugar
50g/2oz/½ cup whole almonds, in
    their skins
fresh mint sprigs, to decorate
Crème fraîche or thick double cream,
    to serve

1 Preheat the oven to 180°C/350°F/
Gas 4. Peel the plantains and cut them
in half lengthways. Put the pieces in a
shallow baking dish, dot them all over
with butter, then spoon over the rum
and orange juice.

2 Mix the orange rind, cinnamon and
brown sugar in a bowl. Sprinkle the
mixture over the plantains.

3 Bake for 25–30 minutes, until the
plantains are soft and the sugar has
melted into the rum and orange juice
to form a sauce.

4 Meanwhile, slice the almonds and dry
fry them in a heavy-based frying pan
until the cut sides are golden. Serve the
plantains in individual bowls, with some
of the sauce spooned over. Sprinkle the
almonds on top, decorate with the fresh
mint sprigs and offer crème fraîche or
double cream separately.

CINNAMON ROLLS

MAKES 24 SMALL ROLLS

INGREDIENTS
For the dough
   400g/14oz/3½ cups strong
     white bread flour
   2.5ml/½ tsp salt
   30ml/2 tbsp sugar
   5ml/1 tsp easy-blend (rapid-rise)
     dried yeast
   45ml/3 tbsp oil
   1 egg
   120ml/4fl oz/½ cup warm milk
   120ml/4fl oz/½ cup warm water

For the filling
   25g/1oz/2 tbsp butter, softened
   25g/1oz/2 tbsp dark brown sugar
   2.5–5ml/½–1 tsp ground cinnamon
   15ml/1 tbsp raisins

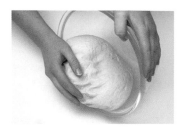

1 Sift the flour, salt and sugar and sprinkle over the yeast. Mix the oil, egg, milk and water and add to the flour. Mix to a dough, then knead until smooth. Leave to rise until doubled in size and then knock back (punch down).

2 Roll out the dough into a large rectangle and cut in half vertically. Spread over the soft butter, reserving 15ml/1 tbsp for brushing. Mix the sugar and cinnamon and sprinkle over the top. Dot with the raisins.

3 Roll each piece into a long Swiss (jelly) roll shape, to enclose the filling. Cut into 2.5cm/1in slices, arrange flat on a greased baking sheet and brush with the remaining butter. Leave to rise again for about 30 minutes.

4 Preheat the oven to 200°C/400°F/ Gas 6 and bake the cinnamon rolls for about 20 minutes. Leave to cool on a wire rack. Serve fresh for breakfast or tea, with extra butter if you like.

PEACH KUCHEN

THE JOY OF THIS CAKE IS ITS ALL-IN-ONE SIMPLICITY. IT CAN BE SERVED STRAIGHT FROM THE OVEN, OR CUT INTO SQUARES WHEN COLD.

SERVES 8

INGREDIENTS

350g/12oz/3 cups self-raising
  (self-rising) flour
225g/8oz/1 cup caster
  (superfine) sugar
175g/6oz/¾ cup unsalted (sweet)
  butter, softened
2 eggs
120ml/4fl oz/½ cup milk
6 large peeled peaches, sliced or
  450g/1lb plums or cherries, pitted
115g/4oz/½ cup soft brown sugar
2.5ml/½ tsp ground cinnamon
sour cream or crème fraîche, to serve

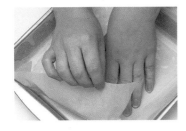

1 Preheat the oven to 190°C/375°F/
Gas 5. Grease and line a 20 x 25 x
2.5cm/8 x 10 x 1in cake tin (pan).

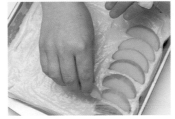

2 Put the flour, sugar, butter, eggs and milk into a large bowl and beat for a few minutes until you have a smooth batter. Spoon it into the prepared cake tin.

COOK'S TIP
To peel ripe peaches, cover with boiling water for 20 seconds. The skin will then slip off easily.

3 Arrange the peaches, plums or cherries over the cake mixture. Mix the brown sugar and cinnamon and sprinkle over the fruit.

4 Bake for about 40 minutes, testing for doneness by inserting a cocktail stick (toothpick) in the centre.

5 Serve the cake warm or cool with the sour cream or crème fraîche.

CARIBBEAN FRUIT AND RUM CAKE

THIS IS A DELICIOUS RECIPE FOR A CAKE THAT IS EATEN AT CHRISTMAS, WEDDINGS AND OTHER SPECIAL OCCASIONS. IT IS KNOWN AS BLACK CAKE, BECAUSE, TRADITIONALLY, THE RECIPE USES BURNT SUGAR.

MAKES 1 CAKE

INGREDIENTS
   450g/1lb/2 cups currants
   450g/1lb/3 cups raisins
   225g/8oz/1 cup prunes, pitted
   115g/4oz/²⁄₃ cup mixed
      (candied) peel
   400g/14oz/2¼ cups dark soft
      brown sugar
   5ml/1 tsp mixed (apple pie) spice
   90ml/6 tbsp rum, plus more
      if needed
   300ml/½ pint/1¼ cups sherry, plus
      more if needed
   450g/1lb/2 cups softened butter
   10 eggs, beaten
   450g/1lb/4 cups self-raising
      (self-rising) flour
   5ml/1 tsp vanilla essence (extract)

1 Wash the currants, raisins, prunes and mixed peel, then pat dry. Place in a food processor and process until finely chopped. Transfer to a large, clean jar or bowl, add 115g/4oz of the sugar, the mixed spice, rum and sherry. Mix very well and then cover with a lid and set aside for anything from 2 weeks to 3 months – the longer it is left, the better the flavour will be.

2 Stir the fruit mixture occasionally and keep covered, adding more alcohol, if you like.

3 Preheat the oven to 160°C/325°F/ Gas 3. Grease and line a 25cm/10in round cake tin (pan) with a double layer of greaseproof (waxed) paper.

4 Sift the flour and set aside. Cream together the butter and remaining sugar and beat in the eggs until the mixture is smooth and creamy.

5 Add the fruit mixture, then gradually stir in the flour and vanilla essence. Mix well, adding 15–30ml/1–2 tbsp sherry if the mixture is too stiff; it should just fall off the back of the spoon, but should not be too runny.

6 Spoon the mixture into the prepared tin, cover loosely with foil and bake for about 2½ hours, until the cake is firm and springy. Leave to cool in the tin overnight, then sprinkle with more rum if the cake is not to be used immediately. Wrap the cake in foil to keep it moist.

COOK'S TIP
Although the dried fruits are chopped in a food processor, they can be marinated whole, if you prefer. If you don't have enough time to marinate the fruit, simmer the fruit in the alcohol mixture for about 30 minutes, and leave overnight.

Add colour and fire to Mexican Sangrita, a refreshing drink based on tomatoes — and chillies! Bring a touch of fire to a Bloody Maria cocktail by pepping it up with Worcestershire and Tabasco sauces. Try a Caribbean pick-me-up with Caribbean Cream Stout Punch or Demerara Rum Punch, sprinkled with freshly grated nutmeg. Finally, as your friends gather round the fireside on a chilly winter day, warm their hearts with tumblers of Spiced Mocha Drink or Mulled Wine.

Spiced Drinks

SANGRITA

THE BLOOD-RED COLOUR OF THIS VERY FIERY YET COOLING BEVERAGE IS REFLECTED IN ITS NAME, WHICH IS DERIVED FROM THE SPANISH WORD FOR "BLOOD".

SERVES 8

INGREDIENTS
    450g/1lb tomatoes, peeled, seeded
        and chopped
    120ml/4fl oz/½ cup orange juice
    60ml/4 tbsp freshly squeezed lime juice
    1 small onion, chopped
    2.5ml/½ tsp granulated sugar
    6 small fresh green chillies, seeded
        and chopped
    50ml/2oz aged tequila *(Tequila Anejo)*
        per person
    salt

COOK'S TIP
Plain white tequila is not suitable for this. Choose one of the amber aged tequilas *(Añejos)*, which are smoother and more gentle on the palate.

1 Put the chopped tomatoes, orange juice, lime juice, chopped onion, granulated sugar and chopped green chillies into a food processor.

2 Process the tomato mixture until very smooth, scraping down the sides if necessary.

3 Pour the tomato mixture into a jug (pitcher) and chill well.

4 To serve, pour into small glasses, allowing about 90ml/6 tbsp per portion. Pour the tequila into separate small glasses. Sip the tomato juice and tequila alternately.

SANGRIA

THIS VERY POPULAR SUMMER DRINK WAS BORROWED FROM SPAIN. THE MEXICAN VERSION IS VERY SLIGHTLY LESS ALCOHOLIC THAN THE SPANISH ORIGINAL.

SERVES 6

INGREDIENTS
    ice cubes
    1 litre/1¾ pints/4 cups dry red
        table wine
    150ml/¼ pint/⅔ cup orange juice
    50ml/2fl oz/¼ cup freshly squeezed
        lime juice
    115g/4oz/generous ½ cup caster
        (superfine) sugar
    2 limes or 1 apple, sliced, to serve

1 Half fill a large jug (pitcher) with ice cubes. Pour in the wine and the orange and lime juices.

2 Add the sugar and stir well until it has dissolved completely.

3 Pour into tall glasses and float the lime or apple slices on top. Serve the sangria immediately.

COOK'S TIP
Sugar does not dissolve readily in alcohol. It is easier to use simple sugar syrup, which is very easy to make and gives a smoother drink. Combine 475ml/16fl oz/2 cups granulated sugar and 450g/1lb water in a jug (pitcher) and set aside until the sugar has dissolved. Stir from time to time. 15ml/1 tbsp simple syrup is the equivalent of 7.5ml/1½ tsp sugar.

VARIATION
Substitute sparkling lemonade for the orange juice for a lighter drink.

BLOODY MARIA

*A CLOSE COUSIN OF THE ORIGINAL VODKA-BASED BLOODY MARY, THIS SIMPLE COCKTAIL
CONSISTS OF WHITE TEQUILA AND TOMATO JUICE MIXED TOGETHER WITH SPICY SEASONINGS.
BE CAREFUL WHEN ADDING THE TABASCO SAUCE – IT'S WICKEDLY HOT.*

SERVES 2

INGREDIENTS
175ml/6fl oz/¾ cup tomato juice
90ml/3fl oz/6 tbsp white tequila
dash each of Worcestershire and
  Tabasco sauces
30ml/2 tbsp lemon juice
salt and ground black pepper
8 ice cubes

COOK'S TIP
When drinks are to be served with ice,
make sure all the ingredients are
thoroughly chilled ahead of time.

1 Combine the tomato juice, tequila,
Worcestershire and Tabasco sauces,
and lemon juice in a cocktail shaker.
Add salt and pepper to taste, and four
ice cubes. Shake very vigorously.

2 Place the remaining ice cubes in
two heavy-based glasses and strain
the tequila over them.

MARGARITA

*TEQUILA IS MADE FROM THE SAP OF A FLESHY-LEAFED PLANT CALLED THE BLUE AGAVE
AND GETS ITS NAME FROM THE TOWN OF TEQUILA, WHERE IT HAS BEEN MADE FOR OVER
200 YEARS. THE MARGARITA IS THE BEST-KNOWN DRINK MADE WITH TEQUILA.*

SERVES 2

INGREDIENTS
½ lime or lemon
120ml/4fl oz/½ cup white tequila
30ml/2 tbsp Triple Sec or Cointreau
30ml/2 tbsp freshly squeezed lime or
  lemon juice
4 or more ice cubes
salt

1 Rub the rims of two cocktail glasses
with the lime or lemon. Pour some salt
into a saucer and dip in the glasses so
that the rims are frosted.

COOK'S TIP
It really is worth going to the trouble of
buying limes for this recipe. Lemons
will do, but something of the special
flavour of the drink will be lost in
the substitution.

2 Combine the tequila, Triple Sec or
Cointreau, and lime and lemon juice in a
jug (pitcher) and stir to mix well.

3 Pour the tequila mixture into the
prepared glasses. Add the ice cubes
and serve immediately.

DEMERARA RUM PUNCH

THE INSPIRATION FOR THIS PUNCH CAME FROM THE RUM DISTILLERY AT PLANTATION DIAMOND ESTATE IN GUYANA WHERE SOME OF THE FINEST RUM IN THE WORLD IS MADE, AND THE TANTALIZING AROMAS OF SUGAR CANE AND RUM PERVADE THE AIR.

SERVES 4

INGREDIENTS

150ml/¼ pint/⅔ cup orange juice
150ml/¼ pint/⅔ cup pineapple juice
150ml/¼ pint/⅔ cup mango juice
120ml/4fl oz/½ cup water
250ml/8fl oz/1 cup dark rum
a dash of angostura bitters
freshly grated nutmeg
25g/1 oz/2 tbsp demerara (raw) sugar
1 small banana
1 large orange

COOK'S TIP
You can use white rum instead of dark, if you prefer. To make a stronger punch, add more rum.

1 Pour the orange, pineapple and mango juices into a large punch bowl. Stir in the water.

2 Add the rum, bitters, nutmeg and sugar. Stir gently until the sugar dissolves.

3 Slice the banana and stir gently into the punch.

4 Slice the orange and add to the punch. Chill and serve with ice.

CARIBBEAN CREAM STOUT PUNCH

A WELL-KNOWN "PICK-ME-UP" THAT IS POPULAR ALL OVER THE CARIBBEAN.

SERVES 2

INGREDIENTS
  475ml/16fl oz/2 cups stout
  300ml/½ pint/1¼ cups evaporated
    (unsweetened condensed) milk
  75ml/5 tbsp sweetened
    condensed milk
  75ml/5 tbsp sherry
  2 or 3 drops vanilla essence (extract)
  freshly grated nutmeg

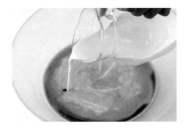

1 Mix together the stout, evaporated and condensed milks, sherry and vanilla essence in a blender or food processor, or whisk together in a large mixing bowl, until creamy.

2 Add a little grated nutmeg to the stout mixture and blend or whisk again for a few minutes.

COOK'S TIP
Stout is a strong, dark beer that originated in the British Isles. It has a strong taste of hops and is made with roasted barley, which gives it its dark colour and bittersweet flavour.

3 Chill for at least 45 minutes until really cold before serving.

INDEX

African spice mixtures 26–7
aji amarillo chillies 11
alfalfa and cucumber
    tortillas 400
Anaheim chillies 9
ancho chillies 9
anis with pumpkin
    soup 89
apple and cinnamon
    crumble cake 476–7
apricot chutney 74–5
aromatic mussel risotto 349
asparagus, Thai 376
aubergines
    beef with aubergine
        curry 302
    potatoes with aubergines
        and chillies 415
avocados
    avocado and sweet red
        pepper salsa 36
    avocado and tomato
        dip 54
    gazpacho with avocado
        salsa 95
Aztecs 6

baharat 27
baked spiced whole
    fish 206–7
baklava 472
Balinese fish curry 235
Balti potatoes 446–7
Balti split peas with green
    and red chillies 418
Balti-style vegetables with
    cashew nuts 417
bamboo shoots with red
    chicken curry 254–5
bananas
    banana ginger cake 478
    spiced nutty bananas 469
barbecue spice mixtures 28–9
barbecue jerk chicken 246
barbecue pork
    spareribs 284–5
basil
    chilli beef with basil 305
    fried jasmine rice with
        prawns and Thai
        basil 353
    stir-fried chicken with
        chilli and basil 259
basmati and nut pilaff 347
beans
    beancurd and green bean
        red curry 413
    beans in hot sauce 374

beef with peppers and
    black bean sauce 300
black bean and chilli
    burritos 401
black bean salsa 51
black-eyed bean stew with
    spicy pumpkin 404
broad bean and
    cauliflower curry 375
chilli bean dip 57
chilli beans with basmati
    rice 343
chilli beans with lemon
    and ginger 414
eggs with tortillas and
    beans 170–1
five-spice squid with
    chilli and black bean
    sauce 193
French beans, rice and
    beef 367
green bean and chilli
    pepper salad 433
hot chilli beans 403
Jamaican black bean
    pot 398
Kenyan mung bean
    stew 402
masala beans with
    fenugreek 441
mussels in chilli and black
    bean sauce 197
peppery bean salad 449
pinto bean salsa 50
red bean chilli 405
refried beans 396–7
rice with dill and spicy
    beans 339
rolls with refried beans
    and chilli 172
spicy bean soup 94
beef
    beef and sweet potato
        salad with mild chilli
        dressing 460

beef and turmeric
    soup 121
beef enchiladas with red
    sauce 290
beef tagine with sweet
    potatoes 296
beef with aubergine
    curry 302
beef with cactus
    pieces 298
beef with peppers and
    black bean sauce 300
chilli beef pizza 295
chilli beef with basil 305
chilli beef with spicy onion
    rings 296
French beans, rice and
    beef 367
Indonesian beef
    patties 286–7
meatballs with
    spaghetti 293
Mexican spicy beef
    tortilla 291
Mussaman beef curry 304
noodles with spicy meat
    sauce 322
shredded beef with
    chillies 301
Thai beef and mushroom
    salad 461
Thai beef salad 456–7
Thai green beef curry 303
Bengali-style vegetables 416
Berbere 27
bird's eye chillies 12
black bean and chilli
    burritos 401
black bean salsa 51
black pasta with squid
    sauce 311
black pepper (*Piper
    nigrum*) 6
black-eyed bean stew with
    spicy pumpkin 404
blackened hot chicken
    breasts 247
bloody Maria 492–3
Bombay potatoes 421
bon-bon chicken with spicy
    sesame sauce 249
braised fish in chilli and
    garlic sauce 204
bread pudding 480–1
bread rolls with refried beans
    and chilli 172
broad bean and cauliflower
    curry 375

brown rice with lime and
    lemon grass 337
Burmese rice and
    noodles 328
butterflied prawns in chilli
    chocolate 148

cabbage
    coleslaw in triple-hot
        dressing 428–9
    spicy cabbage 378–9
    vinegared chilli
        cabbage 428–9
cactus pear salsa 48–9
cactus pieces with
    beef 298
Cajun blackened fish with
    papaya salsa 218–19
Cajun popcorn 154
Cajun spice mixtures and
    bastes 30
cake
    apple and cinnamon
        crumble cake 476–7
    banana ginger cake 478
    Caribbean fruit and rum
        cake 484–5
    peach kuchen 483
    spiced date and walnut
        cake 479
caramel rice pudding 470–1
Caribbean chilli crab
    cakes 191
Caribbean cream stout
    punch 495
Caribbean fish
    steaks 218–19
Caribbean fruit and rum
    cake 484–5
Caribbean lamb curry 283
Caribbean peanut
    chicken 241
Caribbean red bean
    chilli 340
Caribbean spiced fish 229
cascabel chillies 10
catfish fillets with piquant
    sauce 212
cauliflower
    broad bean and
        cauliflower curry 375
    red hot cauliflower 373
cayenne 6, 13
cayenne chillies 11
ceviche of fish with citrus
    fruits 156
chargrilled squid with
    chillies 194

chayotes
    chayote salad 445
    prawns with chayote in
        turmeric sauce 188–9
cheese
    cheese and leek sausages
        with chilli and tomato
        sauce 391
    cheese fritters 138–9
    chilli cheese tortilla with
        fresh tomato and
        coriander salsa 399
    chilli yogurt cheese in
        olive oil 127
    courgettes with cheese
        and green chillies 143
    peppers with cheese and
        chilli filling 142
    salad of roasted shallots,
        chillies and butternut
        squash with feta 438
    spiced feta with chilli and
        olives 127
    stuffed chillies with
        cheese 140–1
    toasted cheese
        tortillas 144
chermouta 29
cherry hot chillies 10
chicken
    barbecue jerk chicken 246
    blackened hot chicken
        breasts 247
    bon-bon chicken with spicy
        sesame sauce 249
    Caribbean peanut
        chicken 241
    chicken jambalaya 358–9
    chicken naan
        pockets 166–7
    chicken satay 161
    chicken sauce
        piquante 242–3
    chicken pepper soup 115
    chicken tikka 166–7

chicken tortillas with Fresno
        chilli salsa 164–5
    chicken with chipotle chilli
        sauce 244–5
    chicken with coconut 239
    chicken, vegetable and
        chilli salad 458
    chilli chicken salad 456–7
    classic chicken
        tandoori 251
    ginger, chicken and
        coconut soup 110–11
    hot and spicy oat-fried
        chicken 240
    hot chicken curry 256–7
    mulligatawny soup 114
    red chicken curry with
        bamboo shoots 254–5
    San Francisco chicken
        wings 160
    scorching chilli chicken 250
    Sichuan chicken with
        kung po sauce 258
    spicy fried chicken 238
    spicy masala chicken 253
    spicy rice with
        chicken 362–3
    stir-fried chicken with
        chilli and basil 259
    tandoori chicken 252
    tangy chicken salad 459
    Thai chicken and chilli
        soup 112–13
    Thai chicken and noodle
        soup 116
    yogurt chicken and
        rice 360
chickpeas
    chickpea breads 78
    parsnips and chickpeas in
        a chilli paste 411
    sweet rice with hot sour
        chickpeas 329
chilled soba noodles with
        nori 138–9
chilli and garlic mustard 33
chilli and garlic prawns 168–9
chilli and pak choi omelette
        parcels 386
chilli and pesto salsa 37
chilli and red onion raita 58
chilli and tomato oil 14
chilli bean dip 57
chilli beans with basmati
        rice 343
chilli beans with lemon and
        ginger 414
chilli beef pizza 295

chilli beef with basil 305
chilli beef with spicy onion
        rings 296
chilli cheese tortilla with
        fresh tomato and
        coriander salsa 399
chilli chicken salad 456–7
chilli chive rice with
        mushrooms 336
chilli con carne 292
chilli courgettes 396–7
chilli crab claws 175
chilli crabs 192
chilli gifts 32–3
chilli pasta 31
chilli pepper baste 30
chilli poori puffs 79
chilli prawns with okra 18
chilli ravioli with crab 313
chilli relish 64
chilli ribs 266
chilli sambal 24
chilli sambal 286–7
chilli spiced onion koftas 126
chilli squash soup 107
chilli strips with lime 70
chilli yogurt cheese in olive
        oil 127
chilli, tomato and spinach
        pizza 394
chilli-spiced plantain
        chips 81
chillied monkfish parcels 155
chillies
    bottled 13
    buying 15
    cooking 16–17
    crushed 13
    cultivating 10
    history 6–7
    hotness 8
    oils 14
    paste 13
    powders 13
    preparation 16–17
    sauces 14
    storing 15
    types 8–12
Chinese chilli noodles 32
Chinese curry powder 21
chipotle chillies 11
chive chilli rice with
        mushrooms 336
chocolate
    butterflied prawns in
        chilli chocolate 148
    Mexican turkey mole 264–5
    spiced mocha drink 488

turkey stew with spicy
        chocolate sauce 262–3
chorizo sausage in olive
        oil 168–9
chunky cherry chilli and
        tomato salsa 40
chutney
    apricot chutney 74–5
    coconut chutney 72–3
cinnamon 6
    apple and cinnamon
        crumble cake 476–7
    cinnamon balls 475
    cinnamon rolls 482
citrus
    ceviche of fish with citrus
        fruits 156
    citrus fish with chillies 209
    fiery citrus salsa 37
    Thai chilli and citrus
        marinade 29
clam sauce with vermicelli 312
classic chicken tandoori 251
classic curry powder 18
classic Mexican tomato
        salsa 38–9
coconut
    chicken with coconut 239
    coconut and nutmeg ice
        cream 467
    coconut and peanut
        relish 424–5
    coconut and pumpkin
        soup 92
    coconut and seafood
        soup 106
    coconut chilli relish 430–1
    coconut chutney 72–3
    coconut fish curry 234
    coconut rice 362–3
    coconut salmon 222
    curried prawns and
        coconut milk 186–7
    curried seafood with
        coconut milk 232–3

manzano chillies 12
Margarita 492–3
marinades
  peri-peri barbecue
    marinade 29
  Thai chilli and citrus
    marinade 29
marinated vegetables on
  skewers 439
masala beans with
  fenugreek 441
masala mashed
  potatoes 378–9
masala prawns and
  rice 354–5
Mayas 6
meatballs with spaghetti 293
Mexican bread pudding 480–1
Mexican rice 338
Mexican spicy beef
  tortilla 291
Mexican spicy fish 208
Mexican turkey mole 264–5
Mexican vinegar
  seasoning 63
mild curry powder 18
miso broth with tofu 91
mixed spiced nuts 80
mixed vegetable pickle
  dip 76
monkfish parcels 155
Montezuma 6
mortar and pestle 15
mulato chillies 9
mulled wine 489
mulligatawny soup 114
mushrooms
  chilli chive rice with
    mushrooms 336
  hot and sour soup 86
  mushrooms with chipotle
    chillies 372
  Thai beef and mushroom
    salad 461
Mussaman beef curry 304
mussels
  aromatic mussel
    risotto 349
  Louisiana shellfish
    gumbo 356–7
  mussels in chilli and black
    bean sauce 197
  pan-steamed chilli
    mussels 152
  pineapple curry
    with prawns and
    mussels 186–7
  spiced mussel soup 104

mustard
  chilli and garlic mustard 33
  cod with chilli and
    mustard seeds 229
  cooking mustard
    seeds 19

nam prik sauce 25
noodles
  Burmese rice and
    noodles 328
  chilled soba noodles with
    nori 138–9
  Chinese chilli noodles 32
  curry fried noodles 316–17
  fish and shellfish rice
    noodles 318
  five-spice vegetable
    noodles 315
  noodle soup with pork
    and Szechuan pickle
    118–19
  noodles with spicy meat
    sauce 322
  sesame noodles with
    spring onions 324–5
  snapper, tomato and
    tamarind noodle
    soup 118–19
  spicy noodle pudding 468
  spicy Szechuan
    noodles 324–5
  stir-fried prawns on crisp
    noodle cake 319
  Thai chicken and noodle
    soup 116
  Thai fried noodles 321
  tomato noodles with fried
    egg 316–17
  tossed noodles with
    seafood 322–3
  traditional Indonesian
    noodles 327
nuoc chan 25
nutmeg 6

coconut and nutmeg ice
  cream 467
nutrition 7
nuts
  Balti-style vegetables
    with cashew nuts 417
  basmati and nut
    pilaff 347
  Caribbean peanut
    chicken 241
  coconut and peanut
    relish 424–5
  gado-gado with
    peanut and chilli
    sauce 443
  hot hot Cajun peanut
    salad 444
  mixed spiced nuts 80
  pistachio pilaff 346
  spiced date and walnut
    cake 479
  spiced nutty bananas 469
  spicy peanut balls 124
  stuffed chillies in a walnut
    sauce 272–3
  tamarind soup with
    peanuts and
    vegetables 99
  vegetables in peanut and
    chilli sauce 438

oils 14, 32
  chilli yogurt cheese in
    olive oil 127
  chorizo sausage in olive
    oil 168–9
  spaghetti with garlic, chilli
    and oil 309
okra
  chilli prawns with
    okra 18
  okra fried rice 334–5
  okra with green mango
    and lentils 446–7
  okra, chilli and tomato
    tagine 389
old-fashioned Philadelphia
  spice powder 28
onions
  chilli and red onion
    raita 58
  chilli beef with spicy onion
    rings 296
  chilli spiced onion
    koftas 126
  deep-fried onions 24
  jalapeño and onion
    quiche 395

kachumbali salad 430–1
  little onions cooked with
    chillies 125
  onion relish 67
  onion, mango and chilli
    relish 72–3
  red onion, garlic and chilli
    relish 66
  seared tuna
    with red onion
    salsa 203
  spiced fish with chillies,
    lemon and red
    onions 215
  tomato and onion
    salad 424–5
orange and ginger sauce
  with avocado
  salad 465

pak choi and chilli omelette
  parcels 386
pan-fried spicy
  sardines 210–11
pan-steamed chilli
  mussels 152
pancakes stuffed with
  lightly spiced
  squash 384–5
papaya
  Cajun blackened
    fish with papaya
    salsa 218–19
  green papaya and chilli
    salad 435
paprika 6, 13
  flash-fried squid
    with paprika and
    garlic 190
parsnips and chickpeas
  in a chilli paste 411
party pizzettes with a hint
  of chilli 149
pasado chillies 10
pasilla chillies 10

pasta 31
  black pasta with squid
    sauce 311
  chilli pasta 31
  chilli ravioli with
    crab 313
  meatballs with
    spaghetti 293
  pasta with sugocasa and
    chilli 308
  penne with chilli and
    broccoli 310
  penne with tomato and
    chilli sauce 314
  pink and green
    salad 451
  scallop conchiglie 454
  spaghetti with garlic, chilli
    and oil 309
  vermicelli with spicy clam
    sauce 312
pastries
  baklava 472
  date and nut pastries 474
peach kuchen 483
peas
  Balti split peas with
    green and red
    chillies 418
penne with chilli and
  broccoli 310
penne with tomato and chilli
  sauce 314
pepperoni and chilli
  pizza 267
peppers (bell)
  avocado and sweet red
    pepper salsa 36
  beef with peppers and
    black bean sauce 300
  peppers filled with spiced
    vegetables 392–3
  peppers with cheese and
    chilli filling 142
  peppery bean salad 449
  roasted pepper and
    tomato salad 426
  sweet potato, pepper and
    chilli salad 442
peppers (*Capsicum*) 6
peri-peri barbecue
  marinade 29
peri-peri prawns with
  aioli 150
Persian rice with a
  tahdeeg 332
pestle and mortar 15
pesto and chilli salsa 37

pickles
  hot Thai pickled shallots
    with chillies 71
  mixed vegetable pickle
    dip 76
  noodle soup with
    pork and Szechuan
    pickle 118–19
  pickled cucumbers 68
  pickled fish 198
pimentón dulce 13
pimiento tartlets 145
pineapple
  fresh pineapple with
    ginger 464
  pineapple curry
    with prawns and
    mussels 186–7
  piquant pineapple
    relish 69
  pork with chillies and
    pineapple 269
pink and green salad 451
pinto bean salsa 50
piquant prawn salad 450
piquant pumpkin and
  coconut soup 88
pistachio pilaff 346
plantain
  chilli-spiced plantain
    chips 81
  plantain soup with corn
    and chilli 100–1
poblano chillies 9
popcorn
  Cajun popcorn 154
  popcorn with lime and
    chilli 81
pork
  barbecue pork
    spareribs 284–5
  chicken jambalaya 358–9
  chilli ribs 266
  deep-fried spareribs
    with spicy salt and
    pepper 268
  noodle soup with pork and
    Szechuan pickle 118–19
  noodles with spicy meat
    sauce 322
  pork casserole with
    chillies and dried
    fruit 270–1
  pork satay sticks 158–9
  pork with chillies and
    pineapple 269
  rice porridge 117
  sweet and sour pork 274

potatoes
  Balti potatoes 446–7
  Bombay potatoes 421
  hot and spicy
    potatoes 419
  masala mashed
    potatoes 378–9
  potato skins with Cajun
    dip 133
  potatoes with
    aubergines and
    chillies 415
  potatoes with red
    chillies 420
  spicy potato salad 448
  spicy potato wedges with
    chilli dip 134
  spicy potatoes 135
  Tex-Mex baked potatoes
    with chilli 299
prawns
  butterflied prawns in chilli
    chocolate 148
  chicken jambalaya 358–9
  chilli and garlic
    prawns 168–9
  chilli prawns with
    okra 18
  curried prawns
    and coconut
    milk 186–7
  curried prawns and
    saltfish 182–3
  firecrackers 174
  fish and shellfish rice
    noodles 318
  fried jasmine rice with
    prawns and Thai
    basil 353
  hot and sour prawn
    soup 110–11
  hot and sour shellfish
    soup 112–13
  king prawns in curry
    sauce 220–1

Louisiana shellfish
  gumbo 356–7
Malaysian prawn
  soup 108–9
masala prawns and
  rice 354–5
peri-peri prawns with
  aioli 150
pineapple curry with prawns
  and mussels 186–7
piquant prawn salad 450
prawns in spiced coconut
  sauce 182–3
prawns in spicy tomato
  sauce 200–1
prawns with chayote in
  turmeric sauce 188–9
salt and pepper
  prawns 180
seafood and
  rice 358–9
spicy prawns with
  cornmeal 185
stir-fried prawns on crisp
  noodle cake 319
stir-fried prawns with
  tamarind 184
Provençal fish soup with
  rouille 103
pumpkin
  black-eyed bean
    stew with spicy
    pumpkin 404
  coconut and pumpkin
    soup 92
  hot pumpkin seeds 82–3
  piquant pumpkin and
    coconut soup 88
  pumpkin seed sauce 59
  pumpkin soup with
    anis 89

quiche, jalapeño and
  onion 395

Ras-el-hanout 27
red bean chilli 405
red chicken curry
  with bamboo
  shoots 254–5
red hot cauliflower 373
red onion, garlic and chilli
  relish 66
red rice rissoles 344–5
red snapper with chilli, gin
  and ginger sauce 214
red snapper, Veracruz
  style 213

red-hot roots 80
refried beans 396–7
ribs
    barbecue pork
        spareribs 284–5
    chilli ribs 266
    deep-fried spareribs
        with spicy salt and
        pepper 268
rice
    aromatic mussel
        risotto 349
    basmati and nut
        pilaff 347
    brown rice with lime and
        lemon grass 337
    Burmese rice and
        noodles 328
    caramel rice
        pudding, 470–1
    chilli beans with basmati
        rice 343
    chilli chive rice with
        mushrooms 336
    coconut rice 362–3
    crab with green
        rice 352
    crispy fried rice
        vermicelli 320
    festive rice 333
    fish and shellfish rice
        noodles 318
    French beans, rice and
        beef 367
    fried jasmine rice with
        prawns and Thai
        basil 353
    Indian pilau rice 334–5
    Louisiana rice 365
    Madras curry with spicy
        rice 368–9
    masala prawns and
        rice 354–5
    Mexican rice 338
    okra fried rice 334–5

Persian rice with a
    tahdeeg 332
pistachio pilaff 346
red rice rissoles 344–5
rice with dill and spicy
    beans 339
rice porridge 117
savoury fried rice 366
savoury spicy rice 341
seafood and
    rice 358–9
spiced rice pudding 470–1
spiced trout pilaff 348
spicy fish and
    rice 354–5
spicy rice cakes 344–5
spicy rice with
    chicken 362–3
squid and chilli
    risotto 350–1
sweet and sour
    rice 342
sweet rice with hot sour
    chickpeas 329
Thai fried rice with
    chillies 361
Thai mixed vegetable
    curry with lemon grass
    rice 330–1
warming spinach and
    rice soup 87
yogurt chicken and
    rice 360
roasted pepper and tomato
    salad 426
roasted serrano and tomato
    salsa 44–5
roasted tomato salsa 42–3
rolls with refried beans and
    chilli 172
rouille 7
    Provençal fish soup with
        rouille 103
rum
    Caribbean fruit and rum
        cake 484–5
    demerara rum punch 494

saffron fish 210–11
salad of roasted shallots,
    chillies and butternut
    squash with feta 438
salmon
    coconut salmon 222
    salmon parcels with
        spiced leeks 224
    salmon with tequila cream
        sauce 223

sushi 364
    Thai-style marinated
        salmon 157
salsa verde 36
salt and pepper
    prawns 180
salt cod in mild chilli
    sauce 205
sambaar powder 19
sambals 24–5
    chilli sambal 24
    nam prik sauce 25
    nuoc chan 25
    sambal blachan 24
    sambal kecap 24
    sambal salamat 25
samosas 131
San Francisco chicken
    wings 160
sangria 490–1
sangrita 490–1
sardines, pan-fried
    spicy 210–11
savoury fried rice 366
savoury spicy rice 341
scallops
    scallop conchiglie 454
    spiced scallops in their
        shells 196
scorching chilli
    chicken 250
Scotch bonnet chillies 12
seafood
    aromatic mussel
        risotto 349
    black pasta with squid
        sauce 311
    butterflied prawns in chilli
        chocolate 148
    Caribbean chilli crab
        cakes 191
    chargrilled squid with
        chillies 194
    chilli and garlic
        prawns 168–9
    chilli crab claws 175
    chilli crabs 192
    chilli prawns with
        okra 18
    chilli ravioli with
        crab 313
    coconut and seafood
        soup 106
    crab with green rice 352
    curried prawns and
        coconut milk 186–7
    curried prawns and
        saltfish 182–3

curried seafood with
    coconut milk 232–3
five-spice squid with
    chilli and black
    bean sauce 193
flash-fried squid with
    paprika and garlic 190
fried jasmine rice with
    prawns and Thai
    basil 353
hot and sour prawn
    soup 110–11
hot and spicy seafood
    soup 105
king prawns in curry
    sauce 220–1
Malaysian prawn
    soup 108–9
masala prawns and
    rice 354–5
mussels in chilli and
    black bean sauce 197
pan-steamed chilli
    mussels 152
peri-peri prawns with
    aioli 150
pineapple curry
    with prawns and
    mussels 186–7
piquant prawn salad 450
salt and pepper
    prawns 180
scallop conchiglie 454
seafood and rice 358–9
Singapore crabs 158–9
spiced mussel soup 104
spiced scallops in their
    shells 196
spicy prawns with
    cornmeal 185
spicy squid salad 455
squid and chilli
    risotto 350–1
stir-fried prawns on crisp
    noodle cake 319
stir-fried prawns with
    tamarind 184
tossed noodles with
    seafood 322–3
vermicelli with spicy clam
    sauce 312
seared tuna with red onion
    salsa 203
serrano chillies 11
    roasted serrano and
        tomato salsa 44–5
    spinach and serrano chilli
        salad 427

sesame
    bon-bon chicken
        with spicy sesame
        sauce 249
    sesame noodles with
        spring onions 324–5
seven-seas curry powder 21
shallots
    hot Thai pickled shallots
        with chillies 71
    salad of roasted shallots,
        chillies and butternut
        squash with feta 438
    Thai shellfish salad with
        chilli dressing and
        frizzled shallots 452–3
shellfish *see* seafood
shredded beef with
    chillies 301
shrimp paste 23
Sichuan chicken with
    kung po sauce 258
Sichuan sizzler 382
Singapore crabs 158–9
Singapore-style curry
    powder 20
smoky chipotle
    sauce 60–1
snapper, tomato and
    tamarind noodle
    soup 118–19
spaghetti with garlic, chilli
    and oil 309
spatchcocked devilled
    poussins 248
spice grinders 15
spice mixes
    baharat 27
    basic barbecue spice
        mix 28
    Berbere 27
    Cajun spice mix 30
    chermouta 29
    chilli pepper baste 30
    harissa 26

Jamaican jerk paste 28
old-fashioned Philadelphia
    spice powder 28
peri-peri barbecue
    marinade 29
Ras-el-hanout 27
Thai chilli and citrus
    marinade 29
tsire powder 26
spice pastes 22–3
    green curry paste 23
    Madrasi masala 22
    shrimp paste 23
    Thai mussaman curry
        paste 23
    Thai red curry paste 22
spice powders 18–21
    Chinese curry powder 21
    classic curry powder 18
    garam masala 19
    Malayan curry powder 21
    mild curry powder 18
    sambaar powder 19
    seven-seas curry
        powder 21
    Singapore-style curry
        powder 20
    Sri Lankan curry
        powder 20
spiced bread pudding 473
spiced date and walnut
    cake 479
spiced feta with chilli and
    olives 127
spiced fish kebabs 200–1
spiced fish with chillies,
    lemon and red
    onions 215
spiced lamb soup 120
spiced mocha drink 488
spiced mussel soup 104
spiced nutty bananas 469
spiced red lentil and
    coconut soup 93
spiced rice pudding 470–1
spiced scallops in their
    shells 196
spiced trout pilaff 348
spices, buying 21
spicy bean soup 94
spicy cabbage 378–9
spicy carrot dip 56
spicy carrots 380
spicy fish and rice 354–5
spicy fried chicken 238
spicy fried dumplings 77
spicy groundnut
    soup 100–1

spicy kebabs 176
spicy lamb stew 280–1
spicy Masala chicken 253
spicy meat fritters 284–5
spicy meat-filled
    parcels 177
spicy meatballs 294
spicy noodle pudding 468
spicy peanut balls 124
spicy pepper soup 102
spicy potato salad 448
spicy potato wedges with
    chilli dip 134
spicy potatoes 135
spicy prawns with
    cornmeal 185
spicy rice cakes 344–5
spicy rice with
    chicken 362–3
spicy root vegetable
    gratin 387
spicy shellfish
    wontons 153
spicy squid salad 455
spicy sweetcorn
    relish 65
spicy Szechuan
    noodles 324–5
spicy tomato and chilli
    dip 55
spicy vegetable
    ribbons 434
spicy vegetables with
    almonds 440
spicy yogurt soup 98
spinach
    spinach and serrano chilli
        salad 427
    warming spinach and rice
        soup 87
spring onions
    sesame noodles with
        spring onions 324–5
    spring onions with
        romesco sauce 377

spring rolls with fiery chilli
    sauce 173
squash
    chilli squash soup 107
    pancakes stuffed
        with lightly spiced
        squash 384–5
    salad of roasted shallots,
        chillies and butternut
        squash with feta 438
squid
    black pasta with squid
        sauce 311
    chargrilled squid with
        chillies 194
    five-spice squid with
        chilli and black bean
        sauce 193
    flash-fried squid
        with paprika and
        garlic 190
    spicy squid salad 455
    squid and chilli
        risotto 350–1
Sri Lankan curry
    powder 20
steamed fish with chilli
    sauce 195
steamed vegetables with
    Thai spicy dip 383
stir-fried chicken with chilli
    and basil 259
stir-fried chilli greens 432
stir-fried prawns on crisp
    noodle cake 319
stir-fried prawns with
    tamarind 184
stuffed chillies in a walnut
    sauce 272–3
stuffed chillies with
    cheese 140–1
stuffed rolls with spicy
    salsa 170–1
sushi 364
sweet and sour pork 274
sweet and sour rice 342
sweet potato
    beef and sweet potato
        salad with mild chilli
        dressing 460
    beef tagine with sweet
        potatoes 296
    sweet potato and jalapeño
        salsa 46
    sweet potato, pepper and
        chilli salad 442
sweet rice with hot sour
    chickpeas 329

swordfish
  tacos 226–7
  with chilli and lime
    sauce 226–7
Szechuan spicy tofu 412

Tabasco 14
tamarind 29
  snapper, tomato and
    tamarind noodle
    soup 118–19
  stir-fried prawns with
    tamarind 184
  tamarind soup with
    peanuts and
    vegetables 99
  trout with tamarind and
    chilli sauce 225
tandoori chicken 252
tangy chicken salad 459
tasty toasts 74–5
tempeh cakes with chilli
    sauce 132
tequila cream sauce with
    salmon 223
Tex-Mex baked potatoes with
    chilli 299
Thai asparagus 376
Thai beef and mushroom
    salad 461
Thai beef salad 456–7
Thai chicken and chilli
    soup 112–13
Thai chicken and noodle
    soup 116
Thai chilli and citrus
    marinade 29
Thai chillies 12
Thai fried noodles 321
Thai fried rice with
    chillies 361
Thai green beef
    curry 303
·Thai mixed vegetable curry
    with lemon grass

rice 330–1
Thai mussaman curry
    paste 23
Thai red curry paste 22
Thai red curry sauce 62
Thai shellfish salad with chilli
    dressing and frizzled
    shallots 452–3
Thai tempeh cakes with
    chilli sauce 132
Thai-style marinated
    salmon 157
three-colour fish
    kebabs 202
toasted cheese tortillas 144
tofu
  beancurd and green bean
    red curry 413
  hot and spicy miso broth
    with tofu 91
  hot and sweet vegetable
    and tofu soup 90
  Szechuan spicy tofu 412
tomatoes
  avocado and tomato
    dip 54
  cheese and leek
    sausages with chilli and
    tomato sauce 391
  chilli and tomato oil 14
  chilli cheese tortilla with
    fresh tomato and
    coriander salsa 399
  chunky cherry chilli and
    tomato salsa 40
  classic Mexican tomato
    salsa 38–9
  gazpacho with avocado
    salsa 95
  okra, chilli and tomato
    tagine 389
  prawns in spicy tomato
    sauce 200–1
  roasted pepper and
    tomato salad 426
  roasted serrano and
    tomato salsa 44–5
  roasted tomato salsa 42–3
  snapper, tomato and
    tamarind noodle
    soup 118–19
  spicy tomato and chilli
    dip 55
  tomato and onion
    salad 424–5
  tomato noodles with fried
    egg 316–17
  tomato salsa 52–3

tortillas
  chicken tortillas
    with Fresno chilli
    salsa 164–5
  chilli cheese tortilla
    with fresh tomato
    and coriander
    salsa 399
  cucumber and alfalfa
    tortillas 400
  desert nachos 146
  eggs with tortillas and
    beans 170–1
  Mexican spicy beef
    tortilla 291
  toasted cheese
    tortillas 144
  tortilla soup 96
  tortilla turnovers 162–3
  tortillas with enchilada
    sauce 146–7
tossed noodles with
    seafood 322–3
traditional Indonesian
    noodles 327
trout
  spiced trout
    pilaff 348
  trout with tamarind and
    chilli sauce 225
tsire powder 26
tuna sushi 364
turkey
  Mexican turkey
    mole 264–5
  turkey stew with
    spicy chocolate
    sauce 262–3
Turkish cold fish 217
turmeric
  beef and turmeric
    soup 121
  prawns with
    chayote in turmeric
    sauce 188–9

vegetables
  Balti-style vegetables with
    cashew nuts 417
  Bengali-style
    vegetables 416
  chicken, vegetable and
    chilli salad 458
  fiery vegetables in coconut
    milk 381
  five-spice vegetable
    noodles 315
  hot and sweet vegetable
    and tofu soup 90
  marinated vegetables on
    skewers 439
  mixed vegetable pickle
    dip 76
  peppers filled with spiced
    vegetables 392–3
  red-hot roots 80
  spicy root vegetable
    gratin 387
  spicy vegetable
    ribbons 434
  spicy vegetables with
    almonds 440
  steamed vegetables with
    Thai spicy dip 383
  tamarind soup with
    peanuts and
    vegetables 99
  Thai mixed vegetable
    curry with lemon grass
    rice 330–1
  vegetable soup with chilli
    and coconut 97
  vegetables in peanut and
    chilli sauce 438
vermicelli with spicy clam
    sauce 312
vinegar
  Mexican vinegar
    seasoning 63
  vinegar chilli fish 206–7
  vinegared chilli
    cabbage 428–9

warming spinach and rice
    soup 87
whole fish with sweet and
    sour sauce 216

yogurt
  chilli yogurt cheese in
    olive oil 127
  spicy yogurt soup 98
  yogurt chicken and
    rice 360